The Green Studio Handbook

Second Edition

DISCLAIMER

The information presented in this book has been assembled, derived, and developed from numerous sources including textbooks, standards, guidelines, professional firms, and the Internet. It is presented in good faith. The authors and the publisher have made every reasonable effort to ensure that the information presented herein is accurate; they do not, however, warrant (and assume no responsibility for) its accuracy, completeness, or suitability for any particular purpose or situation. The information is intended primarily as an aid to learning and teaching and not as a definitive source of information for the design of building systems by design professionals. It is the responsibility of all users to utilize professional judgment, experience, and common sense when applying information presented in this book. This responsibility extends to verification of local codes, standards, and legislation and assembly and validation of local climate data.

COPYRIGHTS AND TRADEMARKS

ENVIRONMENT

All Architectural Press books are published by Elsevier which is part of the Reed Elsevier group. The Dow Jones Sustainability Index has classified Reed Elsevier as a Sustainability Leader citing a score "above the industry average with a good performance in environmental performance and reporting". Environmental best practice extends to all parts of our organization right down to its individual publications. Please see the Reed Elsevier website for further information on Reed Elsevier and the environment: http://www.reedelsevier.com/corporateresponsibility/focusareas/pages/environment.aspx

The Green Studio Handbook

Environmental strategies for schematic design

Second Edition

Alison G. Kwok, AIA
and
Walter T. Grondzik, PE

ELSEVIER

AMSTERDAM • BOSTON • HEIDELBERG • LONDON • NEW YORK • OXFORD
PARIS • SAN DIEGO • SAN FRANCISCO • SINGAPORE • SYDNEY • TOKYO

Architectural Press is an imprint of Elsevier

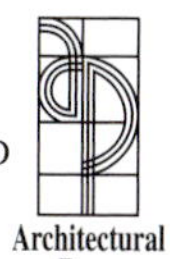

Architectural Press is an imprint of Elsevier
30 Corporate Drive, Suite 400, Burlington, MA 01803, USA
The Boulevard, Langford Lane, Kidlington, Oxford OX5 1GB, UK

First edition 2007
Second edition 2011

British Library Cataloguing in Publication Data
A catalogue record for this book is available from the British Library

Library of Congress Cataloguing in Publication Data
A catalogue record for this book is available from the Library of Congress

ISBN: 978-0-08-089052-4

For information on all Architectural Press publications visit our website at www.architecturalpress.com

Typeset by MPS Limited, a Macmillan Company, Chennai, India
www.macmillansolutions.com

Printed and bound in the United States of America

11 11 10 9 8 7 6 5 4 3 2 1

CONTENTS

PREFACE

The first edition of *The Green Studio Handbook* was written to serve as a reference guide—as well as a source of inspiration for students in design studios and architects in professional practice. It was founded upon the premise that there would be more green buildings if the technics of green—the underlying strategies that save energy, water, and material resources—were more accessible to the designer. This premise remains the driving force behind the second edition.

A student should find *The Green Studio Handbook* a useful introduction to green design strategies and the associated green design process. An architect, already convinced of the merits of green building and familiar with design process, can use the *Handbook* as an accessible supplement to augment his/her basic knowledge of green building strategies.

The Green Studio Handbook is not intended to serve as a green building checklist, nor as a textbook for environmental technology. Instead it provides the information needed to make judgments about the appropriate use of green strategies and to validate design decisions regarding these strategies. It also provides tools for preliminary sizing of strategies and their components during the early stages of design. We hope designers will be able to realistically incorporate such strategies in their schematic design work. Project aesthetics are left to the designer and project context, but numerous examples illustrating the application of strategies are provided to trigger ideas and encourage implementation.

Each strategy in *The Green Studio Handbook* includes a description of principle and concept, suggestions for integrating the strategy into a green building, step-by-step procedures to assist with preliminary sizing of components, and references to standards, guidelines, and further information. Conceptual sketches and examples illustrate each strategy. To further the goal of integrative design, each strategy is linked to relevant complementary strategies.

The Green Studio Handbook is intended for use in university design studios and/or seminar courses and in professional office practice. Astute building owners might also use this book as a way of becoming better informed about green design projects. The focus is upon strategies that have the greatest impact on building form and that must be considered very early in the design process. The book assumes that users have a basic knowledge of environmental technology and the design process and access to conventional design resources such as sun path diagrams, material R-values, thermal load calculation information, lighting standards, air quality guidelines, and the like.

ACKNOWLEDGMENTS

Similar to the design process, *The Green Studio Handbook* is very much a collaborative effort. There are many people to thank. That said, the authors were ultimately responsible for deciding what appears in this book and how information is organized and presented.

Many minds and hands are required to organize the nuts and bolts that hold a project such as this together. For database development, troubleshooting, and sequencing of images (and related file data) for the first and second editions, we extend a very sincere thank you to Theodore J. Kwok (University of Hawaii). The internal production crew for the second edition included Tom Collins, Matt Hogan, and Luzanne Smith. We cannot say enough about their dedication to task, belief in quality, and tireless work ethic. (Kate Beckley and Sam Jensen-Augustine played similar roles on the first edition.) Tom assembled and edited all the case studies—a Herculean effort. Matt developed several drawings, processed many images, and assembled page layouts. Luzanne processed many, many images and developed several new and revised drawings. Many new images included in the second edition were prepared by Jonathan Thwaites. Other images were developed by Ben Vaughn. Image credits in the text denote their specific contributions. Seyad Iman Rejaie Shoshtari processed hundreds of images and contributed others. David Bartley assisted with compilation and verification of the Glossary of Buildings.

Many of the strategy descriptions in the book were first developed in a seminar course on the teaching of technical subjects in architecture offered at the University of Oregon. Alison Kwok was the faculty member in charge of that course—with assistance from Walter Grondzik. Students participating in this class included: Sam Jensen-Augustine, Juliette Beale, Kathy Bevers, Martha Bohm, Jessica Gracie, Dan Goldstein, Jeff Guggenheim, Will Henderson, Daniel Meyers, Daniel Safarik, Alison Smith, Aaron Swain, Amelia Thrall, and Jason Zook. These initial strategies have been substantially morphed, tweaked, and transformed to their present form by numerous rounds of reviews and edits. Nicholas Rajkovich (University of Michigan) and Emily Wright (Einhorn Yaffee Prescott Architecture and Engineering) developed several draft strategies to fill gaps in coverage. Professor Donald Corner (University of Oregon) developed material for the Double Envelope design strategy. These were all done under a tight deadline and competing time demands, so are especially appreciated.

The case studies presented in Chapter 5 were informed by the gracious contributions of materials from design professionals with direct knowledge of the projects. Many thanks to the many architects, engineers, and owners who contributed information, provided reviews, and answered questions. Bruce Haglund of the University of Idaho developed the John Hope Gateway case study. Alison Kwok developed the Passive House case study. Tom Collins developed the other case studies.

Two focused essays were written expressly for the first edition of this work. An essay on the design process was prepared by Laura Briggs (Parsons: The New School for Design) and Jonathan Knowles (Rhode Island School of Design) of Briggs Knowles Design in New York City. An essay on integrated design was prepared by David Posada (with

GBD Architects in Portland, Oregon). For the second edition, these two essays (edited by the authors of this book) have been incorporated into Chapter 2. David Posada also contributed the majority of the information about green building rating systems that appears in Chapter 1.

We would also like to thank Kathy Bevers (Colorado), Martha Bohm (University of Buffalo), Christina Bollo (SMR Architects, Seattle, Washington), Bill Burke (Pacific Energy Center, San Francisco, California), John Quale (University of Virginia), John Reynolds (professor emeritus, University of Oregon), Amelia Thrall, and Emily Wright (EYP) for their insightful comments on draft versions of this work. Their thoughtful concerns have helped improve the final product. As follow-up to his review of the draft manuscript, Bill Burke also wrote drafts of the "part-opener" summaries for the six topics that organize the strategies presented in Chapter 4.

The graphic design for this book—with which we are particularly pleased—was prepared by Noreen Rei Fukumori (NRF Studio, Berkeley, California). Images throughout the book have been provided by numerous students, faculty, design professionals, and professional photographers, many upon short request. All images are credited immediately following the caption. These images are vitally important to the presentation of green design strategies, so these numerous contributions are greatly appreciated. We also thank Tom Arban (Tom Arban Photography) for the provocative cover photo.

The first edition (and by extension, the second edition) relied heavily on drawings from Greg Hartman (who illustrated the topic openers), Amanda Hills, and Jonathan Meendering. Kathy Bevers developed a number of system sizing graphs to replace complex equations. All four amazed us with their ease of depicting green technologies and data in a visually pleasing and inspiring graphic form.

We sincerely thank the staff at Architectural Press for seeing the value in this book and for their diligent efforts to get it produced and into your hands in the form that you see. Special thanks go to Hannah Shakespeare, Commissioning Editor; Mike Travers, Development Editor; Kara Milne, Senior Acquisitions Editor; Carol Barber, Editorial Assistant; Renata Corbani, Project Manager; and Soo Hamilton, Subeditor. We also compliment Fred Rose and Mike Travers for their diligent and creative work on the book's cover.

And last, but not least, we wish to acknowledge the debt owed by many in the environmental buildings movement to the vision, works, writings, and humanity of Malcolm Wells. We believe we can use the wisdom of the past to channel the knowledge of the present to reach our goals for the near future (as embodied in the 2030 Challenge) and beyond.

Alison G. Kwok and Walter T. Grondzik

Green

Green is an important word—it represents one-third of the main title of this book. More critically, green is an important adjective—it accurately describes the limits of what a resource such as this book can rationally and honestly address at this point in time. Green is worthy of discussion.

It would have been easy to name this book *The Sustainable Studio Handbook*. Sustainable, unfortunately, is undefined in any day-to-day operational sense. There is no way (today) to easily demonstrate that a building is sustainable. It is, however, woefully easy to claim so. We do not want to contribute to the essentially meaningless babble about "sustainable" features, "sustainable" systems, and/or "sustainable" buildings that is so common in design circles today. We *do* want to contribute to the ability of designers to produce high-performance green buildings. Sustainability will (and must) come—but it must do so rationally and not through self-assured and totally mistaken declarations of victory that would make the Federal Trade Commission cringe.

Green building design, on the other hand, is a fairly well-defined and understood concept. This has not always been the case, but the development and ready adoption of numerous transparent rating systems (such as LEED, Green Globes, the Building Research Establishment's BREEAM, Smart Homes, Built Smart, EcoHomes, ASHRAE Standard 189, the International Green Construction Code, and others) have allowed the design professions to use the term "green" with confidence and assurance. This confidence extends to discussions with clients and the general public. If a project is claimed to be green, "prove it" would be a logical and reasonable client request. Such proof may be burdensome to assemble, but the quest for verification—against a generally respected national or international benchmark—is not an impossible task.

We define a green building as one that complies with the minimum requirements for certification under one of the several available green building rating systems (such as those noted above). Sustainable buildings and high-performance buildings are another story. Sustainable is still over the horizon. High-performance is here today. A high-performance building goes beyond the minimum requirements of green to achieve outstanding performance. To do so, the design process will adopt a more thorough "systems approach" and go beyond design into operation and maintenance of the building.

Relative to green buildings, which rating system is used is not of too much importance. This book is not intended to assist in the building certification process; it is intended to assist with the design of more environmentally-responsive buildings. Having said this, however, it is useful to discuss green building certifications in order to get a feeling for this powerful force that is causing a serious rethinking of building design and performance.

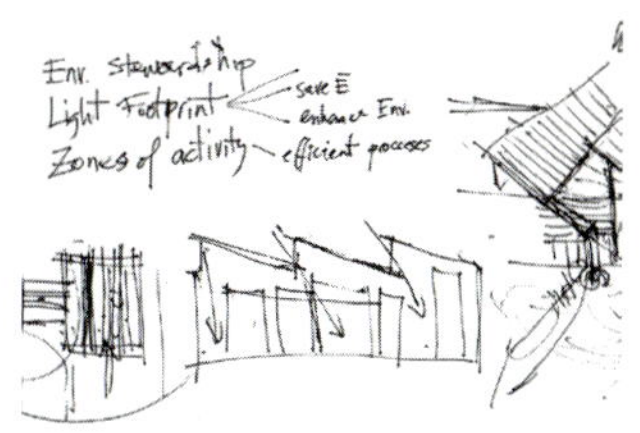

1.1 Exploring intentions with an initial gestural sketch. ALEX WYNDHAM

Green Building Rating Systems

Introduction. How does a designer decide what strategies to use? How green will a proposed project be? How can design and construction practices be changed to produce greener buildings—that may eventually lead to ever-higher performance and eventually sustainability? Rating systems can offer design guidance, serve as a decision-making tool, provide metrics by which to assess environmental impact, and act as a tool for change. Used skillfully, rating systems can promote a more integrated design process, reduce environmental impacts and life-cycle costs, and prompt major changes in the building industry. But like any powerful tool, rating systems can be used clumsily or be misunderstood. In such instances they may lead to unrealistic expectations, added project costs and complexity, and may be "blamed" when a building doesn't perform as expected.

Just as designers grapple with the emerging technologies and long-standing strategies described in this book, they also grapple with the evolving language and shifting requirements of green building rating systems. As strategies are evaluated for their suitability for a given project, so may the framework provided by a particular rating system be evaluated for applicability to a particular project.

Rating Systems Context. Since the Code of Hammurabi, written around 2000 BCE, laws have governed some aspects of building to protect human life. Architects and engineers are legally bound to protect the public's health, safety, and welfare, and governments have adopted codes that define exactly how this is to be achieved. To some extent such codes have made our buildings more green by requiring ventilation, windows, or insulation and prohibiting certain harmful toxins/practices (such as asbestos, lead paint, and chamber pots being emptied onto a street). The public's concern with health and welfare, however, is always tempered by concerns for the cost of building.

Standards and guidelines have a different status than codes. Codes are adopted and enforced by some governmental body (a country, a state, a municipality). Standards and guidelines are enforced by contract law to the extent that they are written into specifications and professional services agreements for building projects. Guidelines are generally not as refined as standards. Often some aspect of design guidance will start as a guideline, be refined into a standard, and eventually be adopted as a code. Most (but not all) green rating systems currently reside at the guideline stage, but they make reference to accepted industry standards in many performance areas in order to avoid reinventing the wheel.

In the long history of codes and standards, green rating systems were born yesterday. Mid-twentieth-century writers, such as Aldo Leopold, began to articulate a land ethic that values conserving nature, not just for what it supplies us, but for its own sake. Rachel Carson's *Silent Spring* exposed how our industries produced chemicals that accumulated in wildlife and plants—to the point where human health and survival were at risk. The OPEC oil embargo of the 1970s jolted Western society and spurred the building industry to improve energy efficiency. Codes requiring better insulation and reduced infiltration/ventilation were quickly implemented (beginning with ASHRAE Standard 90-75).

With relatively little understanding of how building equipment and assemblies interacted in a complex system, these early code requirements often had the unintended consequence of "sick building syndrome." Water vapor and off-gassing of volatile organic compounds from carpets, paints, and glues went unnoticed in leaky, well-ventilated buildings, but tight buildings allowed mold growth and chemical concentrations to trigger widespread illness. Essentially, it became clear to many that environmental responsiveness involved more than reduced energy consumption.

For many years, lawsuits were the primary tools of green building (green environment) advocates. The Clean Air Act, Clean Water Act, and Endangered Species Act passed in the 1960s and 1970s allowed environmentalists to challenge development seen as threatening the environment and human health, but this approach led to a legacy of confrontation between development and the environment that lasted many decades. When a wave of concern for environmentally-responsive buildings entered the collective consciousness in the early 1990s, many unsubstantiated (and unsubstantiable) claims about building (and designer) performance were made. Enter the idea of a green building rating system.

A Sampling of Rating Systems

BRE Environmental Assessment Method (BREEAM) is a voluntary rating system for green buildings that was established in the UK by the Building Research Establishment (BRE) in 1990. Since its inception it has grown in scope and dispersed geographically, being exported in various guises across the globe. Its progeny in other regions include LEED and Green Globes in North America and Green Star in Australia.

LEED began in the United States in 1993 with the formation of a building industry coalition to promote green building strategies and shift the market toward greener products and systems. Using BREEAM as the foundation, LEED sought to dangle a carrot in front of the building industry instead of threatening it with the stick of legal action.

Version 1.0 of LEED (a voluntary, third-party rating system) set a benchmark for green buildings to address the growing problem of "green washing." Since buildings built to code are sometimes described as "the worst building you can build without going to jail" LEED upped the ante by establishing performance levels above code minimums. Since its early focus on institutional/commercial buildings, LEED has expanded coverage to a wide range of building types. Buildings achieve LEED certification based primarily on their potential (as revealed through design and construction documentation—versus in-use performance), and are intended to represent the upper 25% of the market in terms of environmental performance.

LEED has been criticized for not being based in whole or in part on actual performance. As the first rating system to achieve widespread acceptance in the U.S., many believe it would not have been so widely adopted if in-situ performance tracking was central to the ratings.

The Green Globes rating system began in 1996 as a Canadian rating system based upon BREEAM. It was adopted by the Green Building Initiative (GBI) for use in the U.S. in 2002, partly to provide an alternative to LEED. It is intended to provide greater flexibility to design teams with less administrative effort and cost.

The system was initially criticized for being less rigorous than LEED since it relied more on self-reporting of green measures and the governing body was seen as being influenced by industry groups that provided much of the initial funding and administration. As the standard evolved, it has included more rigorous third-party review and the governing body has expanded to represent broader input from the design and construction field.

Much of the debate between advocates of LEED and Green Globes has focused on the issue of certification of wood products. LEED has historically only accepted the Forest Stewardship Council (FSC) certification for sustainably harvested wood, while Green Globes has adopted the Sustainable Forestry Initiative (SFI) standard. SFI was developed with support from the forest products industry, and has been criticized for being less rigorous than FSC.

The Living Building Challenge was launched in 2006 and is operated by the Cascadia Region Green Building Council, a chapter of both the U.S. Green Building Council and Canada Green Building Council. The program was conceived as a means of complementing LEED (and other rating systems) while challenging the industry to move as close to a "fully sustainable" building as possible. Using the metaphor of a flower, the Living Building Challenge (LBC) is comprised of seven performance areas or "Petals": Site, Water, Energy, Health, Materials, Equity, and Beauty. Petals are subdivided into a total of 20 imperatives, each of which focuses on a specific set of issues.

The LBC may have set the highest bar yet for green rating systems: it seeks to create buildings that, like a flower, are autonomous and regenerative. It starts with the concept of "triple-net zero" where a project generates all of its energy on site with renewable energy systems such as PV or wind, harvests all of its water from the precipitation that falls on the site, and processes all of the water and sewage that leaves the site. Materials containing chemicals on a "Red List" such as PVC, formaldehyde, and phthalates are prohibited, except where no alternatives can be found. Rather than choosing from many optional credits, projects must demonstrate they meet all 20 program requirements by showing a full year of operating data.

As both an aspirational challenge and a tool for promoting change, the LBC allows for some exceptions where projects are unable to negotiate code exceptions or find products that meet the requirements. Several candidate projects are currently under construction or have been recently completed, but none had been operating long enough to earn certification at the time of writing.

ASHRAE Standard 189, *Standard for the Design of High-Performance Green Buildings Except Low-Rise Residential Buildings* was released in 2009. Its purpose is to create green building guidance written in the prescriptive language and format of a standard that can be adopted as code or referenced in specifications. Developed jointly with the U.S. Green Building Council (USGBC) and the Illuminating Engineering Society of North America (IESNA), the 189 committee also included stakeholders from the design, construction, and manufacturing industries.

With many similarities to LEED, the standard represents the next step in the progression from guideline to standard to code that signals a maturing body of knowledge and practice.

The **PassivHaus** "standard" was developed in Germany as an extension of the "super insulation" movement of the 1970s. The standard functions much like a rating system in that it provides design guidance, a performance modeling tool, and performance requirements for air tightness that require an integrated, systems approach to building design. The objective is very high levels of energy savings. Applied to both residential and commercial buildings, the standard calls for significantly better insulation, glazing, and envelope air-tightness performance that will allow for a drastic downsizing of heating system capacity. Mechanical ventilation with heat recovery ensures good air quality and reduces heat losses. Many cold climate Passive Houses have been heated comfortably with a heating coil not much bigger than a hairdryer.

By focusing almost exclusively on energy efficiency and air tightness, PassivHaus reflects the belief that climate change is an issue that eclipses concerns such as recycled content, landscape design, or forest certification. Extensive post-occupancy research has shown the PassivHaus modeling tool to be more effective than most at predicting actual building energy consumption, and many of the projects have achieved 70 to 80% reduction in energy use for heating, and 50 to 70% reduction in total energy use. The PassivHaus standard was launched in the U.S. in 2006 by the Passive House Institute U.S. (PHIUS) with the support of the German founders.

The Comprehensive System for Built Environment Efficiency (CASBEE) was developed in Japan in 2005—and was also based upon work of BREEAM and LEED. One notable difference is the creation of four rating tools to address environmental performance at four stages of the building life cycle: pre-design, construction, existing building operations, and renovations. It was also developed to address conditions specific to Japan and Asia, and to be as simple to implement as possible. The program was developed by partners in government, academia, and industry and is managed by JSBC (Japan Sustainable Building Consortium).

The International Green Construction Code (IGCC) represents the evolutionary sequence from a rating system guideline (such as LEED) to a standard (such as ASHRAE 189) to a model code (such as the *International Building Code*). Developed in collaboration with the USGBC, GBI, and ASHRAE, the first public draft was released in 2010.

Instead of a voluntary rating system, the IGCC defines design and construction requirements that can be adopted by building authorities. It still provides flexibility to project teams by giving several options for compliance—both in the types of strategies that can be used and the means by which they are documented.

The National Green Building Standard was created by the National Association of Homebuilders (NAHB) specifically for single family homes, multi-family projects, and associated site work and renovation projects. Released in 2008, it covers very similar territory to the LEED-Homes rating system. LEED-Homes puts a bit more weight on location and site selection issues, with slightly lower rating costs and submission requirements. NAHB's NGBS is seen as comparable to, if slightly less rigorous than, LEED-Homes.

Local green building certifications are also common. Several states and municipalities have developed their own green certifications, especially for residential projects, in response to local demand and context—some having done so before a national rating system was available or widely adopted. With time, these local ratings are likely to be replaced by national/international codes and standards, but may retain favor among builders who wish to differentiate their projects from the rest of the market.

Rating System Challenges

Initially, rating systems provided a voluntary, third-party benchmark that gave greater credibility to the green claims of projects and project designers. Over time they became a roadmap for increasing numbers of mainstream projects that wanted to provide higher performance (whether for market differentiation, perceived benefits for occupants, organizational mission, or long-term cost savings). Now, with growing public and political support for green buildings, requirements for beyond-code performance are beginning to appear in client programs, municipal development agreements, and the building regulations of some government entities. When a previously voluntary system becomes a requirement, whether by law, to qualify for incentives, or fulfill a contractual agreement, several things can happen. Several of these challenges are outlined below.

Industry Pressure. Manufacturers who see the competitiveness of their products as being even slightly disadvantaged by a rating system will be motivated to lobby for requirements that "level the playing field." The more they stand to lose, the harder they will fight.

Growing Pains. Often a nascent, non-profit, an organization developing a rating system may experience rapid growth and the chaos that often comes with it. Such rapid growth will also come with greater scrutiny, potential conflicts of interest, and competition for "market share" in the ratings world.

Moving Targets. Rating systems often require incremental improvements over a baseline (or typical) level of performance. How is that baseline defined? Is a project compared with the average performance of all buildings, or ones built to the current code in a given area? When using software to predict how a building is likely to perform, how much change can be made between the baseline case and the proposed design?

Human Nature. Buildings don't inherently use energy—the occupants and their use of the building do. A carefully designed building can be used in unanticipated ways or by people with different habits, priorities, comfort expectations, or preferences than expected. If the first year's energy bills come back higher than modeled, stakeholders (or grudge holders) may be quick to sound the alarm.

Complexity. As buildings must address more varied, specific, and ambitious requirements, their systems often become substantially more complex. More building trades, more automation, and pressure to embrace the latest, most efficient new technology bring their own systemic chaos. Commissioning strives to de-bug such systems and their interconnections, but large buildings can take up to a year to be tuned properly.

Liability. Projects that fail to achieve their intended goals can prompt owners, developers, or even building occupants to take legal action to recover any perceived loss of funding, marketing advantage, value, or performance. A voluntary rating system, not written in the prescriptive language of codes, can become a legal minefield.

Risk Management. Faced with higher expectations, greater complexity, increased regulatory pressure and/or liability, project teams may spend more time and effort managing rating system requirements to control their risk than doing creative design work.

Point-Chasing. Since no rating system can address all circumstances, designers may have to choose between a strategy with questionable environmental benefits that precisely meets a credit requirement and an alternative strategy with substantial benefits but with questionable credit credentials. When there is little money or liability riding on a particular level of certification, designers are more likely to "do the right thing" than engage in "point chasing."

Applicability/Utility. As long as there have been codes and standards that govern what and how we build, there have been people who have objected to them. Some objections are simply obstructionist, but some are surely well-founded and can improve the quality and relevance of regulatory requirements. To remain vibrant, green rating systems need accessible and transparent procedures for interpretations and appeals. Tension will always exist between requirements language that is too broad or vague to be easily understood and language that is too specific and prescriptive to be applied fairly in the real world. In ambiguous cases, projects should be generally assessed for whether they meet the *intent* of a requirement rather than the exact wording.

Leading Change. Critics will often say "we don't need a rating system to build a better building, a greener building," and this may be true. But if a rating system is going to change practices, improve environmental performance, and increase the demand for greener products throughout the industry, it has to work for the big bulge of the bell curve where most projects are found. There will always be a leading edge of innovators and pioneers who feel any rating system has set the bar too low. But there will be 10 times as many projects for which the rating system is enough of a stretch to prompt significant changes, but not so much of a stretch that it becomes disruptive and infeasible to follow. The challenge is creating a rating system that can be supported by the pioneers, while being both aspirational and achievable to the bread and butter projects that get built by small teams on tight schedules with small margins.

Beyond Green

The terms "green" and "sustainable" are used synonymously by many involved in architectural and engineering design. This is not a good idea. Sustainability is broader in its reach than green, addressing the long-term impacts of the built environment on future generations and demanding an examination of the relationship between ecology, economics, and social well-being. Implicit in this notion (often termed the "triple bottom line") is the suggestion that the design process will seek to examine and address issues beyond the scope of the traditional building design process.

A green building will be energy-efficient, water-efficient, and resource-efficient and address on-site as well as off-site impacts on the environment. This is contributory to sustainability, but not identical with sustainability. We believe that sustainability implies having no net negative impacts on the environment. Paraphrasing the Brundtland (*Our Common Future*) report: sustainability is meeting the needs of the current generation without impairing the ability of future generations to meet their needs. Green design is a precursor to, a component of, a positive step toward sustainable design. Green design is a means—but not the end. We should surely do no less than green, but also must do more.

This book does not presume to address truly sustainable design. Green design and green buildings are a step toward sustainable design and sustainability—and green may honestly be the best that can be accomplished on a large scale in today's societal context. The need (and demand) for green buildings has become increasingly clear. The means for defining specific goals and measurable achievements for green buildings have also been refined through the development of numerous rating systems.

One of the most critical challenges now facing designers—and one of the aspects of "doing more" that must be actively considered—is the problem of climate change fueled by greenhouse gas emissions. Carbon dioxide is a key greenhouse gas and is a major product of our current building design, construction, and operation practices. While green design focuses upon reducing the environmental impacts of energy, water, and material usage (including, presumably, carbon emissions), truly informed designs must *explicitly* reduce the carbon dioxide emissions from buildings. Present-day green design efforts may reduce carbon emissions—but not in a manner that is easily quantified or open to accountability. There is little information currently available to help guide designers toward the use of quantifiably carbon-neutral products and processes and, unfortunately, the time to seriously begin dealing with carbon-neutral design outcomes appears to have been yesterday. Given this quandary, and until such time as clear-cut carbon-neutral design guidance is available, the prudent course seems to be to "green" every building and to attempt to go deeper green than lighter on every green project.

Green building as a concept may someday be obsolete. In the future, what is universally considered a "good," "economical," or "cost-effective" building would also be a green one—but we are not there yet. Order-of-magnitude changes have to come first: an understanding that long-term goals need to trump short-term conveniences; an economic system that better accounts for the costs to society of environmental impacts; and a consensus on how to regulate carbon emissions. Until then, we'll need resources for those who choose to build in ways that reduce impacts on the environment, while being aware of the limits of such resources.

This chapter was written as an essay on green buildings by David Posada, Portland, Oregon. It was adapted for The Green Studio Handbook *by the book's authors.*

NOTES

CHAPTER 2

THE STUDIO

THE DESIGN STUDIO is where the architectural action is. There are many ways for a building to obtain green status (either formally via a rating system or informally through superior performance). It is possible for a green building to do well primarily as a result of active strategies implemented by a consulting engineer. Such strategies are typically implemented during design development and have little impact on building form or orientation. It is also possible to produce a green building primarily as a result of passive (i.e., architectural) systems that are incorporated during conceptual and schematic design. Although the end environmental result of these two approaches may be equivalent, the method of getting there is definitely not. The difference is the architectural design process. And architectural design—in school or in practice—with all its attendant culture (good or bad) occurs within the studio setting.

2.1 Courtyard sketch—bringing daylight into adjacent rooms.
DANIEL JOHNSON

Informed architectural design is the challenge. Architects must be active participants in shaping green buildings—through early, reasoned, appropriate, and passionate integration of green design strategies. As educators, we believe that this process must happen in the school of architecture design studio where students can learn, acquire skills, test solutions, and be supportively critiqued. Then, we sincerely hope, an ingrained green design philosophy will flow into practice—into the workplace studio. Students will be the agents of change. Practitioners will implement change. Studio is the place.

Design Process[1]

> *"The specialist in comprehensive design is an emerging synthesis of artist, inventor, mechanic, objective economist and evolutionary strategist. He bears the same relationship to Society in the new interactive continuities of world-wide industrialization that the architect bore to the respective remote independencies of feudal society."*
>
> Buckminster Fuller, Comprehensive Designing, in *Ideas and Integrities*

Design is a multifaceted pursuit. It is at once cultural, technical, formal, and programmatic. An emphasis on one or another of design's facets affects the outcome of the pursuit and its resulting architectural expression. A comparison of two buildings by two Italian architects practicing in the early twentieth century reveals striking differences emerging from design emphasis. Luigi Nervi's work is defined by structural logic, wherein force diagrams become the form; while Gio Ponte draws upon a compositional logic that prioritizes the development of the surface. While Ponte's buildings also have a structural logic and Nervi's are also compositional, their unique inflections are clear in their works.

Does a focus on ecological (green) design similarly change a building's articulation or does this focus only change the underlying values? This is a question unique to each design team and speaks to the degree to which techniques are concealed or revealed, drawn out or underplayed, and whether the concerns of ecology are

[1] This material on design process appeared in the first edition of the *Green Studio Handbook* and constitutes an essay prepared by Laura Briggs and Jonathan Knowles of BRIGGSKNOWLES Architecture + Design in New York City. The material has been slightly edited for this second edition.

primary or secondary emphases. Nonetheless, the process of design, particularly in the early schematic stages, is by necessity transformed by an ecological focus. Ironically, a focus on environmental performance requires the pursuit of an expanded set of design issues. The process, therefore, requires the architect to assume a greater than normal degree of expertise as naturalist, material scientist, lighting designer, or engineer to be able to converse with specialists in creative ways. The architect's role is transformed from a specialist of form to a generalist of building performance—perhaps a reversion to the earlier days of design. This focus represents an opportunity for innovation and can greatly affect our understanding of design.

Defining the Problem

Schema. The first stage of design includes the moments when the project is conceptualized, the intentions are elaborated, and a geometric logic is settled upon—whether that logic is strict, internalized, or drawn as a gesture. The formal and the abstract must hold together. The first design moves are a graphic sketch or outline, a plan of action, a systematic or organized framework. These moves provide the opportunity to define goals and to set criteria. This moment is but part of the larger process of design. It is a time to set a direction for form and to gather ideas and concepts. It is not a time, however, to close down possibilities or crystallize all relationships. It is the beginning phase and, as such, it is open. The outlines formed in the mind fall on the blank sheet of paper. While it is useful to articulate intent before starting to draw, it is also useful to clarify and sharpen ideas through trial and error. The process of drawing/modeling slowly, tentatively, hypothetically unfolds the direction of the design. While the paper may be blank, the mind itself never is. Behind the first sketch are values, attitudes, assumptions, and sets of knowledge. For better or worse, arbitrariness, inspiration, and other influences seep in when least expected. A strong sense of project and environmental values can help to filter these many impulses.

Intentions. At the beginning moments of a project, it is important to define expectations for building performance. It should be decided whether the building will perform to minimum standards (as embodied in building codes) or will strive to surpass them—which must be the case for a green building. What aspects of performance will be emphasized: energy efficiency, quality of light, or air quality? What extent of green design is to be considered? A net-zero-energy building, a reduction of energy usage, a mimic of nature, or a "wild" architecture that, according to the architect Malcolm Wells, is regenerative in its nature? The intention must be clear because it points to the kind of process, the type of team, and potential strategies and technologies that will be most appropriate for a given project. This process of design requires the architect to be equally pragmatic and speculative.

Criteria. Project criteria are the standards by which judgments and decisions are tested. They are often established by an authority, custom, or general consent; but for innovative projects they are often internally established. What is really meant by green? Who decides? Criteria can be based upon quantitative standards (such as energy efficiency) or upon qualitative criteria (such as a desired lighting effect). Criteria should be realistic so they can be met; they should also be stringent enough to provide a challenge and meet design intent.

Validation. One must be conscious of the types of issues to be framed and the appropriate design methods and strategies to use. The way a designer frames a set of issues speaks to the outcomes. The studio method implies a feedback loop. A knowledge-based profession reflects upon previous efforts and explicitly learns from successes and failures. Collapses occurred during the construction of Chartres. Calculations and formulations about how materials work under the forces of gravity were rethought and the famous cathedral was rebuilt. This is also true with environmental forces, although they are often more subtle, complex, and variable than gravity. A different type of feedback loop is required, not one based upon collapse, but one that is part of the larger discipline—learning from others and learning from analysis. The analysis of an existing project becomes a hypothesis of how things should and do work.

Prioritizing. It is critically important to give order to intentions and goals. Prioritizing goals helps the designer and client to understand what is most important, what can be compromised if necessary, and how flexible are proposed solutions. As with any design process, one works through sets of ideas to get to a clarification of goals. This is particularly important because one strategy can negate or conflict with another.

Research

Data collection. Photographs of the office of Charles and Ray Eames depict large cabinets and walls displaying beautiful objects. These displays frame a space more like a museum than a place of work. The airy room was filled with a marvellous collection of things (in addition to work in progress), all emanating something provocative (i.e., geometric orders and skeletal structures). The image encapsulates an important moment in the design process, which is research.

The Eames' research involved collecting and interpreting a curious assembly of elements that ranged in scale and function. As "copy artists," they drew happily from their surroundings. Their work was as much about research into the way things work as it was the creation of things. Their images were an inspiration. With ecological design, each project requires its own archive. What one chooses to research affects the way one sees the project and, therefore, what he or she makes of it and what can be done. Ecologies work on many scales; therefore research starts with the collection of data at different scales.

Site analysis. The designer must look at the site up close and from afar. One must read the site, and learn from what is apparent, invisible, and ephemeral. The effects of the earth's tilt cause the patterns of sun angles as well as atmospheric stirrings that produce wind.

Some data, such as wind speed or solar insolation, can usually be found synthesized and packaged on the Internet or in a library. Other data, such as noise levels or circulation patterns, must be observed on site. The essence of site analysis is finding the resources and identifying the problems of a site in the context of the project and the designer's values.

It is also useful to look at vernacular architecture, which, of necessity, used the envelope and materials to mitigate climate impacts on a building. Knowledge of an appropriate climate response is implicit in many traditional ways of building and in the living patterns of the occupants. Great projects are sometimes a case of understanding and applying traditional modes of building.

Site selection. Through its interactions with its surroundings (or the lack thereof) every building modifies an external as well as internal climate. Any project creates its own microclimate and has an effect on the conditions subsequently experienced on the site. A new building affects slope, vegetation, soil type, and obstructions. Understanding the effects of various elements of a site, it is then possible to manipulate these elements to modify the microclimate for various purposes. For instance, the planting of a shade tree or the building of a simple wall can positively transform the thermal qualities of a portion of a site. The site selection process emphasizes the relation of building to localized ecological phenomena, but the logic of climate optimization also extends to the scale of the urban as well as to the building.

Form Givers

Daylighting/sunlighting. Light has famously been understood as a form giver throughout the history of architecture. In the Pantheon, Hadrian's architect dramatically captured light from an enormous oculus; all of Alvar Aalto's buildings use light scoops to steal the low sun of the far northern hemisphere. Traditional solar design uses a celebration of southern glazing in combination with thermal mass to provide passive heating. Windows, however, must be carefully sized and arranged to provide a balance between the correct amount of light, well-insulated walls, and solar collection. To arrive at a lighting strategy, appropriate lighting levels should be determined based upon the functions and needs of the various spaces; then potential solutions tested and evaluated using daylighting models or other tools. The effects of light also can be easily studied through ray diagrams expressing the sun's path. The results of such studies should provide for distinct lighting effects—and a distinct building form.

Passive and active strategies. Green buildings are often characterized by an "either/or" approach to passive or active techniques. Passive systems strategically use orientation, form, and apertures to capture and control site resources, whereas active systems deploy pumps, piping, and manufactured devices to collect, store, and redistribute such resources. The choices are often complex and may result in the adoption of a hybrid of the two approaches.

Passive design means that nature (and the architect) does the work. Passive strategies adjust to environmental conditions primarily through the architecture and should be considered before active solutions. This means that the architect must be strategic. It means using resources from the site rather than importing energy from a remote source. The careful placement of walls, windows, and overhangs can help to "green" a project; otherwise mechanical equipment (and engineering consultants) will be forced to do the job.

Hybrid systems often create a symbiosis between the building envelope and the heating and cooling systems, each working to mitigate the use of energy. Building components that have traditionally been static may be designed to move (through computerized controls or biological means), while elements of a mechanized system that appear visually inert are conveying fluids internally. A hybrid system allows the occupant to engage the variability of the surrounding natural environment in unique ways.

It is important to realize when and how often the variable climate of a site goes beyond the comfort zone and thereby begins to define the direction of a project—leading to a logical mix of passive and active systems.

Feedback Loops

A number of design tools can be deployed to predict a building's performance during the design process; these include hand calculations, physical models, computer simulations, and drawings (mapping). The performance of an environmental system is generally more difficult to evaluate than the performance of structure, material, or envelope. One can often envision the effects of weather and stress on materials, but it is difficult to see the movement of tempered air through a room. Powerful predictive computer tools are now available, such as EnergyPlus, DesignBuilder, Energy-10, ECOTECT, and eQUEST. These tools can help a designer to understand and visualize how heat moves in and around the spaces and form of a building. One must be trained to use these programs, however, in order to know what to "see"—as the power and complexity of the programs can be overwhelming.

Drawings and diagrams, documenting the changing phenomena of light and wind, can tangibly attest to what a given site can provide. Each site is unique and has distinctive characteristics. It is possible to sketch where the sun will be, how it changes throughout the day, and the potential for shading. Sun charts and diagrams may be used to quickly obtain information about sun angles. Dynamic computer models provide an alternative way to track the position of the sun. Lighting levels can be predicted mathematically using various daylighting design methods or through daylighting models.

Buildings should be commissioned by an independent authority with the active involvement of the design team. The goal of commissioning is to verify that building equipment and systems have been installed correctly and are working as intended and designed. Post-occupancy evaluation (POE) is a related feedback tool. It is critical that the design professions build a database of POE information (most likely as case studies) to inform future design efforts. Lessons learned from direct experience with system performance in a successful project can be applied to more general situations. Quality diagnostic research captured for use and publicly shared would advance the discipline of environmental design.

Building Organization and Systems

The architectural program (in commissioning terminology—the Owner's Project Requirements) developed by the architect and client determines the underlying potential for building performance. Based upon layout and orientation, the forms implicit in every potential building bear within themselves the possibility of responding well or poorly to a given climate and context. Reyner Banham in his book *The Architecture of the Well-Tempered Environment* points out the clever way Frank Lloyd Wright manipulated form to provide comfort through the use of overhangs, bay windows, and the hearth. The building organization can gather light in the winter, collect and channel wind, and provide shade. The form and shape of the building can guide the flow of natural phenomena. Simple tenets include arranging buildings and vegetation so that solar access is possible during the heating season and placing taller buildings to the north, to avoid overshadowing lower ones.

Transitional spaces. In simple terms, a transitional space is a connection between two environments. A revolving door or a double-doored vestibule are the most common examples. These approaches are useful but have but one purpose. Much more sophisticated concepts of transitional spaces can be seen in the work of Louis Kahn, who mastered the idea that an environmental response can also be architecturally rich. His projects for the Salk Library (unbuilt), the Indian Institute of Management, and the Assembly Hall in Dhaka all use transitional spaces for circulation and to bounce daylight throughout the buildings. These double shell constructions are used for corridors and stairs and are thermally neutral. They are infrequently used by occupants and require less energy; at the same time, they separate the heat of the sun from its daylight. Transitional spaces are essentially buffer zones that provide mediation from exterior to interior and can greatly reduce heat gains on a building and community.

Structure. Structure is form-giving. Different structural systems allow for different opportunities but also have inherent consequences. For instance, a load-bearing masonry wall provides thermal mass that can be used to passively modulate the temperature of a building in both hot and cold climates. Lightweight construction such as wood frame is much more susceptible to abrupt temperature swings and must be effectively insulated, yet is a good choice in climates with little diurnal temperature change or where swings of internal temperature are desired.

Envelope—Material. To design a building detail is to test a hypothesis; but the difference between idea, intention, and the actuality of the full-scale artifact can be immense. The infinite specificity of the real makes it difficult to anticipate exactly how materials will come together, correspond, and behave. For this reason, the conception of a project must be constantly examined throughout its development and grounded in a rigorous process and intuition about the behavior of materials. Material choices and relationships reinforce the spatial organization and the legibility of the idea and vice versa. A detail must have constructional purpose and critical content. Of primary interest is the critical role the building envelope (walls, roof, floor, and openings) plays alongside mechanical systems in providing visual, thermal, and acoustical comfort. The conscientious and rigorous development of a detail becomes a more complex undertaking as the building itself assists in mitigating the variability and extremes of weather. Material choice deals directly with the interrelated nature of structure, construction, and environmental systems in pursuit of the integration of these technologies into the architectural idea.

Envelope—Insulation. Attention to a well-insulated envelope allows the designer to reduce the size of climate control systems. The exterior walls, floors, and roof of a structure should be insulated to a level consistent with climate and codes. Walls, floors, roofs, and fenestration for a green building should exceed code-minimum performance requirements. Infiltration must be controlled; this means air cannot move through unplanned openings in the envelope. Windows and glazed doors should be selected and specified to contribute to the goals of the project—whether this be through solar admittance, daylighting, and/or solar rejection.

A green roof can provide many advantages. It plays an aesthetic role by extending the form of the project and creating a place of refuge. Species of grasses and plants should be selected to require minimal water and maintenance, to shade the project when full grown in the summer, and to provide produce (flowers/herbs/fruits/vegetables) for use in the building. Lightweight soil can provide extra insulation and absorb water to reduce runoff. Rainwater can be used for irrigating a garden or used in a greywater system. A green roof can extend the usable living space of a project in area and in spirit and expand ecological habitat for fauna.

Climate control systems. Green heating and cooling systems use natural ambient conditions to the fullest extent to provide climate control for a building. These ambient energies are typically renewable and non-polluting (reducing carbon emissions and reserving non-renewables for future generations). Passive strategies have the capacity to deliver heating and cooling strictly from environmental resources on site. A green climate control system should be designed to be simple, both in operation and installation.

Design Process in Summary

The design process is never "conventional," although the procedure by which a building takes form generally involves several phases and includes idea generation, testing, and working at multiple scales. Integration of technologies is often viewed as an unwanted task that should be delegated to consulting engineers—instead of being viewed as an ongoing design opportunity. Working with environmental strategies is more than an assembling of parts, or the choosing of systems as if selecting from a menu. Like a great collage, it is important for the parts to blend. In addition, they can be executed with infinite variation.

Each strategy presented in Chapter 4 is like part of a tapestry. One strategy alone does not make a project green. This becomes clear if one considers the strategies outlined. For instance, sizing a photovoltaic (PV) system without first employing stategies for energy-efficiency would produce an untenable PV strategy—not an environmentally-responsive solution. A whole roof of PVs may only be able to provide 20% of the electricity needs of a poorly conceived project. One must balance the quantitative and qualitative. It is important to work with the available strategies as part of a defined intention in order to close the loop.

The best way to use the strategies is to understand their basis in physics, ecology, and chemistry and to match the technology with the need. Avoid using high-end technologies for low-grade tasks. Don't use purified water to flush a toilet or photovoltaic electricity for a hairdryer. It is important to seek common solutions to disparate problems. This is called functional redundancy and is the basis of green design and this book.

Integrated Design[2]

The means for achieving green design goals may be elusive or at least challenging. In some cases a project team may have an intuitive sense for what feels like "the right thing to do," but lack the tools to make a clear argument for why the proposed approach would be effective. Or a designer may be faced with a bewildering choice of green design strategies and not have a clear picture of how to proceed. A committed design team may have a number of promising options on the table but concerns about technical viability or budget implications stifle their implementation. Oftentimes the flow and sequence of the design process do not leave adequate time to explore necessary options or examine alternatives. The goals may be clear, but achieving them remains just out of reach.

Integrated design provides a vehicle for achieving green goals. Recent years have seen great improvements in our technical understanding of energy use in buildings and of systems for making better use of solar heat, light, air, and materials. Numerous buildings (see Chapter 5, for example) have shown vast improvements over conventional norms of energy consumption, human comfort, and environmental impact. The fact that such buildings get built shows that not only are our building forms, materials, and systems evolving, but so are the means by which we design and build them.

Integrated Design Defined

Integrated design is a process that applies the skills and knowledge of different disciplines and the interactions of different building systems to synergistically produce a better, more efficient, more effective, and more responsible building—occasionally for lower first cost, but more typically for lower life-cycle cost. Integrated design

[2] This material on integrated design appeared in the first edition of the *Green Studio Handbook* and constitutes an essay prepared by David Posada, Portland, Oregon. The material has been slightly edited for this second edition.

considers the relationships between elements that have often been seen as unrelated.

Design is a process of inquiry. Every project is unique—presenting a unique response to the particular combinations of site, climate, user, budget, and program that define context. Every building design is a hypothesis about what represents an acceptable, a good, or an outstanding response to these contextual elements. There is much we still don't know or fully understand about building performance, and many opinions about equipment, materials, and systems that can contribute to green solutions are only recently emerging from the ongoing and growing research into the performance of constructed projects.

Design is a process of collaboration. No single person, no single profession, has all of the knowledge or skills required to understand all of the systems, materials, and assemblies that constitute the typical modern building. The best design solutions reflect a collaborative understanding developed through the contributions of many disciplines.

Design is a process of integration. Abundant knowledge must be filtered and the most relevant and applicable principles teased out of the mix. This must be done by a group of people with different backgrounds, expertise, and personalities through the congested channels of meetings, e-mail, voicemail, contracts, and work schedules. It helps if all players are working from a common value set.

Integrated design may best be defined by a comparison with what it is not. It is not necessarily high-tech design. The technological era has resulted in increased specialization and fragmentation of knowledge. Often, when very specialized knowledge is applied to problems the results lead to worse problems—following the law of unintended consequences. While high-tech knowledge is not unwelcome in integrated design, the process fundamentally tries to understand the functioning of the whole system instead of just one technical aspect. Many people see the conventional design process as an inevitable outgrowth of the industrial revolution, as the application of mechanistic ways of seeing how a narrowly defined system behaves. The "machine for living in" has not delivered on its promise; some would say it has made our situation worse.

Integrated design is not sequential design. The conventional design process is often described as "baton passing" from one specialty to another—from designer to drafter to engineer to contractor to subcontractors. Costs increase when one party makes decisions without the input of others, and opportunities for synergistic benefits are missed. Conventional design can be thought of as "knowledge applied in series." Integrated design is "knowledge applied in parallel."

Integrated design is not really design by committee. Input from team members is sought as a way to test concepts within a rapid cycle of design ideation and to discover multiple benefits from unexpected alternatives. It is a way of increasing the overall design intelligence applied to a problem and providing quick reality checks and course corrections. Design leadership is still required, but those leaders need to be sincere in soliciting and integrating the input of other team members.

Integrated design is not the same old process applied under a different set of rules. Design teams are understandably prone to using the methods and approaches they have used in the past. Only by stepping back from a situation and examining the underlying assumptions and rules can a new realm of solutions be made visible. A contemporary parallel can be seen in Amory Lovins' argument that people want hot showers and cold beer—not sticky, black goo. Owners want productivity, occupants want comfort—not HVAC systems or light shelves.

Integrated design is not a point-chasing game. The requirements of rating systems such as LEED can produce, in some cases, a mentality where strategies are adopted not because of their long-term benefits but for the short-term goal of certification. LEED credits can also take on the appearance of an additional layer of pseudo-code requirements and, in an effort to meet such requirements, teams can lose sight of the original intent of the project. By way of analogy, the requirements of the Americans with Disabilities Act have been seen as burdensome or limiting by some, but they have also opened up many designers' eyes to solutions that have improved spatial utility for all users.

Integrated design is not easy. Habits, conventions, contracts, and regulations all evolved in response to a system that grew out of a particular view of what was expected or required. The existing system is designed to address things in a piecemeal fashion. To make buildings, communities, and cities that produce energy, support human health and activity, and improve rather than degrade the environment we cannot apply a design process that created just the opposite.

Integrated design looks at the ways all parts of a complex system interact and uses this knowledge to avoid pitfalls and discover solutions with multiple benefits.

Moving Toward Integrated Design

Establishing commitment. A desire for and commitment to green should ideally start with the owner or client, since they ultimately direct and pay for the work of the design team. Client perseverance and a desire for innovation can persuade reluctant members of the team to keep moving forward. This does not suggest that the design team is a neutral observer of project values. Normally the owner and the design team share similar values and objectives. When appropriate, a charismatic designer can convert an owner to green. If the owner is the green go-getter on a project, however, potential barriers to high-performance can melt away.

Team formation and goal setting. A design team would ideally include people with the experience and expertise to quickly identify new opportunities and solutions. But if it were this easy, we'd already all be doing it. A lack of experience or technical knowledge can be offset by a willingness to explore new territory and to let go of prior assumptions and habits.

Information gathering. Each project discipline should gather information not just dealing with their conventional area of expertise, but expand the search to see how their realm of expertise interacts with and affects other parts of the system. By looking for interactions and foreseeing problems and opportunities, one can identify potential solutions. Brainstorming these solutions provides a starting point for collaborative discussion.

Conceptual and schematic design. The conceptual and schematic design phases are where the design team typically first engages the owner's program (or project requirements). During conceptual design (if all goes well) the owner will be convinced that the design team has a vision worth pursuing. During schematic design the design team convinces itself that the vision sold to the owner is in fact feasible. Rarely do any big ideas (or key strategies) creep into the design process after these initial phases. The potential of many green design strategies will be lost forever if not incorporated during schematic design.

Testing. Once a number of options are on the table, the design team can test the energy, cost, and material consequences of the options. Software models can simulate building energy use; financial models, life-cycle costing, and pro forma can test the economic implications of both long- and short-term costs and returns; the availability, costs, and implications of materials and systems can be explored. This leads to refinement of the developing design solution. Problems inevitably arise that force the team to re-evaluate the strategies being considered—sometimes even the original intent and criteria for the project. If the team has "done its homework" by thoroughly examining the resources and constraints of the site, climate, program, and budget, it will be easier and faster to find alternate solutions. Design intent and criteria should be vigorously defended (unless obviously flawed)—they represent the original project aspirations. This is where owner commitment is critical.

The contractor. The design development phase typically culminates in the preparation of construction documents (drawings and specifications) that become the basis for the general contractor's bidding and hiring of subcontractors. If the contractor joins the design team at this late point, he or she would have little knowledge of the intent and commitment behind the documents, and thus will be more likely to propose substitutions or changes that might alter the original intent. In addition, the owner and design team have not been able to benefit from the contractor's knowledge and experience. The contractor should join the project team early on; he or she would then be familiar with project intents and have a chance to suggest design changes based upon construction process constraints and opportunities.

Quality control. An owner should "get what they have paid for." This requires a quality control function that should be ingrained in the design and construction processes—but often is lacking.

Commissioning is an increasingly common means of ensuring that the owner gets the product they have been led to expect. Commissioning verifies that building systems and assemblies actually function as intended—prior to occupancy. Commissioning is not a construction-phase process; it starts in pre-design and continues through occupancy. A thorough post-occupancy evaluation (POE) of important building performance parameters is also often warranted.

The Philosophy of Integrated Design

Different descriptions have been used to characterize the integrated design process—using language and insights from different fields. A philosopher might see this process as an extension of ethics, expanding the circle of populations or issues considered worthy of ethical treatment. Green design, for example, typically looks at off-site impacts—on people and environments not directly connected to the project. A biologist might see a biophiliac approach. Systems Thinking, Learning Organizations, The Natural Step, The Triple Bottom Line, Whole Building Systems are all different ways of describing a similar process and value system. The integrated design process is based upon an understanding of how the components of a complex system interact; the value aspect is driven by what some call "purposeful" intent, which often has a moral or ethical component.

The notion of "systems thinking" arose in the mid twentieth century and has been applied to many different disciplines—from the social sciences, human resources, and biological sciences to software development and military planning. It is fundamentally different from the Cartesian world view, which studies an object or function in isolation, trying to minimize the interactions of other forces to understand its essential function. Systems thinking realizes that nothing ever occurs in a vacuum. Every element and event is seen as being a part of, and interacting with, a larger system, and that system in turn is part of an even larger system of interactions. Rather than ignore these interactions, systems thinking instead describes the different subsystems and super-systems and clarifies the boundaries that separate one system from the next.

Applying these ideas to building design is sometimes done metaphorically. Integrated design is often facilitated by looking to biological models for guidance. The interaction of many organisms in a biotic environment is akin to the ways that humans interact with their physical and social environments. Biological models can help explain the interactions between different components or the web of relationships and make it easier to see how parts of a building and related social systems can interact.

Author and farmer Wendell Berry describes the notion of "Solving for Pattern," in which good solutions tend to solve many problems simultaneously, and at many different scales. A large-scale monoculture farm deals with pests by applying greater amounts of pesticides; the side effects become as troubling as the initial problem. Solving for pattern sees the problem as one of scale: by bringing the scale of the farm back to what one farmer can oversee, it becomes possible to cultivate a variety of crops and use techniques that reduce pests without large-scale chemical applications. The smaller farm can also contribute to a wider pattern of farmers' markets or local commerce that yields benefits to the family and community as well.

An example of solving for pattern in architectural design can be seen when using building forms that maximize the use of daylight. Not only are electric loads lessened (through appropriate controls), but human comfort and productivity improve, heat gains are lessened, natural ventilation becomes easier, greater articulation of the building form and aesthetic values can result, and circulation and use patterns more conducive to social well-being may evolve.

The ability to understand the patterns of energy, light, water, and air as they apply to the built environment is a step toward developing integrated design skills. For some people thick books or long lectures help to explain these patterns, but for many the quickest route may be to apply appropriate strategies to design problems using quick ballpark estimates, back-of-the-envelope calculations, or general guidelines. Examples of such schematic approaches for many strategies are presented in Chapter 4.

NOTES

CHAPTER 3

THE HANDBOOK

THIS HANDBOOK is intended to provide focused information that will help a designer make rational decisions regarding the use of green building *strategies* during the schematic design phase of a project. Case studies of exemplary projects that illustrate a range of green building types and contexts are included to encourage the use of such strategies and to highlight some of the exceptional green design work being done throughout the world.

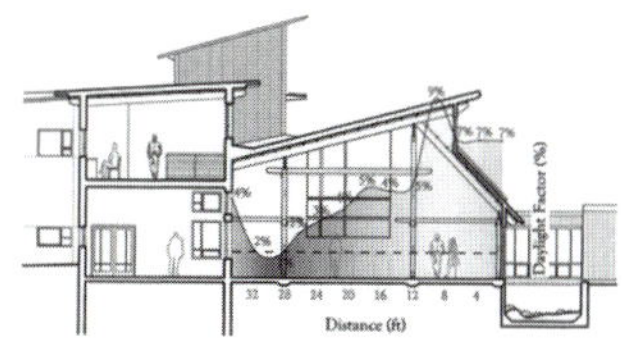

3.1 Schematic drawing showing daylight factors for an interpretive center—measured using a physical daylight model. JONATHAN MEENDERING

The schematic design phase emphasis is intentional. This is where informed decision making can exert the maximum impact on project performance at the least cost. Building form and orientation decisions are made during schematic design—and the negative impacts of poor site and massing decisions are virtually impossible to reverse (other than by the use of mitigating technological fixes—the design equivalent of atonement). We believe that high-performance buildings—specifically green buildings, but also net-zero-energy and carbon-neutral buildings—must aggressively embrace passive architectural strategies. These strategies must be incorporated very early in the design process; typically within the first few days of project development.

During the schematic design phase, an understanding of system potentials is critical to the adoption of appropriate strategies. Likewise, a sense of system sizing requirements is vital to the architectural implementation of many strategies. Will 100 ft^2 of solar thermal collector be required to meet domestic hot water demands or is 1000 ft^2 necessary? Will a 5000 L cistern work for rainfall storage or is 50,000 L capacity necessary? Can a passive cooling system maintain 80 °F under peak design conditions or should the client expect to see 90 °F? During the schematic design phase the essential questions facing a designer are "go/no-go" relative to potential strategies, closely followed by "fit/no-fit" for key components. Nuances are not critical at this stage; being in the right ballpark is.

We believe that an architect must understand the general nature of green strategies (the defining system characteristics, constraints, and variables) and also understand conceptually how each strategy functions. In addition, he or she must be able to make preliminary judgments about system sizing. The main reason we feel this falls into the architect's lap is philosophical; most of these strategies are architectural, that is to say they should be owned by the architect. A second reason is pragmatic: unless the project is being conducted under an integrated design process there is no mechanical, electrical, or civil engineering consultant off whom to bounce ideas during schematic design.

This handbook presents 42 schematic design strategies that are worthy of consideration for a green building project. There are many other strategies that will typically be applied to a green project, but that normally come into play later in the design process—examples include the selection of materials and finishes, HVAC system design, lighting controls, and the like. If a strategy is likely to influence building orientation, form, organization, and/or apertures it is included in this handbook.

The 42 strategies are presented in a consistent format. Each begins with an introduction, followed by a statement of key architecture issues, a discussion of implementation considerations, an overview of design procedures related to the strategy, some examples of the strategy in use in constructed buildings, and resources for further information. Running in parallel with the main text, sidebar information summarizes important contextual concerns for each strategy, provides a worked example of sizing or coordination (if applicable) and suggests design efforts related to the strategy that will occur after schematic design.

Chapter 4 (the heart of this book) presents both active and passive design strategies. Many highly rated green buildings have achieved their status primarily through skillful use of active solutions. Other well-regarded green buildings have taken a primarily passive route to high performance. Most larger-scale green buildings include both types of systems. All 10 of the case study projects presented in Chapter 5 include active as well as passive systems. What's the difference between active and passive?

Simply put, a passive system:

- uses no purchased energy (no electricity, natural gas, ...);
- uses components that are generally also part of another system (windows, floors, ...);
- is closely integrated into the overall building fabric (not tacked on, nor easily removable).

An active system has essentially the opposite characteristics—requiring purchased (non-renewable) energy for operation and employing single-purpose components that are often lightly integrated with other building systems. Active and passive strategies have no inherent goodness or badness—they are simply means to an end. The design team and owner, however, can and should place value on the means. This book, and many green designers, value passive strategies above active. This valuing must be tempered by practicality, and by an understanding of what the various systems can and cannot rationally accomplish in general and in the context of a particular building. A major objective of this book is to provide a sense of "can/cannot" for systems that should generally be considered during schematic design.

It is important to emphasize that this is not a "how to get a green certification" manual. Each certification organization has extensive information to assist with the certification process. This is a "what can I do to get a workable green building" handbook. The difference is subtle, but critical. A green building will exhibit superior environmental performance. A certified green building will amass enough credits to be rated. The two concepts should overlap, and often do—but not always. We'll opt for performance over certification every time.

A conscious decision was made to focus this book on strategies that are not yet in the mainstream, and therefore not necessarily well-addressed by standard design and systems references. Basic design information—such as heat loss calculations, sunpath diagrams and water consumption estimations—are intentionally not included in order to keep this handbook of manageable scope, size, and cost. A few exceptions to this rule will be found in the limited appendices.

Finally, it would be easy to assume, with 42 separate strategies, that each could be used like a catalog of parts. Nothing could be further from the truth. Design strategies are connective—they may support each other or they may clash. Some may be counterproductive in one context and be most beneficial in another context. The strategies are tools that must be manipulated by a skillful designer. This handbook is intended to augment existing design skills.

On an integrated design team, one would ideally be able to turn to an expert and ask: "How do we do this?" This book attempts to be that knowledgeable companion. The integrated design process does not demand long-drawn-out explanations of options and strategies; rather it thrives on concise suggestions of what to consider and how to begin. Such guidance can lead to an initial hypothesis of how a high-performance building may actually work. Getting proof-of-concept regarding potential strategies during schematic design allows the design team to make their first moves really outstanding ones. Schematic design must provide a "thumbs-up" for green design ideas. In-depth modeling, more sketches, and/or testing will be used to evaluate these formative hypotheses during later design iterations.

NOTES

CHAPTER 4

DESIGN STRATEGIES

The green design strategies in this chapter are organized into six major topic areas and include those strategies that most influence schematic design decision making. Each strategy describes an underlying green principle or concept. Sidebar links suggest related strategies and larger design issues to be considered. The heart of each strategy is a step-by-step design procedure to guide the preliminary sizing of building and system components. Where a strategy is more conceptual than physical, the design procedure provides guidance to help incorporate the concept into schematic design thinking. Conceptual sketches illustrate each strategy to reinforce the fundamentals, and photographs show strategies applied to built projects.

NOTES

ENVELOPE

Consideration of the building envelope begins with site selection and the subsequent placement of the building on site, generation of plan and section forms, and the location of windows and skylights. Orienting a building on an east–west axis while placing the bulk of window openings on the north and south elevations makes solar control and daylighting easy to achieve.

Insulation is a crucial part of any green building project. Because reduced energy use is a high priority in any green building, a thick layer of a not-quite-green insulation is usually preferable to an inadequate thickness of a green insulation. That said, presuming adequate insulation values and quality of installation can be achieved, always choose a green insulation over a non-green one.

When selecting materials for structure and envelope, less is often more. Using materials more efficiently conserves resources, reduces waste, and helps reduce construction costs. If using wood framing, make sure spacing and detailing are optimized for resource efficiency. Forest Stewardship Council (FSC) certified framing and/or engineered wood products should be considered. If using concrete, design for efficient use of material and reduce cement content by incorporating fly ash. For steel, develop insulation details that avoid thermal bridging.

During schematic design, consider the benefits of admitting or rejecting solar heat and begin to think about glazing with a solar heat gain coefficient (SHGC) to best address solar concerns and a visible transmittance (VT) to enable daylighting. Glazing selection is shaped by many factors. A wise choice for one project may not be appropriate in another. Overhangs and shading devices can reduce or eliminate the need for solar control glazing.

Consider alternative materials—such as strawbales—for commercial or residential buildings in appropriate climates. Roofing presents several options. A green roof offers many benefits, reducing the urban heat island effect, potentially providing high insulation values, reducing rainwater runoff, and possibly offering habitat for local flora and fauna. If a green roof is not an option, cool roofing materials are preferable in cooling dominated climates. Cool roofing can lessen solar loads on the building and extend the life of the roof by reducing expansion and contraction of materials.

Materials that last longer will reduce the demand for resources and in many cases result in lower life-cycle embodied energy. Quality materials also reduce maintenance costs and thus may be cheaper from a life-cycle perspective even if they involve higher first costs.

ENVELOPE

STRATEGIES

NOTES

SITE ANALYSIS

SITE ANALYSIS is a critical early step in developing a green solution to an architectural problem. The purpose of a site analysis is fundamental: to understand what characteristics of a site may be of benefit, or vice versa, to the design process; for example which site characteristics may be used as resources and which ones are a liability (i.e., a problem that must be resolved). Almost every design project in architecture school that deals with a building includes a requirement for a site analysis. With few exceptions, most of the resulting "analyses" are of little value. In general, the site analysis is often seen as a barrier that must be breached before "design" can begin. In general, most "site analyses" are incomplete descriptions of a few selected site characteristics. In an ideal world, such deficiencies would be less commonly seen in professional practice.

To be useful and successful, a site analysis must consider the type and scale of the proposed project. Is the project a single-family residence, a school, an office, a theater? Is it likely that the project will be envelope-load dominated or internal-load dominated? Is the client seeking minimal code-complying energy performance or a net-zero-energy building? The findings of a site analysis for a single site located in a Memphis, Tennessee suburb (or the Docklands of London, or the steppes of Turkey) will differ under each of these suggested project contexts. A site analysis is really a site-program analysis. The project program is at least as important to the outcome of an analysis as is the site.

A good site analysis must include valuation. What does the design team value on a project? Is daylight seen as a valuable resource, as something to be considered if there is time to do so, or as not worth the time investment? These are subjective values and will vary with the personalities involved with a project as well as with the project itself. A competent site analysis is much more critical for a green or other high-performance building than it is for a just-code-compliant building. Natural site resources (usually associated with passive systems) are more critical to the success of a high-performance project.

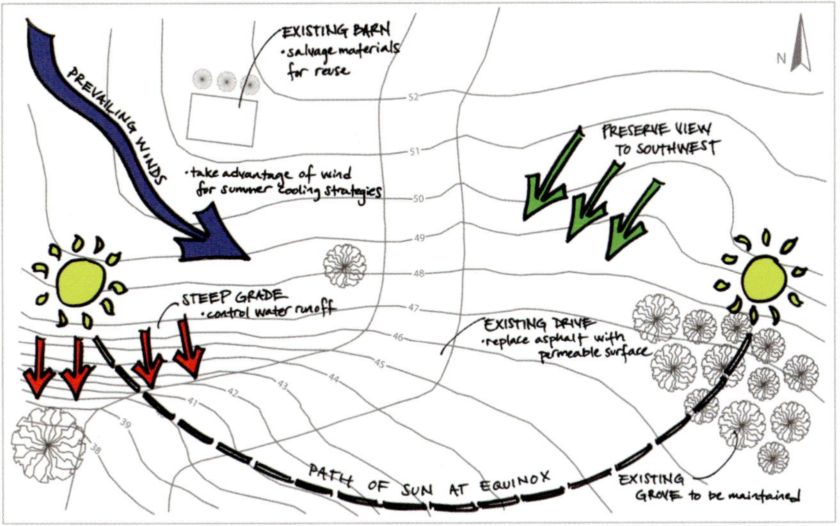

4.1 Typical site analysis; presented in plan and providing a sense of design opportunities. MATT HOGAN

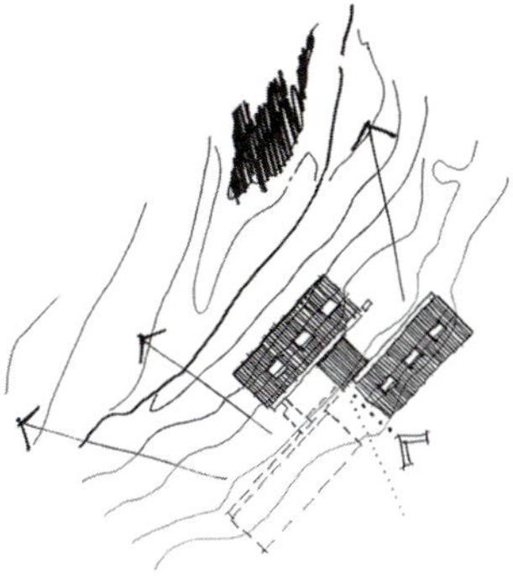

4.2 Conceptual site plan for the Arup Campus, Solihull. ARUP ASSOCIATES

INTENT
To clearly understand the positives and negatives associated with a site vis-à-vis impending design of a project

EFFECT
An understanding of site resources that will facilitate the beneficial use of such resources in a specific project

OPTIONS
Graphic analysis, computer analysis, hybrids

COORDINATION ISSUES
A site analysis is a coordination effort—matching project needs with site resources; results will feed into many green strategies

RELATED STRATEGIES
All passive strategies (daylighting, passive solar heating, passive cooling) and many basic architectural design strategies

PREREQUISITES
Fundamental project objectives, a sense of project scale, design intent, design criteria

Key Architectural Issues

The following are some of the architectural systems that will be influenced by the results of a site analysis. This list is not comprehensive, but typical; project details will change the importance and the specifics of affected architectural systems. Also, the focus herein is green building projects—other issues, such as subsurface conditions, will be an important site issue for many projects.

Daylighting. Successful daylighting depends upon ready access to those portions of the sky vault that can deliver adequate luminance without the need for expensive and complex shading device design. The location of such beneficial sky resources is reasonably generic. The actual availability of access to prime sky resources, however, can be very site-specific. Adjacent buildings, trees, hills, and such can block access to the sky vault and thus to key daylight resources. See the several strategies related to daylighting for further information on sky resources.

Passive Solar Heating. Successful passive solar heating relies upon ready access to direct solar radiation during the underheated period of the year. The extent of the underheated period is influenced by site temperatures (climate)—but also by building envelope design and internal loads (as they affect balance point temperature). Details of building enclosure and plug, equipment, and electric lighting loads will not be known at the time of site analysis. Nevertheless, a building balance point temperature must be estimated to allow the underheated period to be preliminarily defined.

The apparent path of the sun across the sky is generic for any given latitude (and the timing of this path is generic for any given longitude). Obstacles that may impede the flow of direct solar radiation from its "origin" in the sky vault to a passive solar aperture are not generic. As with daylighting, adjacent buildings, trees, and landforms may block radiation that might otherwise be used to heat a building. Such critical obstructions must be identified during site analysis—and will be influenced by site characteristics as well as by intended aperture location.

Passive Cooling. There are numerous passive cooling systems. Some depend upon ambient wind patterns, some upon ambient wet-bulb temperatures, others upon access to the night sky or subsurface soil temperatures. All passive cooling systems require unfettered access to the heat sink that drives their performance. Passive cooling systems usually live on the edge, with little or no excess capacity available under design overheated-period conditions.

In the case of a cross ventilation cooling system, wind velocity, wind speed, and wind direction (during the months of proposed system use) are critical to system success and sizing. A site analysis that values cross ventilation potential will assemble macroclimate information about summer winds, overlay local (microclimate) information about flow-obstructing or flow-enhancing site features, and make projections about the effects of site on cross ventilation potential. Site features and climate patterns that will affect other passive cooling

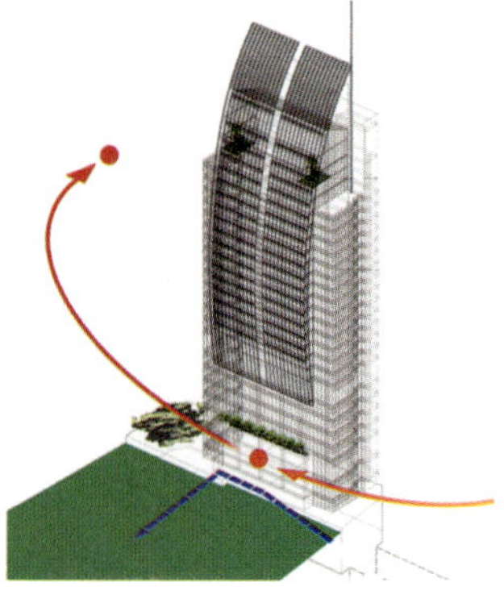

4.3 One Peking Road, an office building in Hong Kong. The facade was designed to work with the path of the sun and permit daylight entry from both the north and south facades. ROCCO DESIGN LTD

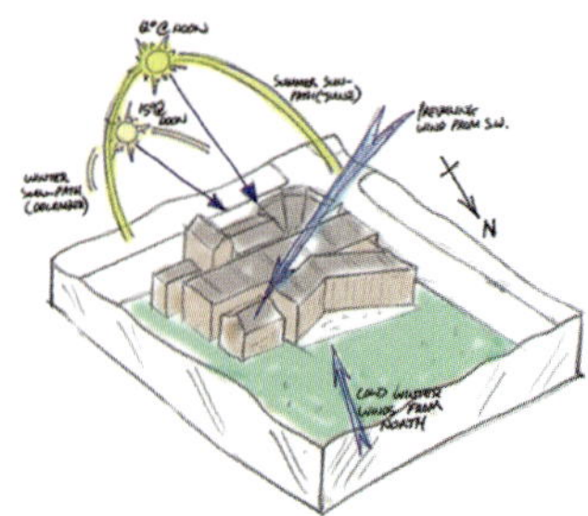

4.4 Site analysis diagram for the John Hope Gateway project in Edinburgh, Scotland. MAX FORDHAM ENGINEERS

systems must likewise be mapped in order to begin to make determinations about locations of buildings, wing walls, and other elements that may enhance or impede wind flow.

Water and Stormwater Runoff. Green buildings often attempt to meet water needs from on-site resources and/or reduce the impact of site runoff. Gauging the potential for such strategies requires an understanding of rainfall rate and patterns, site perviousness, and site contours. Information on these characteristics will be part of a good site analysis—if these strategies are valued.

Acoustics. Even though comfortable architectural acoustics is not an express requirement of most current green building rating systems, the provision of comfortable interior environments is at the heart of most green design efforts. Appropriate acoustics is a part of any such quality environment. From a site perspective, seeking to provide good acoustics normally means reducing noise intrusion. Noise sources are very site-specific and can only be ascertained by a site visit. Noise sources are also time-dependent, so a site visit must be timed to provide information on both typical and "design" noise characteristics.

Air Quality. Although air quality may be broadly characterized on a regional basis, levels of pollutants can and will vary from site to site as a result of localized industrial sources, traffic, and even adjacent buildings. Micro-scale measurements of the many pollutants that may affect building occupants are difficult and expensive to obtain. As a minimum, a site analysis should identify observable, intuitive air quality issues—such as the likelihood of higher CO_2 values near heavy traffic routes. Several on-site measurements of CO_2 patterns in and around occupied buildings have shown measurable differences in ambient CO_2 levels from one side of an urban site to another.

4.5 Climate Consultant wind wheel used as an analysis tool for a project site in San Francisco.

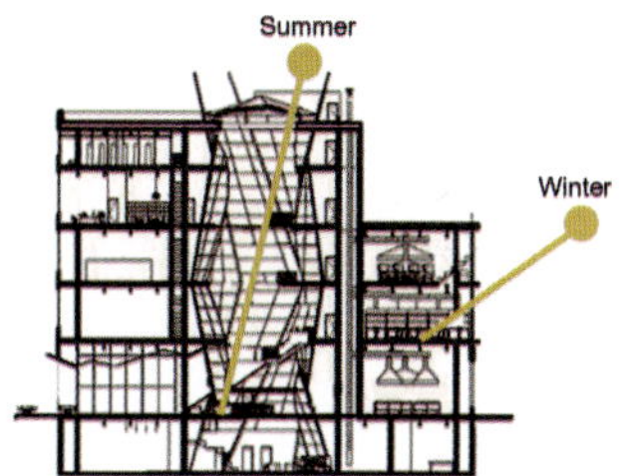

4.6 Section used to study summer and winter solar radiation penetration into an atrium.

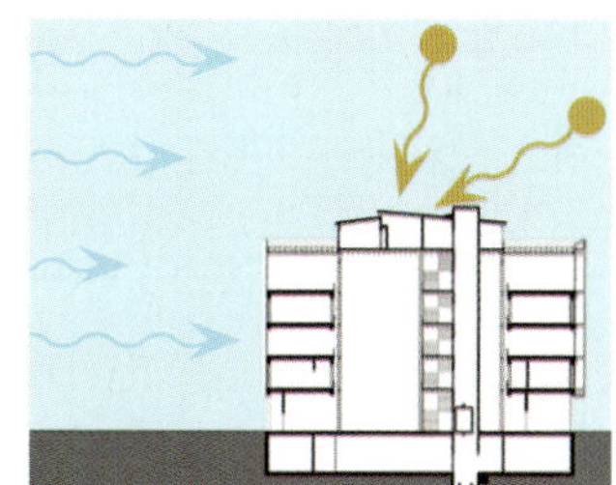

4.7 Section analysis diagram addressing solar position in the winter and summer.

Implementation Considerations

Developing a good site analysis requires a balance between designing a building before site impacts are understood and waiting until all site characteristics are assigned values before designing anything. This is not as difficult as it may sound. A passive solar heating system will generally involve south-facing apertures for reasonable performance. Assuming roughly south-facing apertures during a preliminary site analysis is a reasonable approach that will provide focus and reduce time and resource demands. Should such a south-facing assumption prove to be unworkable later in the design process, a rethinking of the solar access aspects of the site analysis can be conducted.

Some aspects of a site analysis can be done remotely (off site). These include determination of macro-scale phenomena such as solar position data and macroclimate information such as design temperature, solar radiation, rainfall, and wind data. Other aspects can only be ascertained from a physical site visit. These include noise data, view preferences, and solar/sky obstruction data.

It makes sense to assemble available generic (macro-scale) data first, and then visit the site for location-specific (micro-scale) data. Time of observation is critical to some characteristics (noise, traffic density). Time is less important for issues such as views and the mapping of obstructions. Some data, such as views, can be observed and recorded without need for field instrumentation. Other data, such as sound pressure levels, the location and height of trees, or CO_2 levels will require the use of portable instrumentation (in the examples noted: a sound pressure level meter, a compass with inclinometer and a magnetic deviation chart, and a CO_2 meter). Planning will ensure that required instruments are available at the site when needed.

Remember that a sense of the potential "worth" of the characteristics being observed is important. If a resource is seen as exceptionally valuable, it is more likely to be well-described and analyzed than a resource seen as of little concern.

Design Procedure

A site analysis is a part of the building design process—and there is not one correct procedure to be followed. Rather, the following is a suggested procedure that should lead to better outcomes for green projects than is the norm in most academic settings.

1. Establish project design intent.
2. Establish design criteria for each intent. (In building commissioning parlance, the above are collectively termed the Owner's Project Requirements—and define, in substantial detail, what success will look like for the project client.)
3. Develop architectural strategies and systems that will or may be necessary to reach the owner's objectives (daylighting, stormwater mitigation, passive cooling, etc.).
4. Catalog the site resources that will be crucial to the success of the identified strategies (design rainfall, solar radiation magnitude and access, summer wind direction and speed, etc.).
5. Establish a graphic representation by which site analysis findings can be assembled and presented (graphics are suggested as a picture is often worth a thousand words).
6. Ensure that all dimensions (especially height and time) necessary to an understanding of selected site characteristics can be conveyed using the intended graphic vehicle.
7. Access, review, and summarize macro-site data available through off-site research means (climate data, solar path information, regional air quality data, and the like).
8. Determine what instrumentation (such as a sound pressure level meter or anemometer) will be required for site-based micro-scale data collection.
9. Visit the site at appropriate times and observe/record micro-scale information. Improvements in digital data analysis may allow some micro-scale information (such as the height of wind/

SAMPLE PROBLEM

As can be seen in the adjacent design procedure, there is no simple or single means of site design planning. The implications of efficiently using site resources are important for the proper selection and sizing of designated strategies such as PVs, rainwater collection, and daylighting.

solar/sky obstructions) to be obtained remotely, but a site visit will be required for information about noise and ground perviousness.

10. Assemble collected data.
11. Analyze collected data through the filter of project type and objectives.
12. Present data graphically in a manner that supports informed design decision making.

Examples

Ian McHarg, in *Design with Nature*, presented an early, innovative, and creative approach to site analysis involving site plan analysis overlays. In essence, segments of a site were classified across a

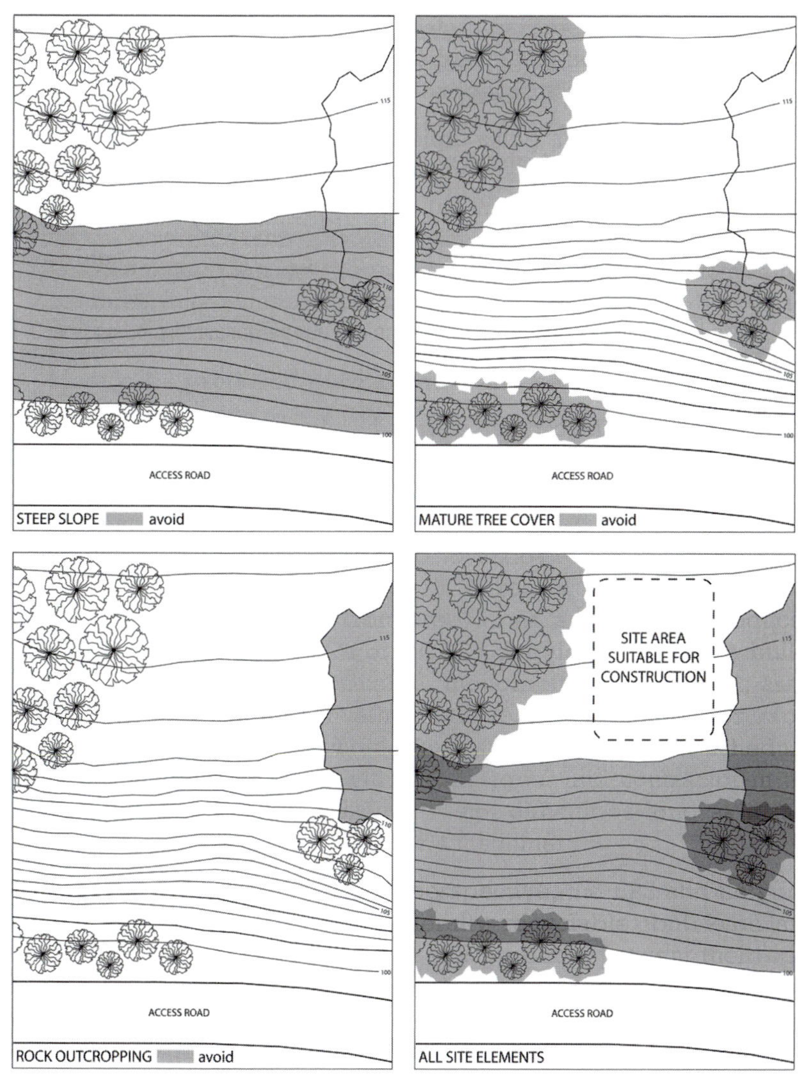

4.8 A site analysis that looks at surface characteristics via the McHarg overlay technique; shaded areas are "valued" as areas to avoid. MATT HOGAN

variety of characteristics (such as slope, existing vegetation, soil quality) and a value assigned to the various classifications. These classifications/values were placed on transparent site plan overlays (layers in today's CAD language). In simple terms, the overlays could value a portion of a site (say, relative to slope) as good, bad, or neutral. Adding overlays (values) for more characteristics built up a composite valuation of portions of a site relative to a proposed project. The overlays act as an integration mechanism across variables.

Victor Olgyay, in *Design with Climate*, presented an approach for analyzing site climate across the seasons. Patterns of dry-bulb temperature and relative humidity for each month of the year were plotted on a thermal comfort zone chart to produce "timetables of climatic needs" relative to human comfort expectations—providing a roadmap to site climate resources and problems. This pioneering site analysis technique is embodied in the "timetable" plots and "psychrometric chart" presentations produced by *Climate Consultant*.

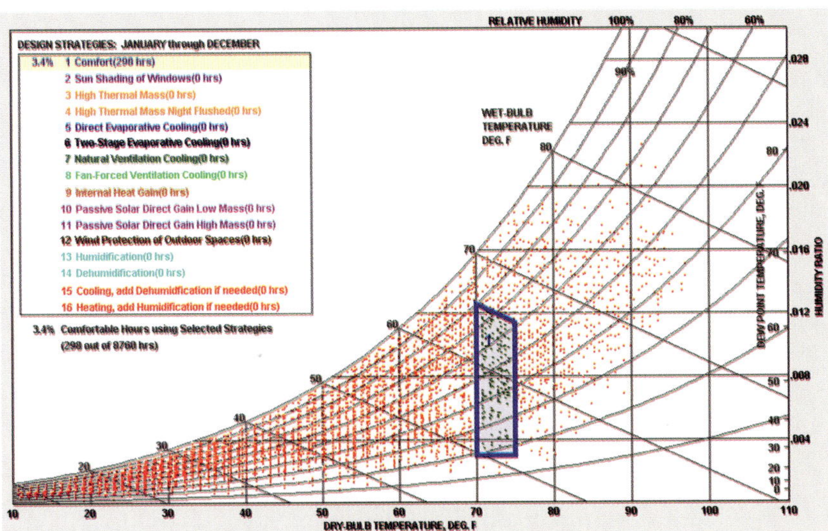

4.9 Sample "psychrometric chart" analysis from *Climate Consultant* that builds upon Olgyay's "timetable of climatic needs" approach. USED WITH PERMISSION

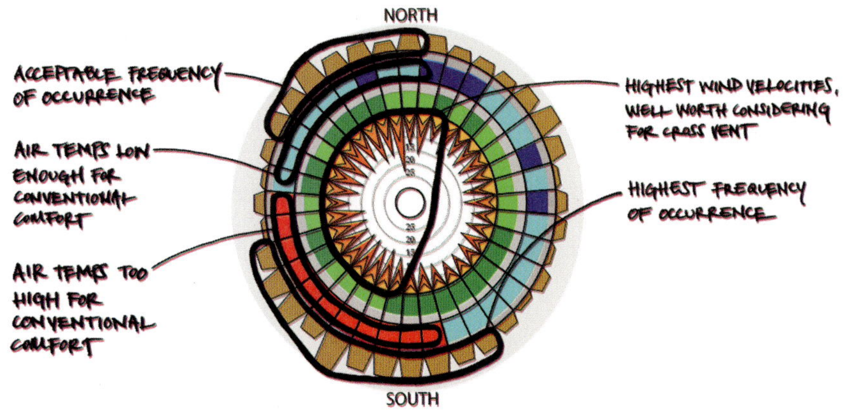

4.10 Wind wheel data presentation from *Climate Consultant* annotated as an analysis of site conditions. MATT HOGAN; WIND WHEEL USED WITH PERMISSION

Climate Consultant, free software developed at UCLA under the direction of Murray Milne, brings the analysis of site climate pioneered by Olgyay into the computer era. Long-term climate data for numerous locales can be accessed and graphically represented using *Climate Consultant*. Unfortunately, most users of this valuable tool make no effort to analyze—and simply show climate data in graphically intriguing ways. This is the fault of the user, not of the tool. *Energy-10*, building energy simulation software distributed by the Sustainable Buildings Industry Council, has climate analysis capabilities embedded within its Weathermaker utility.

BEYOND SCHEMATIC DESIGN

Once site analysis is complete and resource availability, quantity, and direction are understood, an assessment regarding specific approaches to take with daylighting, passive heating and cooling, and access to water and energy can be made. With general knowledge of site resources, the designer can begin schematic design of the building proper.

Further Information

McHarg, Ian. 1995. *Design with Nature* (25th anniversary edition), John Wiley & Sons, New York, N.Y.

Olgyay, Victor. 1973. *Design with Climate: A Bioclimatic Approach to Architectural Regionalism*, Princeton University Press, Princeton, NJ.

UCLA 2010. *Climate Consultant*, Department of Architecture and Urban Design, University of California, Los Angeles. Accessible via Energy Design Tools web page: http://www.energy-design-tools.aud.ucla.edu/

SBIC 2010. *Energy-10*, Sustainable Buildings Industry Council, Washington, DC. http://www.sbicouncil.org/displaycommon.cfm?an=1&subarticlenbr=112

NOTES

INSULATION MATERIALS

INSULATION MATERIALS have traditionally played a vital role in building design for climate control. Their impact on energy efficiency (and thus energy savings) can be substantial. Many insulation materials, however, contain polluting and/or non-biodegradable substances that could seriously decrease the greenness of a project. This strategy provides suggestions on selecting insulation materials that have reduced negative environmental impacts and also provides guidelines on what to watch for regarding thermal insulation during the schematic design phase of a project.

4.12 Installation of faced, formaldehyde-free batt insulation. JOHNS MANVILLE, INC.

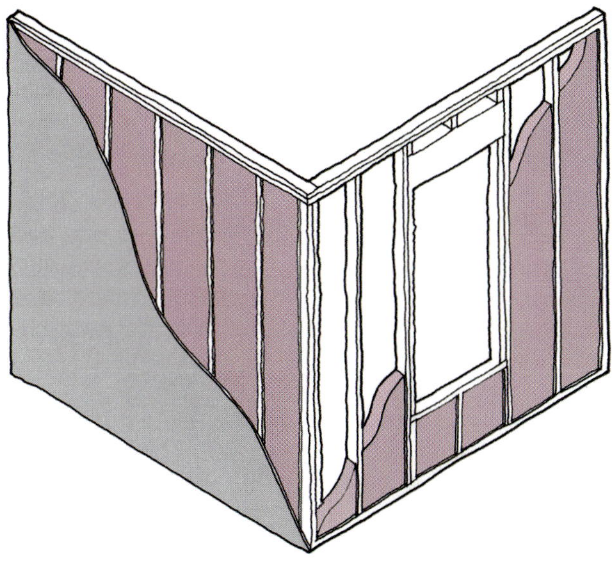

4.11 Wood frame wall section showing traditional installation of insulation between studs. Rigid insulation/sheathing is applied as needed to meet project objectives. NICK RAJKOVICH

Numerous types of insulation materials are available, including:

Plastic foam board (rigid board) insulation. Comprising products such as beadboard (molded expanded polystyrene—EPS) and foamboard (extruded expanded polystyrene—XPS), this category of materials can contain VOCs (volatile organic compounds), is not biodegradable, and may involve fireproofing chemicals of concern to health authorities.

Spray-applied foam insulation (spray-in cavity-fill). Some open-cell polyurethane insulation products are produced with soy oil comprising about 40% of their "poly" components, resulting in foam that is about 25% soy and 75% petrochemically derived. Although these products do not have R-values as high as those of closed-cell polyurethane, they are three to four times as resource-efficient.

Magnesium silicate or cementitious foam (Air Krete®). This product provides a CFC- and HCFC-free insulation alternative. Although it is more expensive than products that use CFCs and HCFCs, it is fire-resistant and has no indoor air quality impact. Its weakest point is its fragility—which may soon be addressed by adding plastics to the mix to reduce brittleness.

INTENT
Energy efficiency, thermal comfort, environmental resource conservation

EFFECT
Reduced heating/cooling loads, improved mean radiant temperatures

OPTIONS
Insulation type, thickness, and location

COORDINATION ISSUES
All aspects of building envelope design

RELATED STRATEGIES
Structural Insulated Panels, Double Envelopes, Green Roofs

PREREQUISITES
Applicable building code requirements, design intent

Cellulose insulation. Installed loose-fill, sprayed damp, or densely packed, cellulose insulation is made from 75–85% recycled newsprint. Embodied energy is about 150 Btu/lb [0.09 kWh/kg]. This insulation contains non-toxic chemical additives which meet U.S. Consumer Product Safety Commission fire-retardancy requirements. There are no significant indoor air quality issues if this product is properly installed, although there are potential risks resulting from dust inhalation during installation and VOC emissions from the incorporated printing inks.

4.13 Application of open-cell polyurethane produced using water as a blowing agent. ICYNENE INC.

Fibrous batt and board insulation. These materials are an insulation mainstay; unfortunately many of these products use formaldehyde as a primary component. Glass fiber products usually use phenol formaldehyde as a binder, which is less likely to emit harmful pollutants than urea formaldehyde. Some major manufacturers have elected not to use formaldehyde binders in their fibrous insulation products.

Loose-fill fiber. Loose-fill glass fiber or blowing wool that does not contain formaldehyde is readily available in applications with R-values ranging from 11 to 60 [RSI 1.9 to 10.6].

Mineral wool. Often used for fire protection of building structural elements, this material is made from iron ore blast-furnace slag (an industrial waste product from steel production that has been classified by the U.S. Environmental Protection Agency as hazardous) or from rock such as basalt.

4.14 "Spider" is a lightweight glass fiber insulation bound with a non-toxic, water-soluble adhesive that also binds to cavity surfaces for gap-free coverage. JOHNS MANVILLE, INC.

Cotton insulation. Batt insulation that is made from recycled denim scraps. Some products use 85% recycled fiber saturated with a borate flame retardant or a combination of borate and ammonium sulfate flame retardants.

Radiant barriers (bubble-backed, foil-faced polyethylene foam, foil-faced paperboard sheathing, foil-faced OSB). These are thin, reflective foil sheets (available in a range of configurations) that reduce the flow of heat by radiant transfer. They are effective only if the reflective surface of the barrier faces an airspace. Proper installation is a key to the success of this type of insulation. Recycled polyethylene products containing 20–40% post-consumer recycled content are available.

Perlite. This is a siliceous rock that forms glass-like fibers. Perlite is usually poured into cavities in concrete masonry units (or similar assemblies). It is non-flammable, lightweight, and chemically inert. Perlite generates very little pollution during manufacturing and poses a minor threat for dust irritation during installation. Its main drawback is its limited range of applications due to its "fluid" character.

Structural insulated panels (SIPs). Comprising "structural" and insulation materials in one assembly, SIPs generally outperform other insulation/construction compositions in terms of R-value per assembly thickness. Building envelopes constructed with SIPs are also virtually airtight when properly installed. (See the Structural Insulated Panels strategy.)

Key Architectural Issues

The primary early design phase implications of thermal insulations involve providing necessary building envelope assembly thickness and addressing unconventional construction approaches—either of which may impact the building footprint and/or the relationships between building planes and openings. In practical terms, a better-insulated envelope is usually a thicker-than-normal envelope. An exceptionally well-insulated envelope may substantially reduce the required size of passive and/or active heating systems, providing opportunities for first and life-cycle cost savings.

4.16 Retrofitting an old uninsulated attic with 12 in. [300 mm] of R-38 [6.7] glass fiber batt insulation improved comfort and reduced heating bills by 40%.

Implementation Considerations

Provide the highest feasible insulation resistance. Remember that codes typically require only minimum acceptable insulation values—not optimum values—and that the cost of energy generally escalates (making more insulation more cost-effective over time). When the use of low-R-value materials makes sense from another perspective, increase material thickness to produce reasonable U-factors.

Given comparable R-value and performance, always choose high-recycled-content insulations over alternatives made from virgin materials. Require that insulation scraps generated on site be recycled. Select/specify extruded polystyrene (XPS) products with low to no ozone-depleting potential. Except when moisture is an issue, use polyisocyanurate instead of XPS or EPS. Rigid mineral insulation works well as a foundation insulation due to its good drainage properties.

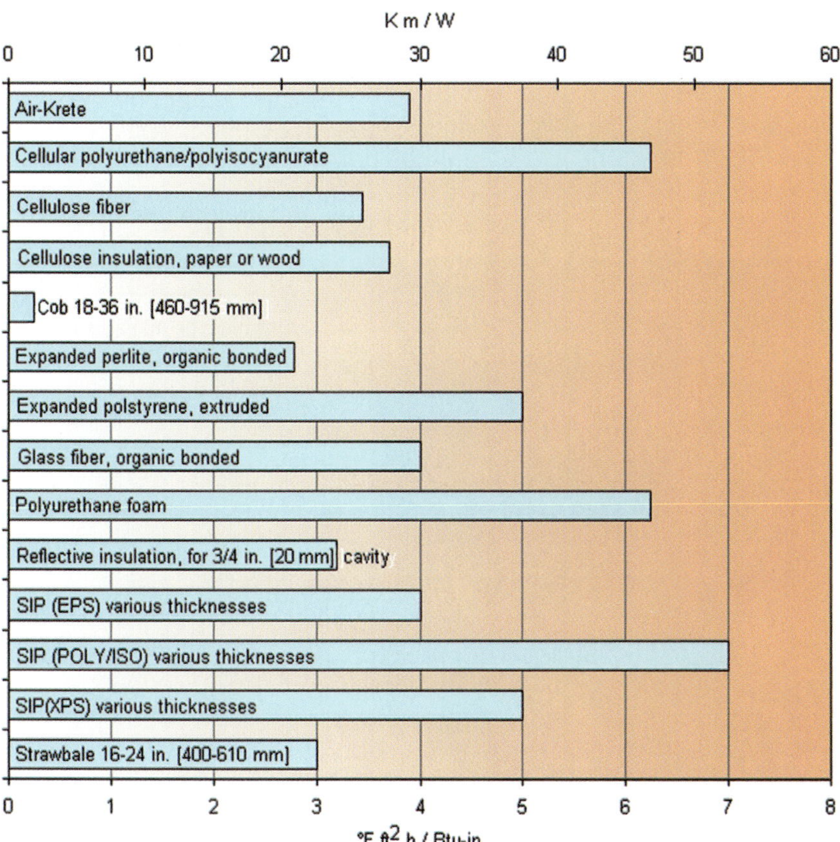

4.15 Thermal resistance values for various insulation and alternative building materials.
KATHLEEN BEVERS

When necessitated by the choice of structural system or detailing, minimize thermal bridging by enclosing highly conductive framing elements with a layer of appropriate insulation. A thermal bridge is an uninsulated or poorly insulated path between interior and exterior environments.

What is considered an environmentally-acceptable thermal insulation material varies from country to country. Be aware of local restrictions and incentives intended to steer selection decisions toward preferred materials. Of particular interest are recent concerns in the U.S. about the environmental impacts of blowing agents and fire retardants used with some thermal insulation materials.

Design Procedure

1. Determine the minimum acceptable insulation R-value (or assembly U-factor) permitted by applicable building codes.
2. This minimum requirement will seldom be appropriate for a green building. Determine whether this minimum insulation requirement meets the intents of the client and design team. If not, establish more appropriate (demanding) insulation values using design guides, client directives, and/or life-cycle cost analysis.
3. Determine whether any likely-to-be-implemented insulation approaches will require unconventional construction or materials assemblies that will impact schematic design decisions. If so, incorporate these considerations into the proposed design solution.
4. Move on with design—remembering the impact that better-than-minimum insulation may have on system sizing and equipment space requirements.

Examples

4.17 Loose-fill glass fiber insulation being blown into an attic. This insulation is often used in existing homes because it is easy to apply in difficult-to-reach areas.

SAMPLE PROBLEM

A single-story strip commercial building is being designed for Hoboken, New Jersey. The building will have a sloped roof with attic and use steel stud wall construction. Hoboken has 6572 HDD65 [3651 HDD18] and 2418 CDD50 [1343 CDD10].

1. Using ASHRAE Standard 90.1 as a benchmark, Hoboken is in climate zone 4A. The minimum roof insulation for an attic construction is R-38 [RSI 6.7]. The minimum wall insulation for metal framing is R-13 [2.3] plus R-7.5 [1.3] continuous. The minimum floor slab edge insulation is R-15 [2.6].
2. Considering the green design intent for this project and the fact that envelope loads will play a big role in building thermal performance, more stringent values from ASHRAE Standard 189.1 are selected. Thus, the roof will be insulated to R-49 [8.6], the walls to R-13 [2.3] plus R-10 [1.8] continuous, and the floor slab to R-10 [1.8] edge plus R-5 [0.9] under.
3. The attic can be insulated using loose-fill blown-in insulation with no impact on construction details. The wall insulation can be accommodated using batt insulation and 6 in. studs and continuous rigid insulation sheathing. The slab insulation can be easily accommodated with conventional rigid board insulation.

4. The impact of the increased envelope resistance will be considered when calculating heating and cooling loads.

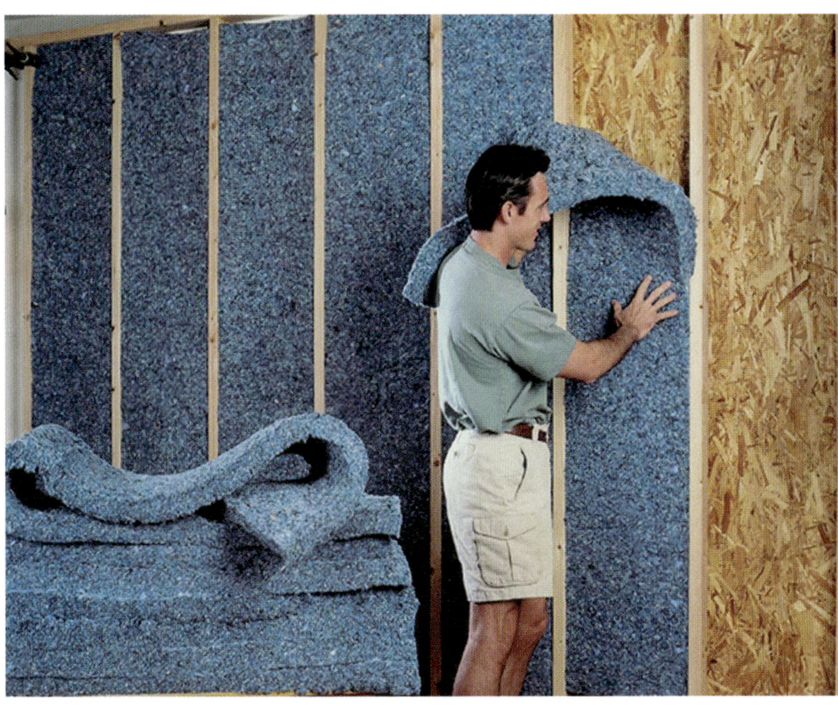

4.18 Installation of cotton batt insulation, made from 85% reycled denim and cotton does not require special clothing or protection. BONDED LOGIC, INC.

4.19 Installation of Air Krete foam, an inert, inorganic, cementitious product made from magnesium oxide (from seawater and ceramic talc). AIR KRETE ® INC.

Further Information

Air Krete, Inc. www.airkrete.com/

Allen, E. and J. Iano. 2008. *Fundamentals of Building Construction*, 5th ed. John Wiley & Sons, Hoboken, NJ.

Bonded Logic, Inc. www.bondedlogic.com/

BREEAM EcoHomes Developer Sheets (Building Research Establishment, Garston, Watford, UK). www.breeam.org/pdf/EcoHomes2005DeveloperSheets_v1_1.pdf

Building Green. www.buildinggreen.com/

Icynene Inc. www.icynene.com/

Johns Manville. www.johnsmanville.com/

Mendler, S., W. Odell and M. Lazarus. 2005. *The HOK Guidebook to Sustainable Design*, 2nd ed. John Wiley & Sons, Hoboken, NJ.

North American Insulation Manufacturer's Association. www.naima.org/

Wilson, A. 2010. "Avoiding the Global Warming Impact of Insulation." *Environmental Building News*, Vol. 19, No. 6, June.

Wilson, A. 2009. "Polystyrene Insulation: Does It Belong in a Green Building?" *Environmental Building News*, Vol. 18, No. 8, August.

Wilson, A. 2005. "Insulation: Thermal Performance is Just the Beginning." *Environmental Building News*, Vol. 14, No. 1, January.

Structural Insulated Panel Association. www.sips.org/

BEYOND SCHEMATIC DESIGN

Detailing of enclosure elements during design development will be critical to the overall success of building envelope performance—particularly with respect to thermal bridging and vapor retarders.

STRAWBALE CONSTRUCTION

STRAWBALE CONSTRUCTION is a strategy for building energy-efficient, low environmental impact buildings. Dry strawbales are set upon a moisture-protected foundation, stacked in a running bond, and secured with rebar or bamboo sticks. The bale wall is then post tensioned with cables or rope to prevent extreme settling. Wire mesh is applied to the constructed bale walls and the resulting assembly is finished with several layers of plaster, spray-applied concrete, or stucco.

4.21 Drilling to place rebar into a strawbale.

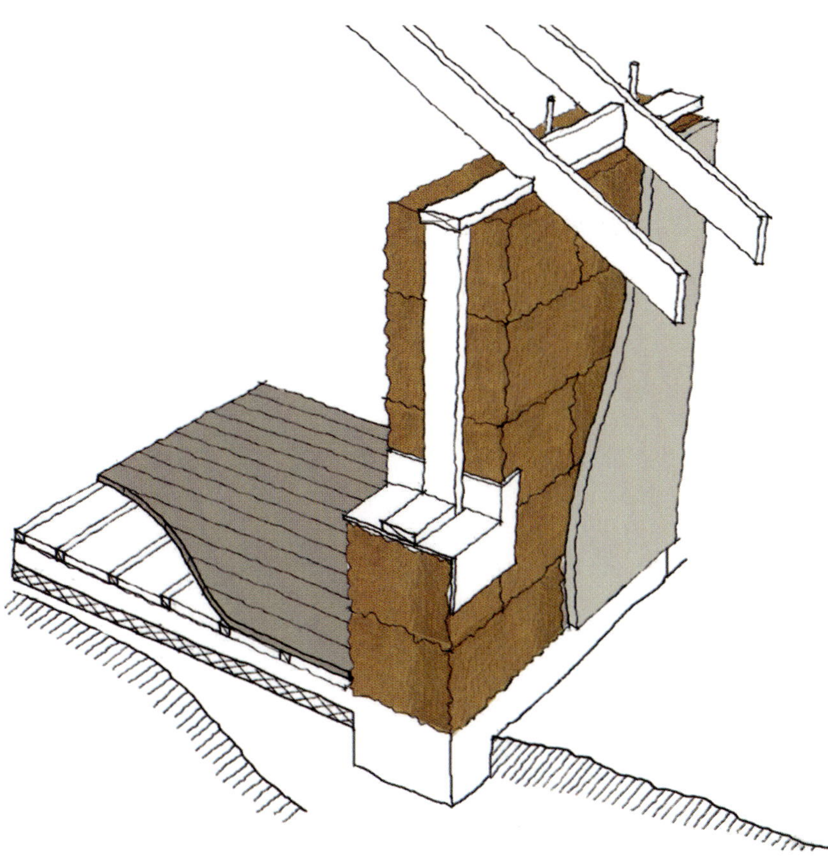

4.20 Diagram showing typical strawbale wall construction. JONATHAN MEENDERING

Early settlers in Nebraska (USA) pioneered strawbale construction methods when faced with a limited timber supply. Many of these century-old structures still stand today as a testament to the viability and durability of strawbale construction.

Straw is a renewable agricultural waste product that is abundantly available, inexpensive, and simple to work with. Bales are typically priced between 1–4 US$ each. They may be used as a structural component of a building as in "Nebraska Style" construction or coupled (as infill) with wood, metal, or concrete framing. "Nebraska Style" is a stressed skin panel wherein the assembly derives its strength from the combined action of bales and a plaster or stucco finish. Used as infill, strawbales carry no appreciable loads (which are borne by an independent structural system). A hybrid system may be adopted to satisfy specific local building code requirements.

INTENT
Climate control, energy efficiency, resource efficiency

EFFECT
Reduced energy consumption for heating/cooling, reduced use of non-renewable building materials, improved interior environmental quality

OPTIONS
Strawbales used as structural elements or as infill, bale characteristics and thicknesses

COORDINATION ISSUES
Climate and site conditions, interior and exterior finishes, heating/cooling systems

RELATED STRATEGIES
Insulation Materials, Cross Ventilation, Stack Ventilation, Direct Gain, Indirect Gain, Isolated Gain, the daylighting strategies

PREREQUISITES
Available material resources, amenable codes

Strawbale walls lend themselves to energy efficient structures. With R-values generally between R-35 and R-50 [RSI 6.2–8.8], the inherent insulating value of straw is a valuable tool in providing viable passive heating and cooling solutions. With a wall thickness of 16 in. [400 mm] or greater providing a substantially massive envelope, strawbale construction can also serve as an effective sound barrier.

Although ideally suited for dry climates, strawbale buildings can be constructed in any area where straw is available, provided careful measures are taken to eliminate moisture infiltration. Misconceptions exist regarding the fire resistance of strawbale construction; a well-constructed wall assembly can have a fire resistance rating higher than that of a typical wood frame building.

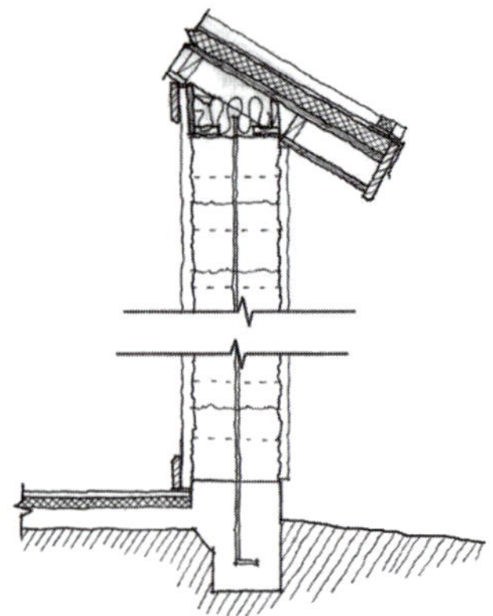

4.22 Section through a strawbale wall. JONATHAN MEENDERING

Key Architectural Issues

During schematic design the most important issue to consider is likely to be wall thickness. Substantially thicker than normal walls that result from strawbale construction must be dealt with in terms of building footprint. Keeping water away from the strawbale construction (via siting, grading, and overhangs) is also a schematic design concern.

4.23 Oak Lodge, Our Lady of the Oaks Retreat Center, in California used strawbales and other strategies to help achieve a low-energy intent. SIEGEL & STRAIN ARCHITECTS

Many important architectural design issues involving detailing will be dealt with later in design. They are noted here because of their overall importance. Water resistance is the key to the long-term success of a strawbale structure. Cracks and holes in the weather skin must be avoided and roof overhangs suitably designed to provide good rain protection. Fenestration elements are susceptible to water penetration and require careful attention to detail. The base of the wall, top plate, and sill should incorporate a moisture barrier. Large wall areas should not be covered with a vapor retarder as it may retain moisture rather than assist with keeping the wall dry.

Foundations should be constructed to limit bale exposure to water by providing a generous elevation above the ground surface and, if possible, above interior floor height. Like any wall system, the insulating value of strawbale walls can be weakened by thermal bridging. Care should be taken to ensure that structural members in a strawbale infill system have minimal thermal bridging capacity. This can be accomplished by insulating the structural elements or encasing structural members within the strawbale assembly (not easy due to the thickness of the bales, which must be retained for thermal performance).

Roof systems are constructed in conventional fashion using a range of systems and materials. When a hybrid wall system is utilized, traditional top plates (adjusted for wall width) support the roof. With Nebraska Style construction, a box frame is common. In either case, the weight of the roof should be distributed to the center of the wall (and not at the edge) to prevent bowing.

4.24 A truth window is often installed in strawbale walls to show their construction. WILLIAM HOCKER

Implementation Considerations

Strawbales are typically available in two- and three-string bindings (wire-bound bales are recommended). Two-string bale dimensions are usually 14 in. [350 mm] high, 30–40 in. [760–1020 mm] long, and

18–20 in. [460–500 mm] wide. Three-string bales measure 14–17 in. [350–430 mm] high, 32–48 in. [810–1220 m] long, and 23–24 in. [580–610 mm] wide. Consider bale dimensions when choosing a foundation type. Bale setting should begin at least 8 in. [200 mm] above grade.

Bale tightness and moisture content are of primary importance when choosing an appropriate source of materials. A good strawbale (for construction) will have a density of 7–8 lb/ft^3 [112–128 kg/m^3]. Bales compacted much beyond 8 lb/ft^3 [112 kg/m^3] have limited air spaces and thus begin to lose thermal resistance. A maximum 20% moisture content is suggested to reduce the danger of mold, mildew, and decomposition within the wall. A moisture meter can be used to determine the moisture content of bales under consideration.

Published information on the thermal resistance of strawbales shows a wide range of values (or, put another way, a range of potential discrepancies). Be cautious when using R-values from the literature. Use values that are most appropriate both technically and contextually; consider local experiences and performance reports.

When selecting individual bales, consistent size is a key criterion. Avoid lopsided bales that will make leveling difficult. Chopped straw bales should be avoided; long-stalk bales provide superior strength. Bales must be free of grain seed that may attract pests. Dry, seedless straw possesses no nutritional value and ensures that the walls are not attractive to insects or rodents. Ask the bale supplier about pesticide and chemical use, if this is of concern (as should be the case with green building design).

All piping, wiring, and plumbing run within bales should be encased in sleeves (insulated as appropriate) for safety.

4.25 Structural timber framing and strawbales are supported on poured-in-place concrete foundations that are the full width of the bales and rise 15–18 in. [380–460 mm] above any water. FREEBAIRN-SMITH & CRANE ARCHITECTS

Design Procedure

1. Establish the general feasibility of strawbales in the context of the proposed project. Are bales readily available? Are they permitted by building code? What size bales are generally available? Are they a generally green product (or do they require extensive irrigation and/or transportation)? Will strawbales provide the intended thermal performance?
2. Ensure that the proposed site is appropriate for strawbale construction relative to water-flow characteristics. Select a building location on site that minimizes potential water problems (i.e., well drained soil, slopes that carry water away from the foundation).
3. Select a structural approach that works in the context of the project and prevailing codes—infill, structural bales, or a hybrid system. Consider the seismic requirements of the locale.
4. Select a foundation type (slab on grade, block, pier, etc.) that best suits the soil characteristics, frost line, and loads.
5. Allow for increased wall thickness when laying out interior spaces, the roof system (including generous overhangs to protect against rain wetting), and fenestration openings.

Examples

4.26 Ridge Vineyard's Lytton Springs Winery in Healdsburg, California used over 4000 rice strawbales and integrates several green strategies including photovoltaics, shading devices (including vines), and daylighting. WILLIAM HOCKER

4.27 At the Lytton Springs Winery, non-load-bearing rice-bale walls are 20–24 ft [6–7 m] tall. The walls serve as infill within a frame of non-treated glulam timber columns and beams. The bales are secured by wire mesh cages (see Figure 4.25). The bales and steel strap seismic cross-bracing were later plastered. FREEBAIRN-SMITH & CRANE ARCHITECTS

SAMPLE PROBLEM

The design of a strawbale building entails the design of an entire building enclosure system. For schematic design, the initial steps described in the design procedure, and knowledge of the available bale size, will allow the designer to work with well-reasoned envelope dimensions.

4.28 At Ridge Vineyard's Lytton Springs Winery in Healdsburg, California, a "breathing" (non-cementitious) earthplaster allows water vapor to pass through the strawbale walls. The plaster was mixed at the site and blown and hand-troweled onto the bales. FREEBAIRN-SMITH & CRANE ARCHITECTS

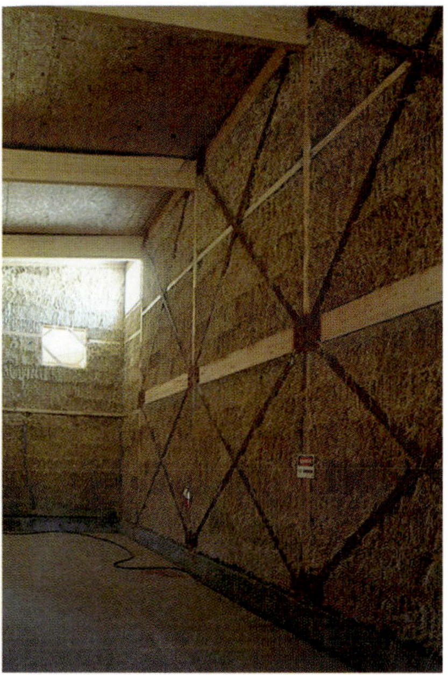

4.29 The entrance to the wine tasting room (left) and other wall openings at the Lytton Springs Winery are shaded by deep roof eaves and vine-covered trellises. Door and window frames are further shaded by recessing them into the 24 in. [600 mm] depth (right) of the strawbale walls. FREEBAIRN-SMITH & CRANE ARCHITECTS

4.30 The Lytton Springs Winery has a daylit tasting room with smooth, earth-plastered strawbale walls and maple cabinetry and woodwork. MISHA BRUK, BRUKSTUDIOS.COM

Further Information

California Straw Building Association. www.strawbuilding.org/

Commonwealth of Australia. Technical Manual: *Design for Lifestyle and the Future—Straw Bale*. www.yourhome.gov.au/technical/pubs/fs58.pdf

Jones, B. 2002. *Building With Straw Bales—A Practical Guide for the UK and Ireland*, Green Books, Totnes, Devon, UK.

Magwood, C. and P. Mack. 2000. *Straw Bale Building—How to Plan, Design and Build with Straw*, New Society Publishers, Gabriola Island, BC.

Steen, A. et al. 1995. *The Straw Bale House*. Chelsea Green Publishing Company, White River Junction, VT.

BEYOND SCHEMATIC DESIGN

Most of the design of a strawbale building is "beyond schematic design." Once deemed feasible in schematic design, the real effort of designing and detailing to ensure structural stability, weather integrity, thermal performance, and acceptable aesthetics begins. This is really no different from other building types—except for the less conventional nature of the fundamental building material and its associated requirements.

STRUCTURAL INSULATED PANELS

4.32 Residential construction in Idaho using SIPs roof panels.
BRUCE HAGLUND

STRUCTURAL INSULATED PANELS (SIPs) consist of an insulating core element sandwiched between two skins. In this structural assembly, the skins act in tension and compression while the core handles shear and buckling forces. SIPs are commonly composed of an expanded polystyrene (EPS) core with adhesive-attached oriented-strand board (OSB) facings. Alternatives to EPS as a core include extruded polystyrene (XPS), polyurethane, polyisocyanurate, and straw. The advantages and disadvantages of these materials, as well as many construction details, are presented by Michael Morley in *Building with Structural Insulated Panels (SIPS)*.

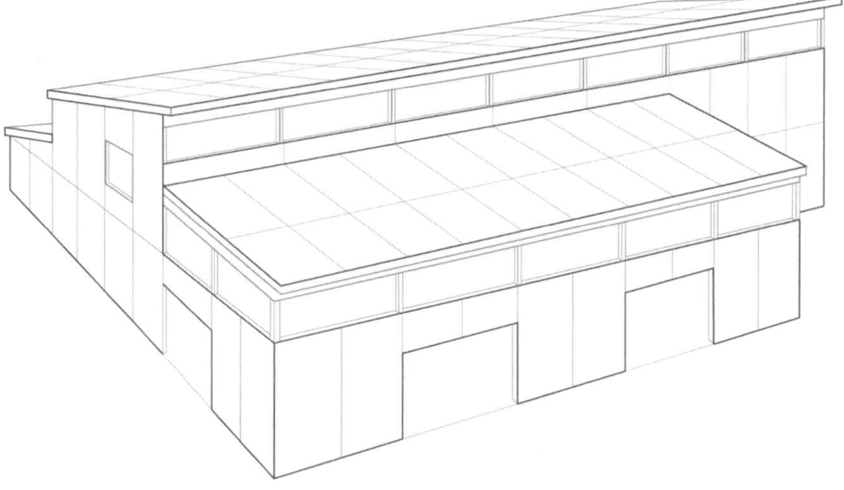

4.31 Conceptual diagram showing the use and assembly of structural insulated panels.
JON THWAITES

Building with structural insulated panels has proven to be an energy-efficient alternative to stick-frame construction primarily because of the limited need for heat-conducting (thermal bridging) studs. The structural strength of this construction method is also superior. Homes built with SIPs have survived tornados in North America and earthquakes in Japan. Another benefit is resource efficiency. Wood for OSB typically originates from tree farms and EPS is produced without ozone-damaging CFCs or HCFCs. A quiet interior in a building that is solidly built is a valuable, though often overlooked, asset that fits with a green design ethic. Due to their potential for rapid assembly, SIPs are a good choice for a project on a tight schedule. Because manufacturers work with the designer and contractor in the production of panels, customization is not difficult as long as it falls within the capacity of a manufacturer's machinery.

From a disassembly and recycling perspective, the EPS and polyurethane components of SIPs are generally recyclable, but foam and adhesive residue on the OSB panels will probably prevent their beneficial reuse. The amount and type of VOCs emitted by SIPs can vary from manufacturer to manufacturer. Some data suggest that SIPs emit lower levels of formaldehyde than standard wooden residential construction (some SIPs may not emit any) but may emit higher levels of other chemicals.

INTENT
Energy efficiency, efficient use of materials, structural integrity, making use of prefabrication

EFFECT
Good overall thermal performance, reduced infiltration, reduced site waste

OPTIONS
Skin and core materials vary, dimensions vary

COORDINATION ISSUES
Site conditions, heating/cooling loads, fenestration, ventilation

RELATED STRATEGIES
All energy conservation strategies, Glazing, Air-to-Air Heat Exchangers, Energy Recovery Systems

PREREQUISITES
A convenient supplier of panels (to reduce transportation requirements and simplify coordination)

Key Architectural Issues

SIPs may be used in conjunction with timber framing, stick framing, steel, and other materials. Typically, SIPs are used for exterior walls and/or bearing walls, with stick framing used for interior partitions. Interior gypsum board, a finished ceiling surface, and a fire-retarding finish are some of the options that may be incorporated into a SIPs assembly at the factory, rather than on site. Cement tile backerboard for stucco, cementitious plank, and other materials may be factory-applied on the exterior skin.

SIPs may be used for walls, roofs, and/or floors. Top and bottom plates, headers, and trimmers are still necessary to enclose the foam core, thus sealing the envelope. Non-structural panels are available for use in conjunction with timber or steel framing systems—with a range of options for interior and exterior facings. Because these framing systems are not inherently energy-efficient, some builders have used SIPs to enclose conventional structural frames.

Implementation Considerations

To reduce field costs and resource wastage, a building designer using SIPs must consider the modular nature of these panels and work within established dimensions to minimize field cutting. To simplify construction, site access for a crane to unload, raise, and place the panels is necessary.

When using SIPs in long-span floors or roofs, creep may cause a panel's facings to pull away from the core. To avoid this problem, confirm the viability of intended applications with the panel manufacturer and/or project structural engineer.

Gypsum board (drywall) facings may be required in order to meet fire code ratings. Verify requirements with the local jurisdiction. A pest control barrier should be provided to prevent carpenter ants and termites from nesting in the insulating core of the SIPs. The use of stick framing behind kitchen sinks (and similar locations) will simplify plumbing installation.

Because SIPs construction can greatly reduce infiltration, ensure that adequate ventilation (active or passive) is provided for acceptable indoor air quality. (See, for example, the strategy addressing Air-to-Air Heat Exchangers.) Select a SIPs manufacturer who has had panel performance tested (and reported) by a third party.

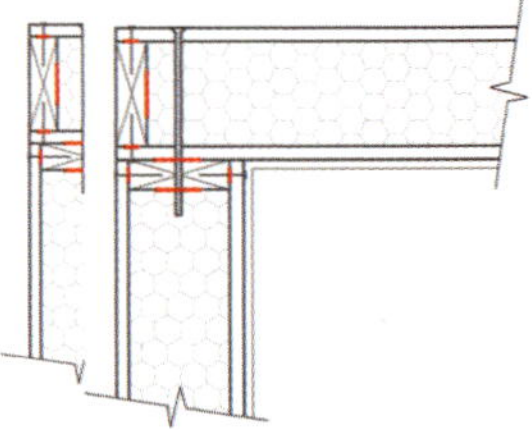

4.33 SIP corner assembly detail. JON THWAITES with permission of the Structural Insulated Panel Association (SIPA)

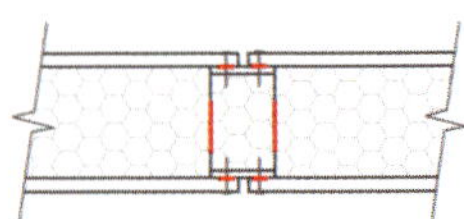

4.34 SIP spline connection detail. JON THWAITES with permission of the Structural Insulated Panel Association (SIPA)

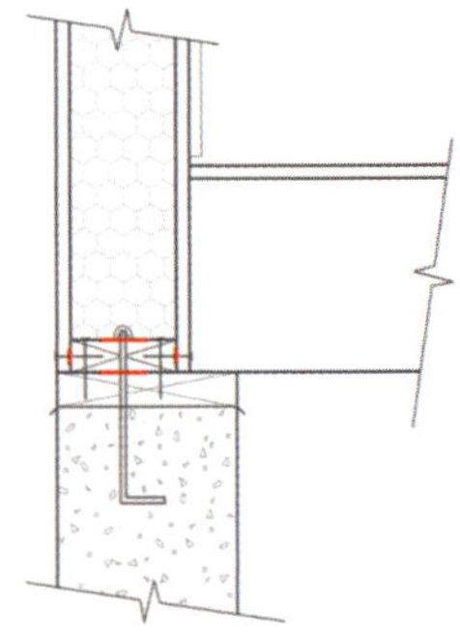

4.35 SIP foundation connection detail. JON THWAITES with permission of the Structural Insulated Panel Association (SIPA)

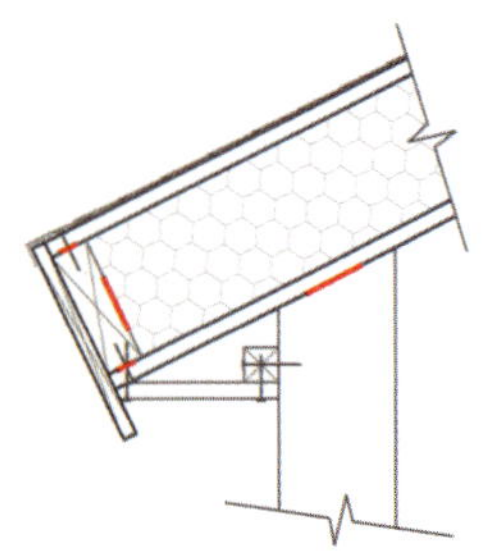

4.36 SIP roof connection detail. JON THWAITES with permission of the Structural Insulated Panel Association (SIPA)

Design Procedure

1. Determine what panel sizes are readily and locally available. Dimensions for SIPs vary between manufacturers. A typical panel is 4 or 8 ft [1.2 or 2.4 m] wide and 8 to 24 ft [2.4 to 7.3 m] long, usually available in 2 ft [0.6 m] increments. Other dimensions, however, are often available, as are curved panels. Openings are most efficiently done at the manufacturing plant using computerized layout tools; a precision of 1/8 in. [3 mm] is common. A factory is also more likely to have a waste materials recycling program than a job site.
2. Determine the minimum R-value (or maximum U-factor) permitted by building code for those envelope elements to be assembled of SIPs. These requirements will usually be different for wall, roof, and floor assemblies. Select panels of appropriate thickness and composition to meet code minimums—or, more likely, to exceed them. The R-value of a SIP increases as panel thickness increases. Standard thicknesses for SIPs, including the insulating core and standard OSB facings, are 4.5, 6.5, and 8.25 in. [115, 165, and 210 mm]. Thicker panels (10.25 and 12.25 in. [260 and 312 mm]) are also available.
3. Investigate building framing and enclosure. A study model is suggested as a means of validating roof panel layouts and addressing complex assembly geometries.

The Structural Insulated Panel Association (www.sips.org/) provides a listing of North American SIPs manufacturers. Manufacturers will typically provide information regarding:

- permissible loadings (axial and transverse)
- available R-values
- standard dimensions
- assembly and connection details
- third-party test results
- consultation services available.

SAMPLE PROBLEM

The design of a building using SIPs involves the design of an entire building system. For schematic design, the initial steps are described in the design procedure and the selected panel sizes will allow the designer to estimate envelope dimensions.

Examples

4.37 This apartment building (under construction in Massachusetts) is close to an airport. SIPs and triple glazing were selected to provide the necessary noise control. AMELIA THRALL

4.38 Combining SIPs (to the right) and conventional interior framing—to use the respective assets of each method to best advantage. AMELIA THRALL

4.39 The Not-So-Big Showhouse in Orlando, Florida used SIPs. Visit www.notsobigshowhouse.com/2005/virtualtour/ to view a video that includes footage shot in a SIPs factory and a crane setting the dormer of the home into place.

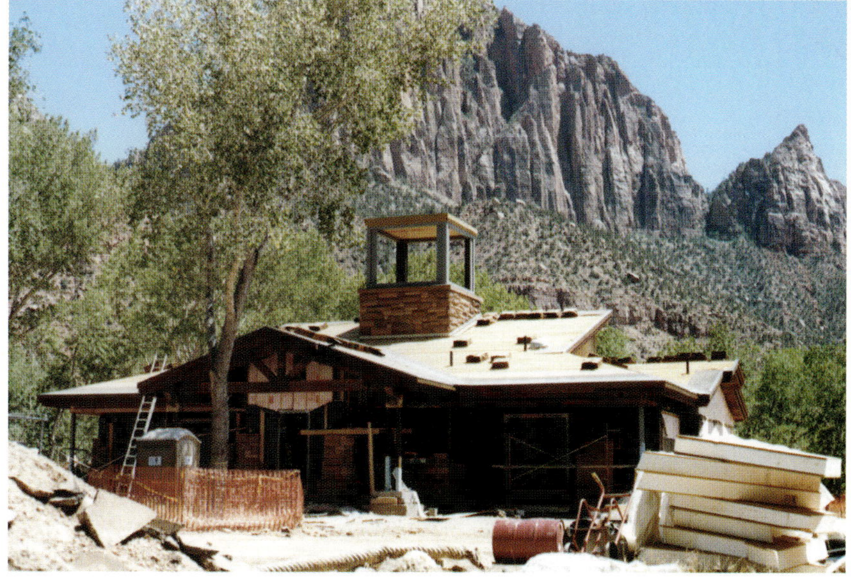

4.40 Zion National Park Visitor's Center under construction; the roof uses structural insulated panels. Paul Torcellini, DOE/NREL

Further Information

Build It Green. "Structural Insulated Panels." www.buildit-green.co.uk/about-SIPs.html

Morley, M. 2000. *Building with Structural Insulated Panels (SIPS)*, The Taunton Press, Newtown, MA.

Sarah Susanka's Not So Big Showhouse 2005. www.notsobigshowhouse.com/2005/

Structural Insulated Panel Association. www.sips.org/

BEYOND SCHEMATIC DESIGN

Much of the effort involved in designing a SIPs-based building will occur after schematic design, during detailing and specification. The key issue relative to SIPs during schematic design is applicability. Planning for SIPs must start early in the design process; detailing for SIPs can come later.

NOTES

GLAZING is a term applied to those portions of a building enclosure system that are transparent or translucent—whether made of glass or plastic. Although the details of glazing material properties and performance will normally not be addressed during schematic design, the extent (size, number, and location) of glazing elements is usually an important decision that will be considered quite early during the design process. Most glazing materials, by their very nature, will have impacts on building performance that are disproportionate to their surface area. Thus, a basic understanding of the goals of glazing and the properties of glazing materials will be useful during schematic design.

Glazing is generally used for one or more of five key reasons: (1) for its architectural appearance; (2) to admit daylight; (3) to admit direct solar radiation; (4) to provide opportunities for views; (5) to allow for airflow (through operable units). These objectives are not necessarily always in alignment—in fact, clashes between glazing objectives are fairly common—and success in implementation will respond to managing such clashes and understanding the various physical properties that define glazing performance.

4.42 Cutaway view of triple-glazed window and framing for PassivHaus-certified window with a low (0.11 [0.63]) U-factor.

4.41 Arizona State University's Biodesign Institute featuring a glazed north facade versus an opaque, brick west facade. JOSH PARTEE

INTENT
To make early design decisions regarding glazing that will make later design decisions easier

EFFECT
Glazing decisions will directly affect project aesthetics, energy performance, visual and thermal comfort, and occupant satisfaction

OPTIONS
There are hundreds of glazing options available

COORDINATION ISSUES
Glazing decisions will be coordinated with almost every aspect of design for perimeter spaces

RELATED STRATEGIES
Site Analysis, all passive strategies (daylighting, passive solar heating, passive cooling), Double Envelopes

PREREQUISITES
Fundamental project objectives, a sense of project scale, design intent, design criteria

Key Architectural Issues

Appearance, daylight admittance, solar radiation admittance, views, airflow, and acoustics are primary factors involved in decision making and planning for glazing elements in any project. The energy-related issues become more important on a green project.

Architectural appearance. This design objective is often seen as the "art" side of architecture rather than the "science" side, and quantitative analyses are often disconnected from initial objective considerations of building performance and occupant satisfaction. A designer (or owner) who truly wants a glass box must plan for the thermal consequences of such a decision.

Daylight admittance. Glazing allows radiation to pass without being substantially converted to another form of energy (such as heat). North glazing is good for daylighting under both clear and overcast sky conditions. South glazing, with appropriate shading, is also great for daylighting. The "appropriate shading" caveat is critical; without shading, winter and/or summer sun angles will likely lead to problems related to the admittance of direct solar radiation. East and west facing windows will receive adequate daylight illuminance throughout most of the year, but are the most difficult orientations to shade. Toplighting with shaded skylights, monitors, or clerestories can also be used. Daylighting can work in concert with well-designed passive solar heating, but may conflict with orientation requirements for cross ventilation or views. During schematic design, glazing elements need to be sized and placed—and they will usually have a demonstrable effect on building form and massing.

4.43 Glazing for passive solar heating.

Solar radiation admittance. Daylighting does not require direct solar radiation—passive solar heating does. If an element of glazing is to be used for both purposes, careful attention to shading device design is necessary to mitigate the potential for year-round glare and unwanted solar gains during the overheated portions of the year. Passive solar heating requires appropriately placed glazing and internal thermal mass to absorb radiation and store the resulting heat for delayed introduction into the space being conditioned. Appropriately placed glazing for solar heating will generally face south. Deviations from south are acceptable, but will change the timing of solar collection (east earlier than south and west later than south) and magnitude of collected energy. The effect of orientation on solar heating systems is discussed in a number of passive heating design guides.

4.44 All-glass facade (aesthetics).

Views. Views are an important consideration in most green buildings. Views provide both amenity and physical relief from eyestrain. The provision of views for building occupants has long provided a credit in the LEED-NC green building rating system. Because they are so site-specific, what orientations may be associated with "good" views for any given project is impossible to determine without a site analysis.

Airflow. The placement of operable windows for a stack ventilation passive cooling system is generally independent of orientation. Window orientation in a cross ventilation system, on the other hand, is critical to the success of the system. Air inlets and outlets must be located to engage the prevailing wind directions during the intended times of cross ventilation system operation.

4.45 Glazing-integrated PV (a form of BIPV). JIM TETRO PHOTOGRAPHY, FOR U.S. DOE

Implementation Considerations

In many jurisdictions, building codes will influence the design of the glazing elements in a building envelope. In residential projects this may involve a minimum glazing area that is considered appropriate for amenity and emergency egress. In most building types this will also involve a prescriptive maximum glazing area (usually expressed as a percentage of overall wall area) that is considered acceptable from an energy-efficiency perspective. Such upper limits on glazing area can usually be exceeded by a design team that chooses to bypass the code's prescriptive requirements for either a tradeoff or simulation approach. The key point for a designer to consider is that excessive glazing areas degrade building energy (and carbon) performance.

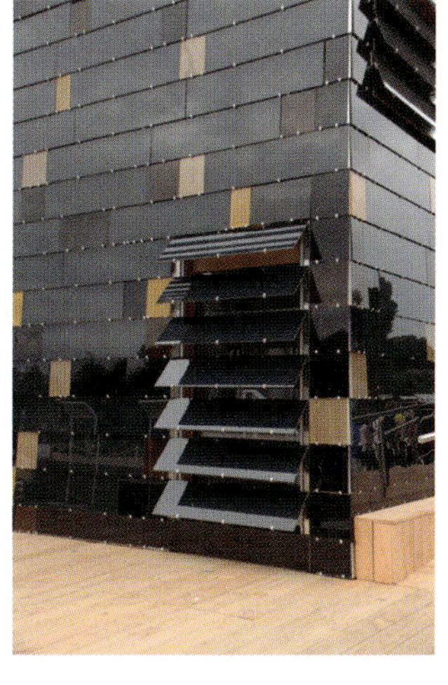

4.46 BIPV cladding integrated with operable windows.

TABLE 4.1 Example of prescriptive glazing requirements for climate zone 5 (temperate) from *ASHRAE Standard 90.1-2007* and recommendations from *ASHRAE Standard 189.1-2009*. [multiply I-P U by 5.678 for SI U]

FENESTRATION ASSEMBLY WITH VERTICAL GLAZING BETWEEN 0–40% OF WALL AREA	MAXIMUM U		MAXIMUM SHGC	
	90.1	189	90.1	189
If non-metal frame	0.35	0.25	0.40	0.35
If metal frame				
Curtainwall/storefront	0.45	0.35	0.40	0.35
Entrance door	0.80	0.70	0.40	0.35
All others	0.55	0.45	0.40	0.35

The following is a brief summary of key glazing material properties relevant to green building design. Making decisions about the intended extent of glazing during schematic design without a good feel for these properties will usually result in a need to "fix" problems later in the design process.

4.47 Glazing for view.

U-factor. U-factor is used to express the ability of a glazing assembly to resist convective heat flow (see Glossary). A window with half the U-factor of another window will permit half as much heat flow. Glass and most plastics have very poor thermal resistance values; it is the attached air films and inter-pane spaces that provide resistance to heat flow.

Solar heat gain coefficient. Solar heat gain coefficient (SHGC) is used to express the ability of a glazing assembly to resist the flow of shortwave solar radiation (see Glossary). In a cooling-dominated climate, glazing with a low SHGC will reduce cooling loads—thus reducing energy consumption.

Visible transmittance. Similar to solar heat gain coefficient, visible transmittance (VT) is used to express the percentage of incident light that will be transmitted through a glazing assembly (see Glossary). VT and SHGC are nearly identical for many glazing products, but glazing can be designed to selectively block IR and UV, but allow the visible wavelengths to pass.

ε (specifically, low ε). ε stands for emissivity, the ability of a building material to emit longwave radiation (see Glossary). A low-ε coating on glazing can reduce longwave radiation losses and improve the ability of the glazing to block heat flow (improving its U-factor).

Operable area. The architectural key to the success of a passive ventilation system is inlet/outlet area. Outdoor air must be allowed into and out of a building, typically via windows (although other devices can be used). It is the operable area of an opening that establishes (along with other variables) ventilation cooling potential. Thus, selection of windows for ventilation must consider operable area.

Air tightness. In addition to convection and radiation losses/gains, heat can also flow via infiltration (unintended leakage of air). This concern need not be addressed during schematic design, but tight windows/skylights should be specified during design development.

Sound transmission loss. From an acoustics perspective, sound transmission loss (TL) or sound transmission class (STC) are key properties that will define the ability of a glazing assembly to block sound (noise); the higher the TL or STC the better the sound blocking performance. This issue should be considered during schematic design.

Glazing Trends

Three categories of advanced glazing products will have a profound impact on facade design, particularly as the market increasingly demands green (and even higher-performance) buildings that exceed code requirements. In addition, retrofitting of existing buildings using high-performance glazing systems will help pave the way for envelopes that transfer daylight and exclude unwanted solar radiation.

4.48 Glazing-integrated PV provides walkway shading at the Habitat Research and Development Centre in Namibia. NINA MARITZ

High-Performance Glazing. This category of glazing solutions deals with the traditional performance characteristics of static fenestration components: U-factor, SHGC, and visible transmittance. Improvements (including low-ε coatings, high-tech fill gasses, and multiple panes) to window products have pushed U-factors from a low of 0.50 or so down to around 0.25. The most thermally resistive window currently listed by the National Fenestration Rating Council (NFRC) has a U-factor of 0.09. This was unheard of a decade ago. Similar improvements in SHGC capabilities are also being seen. The primary issue with visible transmittance is obtaining high values (for daylighting and views) in the face of reduced SHGC values—which leads to the next category of glazing innovations.

4.49 Glazing-integrated PV as an entry canopy at The Helena Apartment Tower in New York City. FX FOWLE ARCHITECTS, PC

Dynamic Glazing. A dynamic glazing product has modifiable transmission properties—either across the full solar radiation spectrum or within one portion of the spectrum (such as the visible portion). The fundamental rationale for dynamic glazing is that one glass type does not fit all situations; as environmental or occupancy conditions change, so too may the need for daylight, solar control, or privacy. Several approaches to dynamic glazing are currently in use/development, including electrochromic layers or coatings, suspended particles, and liquid crystals. Dynamic glazing may be user-controlled or respond automatically to environmental conditions via a control system. Cost-effectiveness is the major constraint to widespread adoption.

Glazing Integrated Photovoltaics. There are two basic types of glazing-integrated photovoltaics (one possible approach to building integrated photovoltaics, BIPV): glazing that pairs opaque PV cells with transparent glass (in a checkerboard-like arrangement) and glazing that is essentially a transparent PV module. The paired glazing approach can deliver 10–12 peak W/ft^2 [129 W/m^2] for the PV portion of the assembly. This technology is best used where unimpeded views and daylighting are not critical. Current generation transparent PV glazing can deliver 4–5 peak W/ft^2 [43–54 W/m^2] of PV array area. The cost-effectiveness of glazing-integrated PV is project-dependent.

Design Procedure

The first step in designing with glazing is to establish design intents. The second step is to establish design criteria. In commissioning circles these are collectively known as the "Owner's Project Requirements." The design team, however, may contribute as much to these requirements as the typical owner. Local building regulations will also have something to say about minimum glazing performance. The impact of glazing decisions will normally be greater in green/high-performance building situations than in code-minimum design solutions.

The following is a suggested procedure that should lead to a rational approach to glazing design for green projects:

1. Establish project design intent.
2. Establish design criteria for each intent. (Intent and criteria are collectively termed the Owner's Project Requirements and define, in substantial detail, what success will look like for the project client.)
3. Consider how daylighting, passive solar heating, natural ventilation, and views will contribute to the achievement of the Owner's Project Requirements. In high-performance green buildings these aspects will usually be very important to success.
4. Rank these considerations in order by impact on project ability to deliver the Owner's Project Requirements.
5. Conduct a thorough site analysis to understand the potential of each consideration (daylighting, views, passive heating, ventilation) relative to a given site and in the general context of the project.
6. Rank the considerations in order not just of impact, but also project potential.
7. Make design decisions that increase the ability of high-impact glazing systems to succeed.
8. See if slight compromises in design decisions (such as building orientation) may allow other systems to more positively contribute to project objectives.
9. Do not compromise so much that the building reflects a lowest common denominator mentality relative to glazing effectiveness.

SAMPLE PROBLEM

An owner in Tonopah, Nevada wants a small office building to perform better than code-minimum and to provide for ample daylight. The design team takes the following steps:

1. Glazing intent: exceed code requirements and support daylighting.
2. Glazing criteria: Maximum U-factor: 0.45 Btuh/ft^2 °F [2.56 W/m^2 °C] from ASHRAE Standard 189.1; maximum SHGC: 0.35; minimum VT 0.7.
3. Daylighting was described as important by the owner; a site analysis indicates that there are views from all building facades, passive heating is of little concern, while cross ventilation is worthy of consideration.
4. Glazing considerations in order of importance are: U-factor, SHGC, VT, and view potential (client driven); operable windows (design team option).
5. Site analysis is partly discussed in 3 above.
6. Further analysis suggests no change in ranking of considerations.
7. A conflict exists between the desired SHGC and VT values. A preliminary review of commercial window products shows that a window with

4.60 Double envelope facade at RiverEast Center, Portland, Oregon.

Further Information

Boake, T.M. 2003. "Doubling Up." *Canadian Architect*, Vol. 48, No. 7, July.

Boake, T.M. 2003. "Doubling Up II." *Canadian Architect*, Vol. 48, No. 8, August.

Diprose, P. and G. Robertson. 1996. "Towards a Fourth Skin? Sustainability and Double-Envelope Buildings." www.diprose.co.nz/LinkClick.aspx?fileticket=pTymiye%2FamE%3D&tabid=16756&mid=24014

Hausladen, G., M. de Saldanha and P. Liedl. 2008. *ClimateSkin: Building-Skin Concepts that Can Do More with Less Energy*, Birkhauser, Basel.

Herzog, T., R. Krippner and W. Lang. 2004. *Facade Construction Manual*, Birkhauser, Basel, Switzerland.

Oesterle, E. et al. 2001. *Double-Skin Facades: Integrated Planning*. Prestel, Munich.

BEYOND SCHEMATIC DESIGN

It has been said that "the devil is in the details." That saying clearly applies to double envelope facades. Much of the design work on a double envelope will occur during design development—including extensive modeling of the system's performance. Proposed configurations may be tested through physical mockups or computer simulations (including computational fluid dynamics analyses) to optimize ventilation performance and understand overall thermal performance.

GREEN ROOFS

GREEN ROOFS can be used to provide for rainwater detention or retention, to increase the thermal resistance and capacitance of a building roof, to reduce the urban heat island effect, and to provide green space for animals and people on what would otherwise be a hard-surfaced area. Green roofs are of two basic types: extensive and intensive.

Extensive green roofs have a relatively shallow soil base, making them lighter, less expensive, and easier to maintain than intensive green roofs. Extensive roofs usually have limited plant diversity, typically consisting of sedum (succulents), grasses, mosses, and herbs. They are often not accessible by building tenants, but may provide for "natural" views from adjacent rooms or neighboring buildings.

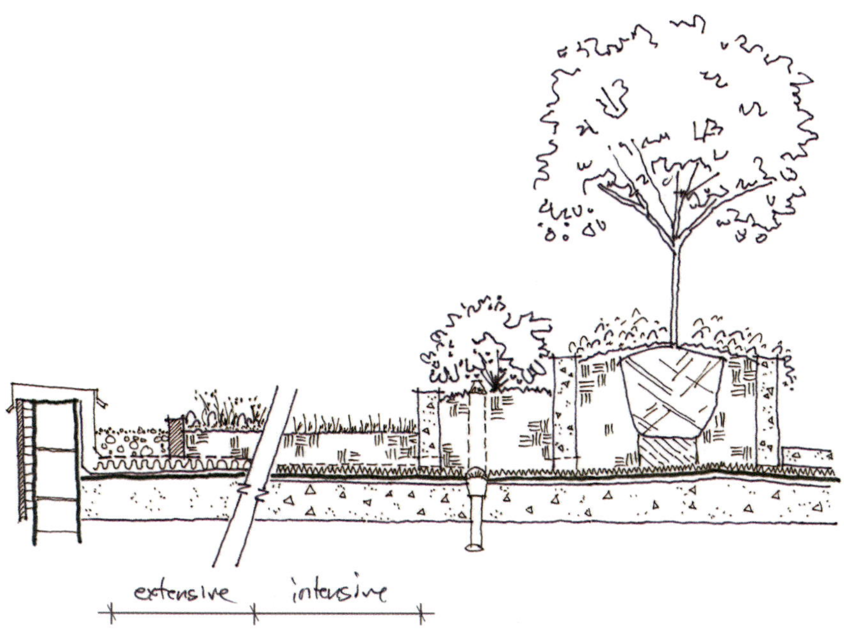

4.61 Cross-section through green roofs—illustrating the difference between an extensive and an intensive approach. BEN VAUGHN

Extensive green roofs can work at slopes of up to 35 °, although slopes above 20 ° require a baffle system to prevent soil slump. These roofs can be used in both urban and rural settings, are applicable to a wide variety of building types, and can be used in both new and existing construction.

From 2 to 6 in. [50–150 mm] of some kind of lightweight growing material (often a mineral-based mixture of sand, gravel, and organic matter) is required for an extensive green roof. In addition to the growing medium, a drainage system for excess rainwater and a protective barrier for the roof membrane are required. Because plant roots bond to underlayment fabrics to create a unified whole, there is

4.62 Green roof at Oregon Health Sciences University in Portland.

INTENT
Site enhancement, climate control

EFFECT
Stormwater retention/detention, improved envelope performance, reduced urban heat island effect, creation of a green space, water and air quality mitigation

OPTIONS
A range of strategies—from a minimal, non-accessible extensive green roof to a large, fully-accessible forested intensive green roof

COORDINATION ISSUES
Structural system, roof insulation, storm drainage, roof access, irrigation system (if required), rooftop elements (plumbing vents, exhaust fans)

RELATED STRATEGIES
Site Analysis, Water Reuse/Recycling, Pervious Surfaces, Insulation Materials

PREREQUISITES
An appropriate roof area, the potential to access the roof for maintenance

no need to provide additional ballast against roof uplift unless the roof is located in an unusually high wind area, such as on a high-rise building or in a coastal area.

Intensive green roofs have a deeper soil base than extensive green roofs. They are not limited in terms of plant diversity (as are shallower extensive green roofs) and often feature the same kinds of landscaping as local gardens. Intensive green roofs can provide park-like accessible open spaces, and often include larger plants and trees as well as walkways, water features, and irrigation systems. The deeper soil base required for these roofs and the weight of the plants combined with the weight of water that may saturate the soil make them much heavier than extensive green roofs or conventional roofs. This extra weight requires a substantial building structure, and results in a roof that is more expensive to build. Intensive green roofs are feasible only on flat-roofed buildings.

While intensive green roofs involve more cost, design time, and attention than other roofs, this approach provides the broadest palette by which the roof can become an exciting and vibrant environment. A great diversity of habitats can be created, including those with trees. These types of roofs are often accessible to people for recreation, for open space, even for growing food. Intensive green roofs are more energy-efficient than extensive green roofs, and their roof membranes are typically more protected and last longer. The deeper soil base provides greater stormwater retention capacity. Growing media depth for intensive green roofs is typically 24 in. [600 mm].

4.64 Green roof on Multnomah County Central Library, Portland, Oregon.

4.63 A green roof covers the restaurant at the Eden Project near St Austell in Cornwall, England, UK.

4.65 Examples of sedums used as roof cover (top two images) and a modular tray green roof system (bottom image).

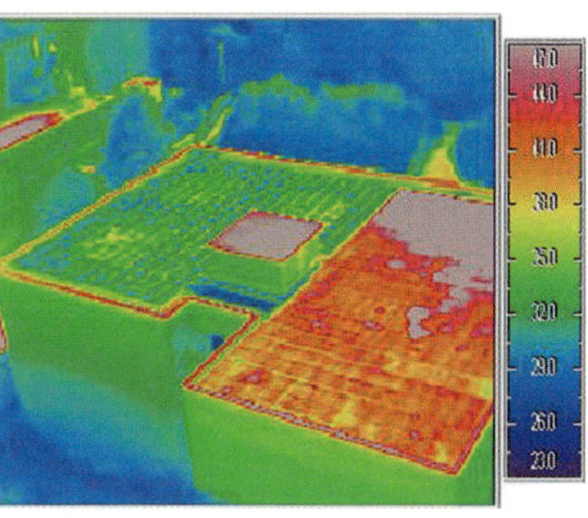

4.66 Experimental green roof on a building (left) at Yokohama National University, Yokohama, Japan. The left side of the roof has pallets of clover; the right side is a conventional exposed roof surface. Infrared thermography (right) shows the effect of the green roof on external surface temperatures. ECOTECH LABORATORY

4.67 Lecture hall located below an experimental green roof at Yokohama National University. ECOTECH LABORATORY

4.68 Thermograph taken at 3:00 PM in classroom below the green roof. Temperatures average 90 °F [32 °C]. ECOTECH LABORATORY

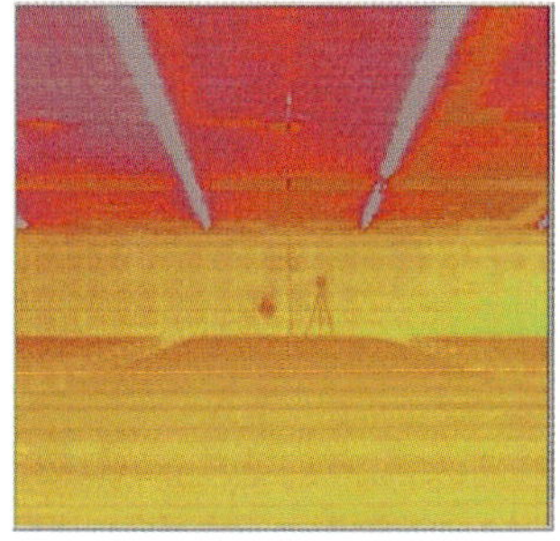

4.69 Thermograph taken at 3:00 PM in classroom without a green roof. Temperatures average 100 °F [38 °C] in the seating area and 108 °F [42 °C] at the ceiling. ECOTECH LABORATORY

The layers of a green roof can vary depending upon the specific type of green roof selected. Generally, insulation will be placed on top of the roof deck. Above this will be a waterproof membrane, a root barrier, a drainable layer, a filter membrane, and finally growing media for the plants. Drainable insulation planes are also commonly used, where the waterproofing is located at the structural surface. Consideration of winter rainfall patterns and likely rainwater temperatures should inform drainage plane decisions. Depending upon the weight of the soil base and plants, additional structure may be needed on top of the insulation layer. Careful attention should be given to vapor retarder location.

Key Architectural Issues

Successful green roofs require a building massing that provides appropriate solar exposure for the intended types of vegetation. Shading from adjacent buildings or trees can have a big impact on the success of rooftop plantings. Building massing can also be used to create rooftop surfaces that are relatively protected from wind. Building form will also determine how building occupants can interact with a green roof. A green roof is a user amenity only if it is at least visible to occupants. If it is also accessible to building users, greater integration of the green roof with appropriate interior spaces is desirable. Structural system design, careful detailing of drainage systems, irrigation systems, and penetrations of the roof membrane are key concerns.

Implementation Considerations

Hardy, drought resistant, low-height plants should be selected for extensive green roofs. Plants on such a roof experience higher wind speeds, more solar radiation, have a thinner soil base, and much less access to groundwater resources than plants in conventional locations. As a result, plants on a green roof experience high evapotranspiration losses, making drought-resistant plants a reasonable choice. Windburn is also a concern. In North American frost zones 4–8 (see www.emilycompost.com/zone_map.htm) at least half of the plants on extensive green roofs should be sedums. In colder climates, grass-dominated covers are recommended. Many extensive green roof plantings turn brown in the winter, and this color change should be anticipated.

Although extensive green roofs are generally not open (other than to maintenance personnel), a safe and viable means of access should be provided to simplify construction and encourage maintenance. A safety railing should be provided at the roof perimeter.

Intensive green roofs create an opportunity to incorporate trees into the roofscape. Trees and other heavy elements should be placed directly over columns or main beams. The area directly underneath a tree can be deepened if necessary. Rooftops experience higher wind velocities than found at ground level. To protect plants and occupants, roof gardens should include both a windbreak and a railing (perhaps provided by a parapet wall). Trees must be anchored against the wind, while avoiding the use of stakes that might puncture the roof membrane. Tension cables are sometimes attached to the root ball and to the roof structure below the soil surface. Pavers should be as light as possible to reduce the dead load on the roof.

Design Procedure

1. Establish the desired function(s) of the green roof with respect to project design intents. Typical functions include:
    - providing a visual amenity for building occupants
    - providing an occupiable green space
    - reducing building energy consumption
    - stormwater retention/detention.
2. Determine if an intensive or an extensive green roof is most appropriate to achievement of the design intents and desired functions.
3. Determine the amount of sun and shade that the proposed green roof area will receive during the year. A sunpeg chart and simple massing model are recommended as easy-to-use tools. Adjust location of the green roof area as necessary to achieve adequate solar exposure.
4. Establish the types of plantings desired, taking into consideration sun/shade patterns, available rainfall, and likely wind speeds. Consultation with a local landscape specialist is recommended.
5. Determine the soil depth required to support the desired plantings—see Table 4.2 for minimum depths for various planting types.

SAMPLE PROBLEM

An ecological housing co-op in North Carolina is interested in a green roof for its communal dining building. The roof is approximately 30 by 20 ft [9.1 by 6.1 m], with a south-facing 20° slope.

1. The roof will be visible from the ground but not accessible by residents. It should retain stormwater, mitigate heat island effects, and serve as a symbol of the community's commitment to green solutions.
2. An extensive green roof is appropriate for the sloped, inaccessible, low-maintenance roof desired—and fits the client's budget.
3. The building is surrounded by low buildings, a lawn, and a parking area. Little shading of the roof is likely and solar exposure will be similar to that of ground plantings.

6. Estimate the dead weight of the proposed green roof (assuming a fully saturated condition) to permit an estimate of the size (depth) of the supporting structural system (see Tables 4.2 and 4.3).
7. If the green roof approach seems feasible, adopt this strategy and proceed with design. Consider how to incorporate access for maintenance and irrigation (if required).

TABLE 4.2 Minimum soil depths for green roof planting. ***TIME-SAVER STANDARDS FOR LANDSCAPE ARCHITECTURE*, 2ND ED.**

PLANTING	MINIMUM SOIL DEPTH[a]
Lawns	8–12 in. [200–300 mm]
Flowers and ground covers	10–12 in. [250–300 mm]
Shrubs	24–30 in. [600–750 mm][b]
Small trees	30–42 in. [750–1050 mm][b]
Large trees	5–6 ft [1.5–1.8 m][b]

[a] above filter fabric and drainage medium
[b] dependent upon ultimate plant size

TABLE 4.3 Approximate weights of green roof materials. ***TIME-SAVER STANDARDS FOR LANDSCAPE ARCHITECTURE*, 2ND ED.**

MATERIAL	DRY lb/ft³ [kg/m³]	WET lb/ft³ [kg/m³]
Sand or gravel	90 [1440]	120 [1929]
Cedar shavings with fertilizer	0.3 [149]	13 [209]
Peat moss	9.6 [154]	10 [166]
Redwood compost and shavings	15 [2387]	22 [357]
Fir and pine bark humus	22 [357]	33 [535]
Perlite	6.5 [104]	32 [521]
Topsoil	76 [1216]	78 [1248]
Concrete		
Lightweight	90 [1400]	—
Precast	130 [2080]	—
Reinforced	150 [2400]	—
Steel	490 [7840]	—

4. Plantings are selected considering climate. The site experiences over 100 sunny days per year. Winters are generally mild, with occasional frosts and snow. Summers are long, hot and humid. Yearly rainfall is approximately 50 in. [1.3 m]. Considering the above and the thin soil layer in an extensive green roof, succulents and drought-resistant plants are selected.
5. A preliminary soil depth of 10 in. [250 mm] of lightweight medium is selected, to be placed atop a 4 in. [100 mm] drainage layer.
6. The estimated roof dead load due to the green roof elements is: $(10/12)(70) + (4/12)(120) = 98$ lb/ft³ [1570 kg/m³]. The weight of the structure and insulation plus live loads must be added to this value.
7. This green roof approach is considered feasible.

Examples

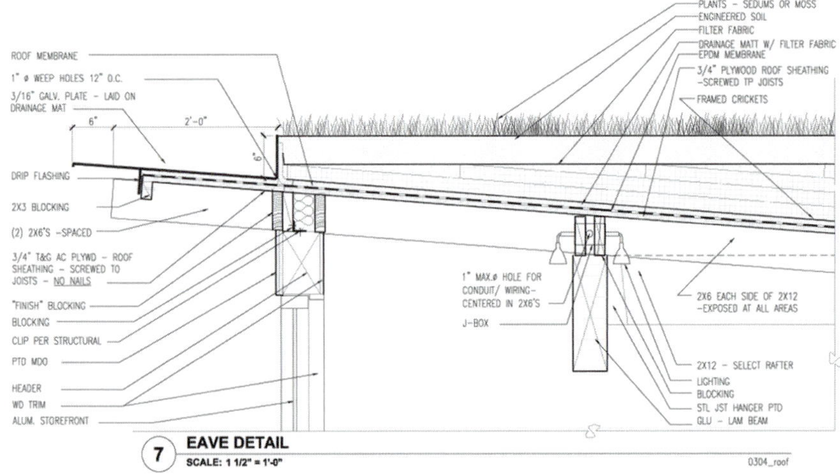

4.70 Construction detail of a green roof over the garage/living area of a residence in Seattle, Washington. MILLER | HULL PARTNERSHIP

4.72 The green roof on the Roddy/Bale garage/studio in Seattle, Washington has a variety of native plants and ground cover. MILLER | HULL PARTNERSHIP

4.71 Extensive, modular green roof on Seattle Hyatt Olive 8 hotel.

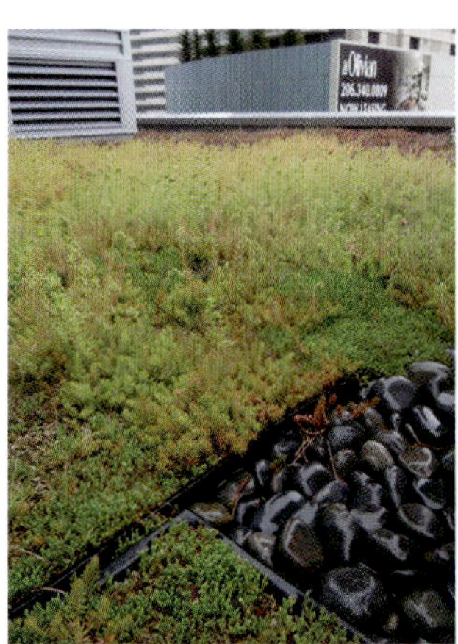

4.73 Close up view of the Hyatt Olive 8 hotel roof, showing the modular design of the green roof.

Further Information

British Council for Offices. 2003. Research Advice Note: "Green Roofs." www.bco.org.uk/research/researchavailabletobuy/detail.cfm?rid=45&cid=0

Centre for Architectural Ecology, Collaborations in Green Roofs and Living Walls. commons.bcit.ca/greenroof/

Earth Pledge. 2004. *Green Roofs: Ecological Design and Construction*, Schiffer Publishing, Atglen, PA.

Green Roofs for Healthy Cities. www.greenroofs.net/

Harris, C. and N. Dines. 1997. *Time-Saver Standards for Landscape Architecture*, 2nd ed. McGraw-Hill, New York.

Oberlander, C.H., E. Whitelaw and E. Matsuzaki. 2002. *Introductory Manual for Greening Roofs for Public Works and Government Services Canada*, Version 1.1. www.bluestem.ca/pdf/PWGSC_GreeningRoofs_wLink_3.pdf

Osmundson, T. 1997. *Roof Gardens: History, Design, and Construction*, W.W. Norton, New York.

Velazquez, L. 2005. "Organic Greenroof Architecture: Design Consideration and System Components" and "Organic Greenroof Architecture: Sustainable Design for the New Millennium". *Environmental Quality Management*, Summer.

Weiler, S. and K. Scholz-Barth. 2009. *Green Roof Systems*, John Wiley & Sons, Hoboken, NJ.

BEYOND SCHEMATIC DESIGN

During design development, a green roof will be optimized and detailed. A landscape architect will likely be involved to ensure the survivability, compatibility, and vibrancy of plantings. The roof structure will be analyzed and detailed. If the building (or roof, due to height) is in a high wind area, detailed wind studies may be done to estimate wind speeds on the roof and to determine the best placement of windbreaks and walls and tree anchorage requirements.

NOTES

LIGHTING

The controlled distribution of daylight in buildings is a cornerstone of green design. Daylighting is a key to good energy performance, as well as occupant satisfaction, productivity, and health. Daylighting must be addressed early in schematic design because requirements for successful daylighting usually have major implications for building massing and zoning of activities.

Toplighting (daylighting through skylights, roof monitors, etc.) and sidelighting (daylighting through vertical windows at the building perimeter) lead to different sets of coordination issues for designers. Toplighting allows even levels of diffuse light to be distributed across large areas of a building. For this reason, successful toplighting is typically easier to achieve and requires less complex electric lighting controls. Sidelighting tends to be more complex. Size, location, visual transmittance, and energy performance characteristics of glazing must be carefully refined. Glare control, involving window overhangs, interior light shelves, glazing choices, as well as interior shades or blinds, is critical. Because daylight illuminance drops off with distance from a window, electric lighting controls become more complex.

It is important to distinguish between sunlight and daylight. In most situations, direct sunlight brings excessive heat and light leading to visual and thermal discomfort. Skylights designed to provide daylighting should contain diffusing (rather than clear) glazing. Controlling solar gain through skylights is critical to building energy efficiency. Vertical glazing design must include glare and heat control. Large areas of unprotected glass do not result in quality daylighting.

The importance of viable and working controls for electric lighting cannot be overstated. Unless electric lighting is dimmed or turned off, there will be no savings of electricity or reductions in cooling load. Without controls, even a well-designed daylighting system will require the use of more, not less, energy.

Interior finishes and furnishing are very important in a daylit building. Ceilings and walls should be light colored with high reflectance. Office partitions and cubicles should be as low as possible while meeting privacy needs. These requirements must be communicated to the client and interior designer or the architect's intentions for daylighting may not be achieved.

If a project is to be certified under the USGBC LEED-NC rating system, note that the credits for daylight and views under Indoor Environmental Quality address daylight as an amenity for building occupants, not as an energy-efficiency strategy. A well-designed and controlled daylighting system will also reduce energy use. Thus, daylighting can result in additional points under the Energy & Atmosphere category.

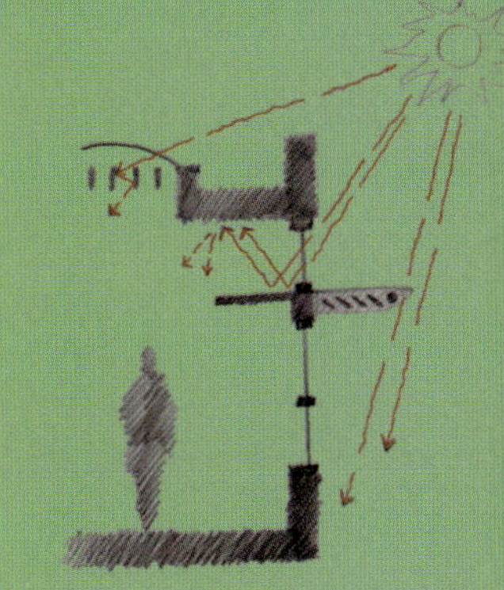

STRATEGIES

Daylight Factor
Daylight Zoning
Toplighting
Sidelighting
Light Shelves
Internal Reflectances
Shading Devices
Electric Lighting

NOTES

DAYLIGHT FACTOR

DAYLIGHT FACTOR (DF) is a numerical ratio used to describe the relationship between indoor and outdoor daylight illuminances (typically under overcast sky conditions). In order to make sense of daylighting system performance and the many design strategies used to deliver daylight, it is critical to understand this key measurement that is universally used to assess daylighting performance.

4.75 Exterior view of a typical daylighting study model.

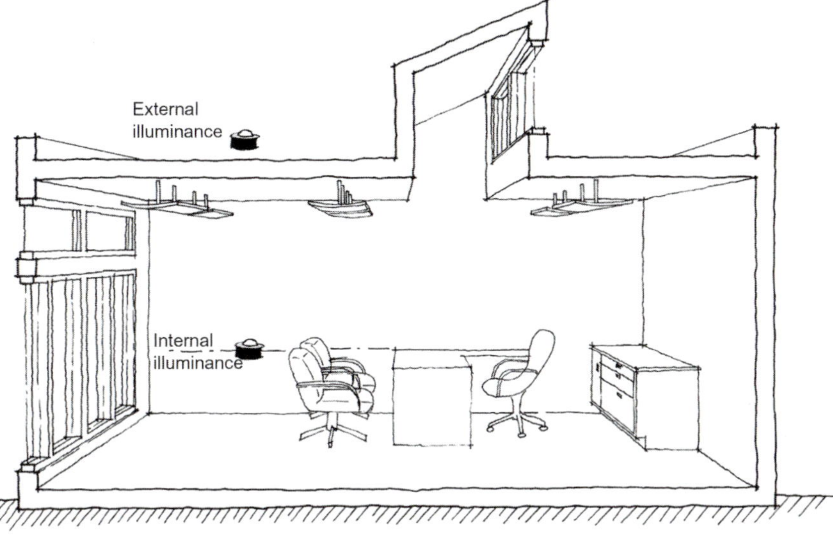

4.74 The fundamental concept of daylight factor—the relationship between indoor and outdoor daylight illuminances. JONATHAN MEENDERING

Because sky conditions are always changing, daylight illuminance is exceptionally variable throughout a typical day/month/year. It is not, therefore, possible to flatly state that the daylight illuminance at some point in a building will be "x" footcandles [lux]. Whatever value for "x" is stated will be incorrect most of the time (under different exterior conditions). Absolute values of daylight illuminance are often not a useful metric for design. As a ratio (a relative measure) daylight factor is generally stable across time and therefore much more useful and usable as a design tool—although at some point in the design process a daylight factor will typically need to be related to a delivered illuminance value.

As suggested in Figure 4.74, daylight factor equals the internal daylight illuminance at a specific point divided by a reference external daylight illuminance. DF is dimensionless (the illuminance units cancel) and is expressed either as a percentage (for example, 2.5%) or as a decimal (0.025). Daylight factor is position-specific; there will be a range of daylight factors in any given space. Daylight factor literally represents the efficiency of the entire daylighting system in delivering daylight from the exterior environment to a specific point within a building.

INTENT
Used as a daylighting performance quantifier

EFFECT
Normalizes variations in daylight illuminance over time

OPTIONS
Expressed as either a percentage or decimal value

COORDINATION ISSUES
Not applicable

RELATED STRATEGIES
Site Analysis, Glazing, Sidelighting, Toplighting, Light Shelves, Shading Devices, Internal Reflectances

PREREQUISITES
Not applicable

Daylight factor is used both as a design criterion (a design target) and as a measure of actual system performance. As a design criterion DF may be set to meet an internally established client goal, to meet some externally mandated or suggested minimum performance, or to meet an explicit energy efficiency or passive system contribution threshold. Recommendations for minimum daylight factors may be obtained from numerous resources.

Key Architectural Issues

The daylight *factor* experienced at a given point in a particular building space depends upon a number of design considerations including:

- size of daylight apertures (windows, skylights, etc.);
- location of daylight apertures (sidelighting, toplighting, etc.);
- access to daylight (considering the site, building, and room contexts);
- room geometry (height, width, and depth);
- location of the point of interest relative to apertures;
- visible transmittance (VT) of glazing;
- reflectances of room surfaces and contents;
- reflectances of exterior surfaces affecting daylight entering the aperture;
- the effects of daylighting enhancements (such as light shelves).

The daylight *illuminance* experienced at any given point in a building depends upon the factors noted above and:

- the building's global location and prevailing climate;
- the time of day/month/year;
- the current sky conditions.

Having information about the daylight factor at some location within a building allows a designer to estimate daylight illuminance on the basis of available exterior illuminance. For example, the expected illuminance (E) at point "A" in some room at 10:00 A.M. on March 25 is found as follows:

$$E = (\text{DF at point ``}A\text{''})(\text{exterior illuminance})$$

where the "exterior illuminance" is the design exterior illuminance likely to prevail at the building site at 10:00 A.M. on March 25.

The actual daylight illuminance experienced at point "A" in this room at 10:00 A.M. on any specific March 25 will be modified by the particular weather conditions existing at that time.

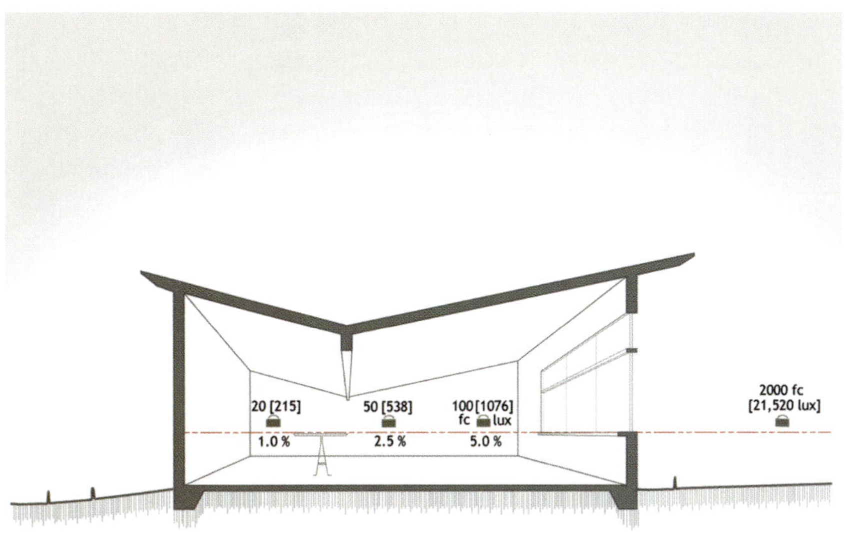

4.76 Daylight factor versus illuminance as a measure of daylighting. The illuminance values will change throughout the day, while the daylight factors will be reasonably constant throughout the day (under similar sky conditions). JON THWAITES

4.77 Daylight factor can be measured in the field (such as in this residence) using paired illuminance meter readings.

4.78 Scale models (such as of the residence shown above) can be used to predict daylight factor during design. Surface reflectances must be carefully modeled for accurate predictions.

Implementation Considerations

As a design criterion. Using daylight factor as a design target is straightforward. Simply set DF criteria for various spaces (and/or locations within spaces) that are appropriate to the design context—remembering that a given DF target will represent different illuminances in different climates and at different times. These targets may come from the client, from codes, from standards or guidelines, or from the environmental or economic values of the design team. DF criteria are often expressed as minimum targets (for example, a DF of no less than 4%). DF criteria may also be derived from a design intent to displace (wholly or in part) electric lighting. In this case, a target DF would be established on the basis of required design illuminance values. Stated another way: sometimes DF criteria will be set based upon a general sense that this or that DF represents a "good" or "reasonable" effort. In other cases, DF targets are explicitly linked to a specific outcome (such as no use of electric lighting between the hours of 10:00 A.M. and 4:00 P.M.).

The U.S. Green Building Council's LEED NC-2.1 system established a minimum DF of 2% (with conditions) as the threshold for a LEED daylighting credit (the current LEED-NC system is a bit less direct). The British Research Establishment's EcoHomes program requires a minimum 2% average DF in kitchens and a 1.5% minimum average DF in living rooms, dining rooms, and studies. Other minimum daylight factor requirements or recommendations can be found in the building codes or lighting standards of many countries. In the absence of other criteria, Table 4.4 provides general recommendations for target daylight factors that have been extracted from several North American and United Kingdom sources. High daylight factors need to be considered with caution as they may bring the potential for glare.

From a subjective perspective, the following user responses to daylight factors have been suggested:

- With a DF of less than 2%, a room will seem gloomy. Electric lighting will be required for most of the daylight hours.
- With a DF between 2% and 5%, a room will feel that it is daylit, although supplementary electric lighting may be needed.
- With a DF greater than 5%, a room will feel vigorously daylit. Depending upon the task at hand, electric lighting may not be necessary during daylight hours.

4.79 A computer simulation, such as Radiance, can provide daylight factor predictions and facilitate qualitative evaluation of a proposed design. GREG WARD

TABLE 4.4 Suggested daylight factor criteria (under overcast skies)

SPACE	AVERAGE DF	MINIMUM DF
Commercial/Institutional		
Corridor	2	0.6
General Office	5	2
Classroom	5	2
Library	5	1.5
Gymnasium	5	3.5
Residential		
Dining Room/Studio	5	2.5
Kitchen	2	0.6
Living Room	1.5	0.5
Bedroom	1.0	0.3

As a performance predictor. There are a number of analog, digital, and correlational methods that can be used to predict the daylight factor likely to be experienced at some point in a building while it is being designed. These methods (in order of potential accuracy) generally include:

- A range of performance guidelines for use in the early stages of design that attempt to correlate a proposed design with the measured performance of previously built spaces. These methods typically give rough feedback on whether a daylight strategy can meet established performance criteria. The 2.5 H rule that suggests usable daylight will penetrate a space to 2.5 times the window head height is an example of this type of method.
- Scale models (daylighting models) that attempt to physically represent a proposed design—predicted DF is measured in an appropriate setting with paired illuminance meters.
- Computer simulations that attempt to represent a proposed design numerically—predicted DF is given as a numerical or graphic output.

As a measure of constructed performance. Daylight factor is easily measured in a completed building with the use of paired illuminance meters. The measurement of in-situ DF values should be an element of any serious post-occupancy evaluation (POE) of a daylit building.

Design Procedure

1. Based upon recommendations or requirements that are most applicable to the context of the project, establish daylight factor criteria for the various spaces in the building being designed. These will typically be minimum values for rooms, rather than point-specific targets.
2. Select the daylighting approach or combination of approaches most likely to provide performance that will match the criteria established in Step 1. Daylighting approaches include sidelighting, toplighting, and special designs involving light pipes or guides. See the Toplighting and Sidelighting strategies that follow.
3. Size daylighting apertures using available schematic design guidance or trial and error.
4. Model the daylighting performance (including daylight factors) of the proposed daylighting system. Modeling tools include physical scale models, computer simulations, and hand calculations.
5. Adjust selected daylighting design parameters (aperture size, glazing transmittance, surface reflectances, light shelves, etc.) as necessary to meet established daylight factor criteria.
6. Revalidate the daylighting design using modified parameters; iterate as necessary to meet design criteria.

Examples

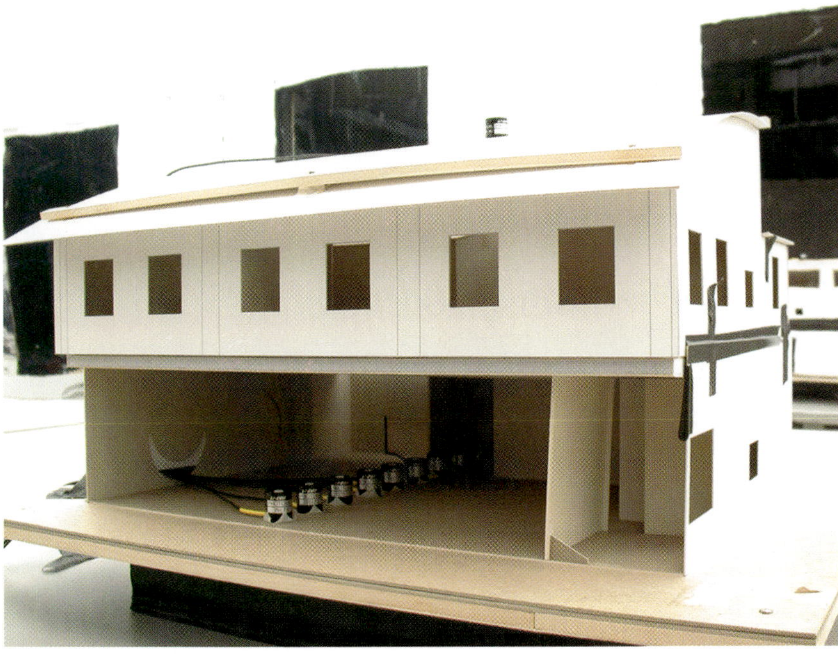

4.80 Daylight model placed in an artificial sky with several interior photosensors and a single exterior sensor (on roof) to measure illuminances and determine daylight factors. The model is "unglazed" and the additional daylight this admits will be corrected for when calculating DF. ROBERT MARCIAL

SAMPLE PROBLEM

The design team for a small stand-alone dentist's office in Alpine, Texas intends to daylight the building in accordance with recommended LEED guidelines.

1. LEED recommends the following daylight factor criteria: a minimum DF of 2% for 75% of the normally occupied spaces.
2. A sidelighting approach is selected as views are considered important by the design team.
3. Using available design guidelines (see the Sidelighting strategy) windows are sized to provide the target daylight factor. Building layout is critical to the success of this daylighting approach.
4. A physical daylighting model is used to test the proposed daylighting design.
5. The proposed design provides minimum DFs of over 2.5% in all spaces except for two, where the minimum is below 2%. The aperture sizes in these spaces are increased.
6. Retesting confirms that the minimum 2% daylight factor is provided in 80% of all occupied spaces.

4.81 Daylight model being tested outdoors under an overcast sky with an interior and exterior photosensor to measure illuminances and calculate daylight factor.

Further Information

British Standards. 2008. *Lighting for Buildings: Code of Practice for Daylighting* (BS 8206-2), BSI British Standards, London.

Brown, G.Z. and M. DeKay. 2001. *Sun, Wind & Light: Architectural Design Strategies*, 2nd ed. John Wiley & Sons, New York.

Grondzik, W. et al. 2010. *Mechanical and Electrical Equipment for Buildings*. 11th ed. John Wiley & Sons, Hoboken, NJ.

IESNA. 1999. *Recommended Practice of Daylighting (RP-5-99)*, Illuminating Engineering Society of North America, New York.

Moore, F. 1993. *Environmental Control Systems: Heating, Cooling, Lighting*, McGraw-Hill, Inc., New York.

Square One Research. Lighting Design, Daylight Factor. www.squ1.com/archive/

BEYOND SCHEMATIC DESIGN

Although daylight factor plays an important role in benchmarking daylighting during schematic design, it is equally valuable as a performance indicator during design development and post-occupancy evaluations. Several green building rating systems use a minimum daylight factor as a threshold for daylighting credits.

DAYLIGHT ZONING

DAYLIGHT ZONING is the process of grouping various spaces in a building with similar luminous requirements into appropriate daylighting zones, thereby simplifying design and enabling lighting control cost savings. Daylighting schemes can then be developed and tailored to meet the particular needs and conditions of associated spaces with similar daylighting needs—thus optimizing the design strategy for each zone.

Several rooms with similar characteristics with respect to lighting might be grouped to form a zone, or a single room might be treated as a zone. Combining spaces into daylight zones is commonly done while considering three characteristics of a space:

- **Function.** The type of visual activities that predominate within a space will establish the lighting requirements that will permit the activity to be performed to a level of quality as defined by design intent.
- **Usage schedule.** The primary time(s) of use of a space and how those times relate to daylight availability will determine daylight potential and influence zoning.
- **Location and orientation.** The location of a space relative to the daylight source (e.g., next to an exterior wall, within an interior atrium, etc.) and the orientation of the space (e.g., a space with an aperture facing north versus a west-facing aperture) will help to determine how daylight can be used.

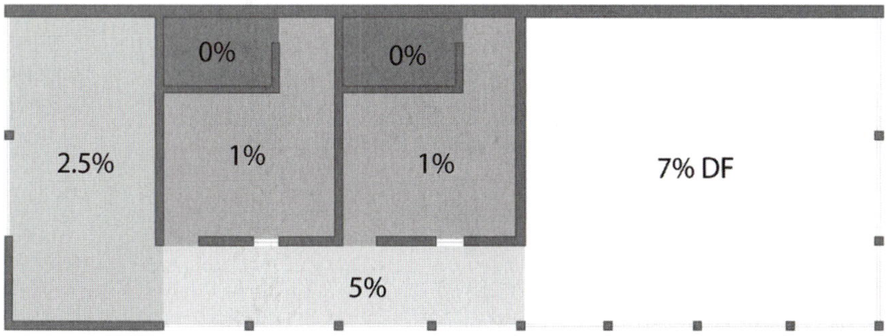

4.82 Example of a daylight zoning diagram. JON THWAITES

While function and usage schedule are primarily determined by the building program, the designer has control over the location and orientation of a space and can use these decisions to optimize the effectiveness of daylighting schemes. In addition, other factors that may be important to consider in the zoning process include visual comfort, thermal comfort, fire and smoke control, and building automation opportunities and requirements.

Key Architectural Issues

Daylight zoning can dramatically affect a building's orientation, massing, plan layout, and section and should be a guiding factor during schematic design. Optimizing daylight access for zones

4.83 Isolux plot of measured daylight distribution in an office building—zones are evident. WYATT HAMMER

INTENT
Optimized daylighting design

EFFECT
Energy efficiency, building organization, potential for coordination with electric lighting

OPTIONS
Not applicable

COORDINATION ISSUES
Daylighting strategy, daylight factor, electric lighting, glazing, shading devices, ceilings, finishes

RELATED STRATEGIES
Site Analysis, Glazing, Daylight Factor, Internal Reflectances, Shading Devices, Light Shelves, Electric Lighting

PREREQUISITES
Building program, preliminary spatial layout, lighting design criteria

where lighting needs can be largely met by daylighting suggests maximizing the building perimeter and the use of toplighting for critical interior spaces. The use of atria and/or light courts may also be appropriate. Daylighting decisions often result in a building with a higher skin-to-volume ratio than a typical compact (electrically lit) building.

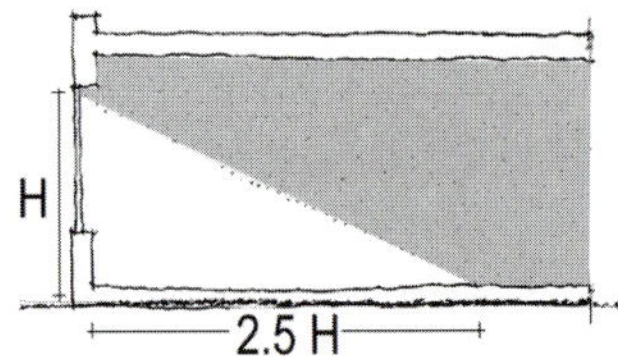

4.84 Illustration of the 2.5 H daylighting guideline. KATE BECKLEY

Implementation Considerations

The building program or schedule of usage may complicate daylight zoning efforts because the particular mix of space types (and/or times of usage) does not accommodate a logical assemblage of daylit spaces. Sometimes what makes sense from a daylight zoning point of view does not work from a functional point of view. The design team will need to resolve any such conflicts.

Site conditions may constrict solar access such that it is not possible to utilize daylighting as much as desired or to accommodate a desired zoning scheme while addressing required design adjacencies and circulation needs.

Glazing, light shelves, and shading devices should be selected and designed to reinforce proposed daylight zoning schemes. Interior partition arrangement can have a dramatic impact on daylight distribution and thus on daylighting zones.

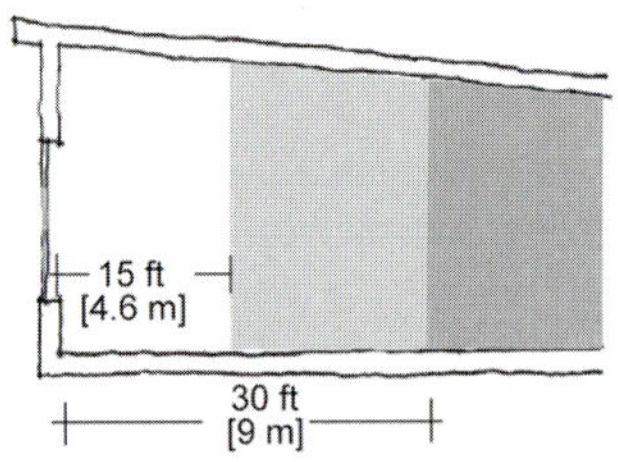

4.85 The 15/30 daylighting guideline—although not linked to a specific window height, there is a presumption that an adequate and appropriate sidelighting aperture has been provided. KATE BECKLEY

Design Procedure

1. List and define the types of spaces that will be present in the building.
2. Determine required ambient and task illuminance values for the various space types based upon the visual activities that will be performed. Recommended illuminance levels may be found in the *IESNA Lighting Handbook* and similar resources.
3. Outline an anticipated schedule of usage and daylighting potential for each space type in a table (as per the example in Table 4.5).
4. Group rooms into zones based upon similar lighting needs (considering ambient and task needs), complementary schedules, corresponding uses, and thermal comfort requirements.
5. Arrange building massing, plans, and sections to allow these zones to optimize daylighting potential by placing zones with higher illuminance needs nearest daylighting apertures, and zones with lower illuminance needs further from daylighting apertures.
6. Verify the potential performance of daylighting strategies for each of the different daylight zones. Two general guidelines—the 2.5 H rule and the 15/30 rule—are useful tools in this regard during the schematic design phase (as explained below).

SAMPLE PROBLEM
The use of daylight zoning is illustrated in Figure 4.82. Application of the 2.5 H and 15/30 rules is illustrated in the Sidelighting strategy.

TABLE 4.5 Example illuminance and usage schedule analysis

SPACE TYPE	ILLUMINANCE EXPECTATIONS		USAGE SCHEDULE	DAYLIGHTING POTENTIAL
	AMBIENT	TASK		
Retail	High	High	10 A.M.–5 P.M.	Little
Meeting Room	Low	High	8 A.M.–5 P.M.	Ambient
Restroom	Low	Low	10 A.M.–5 P.M.	Ambient and Task
Office	Low	High	8 A.M.–6 P.M.	Ambient
Gallery	Low	High	10 A.M.–5 P.M.	Ambient

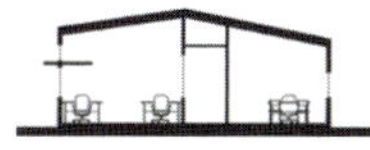

4.86 Plan and section of building proposal used for analysis shown in Fig. 4.87. WYATT HAMMER

Most rooms in a large building have, at most, one exterior wall with access to daylight. Windows along an exterior wall can contribute to the most commonly used daylighting strategy—sidelighting. With sidelighting, daylight levels in a room will tend to be higher on the aperture side of the room and decrease moving away from the aperture wall. The 2.5 H guideline (as shown in Figure 4.84) can be used to estimate how far into a room usable daylight derived from sidelighting will reach. This rule suggests that significant levels of daylight will only reach into the room a distance of 2.5 times the height of the aperture window.

In large, multistory buildings the ability to utilize daylighting wisely is often a result of the shape of the plan and the adjacency of a particular space to an exterior wall. Figure 4.85 shows a relatively common spatial arrangement that leads to the 15/30 guideline, which is also useful for schematic design. This rule suggests that with good window design, on average a 15-ft [4.6 m] deep zone next to a window can be illuminated predominately by daylighting, and a secondary 15-ft [4.6 m] deep zone (between 15 and 30 ft [4.6 and 9.1 m] from the window) can be illuminated by daylighting supplemented by electric lighting. Spaces farther than 30 ft [9.1 m] from a window will need to be lit entirely by electric lighting, if there is no opportunity for toplighting or sidelighting from a second source.

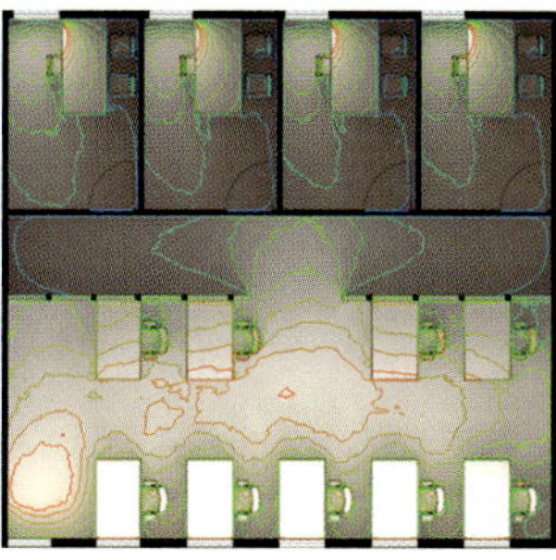

4.87 Daylighting performance prediction developed using Autodesk Ecotect with Radiance lighting simulation and rendering tools. WYATT HAMMER

Examples

4.88 Daylit computer area in the Queen's Building at DeMontfort University in Leicester, UK, showing coordination of electric lighting fixtures with sidelighting zones. THERESE PEFFER

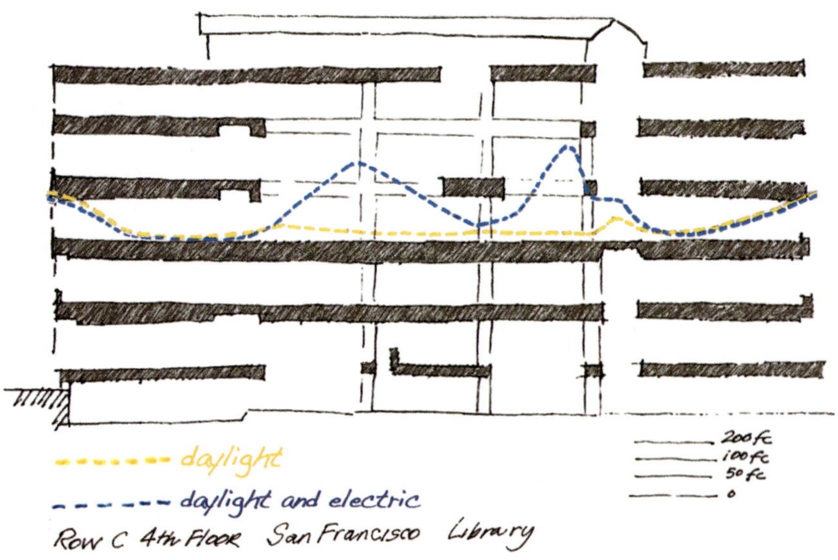

4.89 Illuminance measurements taken throughout the San Francisco Public Library in San Francisco, California with the electric lighting on and off suggest the designer zoned particular spaces for daylighting from windows and skylights. REDRAWN BY LUZANNE SMITH FROM A VITAL SIGNS CASE STUDY PROJECT

4.90 Three distinct daylight zones—reading cubicles, corridor, and stack area—in the Mt. Angel Abbey Library in St. Benedict, Oregon.

Further Information

Ander, G.D. 2003. *Daylighting Performance and Design*, 2nd ed. John Wiley & Sons, New York.

Baker, N., A. Fanchiotti and K. Steemers (eds). 1993. *Daylighting in Architecture: A European Reference Book*. Earthscan/James & James, London.

Bell, J. and W. Burt. 1995. *Designing Buildings for Daylight*, BRE Press, Bracknell Berkshire, UK.

Brown, G.Z. and M. DeKay. 2001. *Sun, Wind & Light: Architectural Design Strategies*, 2nd ed. John Wiley & Sons, New York.

CIBSE. 1999. *Daylighting and Window Design*, The Chartered Institution of Building Services Engineers, London.

CIBSE. 2009. *Code for Lighting*, The Chartered Institution of Building Services Engineers, London.

DiLaura, D. et al. (ed). 2011. *The Lighting Handbook*. 10th ed. Illuminating Engineering Society of North America, New York.

Guzowski, M. 2000. *Daylighting for Sustainable Design*, McGraw-Hill, New York.

Moore, F. 1985. *Concepts and Practice of Architectural Daylighting*, Van Nostrand Reinhold, New York.

BEYOND SCHEMATIC DESIGN

During design development, careful consideration and design of daylighting controls—time clocks, photocontrols (open loop versus closed loop), and switching versus dimming—is critical to an energy-saving daylighting system. Open loop controls sense incoming daylight and raise electric lighting to a predetermined level to augment the daylight. Closed loop controls sense the combined effect of daylight and electric light in the space, and raise the electric lighting until a target illuminance is met. Open loop systems are cheaper and easier to commission. If a building doesn't require a complex control system, simpler is better. Industrial (and many retail) buildings can use switching strategies instead of dimming. Switching is cheaper and the controls are simpler.

NOTES

TOPLIGHTING

TOPLIGHTING is a daylighting strategy that uses apertures located at the roof plane as the point of admission for ambient daylight. Any system that delivers daylight onto a horizontal task plane generally from above is considered a toplighting strategy. Such approaches include skylights, sawtooth roof glazing arrangements, or clerestories located high within a space (often in concert with a reflecting ceiling plane).

Toplighting allows for the consistent introduction of daylight into a space while allowing for reasonably easy control of direct glare. Any toplighting strategy must address the control of direct solar radiation, as such intense radiation/light can cause glare and adds unnecessary heat gains to a space. Toplighting is an ideal strategy under overcast sky conditions because overcast skies have a greater luminance at the zenith (overhead) than at the horizon. Toplighting is usually easily coordinated with electric lighting systems.

4.92 Skylight with large splayed distribution surfaces at Mt. Angel Abbey Library in St. Benedict, Oregon.

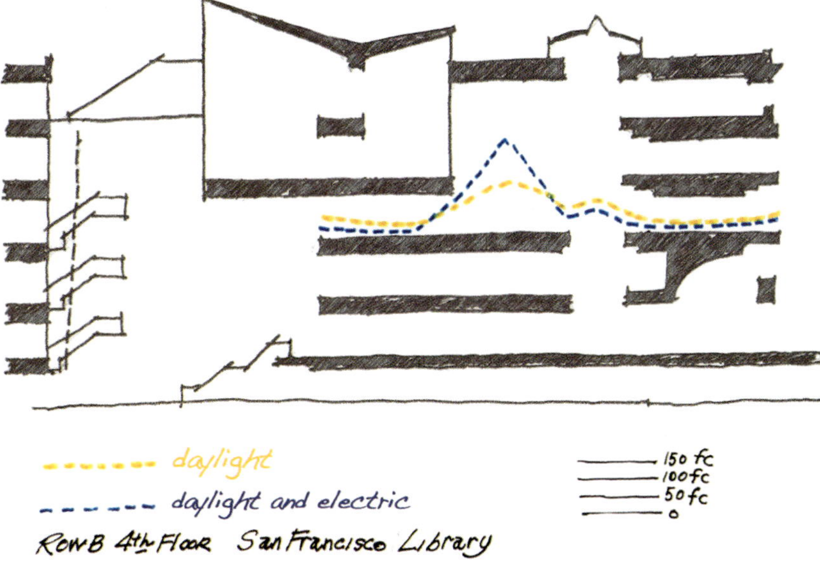

4.91 Conceptual diagram of a toplighting system at the San Francisco Public Library in San Francisco, California. Illuminance measurements with the electric lighting on and off show the light distribution through the space and the influence of daylight from the skylights. REDRAWN BY LUZANNE SMITH FROM A VITAL SIGNS CASE STUDY PROJECT

INTENT

Task visibility, energy efficiency, occupant satisfaction

EFFECT

Reduced consumption of electricity, a high likelihood of improved occupant satisfaction, potentially reduced cooling loads

OPTIONS

Numerous options for apertures and their integration into roof forms, various shading devices and techniques

COORDINATION ISSUES

Design intent, spatial functions and tasks, building/aperture orientation, solar heat gain, electric lighting system controls

RELATED STRATEGIES

Glazing, Daylight Factor, Daylight Zoning, Sidelighting, Electric Lighting, Internal Reflectances, cooling strategies, building envelope strategies, Shading Devices

PREREQUISITES

Design intent, preliminary spatial layout, daylight factor criteria

Key Architectural Issues

Toplighting liberates the walls of a space. Daylighting from above, rather than from the sides, allows for greater latitude in how the walls of a space are used. Additionally, light scoops, clerestories, roof monitors, and skylights all provide opportunities for architectural expression in the building form. An inherent limitation to toplighting is single story construction (or toplighting only the uppermost floor of a multistory building). A toplit building can, however, have great depth—as lighting access is not limited to the walls (and is freed of the 2.5 H rule). Toplighting encourages the activation of the ceiling plane, an area often forgotten in the design process.

ENVELOPE LIGHTING HEATING COOLING ENERGY PRODUCTION WATER & WASTE

Implementation Considerations

Proper detailing is essential in toplighting strategies. No amount of daylight will convince users that a leaky roof is acceptable. Direct solar radiation must also be addressed. Toplighting could exacerbate solar gain in the summer by allowing high altitude sun angles to enter a space—if not properly shaded (e.g., if using a skylight instead of a more controllable sawtooth monitor). Direct solar radiation can cause substantial visual discomfort due to excessive contrast. While a "dazzle" effect is sometimes desirable, it is inappropriate for tasks on the work surface. Finally, consider that regardless of interior illuminance most building users want a visual connection to the outdoors, which will not be provided by translucent skylights.

Design Procedure

This procedure presumes that the merits of toplighting versus sidelighting have been considered and toplighting has been selected as the approach of interest. This does not preclude the use of combined toplighting and sidelighting systems. Illuminances are additive, such that the contribution of one system can be linearly added to that of another system.

1. Establish target daylight factors for the various spaces and activities to be toplit. See the Daylight Factor strategy for suggested daylight factors.
2. Arrange the building spaces and floor plan layouts such that those areas to be toplit have a roof exposure.
3. Determine what type of toplighting aperture (e.g., skylight, clerestory, sawtooth, light scoop, roof monitor) is most appropriate for the space, building orientation, sky conditions, and climate. This is a complex design issue and there is no single best answer (although horizontal skylights should generally be avoided in hot climates).
4. Evaluate different glazing options for the aperture. In general the glazing should have a high visible transmittance (VT) value to maximize daylight entry. In hot climates a low solar heat gain coefficient (SHGC) is generally desirable to minimize solar heat gains. Often a compromise between VT and SHGC is in order. Manufacturers' catalogs are suggested as a valuable source of current information.
5. Estimate the size of daylighting apertures required to provide the target daylight factors as follows (derived from Millet and Bedrick, 1980):

$$A = ((DF_{avg})(A_{floor}))/(AE)$$

where,

A = required area of aperture, ft^2 [m^2]

DF_{avg} = target average daylight factor

SAMPLE PROBLEM

A 4500 ft^2 [418 m^2] ball-bearing factory in Brazil will be toplit to lower energy costs and provide a more pleasant working environment.

1. A daylight factor of 4–8% is considered appropriate for fine machine work. The designer selects a 6% DF.
2. The factory is a single story building; all spaces have roof exposure.
3. The design team decides to use a vertical roof monitor aperture to more easily control the intense direct solar radiation that occurs in this climate.
4. A high VT glass is chosen because the aperture will be shaded by external shading devices (rather than via a low SHGC provided by the glazing itself).
5. For a vertical monitor the area of glazing is estimated as: (DF) (floor area)/AE

$$A = (0.06)(4500\ ft^2)/(0.2)$$
$$= 1350\ ft^2 [125 m^2]$$

1350 ft^2 [125 m^2] of monitor glazing will be distributed evenly across the roof to facilitate a balanced distribution of daylight.

A_{floor} = illuminated floor area, ft^2 [m^2]

AE = aperture effectiveness factor (see Table 4.6)

TABLE 4.6 Toplighting aperture effectiveness (AE) factors

APERTURE TYPE	AE FACTOR
Vertical monitors/clerestories	0.20
North-facing sawtooth	0.33
Horizontal skylights	0.50

Note the inherent luminous efficiency of horizontal skylights expressed in the above values (while remembering their potential for unwanted heat gain).

6. Arrange surfaces adjacent to the toplighting apertures to diffuse entering light to reduce contrast (a potential cause of glare) and more evenly distribute daylight throughout the space.
7. Evaluate the need for shading for the toplighting apertures and design appropriate devices to provide the necessary shading. The assumption that daylighting provides more energy-efficient illumination than electric lighting is dependent upon the exclusion of direct solar radiation from daylighting apertures. Failure to provide appropriate shading will result in increased cooling loads and the potential for glare.

6. The roof form is designed to improve the diffusion and distribution of daylight—to the extent practical in schematic design.
7. A shading device to block direct solar radiation during the summer is designed; the device also facilitates a more diffuse distribution of light.

Examples

4.93 Pod monitor skylight at the Arup Campus Solihull in Blythe Valley Park, Solihull, UK. One of the dual-function roof pods as seen from the roof (left) and from the floor below (right). ARUP ASSOCIATES | TISHA EGASHIRA

4.94 Toplighting and sidelighting provide ample daylight in Kroon Hall, Yale School of Forestry and Environmental Studies, New Haven, Connecticut. ROBERT BENSON PHOTOGRAPHY

4.95 Skylight and clerestory monitors on the roof (left) of the administration building at Guandong Pei Zheng Commercial College in Huadu, China; resulting toplighting distributed by lightwells (right) provides illumination for four floors along a circulation corridor.

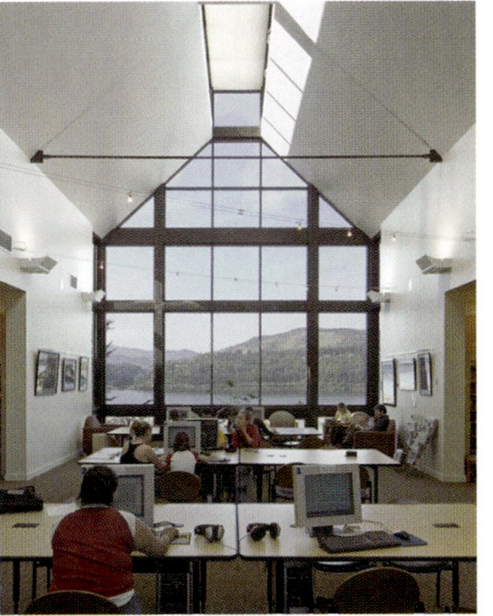

4.96 The Hood River Public Library (left) in Hood River, Oregon uses daylight and natural ventilation strategies; a long, clerestory monitor (right) illuminates the main reading area in the Library addition. FLETCHER, FARR, AYOTTE, INC.

4.97 A glass canopy over the Great Court spans between the old and new portions of the British Museum in London, England and provides delightful toplighting.

4.98 Toplighting washes brick walls with light in an interior courtyard in Montepulciano, Italy.

4.99 Innovative toplighting system in classroom at the Mt. Angel Abbey Annunciation Academic Center, St. Benedict, Oregon. ENERGY STUDIES IN BUILDINGS LABORATORY, UNIVERSITY OF OREGON

Further Information

Evans, B. 1981. *Daylight in Architecture*, Architectural Record Books, New York.

Grondzik, W. et al. 2010. *Mechanical and Electrical Equipment for Buildings*. 11th ed. John Wiley & Sons, Hoboken, NJ.

IEA 2000. *Daylight in Buildings: A Source Book on Daylighting Systems and Components*, International Energy Agency. gaia.lbl.gov/iea21/ieapubc.htm

Millet, M. and J. Bedrick. 1980. *Graphic Daylighting Design Method*, U.S. Department of Energy/Lawrence Berkeley National Laboratory, Washington, DC.

Moore, F. 1985. *Concepts and Practice of Architectural Daylighting*, Van Nostrand Reinhold, New York.

Whole Building Design Guide, "Daylighting." www.wbdg.org/resources/daylighting.php?r=mou_daylight

BEYOND SCHEMATIC DESIGN

The preliminary sizing of apertures undertaken during schematic design will be verified by more accurate modeling studies during design development. Aperture details (including shading and diffusing elements) will be finalized during design development, along with integration of daylighting and electric lighting controls. Commissioning of daylighting-related controls is strongly recommended.

SIDELIGHTING is a daylighting strategy that uses apertures located in a wall plane as the point of admission for ambient daylight. Any system that delivers daylight onto a horizontal task plane generally from the side is considered sidelighting. Sidelighting approaches often utilize windows as the daylight aperture—but glass block, low clerestories, and vertical openings into light courts or atria would also be considered sidelighting approaches.

4.100 Conceptual diagram of a sidelighting system showing typical light distribution pattern in a space, and attention to aperture detail. JON THWAITES

The same windows that allow daylight into a building can provide a visual connection to the outside. The relationship of window height (and hence ceiling height) to room depth is an important consideration with respect to daylight factor. Window height is also a key determinant of views (along with site conditions). Sidelighting systems often involve two distinct apertures—a lower view and daylight window, and an upper daylight-only window associated with a light shelf.

Most daylighting systems should be designed such that no direct solar radiation enters the building through the apertures. First, the direct solar component is not needed to provide adequate daylight factors (illuminance) in most climates during most of the day. Second, direct solar radiation brings unwanted heat gain—which, if admitted into a building, will greatly decrease the luminous efficacy of daylight. Third, direct solar radiation admittance greatly increases the potential for direct glare experiences. Thus, some form of shading should be used in conjunction with sidelighting—the general exception being north-facing windows. Admittance of solar radiation via sidelighting

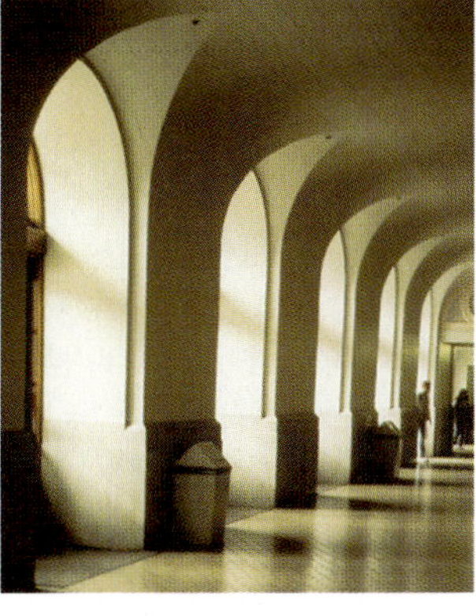

4.101 Sidelighting a corridor using glazed recessed doors; the Hearst Memorial Gymnasium, University of California Berkeley.

INTENT
Task visibility, energy efficiency, occupant satisfaction, views

EFFECT
Reduced consumption of electricity, improved occupant satisfaction, potentially reduced cooling loads, visual relief

OPTIONS
Numerous options for apertures, shading devices, light shelves, light courts, and atria

COORDINATION ISSUES
Design intent, spatial functions and tasks, building/facade orientation, solar heat gain, electric lighting system controls

RELATED STRATEGIES
Site Analysis, Glazing, Daylight Factor, Daylight Zoning, Toplighting, Light Shelves, Direct Gain, Shading Devices, Internal Reflectances, Electric Lighting, cooling strategies, building envelope strategies

PREREQUISITES
Design intent, preliminary spatial layout, daylight factor criteria

apertures as part of a direct gain passive heating system is an exception to the direct solar radiation exclusion discussed above.

Key Architectural Issues

Windows have a rich architectural history, from Gothic cathedrals to the modern glass curtain wall and double envelope. Windows, however, are not synonymous with sidelighting. How a given window sees the sky (or not), how it is detailed, how it relates to the task plane and bounding room surfaces, and the type of glazing used are all important to a daylighting system. The relationship between windows and interior surfaces is a critically important design consideration, as such surfaces act as secondary light sources and assist with distribution and diffusion of daylight.

Sidelighting favors tall, shallow rooms. Sidelighting is a very visible design strategy because the apertures have a dominant presence. Windows often define the character of a building facade.

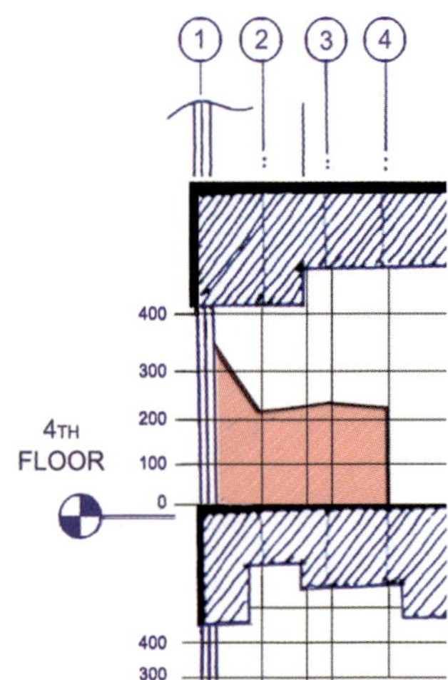

4.102 Incremental measurements of illuminance adjacent to a window in the reading area of the San Francisco Public Library in San Francisco, California.
REDRAWN BY LUZANNE SMITH FROM A VITAL SIGNS CASE STUDY PROJECT.

Implementation Considerations

Glazing selection is important to toplighting, but is especially so to sidelighting. Daylight aperture glazing should have a high visible transmittance (VT) value, but also often needs to meet building/energy code requirements for solar heat gain coefficient (SHGC). Large areas of glazing can affect mean radiant temperatures in perimeter spaces, so an appropriate U-factor to mitigate glazing surface temperatures is another consideration.

A daylighting system will save no energy unless it can displace electric lighting. It is thus critical that the daylighting and electric lighting systems in a space be closely coordinated and that appropriate controls to dim or turn off unnecessary electric lamps be provided. Continuous dimming controls have proven to be well accepted by users, but difficult to properly implement and maintain in practice.

Design Procedure

This procedure presumes that the merits of sidelighting versus toplighting have been considered and sidelighting has been selected as the approach of interest. This does not preclude the use of combined sidelighting and toplighting systems. Illuminances are additive, such that the contribution of one system can be directly added to that of another system.

The design of a sidelighting system is not a purely linear process. Several iterations are often necessary to determine the most appropriate implementation.

1. Establish target daylight factors for each space and activity. Recommended daylight factors for various spaces can be found in the Daylight Factor strategy.
2. Arrange program elements into a footprint that maximizes wall area (surface area to volume ratio)—using, for example, U-shaped buildings, courtyards/atria, long thin building plans. Maximize opportunities for daylighting without direct solar radiation by focusing upon the north and south orientations as prime

SAMPLE PROBLEM

A multistory office complex will be daylit by sidelighting in order to provide views for most workspaces.

1. A minimum daylight factor (DF) of 2.5% is desired for the primary workspaces.
2. The majority of offices are arranged around a U-shaped opening facing south. This maximizes the facade area available for windows while providing some self-shading by the building itself.
3. Primary workspaces are located along the periphery while service elements are placed in the interior.

locations for daylight apertures. East and west apertures require careful consideration of shading devices to reduce the potential for direct glare and unwanted solar gains.

3. Organize the building floor plan with spaces that will benefit the most from daylighting located along the perimeter of the building. Spaces with a lesser need for daylight (or lower illuminance requirements) can be placed in the interior and arranged to borrow light from perimeter spaces.

4. Determine the depth of the space to be daylit, as required by programmatic needs. Depth is the distance inward from the perimeter wall.

5. Divide the depth of the room by 2.5 to determine the minimum top-of-window (head) height needed to effectively sidelight a space of this depth.

6. Verify that the required window head height (measured from the floor) is acceptable (or feasible). Not all of the window height needs to be "view" window. Areas above a reasonable view height can be glazed solely for daylight admittance. When this approach is taken, the two window elements are often separated by a light shelf (see the strategy on Light Shelves).

7. Multiply the proposed window width by 2 to determine the extent of horizontal (parallel to the window plane) light penetration. Ensure that the window width is adequate to provide daylight coverage across the full room width. (This approximation assumes a reasonably even distribution of glazing across the width of the window wall.)

8. Modify the proposed glazing width and head height as required to work within the above constraints.

9. Determine the required area of daylighting aperture by using the following estimates (derived from Millet and Bedrick, 1980):

$$A = ((DF_{target})(A_{floor}))/(F)$$

where,

A = required area of aperture, ft^2 [m^2]

DF_{target} = target daylight factor

A_{floor} = illuminated floor area, ft^2 [m^2]

$F = 0.2$ if the target is an average daylight factor OR

$= 0.1$ if the target is a minimum daylight factor

Note: any window area below task height is of little use for daylighting.

10. Refine the design to maximize the effectiveness of daylight admitted via sidelighting. Arrange primary building structural elements to maximize light penetration into the space. For example, primary beams should run perpendicular to the fenestration plane. Verify appropriate visual connections with the exterior via any view windows. Analyze the potential for glare. Design shading as required by the orientation of the window (see the Shading Devices strategy).

4. A depth of 20 ft [6.1 m] is proposed for the open-plan workspaces.

5. The required height of the top of the window is (20 ft/2.5 m) = 8 ft [2.4 m] .

6. Local building ordinances limit floor-to-floor height to 12 ft [3.7 m]. A maximum window height of 8 ft [2.4 m] plus 30 in. [760 mm] to account for task height is marginally feasible (considering a reasonable plenum depth). Reducing the workspace depth to 15 ft [4.6 m] might be considered.

7. A window more or less the width of the space (less mullions) is proposed, so window width is not a limiting factor.

8. No adjustments to proposed window width are required.

9. Considering a unit width (1 ft or 1 m) of floor, the required area of aperture to obtain a minimum DF of 2.5% across a 20 ft [6.1 m] depth is:

$$A = (0.025)(20)/(0.1)$$
$$= 5\ ft^2\ [0.5\ m^2]$$

The proposed window area is feasible and fits within the constraints of the design, while providing the target daylight factor.

10. Refine elements of the proposed design to minimize glare, control direct solar gain, and beneficially diffuse daylight.

Examples

4.103 Bilateral sidelighting from view windows and clerestories in classrooms at the Druk White Lotus School, Ladakh, India. CAROLINE SOHIE, ARUP + ARUP ASSOCIATES

4.104 A lounge in the Christopher Center at Valparaiso University, Indiana, demonstrates a "wall washing" daylighting technique with the glazing aperture directly adjacent to a light-colored wall. KELLY GOFFINEY

4.105 Sidelighting through tall windows (left) and toplighting via a skylight (right) at the Raffles Hotel in Singapore.

4.106 North-facing clerestories and operable windows at reading areas provide diffuse sidelighting at the Mt. Angel Abbey Library in St. Benedict, Oregon.

4.107 ODS School of Dental Hygiene board room with bilateral sidelighting, Bend, Oregon.
JOSH PARTEE

Further Information

Evans, B. 1981. *Daylight in Architecture*, Architectural Record Books, New York.

Grondzik, W. et al. 2010. *Mechanical and Electrical Equipment for Buildings*. 11th ed. John Wiley & Sons, Hoboken, NJ.

IEA 2000. *Daylight in Buildings: A Source Book on Daylighting Systems and Components*, International Energy Agency.

Millet, M. and J. Bedrick. 1980. *Graphic Daylighting Design Method*, U.S. Department of Energy/Lawrence Berkeley National Laboratory, Washington, DC.

Moore, F. 1985. *Concepts and Practice of Architectural Daylighting*, Van Nostrand Reinhold, New York.

Whole Building Design Guide, "Daylighting."
www.wbdg.org/resources/daylighting.php?r=mou_daylight

BEYOND SCHEMATIC DESIGN

Preliminary estimates of sidelighting performance will be refined via more detailed analysis during design development. Glazing, shading, and distribution elements will be considered, selected, and specified. Electric lighting and control systems will be addressed during design development. Controls for integrating daylighting and electric lighting must be commissioned.

LIGHT SHELVES are used to provide a more even distribution of daylight entering a building through sidelighting apertures (typically windows). Light bounces off the reflective surfaces of the shelf, and subsequently off the ceiling of a room, and creates a more even illuminance pattern than would occur without a light shelf. The form, material, and position of a light shelf determine the distribution of incoming daylight. A light shelf may be placed on the exterior or interior of a building or both; the defining element is that there is glazing directly above the plane of the shelf. The glazing above a light shelf is solely for daylighting. Glazing below a light shelf can provide for view, as well as daylighting.

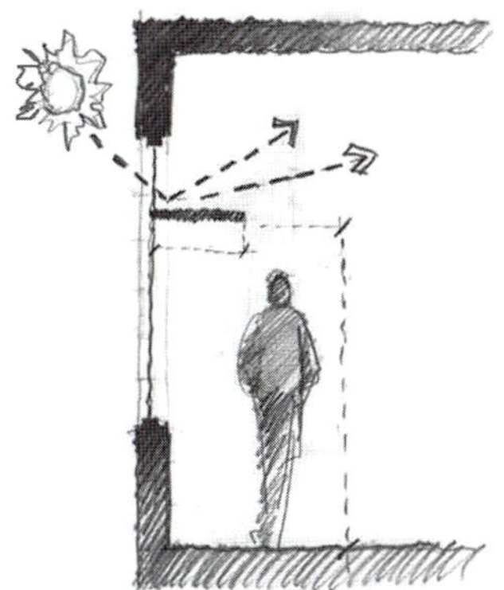

4.109 Conceptual sketch of a light shelf in an office. GREG HARTMAN

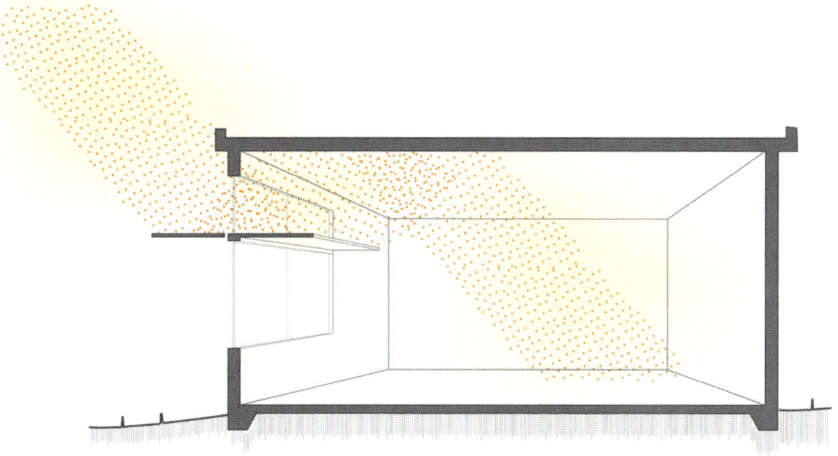

4.108 Section through an exterior wall with sidelighting apertures, showing typical placement of a light shelf. JON THWAITES

By redirecting incoming daylight and increasing light diffusion, a well-designed light shelf will add to the physical and visual comfort of a space and reduce the use of electric lighting by increasing daylight factors away from the aperture and reducing contrast caused by daylighting within a space. An exterior light shelf may also serve as a sunshading device for lower glazing areas, thereby reducing cooling loads by reducing solar gains.

Light shelves are often used in offices and schools where an even distribution of daylight is desirable for visual comfort and a more even distribution of daylight can reduce electric lighting costs.

Key Architectural Issues

A light shelf does not need to look like a shelf. With an understanding of sky conditions, the path of the sun and its seasonal variations, and the use and layout of a space, creative options can enhance the facade of a building. Light shelves should be considered in conjunction with the type, size, and placement of daylight apertures, reveals, walls, ceilings, materials, and furniture. Designing in section–and with consideration of these related elements—it should be possible

INTENT
More even and somewhat deeper distribution of daylight, reduction of glare potential

EFFECT
Reduced electrical lighting usage, potential for reduced cooling load

OPTIONS
Exterior, interior, or combination shelves; fixed or adjustable

COORDINATION ISSUES
Ceiling design, daylighting aperture, glazing, internal partitions, orientation, shading, heat gain

RELATED STRATEGIES
Site Analysis, Glazing, Daylight Factor, Internal Reflectances, Shading Devices

PREREQUISITES
Preliminary room layout (geometry), information on room orientation, site latitude, sun angles, site obstructions

to maximize the amount and optimize the placement of light that is redirected by a light shelf.

A light shelf is often an appropriate solution to the problem of providing a reasonably even distribution of daylight in a building with unilateral sidelighting. In some situations (such as very deep spaces or where ceiling height is restricted) other methods of redirecting daylight, such as light scoops, light pipes, prismatic devices, and anidolic zenithal collectors may be more appropriate. A bilateral aperture arrangement is very appropriate for deep spaces.

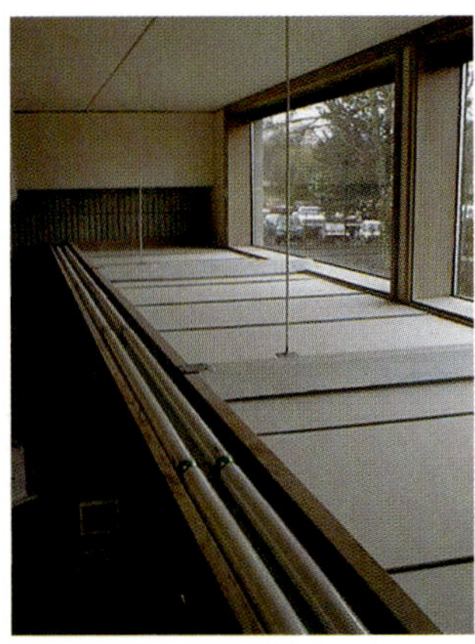

4.110 A matte, light-colored finish on the top of this light shelf diffuses daylight in multiple directions. Fluorescent lighting fixtures are integrated along the edge of the shelf.

Implementation Considerations

Orientation. Light shelves can be effective shading devices on south-facing facades in the northern hemisphere. Light shelves will typically capture direct solar radiation, as well as diffuse light, for redistribution when located on a south facade; this benefit must be tempered, however, against the additional cooling load contributed by this captured solar radiation.

Shelf height and angle. Light shelves should be located above eye level to reduce the potential of glare from the reflective upper shelf surface. Depending upon the use of the area adjacent to the windows, light shelves may also need to be above head height. Horizontal light shelves are very common because they can provide a balance of light distribution, glare control, shading performance, and aesthetic potential. Tilted light shelves, however, may provide better performance (a design decision to be verified during design development).

Ceiling. A high ceiling is desirable for light shelf applications. If floor-to-floor height is tight, sloping the ceiling upward toward the window aperture may prove useful (although the effect of this move is in question).

Windows. Higher windows allow daylight to penetrate deeper into a space. Above a light shelf, clear, double-paned glazing is recommended for most climates. A horizontal louvered shading device may be installed between the panes. If there is view glazing below a light shelf, make a climate-appropriate, view-supporting, glazing selection.

Shading. Use horizontal blinds for the glazing above a light shelf as necessary to block direct solar radiation and (when oriented at roughly 45 °) to direct light to the ceiling. Design a separate shading solution to protect glazing below the light shelf from solar gain.

Finishes. Consider splaying window reveals and frames to reduce contrast. A specular (mirror-like) finish on a light shelf may increase daylight levels, but can also become a potential source of glare. A semi-specular (but still quite reflective) finish is generally preferable. A matte finish will also provide more diffuse light distribution (Figure 4.110). The ceiling and walls of a daylit space should be smooth and reflective, but not so much that they become a potential source of glare. Consider the effect that partition design, furniture layout, and interior finishes will have on increasing daylight penetration and reducing glare. Consider the interrelated effect of all interior design decisions.

Maintenance. Consider how interior and/or exterior light shelves might be maintained. Dust and debris reduce the reflectivity of a light shelf. Interior light shelves can be designed to fold down for easy maintenance. For exterior light shelves, consider rain runoff, snow collection, and disruption of potentially beneficial airflow patterns along the facade.

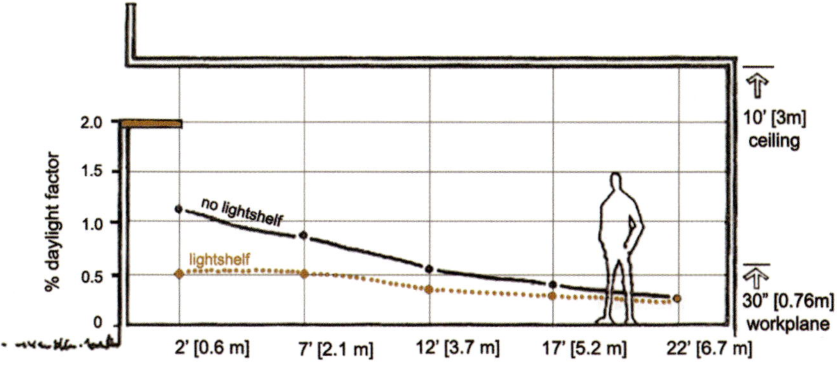

4.111 Effect of the position of a white-colored light shelf on interior illuminance (daylight factor), with clear glazing and overcast sky. No light shelf (a) and interior light shelf (b).
REDRAWN BY LUZANNE SMITH WITH PERMISSION FROM FULLER MOORE

Design Procedure

1. Determine if an external, internal, or combination light shelf is most appropriate for the intended use of the space. An exterior light shelf can even out daylight levels in a space while providing protection from solar gain through the lower glazing. An interior light shelf may decrease daylight levels, particularly in the window vicinity, but provide for more even light distribution with less contrast within a space (see Figure 4.111).
2. Sketch the proposal in section. For an exterior south-facing light shelf, estimate the depth as roughly equal to the difference between the height of the shelf and the work plane. For an interior light shelf, estimate the depth of the shelf as roughly equal to the height of the glazing above it. The top surface of a light shelf should be at least 2 ft [0.6 m] from the ceiling. The ceiling height should be at least 9 ft [3 m].
3. Create a daylighting model to test the proposed design. The model must be large enough to evaluate the rather subtle effects of light shelves and to allow incremental measurements to be made in the space of most interest. See Moore or Evans for recommendations on preparing daylighting models.

SAMPLE PROBLEM

Sidelighting will be used for a 50 ft × 100 ft [15.3 × 30.5 m] open office space in a four-story building in Boca Raton, Florida. The window faces south. Ceiling height is 10 ft [3.1 m]; window height is 6 ft [1.8 m] with 2 ft [0.6 m] above the light shelf and 4 ft [1.2 m] below with a 3 ft [0.9 m] sill height. The work plane height is 2.5 ft [760 mm].

1. The initial light shelf design proposes a combined (interior and exterior) light shelf.
2. Using the preliminary depth rules, the interior light shelf depth is proposed as 2 ft [0.6 m] and the exterior extension depth as $(4 + 3 - 2.5) = 4.5$ ft [1.4 m].

ENVELOPE LIGHTING HEATING COOLING ENERGY PRODUCTION WATER & WASTE

Examples

4.112 Light shelf in a classroom at Ash Creek Intermediate School, Independence, Oregon. Over time, teachers placed items on top of the light shelves, which interfered with the daylighting effectiveness.

4.113 Specular reflectors (another way of thinking about light shelves) at the top of an atrium in the Hong Kong Shanghai Bank, Hong Kong, direct daylight to floors below.

3. Study the performance of this proposed design using either physical models or appropriate computer simulations. Adjust the design as suggested by the modeling studies and the intended performance.

4.114 Daylighting windows with light shelves at the Lillis Business Complex, University of Oregon. EMILY J. WRIGHT

4.115 Close-up view showing perforations and curvature of light shelves at Lillis Business Complex. SRG PARTNERSHIP

Further Information

Evans, B. 1981. *Daylight in Architecture*, Architectural Record Books, New York.

IEA. 2000. *Daylight in Buildings: A Source Book on Daylighting Systems and Components*, International Energy Agency.

LBL. 1997. "Section 3: Envelope and Room Decisions," in *Tips for Daylighting With Windows*. Building Technologies Program, Lawrence Berkeley National Laboratory.
btech.lbl.gov/pub/pub/designguide/index.html

LRC. 2004. *Guide for Daylighting Schools*, Developed by Innovative Design for Daylight Dividends, Lighting Research Center, Rensselaer Polytechnic Institute, Troy, NY.
www.lrc.rpi.edu/programs/daylighting/pdf/guidelines.pdf

Moore, F. 1985. *Concepts and Practice of Architectural Daylighting*, Van Nostrand Reinhold, New York.

NREL 2003. *Laboratories for the 21st Century: Best Practices*, "Daylighting in Laboratories" (DOE/GO-102003-1766). National Renewable Energy Laboratory, U.S. Environmental Protection Agency/U.S. Department of Energy.
www.labs21century.gov/pdf/bp_daylight_508.pdf

BEYOND SCHEMATIC DESIGN

The performance of a light shelf (as estimated during schematic design) will be verified and optimized during design development. Controls are the key to reducing energy use in a daylit building. Photosensor control for each row of lights, running parallel to the light shelf, is recommended. A light shelf must not interfere with sprinkler operation, air diffuser performance, or natural ventilation airflows. Occupants will need to learn how (and should be trained via a User's Manual) to use any operable sun control devices. Establish a reasonable and documented maintenance (cleaning) schedule and routine.

Dirt accumulation and wear and tear will reduce surface brightness over time—an effect captured in a value called "light loss" or "maintenance" factor. One (of several) key light loss factors is the room surface dirt depreciation factor, which is a function of room dimensions, atmospheric dirt conditions, and an estimate of cleaning/refurbishment intervals. This factor can reasonably range from 0.50 (in a terribly dirty environment) to 0.95 (in a pristine, well-maintained environment). The effect of dirt depreciation must be considered during the design process and results in a need for greater initial illuminance (so that an acceptable maintained illuminance is available over time). The relationship between initial, maintained, and design illuminance is as follows (where design illuminance represents the design criterion): initial illuminance $\geq$ maintained illuminance $\geq$ design illuminance.

4.119 A precision luminance meter can be used to accurately measure the amount of light leaving a surface (i.e., surface brightness) in cd/m^2 or ft-L.

4.118 An illuminance meter can be used to roughly estimate luminance. Measure the illuminance at the surface (left) and then measure the amount of light leaving (reflected from) the surface (right). The quantity of reflected light divided by the quantity of incident light is the surface reflectance. (Make sure that self-shadowing does not unduly interfere with the measurements.)

Design Procedure

1. Make sure that the window jamb and sill have a high reflectance, as they can make excellent reflectors. Splay deep jambs away from the window. Both of these design recommendations will increase daylight throughput as well as decrease the contrast between the interior and exterior environments (reducing glare potential).
2. The ceiling is the most important surface for daylighting. Choose a ceiling paint or tile that has a reflectance of 90% or higher to maximize light distribution within the space. Recommended minimum surface reflectances for energy-efficient lighting design are shown in Table 4.7. Use the upper limits of the reflectance ranges for spaces with more difficult daylighting constraints or requiring higher design illuminances.
3. Angling the ceiling toward the source of incoming light can increase the amount of light that is reflected. This works especially well with daylight coming from clerestory windows. Assuming (even if not truly correct) that light is reflected at an

SAMPLE PROBLEM

The adjacent procedure is best applied through use of a physical model.

angle equal to its incidence angle can assist in making decisions regarding ceiling surface angles.

4. Choose light-colored furniture, fixtures, and equipment as they can significantly affect light distribution within a space (see Tables 4.8 and 4.9 for typical reflectances).

TABLE 4.7 Recommended reflectances for interior surfaces in different spaces. THE IESNA LIGHTING HANDBOOK, 9TH ED.

SURFACE	RECOMMENDED REFLECTANCES		
	Offices	Classrooms	Residences
Ceilings	80%	70–90%	60–90%
Walls	50–70%	40–60%	35–60%
Floors	20–40%	30–50%	15–35%
Furnishings	25–45%	30–50%	35–60%

TABLE 4.8 Reflectances of common building and site materials. EXCERPTED FROM HOPKINSON ET AL. (1966) AND ROBBINS (1986)

MATERIAL	REFLECTANCE
Aluminum	85%
Asphalt	5–10%
Brick	10–30%
Concrete	20–30%
Gravel	20%
Plaster, white	40–80%
Water	30–70%
Vegetation	5–25%

TABLE 4.9 Reflectances of typical paint colors

COLOR	REFLECTANCE
White	80–90%
Pale blue	80%
Canary yellow	75%
Lemon yellow	65%
Dark cream	60%
Light blue	55%
Light green	50%
Light brown	50%
Apricot	45%
Apple green	40%
Medium brown	35%
Red-orange	30%
Dark red, blue, gray	15%
Black	5%

There is a great deal of variance among paint colors, names, and reflectances; the above are rough approximations.

Examples

4.120 Translucent and tinted side apertures introduce daylight and modify its color as it falls on concrete floors and ceilings at the Laban Centre in London, England. DONALD CORNER

4.121 Colored walls within the light-capturing aperture in the St. Ignatius Chapel in Seattle, Washington reflect "borrowed" color onto otherwise white walls.

4.122 Twelve-story, central atrium at Genzyme Center, Cambridge, Massachusetts. Fixed mirrors at the top of the atrium direct daylight to prismatic louvers; the light then interacts with hanging prismatic mobiles, reflective panels, and reflective bounding walls. ANTON GRASSL, COURTESY OF BEHNISCH ARCHITEKTEN

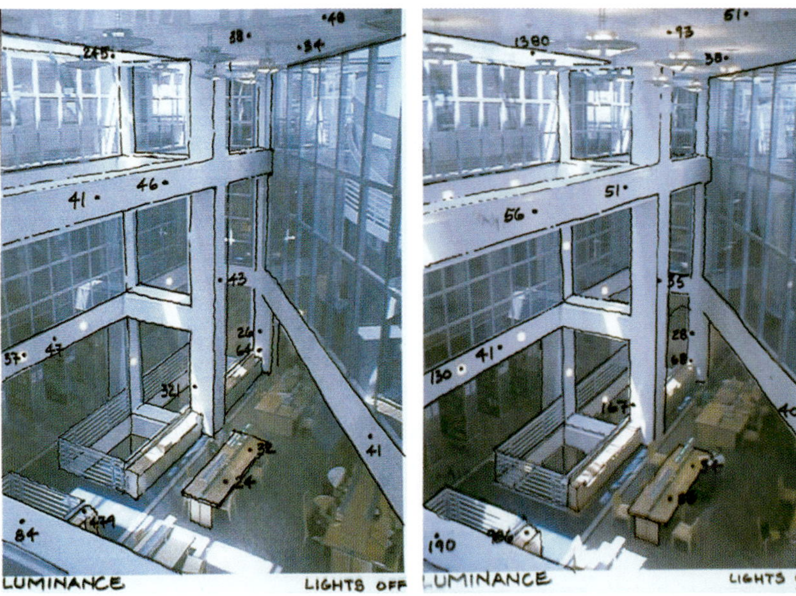

4.123 On-site luminance measurements (cd/m^2) in the San Francisco Public Library with electric lighting off (left) and electric lighting on (right). Part of a Vital Signs case study to examine the influence of light-reflective surfaces in daylit zones.

Further Information

Brown, G.Z and M. DeKay. 2001. *Sun, Wind and Light: Architectural Design Strategies*, 2nd ed. John Wiley & Sons, New York.

DiLaura, D. et al. (ed). 2011. *The Lighting Handbook*. 10th ed. Illuminating Engineering Society of North America, New York.

Grondzik, W. et al. 2010. *Mechanical & Electrical Equipment for Buildings*. 11th ed. John Wiley & Sons, Hoboken, NJ.

Hopkinson, R., P. Petherbridge and J. Longmore. 1966. *Daylighting*, Heinemann, London.

Rea, M. 2000. *The IESNA Lighting Handbook*, 9th ed. Illuminating Engineering Society of North America, New York.

Robbins, C. 1986. *Daylighting: Design and Analysis*, Van Nostrand Reinhold, New York.

BEYOND SCHEMATIC DESIGN

Schematic design phase assumptions regarding reflectances of surfaces and furnishings must be passed on to the design development phase. Failure to communicate this critical information could result in decisions that degrade intended system performance. The importance of maintaining surface reflectances after occupancy should be conveyed to the building owner (ideally, via a User's Manual).

SHADING DEVICES

SHADING DEVICES can significantly reduce building heat gains from solar radiation while maintaining opportunities for daylighting, views, and natural ventilation. Conversely, carefully designed shading can admit direct solar radiation during times of the year when such energy is desired to passively heat a building. While the window (or skylight) is often the focus of shading devices, walls and roofs can also be shaded to help reduce heat gains through the opaque building envelope.

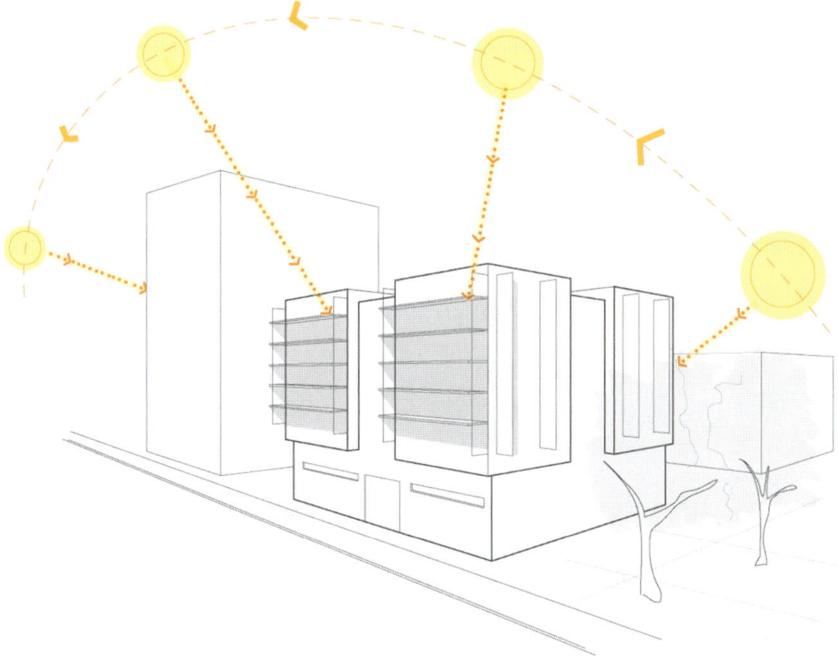

4.124 Effective shading design is dependent upon a number of physical variables, such as the path of the sun, nearby obstructions, time of day, orientation, and latitude. JON THWAITES

Radiation is an energy form that does not require a material medium through which to travel. Energy from the sun reaches the earth entirely through radiation. Solar radiation consists of visible (light), ultraviolet, and infrared radiation components. When solar radiation strikes a surface, the radiation may be reflected, absorbed, or transmitted depending upon the nature of the surface. For example, a fair percentage of solar radiation passes through a typical window, while some of that transmitted solar radiation striking a floor will be absorbed (as heat) and some will be reflected.

The percentage of solar radiation that passes through a window and into a building depends upon the properties of the glass and the window assembly. Solar heat gain coefficient (SHGC) is a dimensionless number (generally falling between 0 and 1) that gives an indication of how much of the solar radiation incident upon a glazing assembly reaches the inside of a building. An SHGC of 1 means that 100% of incident solar radiation passes through the window or skylight. An SHGC of 0.2 indicates that 20% of the incident solar radiation is

4.125 Movable shading devices on the Royal Danish Embassy, Berlin, Germany. CHRISTINA BOLLO

INTENT
Energy efficiency (through screening of solar radiation when not needed and admitting it when desired), visual comfort

EFFECT
Reduced cooling load, solar access when desired, reduced glare

OPTIONS
Devices internal, integral, or external to the building envelope, operable or fixed

COORDINATION ISSUES
Building orientation and footprint, passive and active heating and cooling, natural ventilation

RELATED STRATEGIES
Site Analysis, Glazing, Sidelighting, Toplighting, Cross Ventilation, Direct Gain, Indirect Gain, Isolated Gain

PREREQUISITES
Site latitude, window/wall orientation, skylight tilt/orientation, massing of neighboring buildings and trees, a sense of building heating and cooling loads

passed into the interior of the building. (It is important to remember that a window also transmits heat via conduction and convection.) Shading coefficient (SC) is an alternative (and more historic) measure used to quantify shading. Shading coefficient is the ratio of radiant heat flow through a particular window relative to the radiant heat flow through 1/8-in. [3.2 mm] thick, double strength, clear window glass. Shading coefficient only applies to the glazed portion of a window or skylight; solar heat gain coefficient applies to the glazing–frame combination.

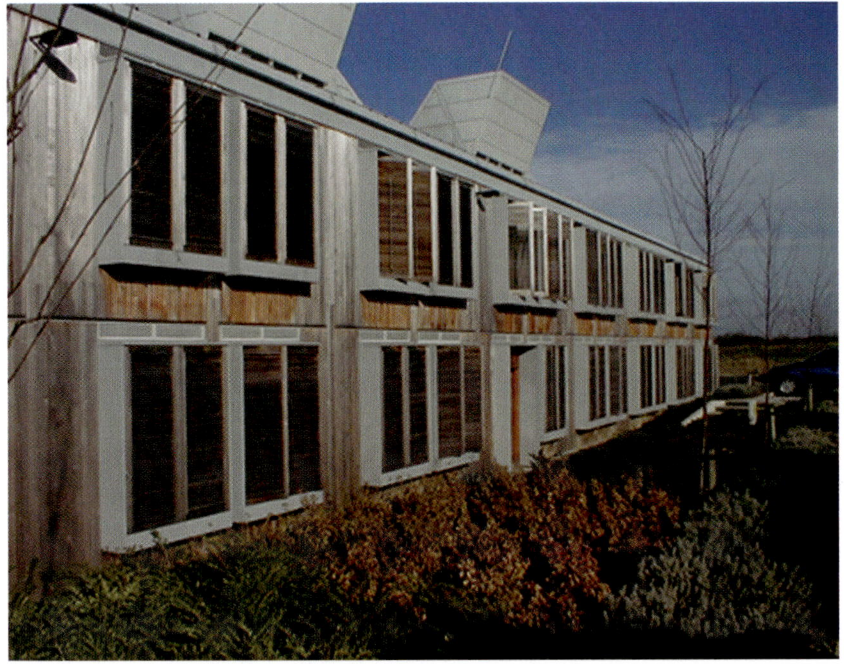

4.126 External wood shutters with horizontal louvers protect operable windows on the southeastern facade of Arup Campus Solihull, England. TISHA EGASHIRA

Shading building envelope elements from direct radiation can dramatically lower heat gains during the cooling season. If the shading is from an internal device (like a blind), solar radiation gain through the window can be reduced on the order of 20%. However, if the shading is provided by an external device (as in Figure 4.126), the heat gain can be reduced by up to 80%. The preferred hierarchy for shading device placement is: external to the glazing, integral with the glazing, and then internal to the glazing.

Knowing the applicable sun paths at different times of the year allows the designer to create a shading device that provides shade when it is desirable to do so. Some shading devices use adjustable/movable parts to optimize shading effects for a particular time of day or year. Louvers can be moved to admit light or to block it, depending upon time of day, season, or orientation. Fixed shading devices are generally positioned to account for the difference between the high summer and low winter sun positions to shade in summer and allow sun in winter.

4.127 Arup Campus Solihull, England. This three-image sequence shows exterior shading devices on the southeast facade of the lower pavilion. They are controlled by the building management system, but with user override. TISHA EGASHIRA

Key Architectural Issues

The massing and orientation of a building are key determinants in designing a building that can be easily shaded. The east and west sides of a building are difficult to shade because of the low altitude of the rising and setting sun in the eastern and western skies. A building with long north and south facades and short east and west facades is much easier to shade. The north side of a building generally receives little direct solar radiation while the south side of a building sees high solar altitude angles during the summer months and low angles during the winter months.

A shading device should not compromise the other amenities that a window can provide—namely daylighting, views, and breezes. External shading devices do not necessarily have to be separate objects attached to a building exterior. Recessed window openings and facade geometry can allow a building to act as its own shading device.

Design Tools

Several tools are available for analyzing the extent and pattern of shade that will be provided by a particular shading device at varying latitudes, orientations, and times of the year. A sun path chart (or Sun Angle Calculator) can quickly provide the sun's altitude and azimuth angles for any specific latitude, month, day, and time of day. This graphic tool will also provide the profile angle, which is the key angle for determining the extent of shading that a device will provide. The percentage of a window shaded on various dates can be determined.

The solar transit (Figure 4.129) is a device that can trace the path of the sun in the sky for any particular day of the year, on site. This is useful for determining the hours of sun available at a particular spot on a site. The solar transit method automatically takes into consideration obstructions to the sun such as neighboring buildings and/or trees. Various computer software packages will simulate the effects of solar radiation on three-dimensional virtual models. A simple massing model of a house (Figure 4.130), for example, clearly shows patterns of shade and direct sunlight on building surfaces and the adjacent site. At the site scale, a fisheye lens can be used to take a photograph of the skydome at a particular point on a site. A sun path chart overlaid on the photo can determine the times during the year when that portion of the site will be shaded by obstructions (Figure 4.128).

A three-dimensional physical model with a sunpeg chart can be a powerful tool to quickly study shading at various times of the year. The sunpeg chart is affixed to the physical model with the proper orientation (north arrow on the sunpeg chart pointing to north on the model). The model can be rotated and tilted under a directional light source while the sunpeg chart indicates the date and time when the shading seen would actually be produced.

4.128 Sunpath chart overlain onto a fisheye photo of the sky. ROBERT MARCIAL

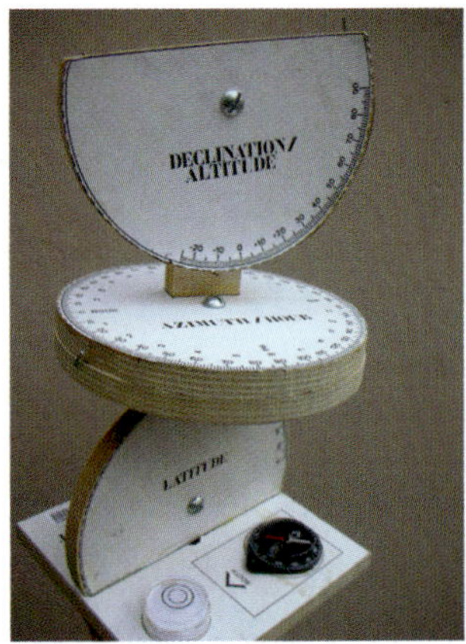

4.129 The solar transit is a useful device to trace the sun's path across the sky and create horizon shading masks for a particular location.

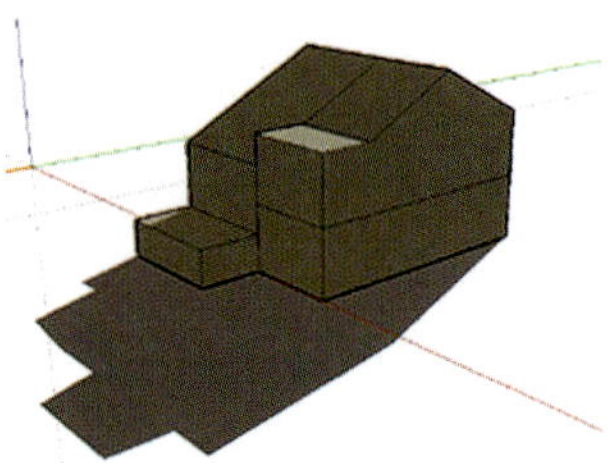

4.130 Cast shadows provided by a simple computer rendering of a massing model reveal patterns of solar irradiation and shading on a building and its site.

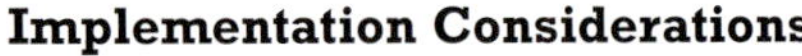

Implementation Considerations

Reflective surfaces on the top side of strategically placed horizontal sunshades can reflect light (and other radiation components) into a building. This can be used to bring more daylight into a building while simultaneously shading the majority of a window.

Shading from plants can often be more effective than from a fixed shading device because sun angles do not always correlate to ambient air temperature (and the resulting heating or cooling loads). For example, the sun angles on the spring equinox (March 21) are identical to the sun angles on the fall equinox (September 21). In the northern hemisphere, however, it is typically much warmer in late September than it is in late March, requiring more shading in September than in March. Deciduous plants respond more to temperature than to solar position. Leaves may not be present in early March, allowing sun to warm a building, while they are still on the trees in September, providing shading.

Design Procedure

1. Determine the shading requirements. Shading requirements are building- and space-specific and are dependent upon many variables including climate, building envelope design, building/space functions, visual comfort expectations, thermal comfort

expectations, and the like. It is impossible to make generic statements about this first critical step in the design procedure.

2. Determine whether shading will be interior, exterior, or integral to glazing; whether movable or fixed. The project budget, facade design intents, importance of views and daylighting (among other considerations) will help determine which is most appropriate.
3. Develop a trial design for the shading device. Examples of shading devices and their applications (as richly illustrated in *Solar Control and Shading Devices*) can greatly assist in this step.
4. Check the performance of the proposed shading device—using shading masks, computer simulations, or scale models as most appropriate to the project context and designer's experiences.
5. Modify the shading device design until the required performance is obtained and the design is considered acceptable with respect to other factors (daylighting, ventilation, aesthetics, etc.).

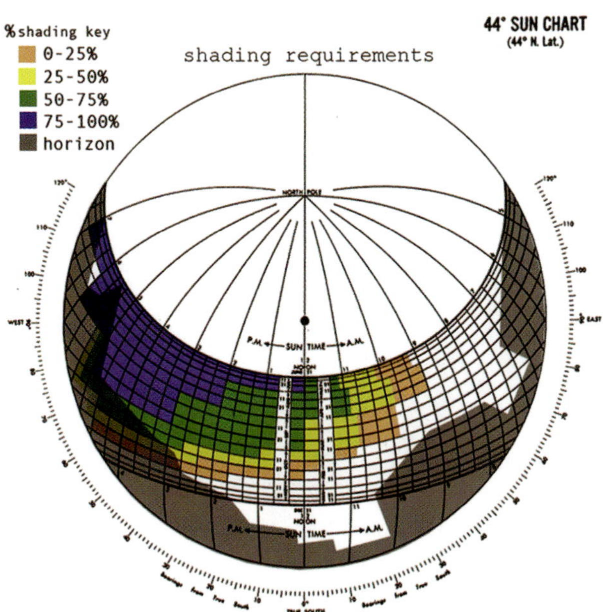

4.131 Building shading requirements superimposed on a sunpath chart. RUSSELL BALDWIN, DOUGLAS KAEHLER, ZACHARY PENNELL, BRENT STURLAUGSON

SAMPLE PROBLEM

An office building in Eugene, Oregon with a south facade experiences high summer solar heat gains. Analysis of climate, internal heat gains, and building envelope yields the shading requirements shown in Figure 4.131. A bay of the south facade was modeled with a sunpeg chart to check the performance of a proposed shading device at two opposite times of the year (Figures 4.132 and 4.133).

4.132 Performance of proposed shading device at 3:00 PM on June 21.

4.133 Performance of proposed shading device at 1:00 PM on December 21.

Examples

4.134 South-facing facade with horizontal shading louvers on the Burton Barr Central Library in Phoenix, Arizona.

4.135 North-facing facade of the Burton Barr Central Library with "sail-fins" to shade against early morning and late evening sun during the summer months.

4.136 1 Finsbury Square in London, England, uses classic, stout, shading overhangs attached to a glass curtain wall.
DONALD CORNER

4.137 The Menara Mesiniaga in Kuala Lumpur, Malaysia, has horizontal shading bands to block the high equatorial sun.

4.138 Vertical fins provide shading from the western sun at Casa Nueva, Santa Barbara County Office Building in Santa Barbara, California. WILLIAM B. DEWEY

4.139 Highly articulated vertical shading elements on the Mod 05 Living Hotel, Verona, Italy. CIRO FRANK SCHIAPPA/FUSINA 6

Further Information

Olgyay, A. and V. Olgyay. 1957. *Solar Control & Shading Devices*, Princeton University Press, Princeton, NJ.

Pacific Energy Center, Application Notes for Site Analysis, "Taking a Fisheye Photograph . . ." www.pge.com/pec/ (search on "fisheye")

Pilkington Sun Angle Calculator. Available through the Society of Building Science Educators. www.sbse.org/resources/index.htm

Solar Transit Template. Available through the Agents of Change Project, University of Oregon. aoc.uoregon.edu/loaner_kits/index.shtml

BEYOND SCHEMATIC DESIGN

Refined calculations of building heating and cooling loads, which impact the extent and timing of desired shading, will typically be made during design development. Ease of maintenance, cleaning of shading elements (birds like them), thermal breaks as appropriate, structure, and detailing to avoid trapping heat will be addressed.

ELECTRIC LIGHTING

ELECTRIC LIGHTING systems are one of the most energy-intensive components of modern buildings. A 2006 International Energy Agency report (by Paul Waide) indicates that lighting accounts for around 19% of global electrical energy consumption and contributes carbon dioxide emissions equivalent to 70% of that caused by passenger vehicle emissions. The same report suggests that using compact fluorescents in place of incandescent lamps, high-efficiency instead of low-efficiency ballasts, and replacing mercury vapor HID (high intensity discharge) lamps with more efficient alternatives would reduce global lighting demand by up to 40%—with a concomitant impact on global electricity use.

4.141 Daylight-integrated electric lighting controlled by photosensors in a classroom at Clackamas High School in Clackamas, Oregon.

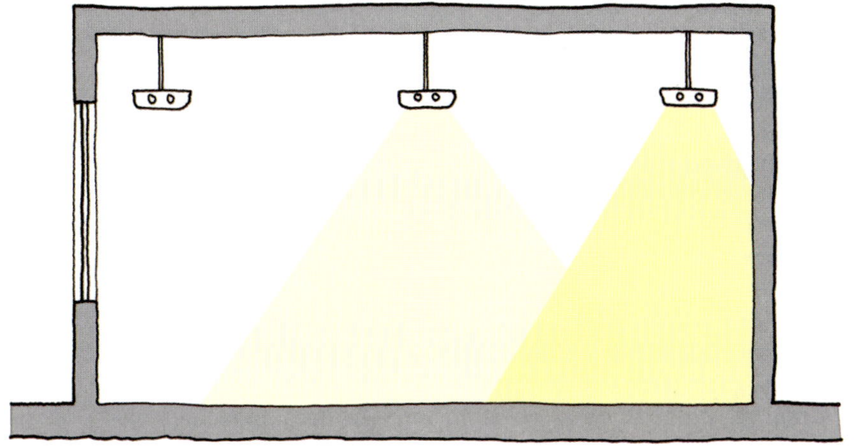

4.140 The conceptual basis of energy efficiency in electric lighting system design (use only what is needed). NICHOLAS RAJKOVICH

A "green" electrical lighting system will reduce lighting energy consumption, can (and most likely will) reduce energy consumption for space cooling, and should improve the visual comfort environment of a building—relative to a less efficient system. To maximize efficiency, electric lighting should be treated as a supplement to, not a replacement for, daylighting. A wide range of techniques is available to maximize the efficiency and quality of electric lighting systems. Technologically-based strategies include the selection of appropriate lamps, luminaires, and lighting controls. Architecturally-based strategies include: the design of appropriate spatial geometries; the selection of appropriate surface finishes; and the thoughtful positioning of luminaires relative to spatial geometries, other system elements (such as ductwork), and sources of daylight.

Several key indices are used to express various efficiency aspects of electric lighting systems. These include:

Luminous efficacy. A measure (in lumens/watt) of the light output of a lamp per watt of electrical input. The higher the luminous efficacy, the more light produced per watt of consumption. Luminous efficacies of commercially available lamps range from a low of around 20 to a high of around 120—a six-to-one ratio (see Figure 4.142). All

INTENT
Visual performance, visual comfort, ambience, energy efficiency

EFFECT
Illuminance, luminance

OPTIONS
Innumerable combinations of lamps, luminaires, spatial geometries, and controls; daylight integration

COORDINATION ISSUES
Daylighting design, furniture and partition layout, automatic control systems

RELATED STRATEGIES
Glazing, Daylight Factor, Internal Reflectances, Toplighting, Sidelighting

PREREQUISITES
Established design intent and criteria, local lighting codes/standards (if applicable)

4.146 Integrated electric lighting and daylighting in a reading area of the Christopher Center at Valparaiso University, Indiana. KELLY GOFFINEY

Further Information

DiLaura, D. et al. 2011. *The Lighting Handbook.* 10th ed. Illuminating Engineering Society of North America, New York.

The European Greenlight Programme. www.eu-greenlight.org/

International Association for Energy-Efficient Lighting. www.iaeel.org/

Nelson, D. 2010. Whole Building Design Guide, "*Energy Efficient Lighting*," National Institute of Building Sciences, Washington, DC.

U.S. Department of Energy, Energy Efficiency and Renewable Energy, *Sustainable Design Guide*, Chapter 5: "Lighting, HVAC, and Plumbing." apps1.eere.energy.gov/buildings/publications/pdfs/commercial_initiative/sustainable_guide_ch5.pdf

Waide, P. 2006. *Light's Labour's Lost*, International Energy Agency, Paris.

BEYOND SCHEMATIC DESIGN

The entire design of electric lighting systems is often undertaken during design development—in many cases by a consultant (lighting designer or electrical engineer). This is not wise for a green project. During design development, lamps, luminaires and controls are selected, coordinated, and specified. Commissioning of all types of automatic lighting controls is strongly recommended—as they are notoriously prone to poor installation and/or calibration.

HEATING

In thinking schematically about heating a building, an understanding of the extent of the heating loads is critical. In single-family homes, heating loads tend to be larger than cooling loads (except in very mild or hot climates). Larger (internal load dominated) buildings tend to have significant cooling loads due to occupancy, lighting, and equipment—along with a low surface-to-volume ratio. It is not unusual for a large office building to be in permanent cooling mode at the building core, with heating required only at the perimeter—and with a high-performance facade it is possible to virtually eliminate perimeter heating. Thus, the heating strategies covered in this book are most appropriate for residential or small-scale commercial/institutional buildings.

The simplest way to heat a building is with direct solar gain, admitting solar radiation during the heating season and storing it in thermally massive materials. Direct gain is very effective in a well-insulated building with good windows. It can bring glare, however, and cause deterioration of interior finishes and furnishings. It is best suited where occupants can move about as conditions change over the course of the day, such as in a residence or library reading room. Direct gain heating is problematic in offices, where workers typically are not free to move to another workspace.

With indirect gain, a massive assembly (such as a Trombe wall or roof pond) absorbs solar radiation without directly admitting the sun into the occupied space. The collected heat gradually conducts through the thermal mass, and radiates and convects to the occupied spaces later in the day. Indirect gain can be combined with direct gain to balance heating over the course of a day.

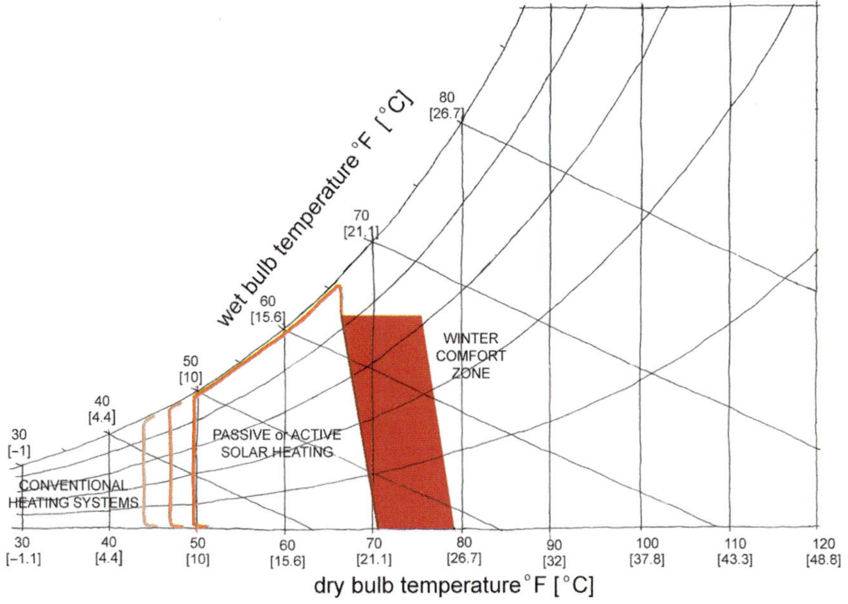

4.147 Applicability of building heating strategies. ADAPTED FROM *ENERGY CONSERVATION THROUGH BUILDING DESIGN*

STRATEGIES

A sunspace absorbs and stores solar heat that can be drawn off for use in occupied spaces as needed. Usually the thermal storage space is not occupied, so temperatures need not be maintained in the comfort zone. In fact, the sunspace may be most effective in providing heat if temperatures rise (and drop) well beyond the comfort zone.

Active heating systems can also contribute to the greening of a project. Active solar thermal collectors can provide for all of a building's domestic water heating needs. Active collectors can also contribute to space heating. Ground source heat pumps use the refrigeration cycle to move heat from one location to another. A ground source heat pump uses the soil as a source of heat during the heating season and as a heat sink during the cooling season. Because the ground temperature is warmer than the outside air during the winter (and cooler during the summer) a ground source heat pump is more efficient than an air source heat pump (which in turn is more efficient than most other active alternatives).

DIRECT GAIN systems are generally considered to be the most basic, simple, and cost-effective means of passive solar heating. During the heating season, solar radiation enters generally south-facing glazing and is then absorbed by and heats interior mass. Properly sized storage mass can provide steady and reliable heating performance. During the cooling season, solar radiation can be blocked with appropriate shading devices (including landscaping). The defining design and operational feature of a direct gain system, suggested in Figure 4.148, is the fact that occupants inhabit the building heating system.

4.149 The concrete floor and partition wall absorb solar radiation from window apertures at the Aldo Leopold Legacy Center, Baraboo, Wisconsin.

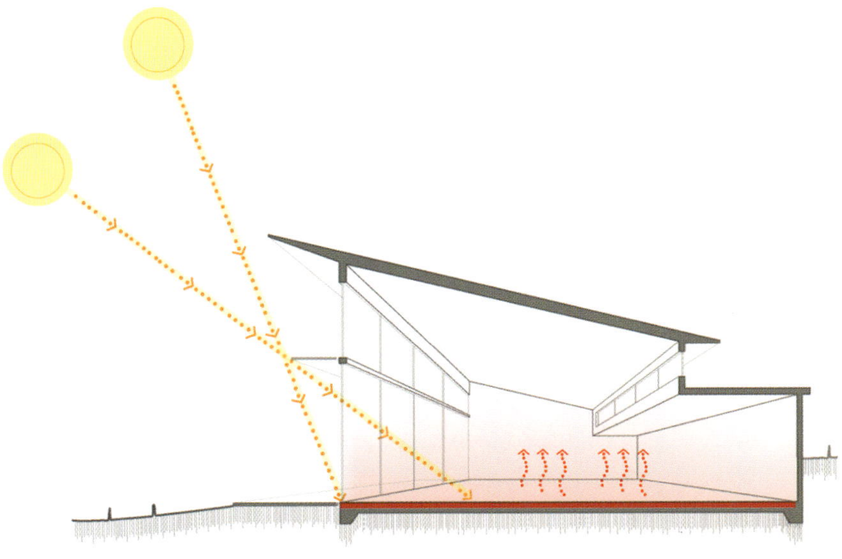

4.148 A direct gain system uses thermal mass to absorb and store solar energy to heat a building. Shading devices control unwanted summer sun. JON THWAITES

INTENT
Climate control (heating), thermal comfort

EFFECT
Use of a renewable resource, passive heating, energy efficiency

OPTIONS
One fundamental approach, but with numerous options for individual elements (aperture, collection, storage, distribution, control)

COORDINATION ISSUES
Passive cooling, active heating, daylighting, interior furnishings, occupant controls

RELATED STRATEGIES
Site Analysis, Glazing, Night Ventilation of Mass, Indirect Gain, Isolated Gain, Shading Devices

PREREQUISITES
Suitable climate, suitable site, suitable building type, appropriate design intent

Key Architectural Issues

Although direct gain systems perform surprisingly well in a variety of climates and building types, cloudless winters and smaller, skin-load dominated buildings make for an ideal application of this strategy.

The building axis for a direct gain system should run generally east–west to maximize solar exposure (and heat gain) on the south-facing aperture. As long as the aperture is within 15 ° of true south (or north, in the southern hemisphere), the building will receive roughly 90% of maximum winter solar heat gains. Shifting the aperture toward the east or west will somewhat shift the timing of these heat gains.

The distribution of functional spaces (Figure 4.150) in a direct gain building is an important consideration. South-facing rooms will benefit from direct solar heating, while north-facing ones will not. Those areas with direct gain aperture will also receive more daylight than rooms with primarily opaque walls. Placing lesser-used spaces (i.e., closets, bathrooms, circulation, service spaces) along the north wall can provide a buffer on the under-heated northern facade, and reduce the need to transfer heat from the southern spaces.

Night ventilation of mass for passive cooling in the summer is a logical complement to a direct gain passive heating system. Coordination of prevailing summer (cooling) wind directions with the elongated southern solar exposure is necessary if this combination of systems is to succeed.

It is important to recognize that a direct gain system will have large glazing areas, therefore it is also important to take steps to mitigate glare and reduce nighttime heat losses. Using light-colored surfaces and furnishings near windows can help reduce glare potential by reducing contrast. The use of some type of movable insulation or high-performance glazing can help reduce nighttime heat losses. Furniture and carpets in the path of direct sunlight may fade if not selected with this exposure in mind—they will also interfere with the absorption and storage of solar energy.

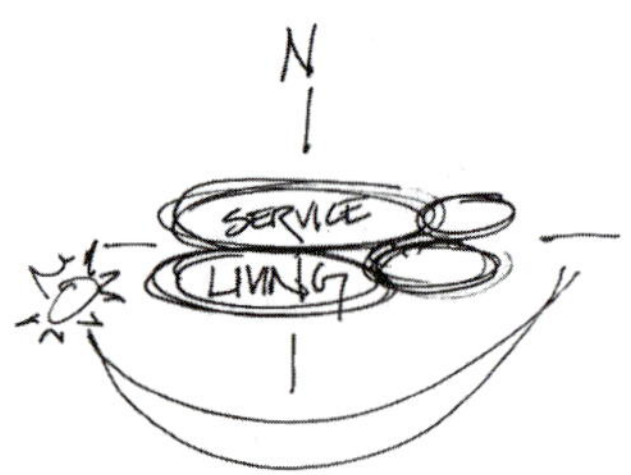

4.150 Unoccupied or service spaces can be placed along the cooler non-solar facade, leaving the warmer side for living spaces. KATE BECKLEY

Implementation Considerations

Sloped glazing is often considered as a way to maximize solar collection. Left unshaded, however, such a solution may increase unwanted summer gains. Sloped glazing, however, is more difficult to keep clean than vertical glazing. Shading tilted glazing is also more difficult than shading vertical glazing. Deciduous vegetation can be used to control seasonal heat gains. Remember that even bare trees provide some shading effect that may reduce system performance.

The color of the absorber surface/thermal mass is an important consideration. Dark colors (with an absorptance of 0.5–0.8) work best. Most unpainted masonry materials will perform reasonably well. Because even reflected radiation can contribute to heating, low thermal-mass surfaces (ceilings, partitions) should be painted a light color in order to reflect radiation onto the identified thermal storage surfaces.

TABLE 4.10 Thermal properties of various materials

MATERIAL	SPECIFIC HEAT		DENSITY		HEAT CAPACITY	
	Btu/lb°F	kJ/kg K	lb/ft^3	kg/m^3	Btu/ft^3°F	kJ/m^{3}K
Water	1.0	4.18	62.4	998	62.4	4172
Brick	0.22	0.92	120	1920	26.4	1766
Concrete	0.19	0.79	150	2400	28.5	1896
Air	0.24	1.00	0.075	1.2	0.018	1.2

As the simplest of the passive solar heating approaches, direct gain systems have certain limitations. Sunnier than average conditions, for example, can lead to overheating—as the heat storage capacity of the building is exceeded. The opposite can occur during cloudy periods. Because of this, it is important to include a certain degree of occupant control (i.e., movable shades or operable exhausts to temper overheating). A backup active (mechanical) heating system is commonly required—both to provide for heating loads that cannot be met passively with a reasonably sized system and for use during periods of extreme (cold or cloudy) weather. Provision of a backup system will affect system economics.

Thermal storage mass should generally not exceed a thickness of 4–5 in. [100–125 mm]. Any additional mass required to provide adequate storage should be provided by additional surfaces. Increasing thickness is progressively less effective and distributed storage can help keep a room evenly heated. Because the absorber surface is also the top of the thermal storage in most direct gain systems, the location of storage mass is constrained by solar exposure. Secondary storage (not receiving direct solar radiation) is much less effective in controlling overheating. Any mass should be exposed as much as possible, so limit the use of rugs or carpets (which act as insulators).

South glazing should have an SHGC (solar heat gain coefficient) of 0.60 or higher (the higher the better, as shading is best provided by other means) and a U-factor of 0.35 [2.0] or less. Non-solar glazing should be selected to optimize building envelope performance. To help keep heat from migrating out of windows at night, use insulating shades or panels to cover the glazing at night—or low U-factor (but high transmission) glazing.

In a building subdivided into rooms (practically speaking, most buildings), the direct gain heating system only heats the rooms with a solar aperture—unless serious efforts are made to ensure the distribution of collected heat to adjacent or distant non-aperture rooms. This can place severe limitations on the applicability of direct gain systems in larger buildings or where there are complex room arrangements.

Design Procedure

The purpose of the procedure outlined herein is to establish the general sizes of system components during the schematic design phase of a project. These rough estimates will be refined and optimized during design development.

The first, and most important, step in the design of a passive solar heating system is to minimize the rate of heat loss through non-south-facing envelope components (including infiltration losses). This is a design concern that is typically addressed in the later phases of design—as specific components are selected and specified. Some opportunities to minimize losses, however, will be lost if not made during schematic design—earth berming, building form, and

SAMPLE PROBLEM

A 1000 ft^2 [93 m^2] building located in Minneapolis, Minnesota will be heated by a direct gain passive solar heating system.

1. For this cold climate building a glazing area ratio of 0.4:1 is considered appropriate. Thus, the estimated glazing area is:

   $(1000\ ft^2)\ (0.4) = 400\ ft^2$ [37 m^2].

orientation, for example. The bottom line is that it makes little sense to attempt to heat a leaky or poorly insulated building with solar energy (or any form of energy for that matter). This step of the design process has been described as providing "insulation before insolation."

1. Estimate the required size of solar apertures (glazing). Use the ranges given below logically—a value toward the higher end being appropriate for a moderately well-insulated building, a colder climate, and/or a climate with limited solar resources.
   - For a cold to temperate climate, use a solar glazing area of between 0.2 and 0.4 ft^2 [m^2] of south-facing, appropriately-glazed aperture for each ft^2 [m^2] of heated floor area. In mild to temperate climates, use between 0.10 and 0.20 ft^2 [m^2] of similar aperture for each ft^2 [m^2] of heated floor area.
2. Estimate the amount of thermal storage required to support the proposed glazing. A general rule is to provide a concrete mass of 4–6 in. [100–150 mm] thickness that is about three times the area of the solar glazing. This assumes the mass is directly irradiated by solar radiation. A ratio of 6:1 is generally recommended for mass that receives only reflected radiation. Primary and secondary thermal mass can be mixed within reason.
3. Estimate the "non-south" building envelope (excluding conduction/convection losses through solar apertures) and total building infiltration heat loss rate—per degree of temperature difference. Multiply this hourly unit heat loss by 24 to obtain the total heat loss per day (essentially this is the heat loss per day per degree day); this value is called the net load coefficient (NLC).
4. Divide the overall NLC by the total floor area, and check the unit NLC against the data presented in Table 4.11.

TABLE 4.11 Overall heat loss criteria for a passive solar heated building. BALCOMB, J.D. ET AL. *PASSIVE SOLAR DESIGN HANDBOOK*, VOL. 2

ANNUAL HEATING DEGREE DAYS Base 65 °F [18 °C]	TARGET NLC Btu/DDF ft^2 [kJ/DDC m^2]
Less than 1000 [556]	7.6 [155]
1000–3000 [556–1667]	6.6 [135]
3000–5000 [1667–2778]	5.6 [115]
5000–7000 [2778–3889]	4.6 [94]
Over 7000 [3889]	3.6 [74]

5. If the estimated NLC is greater than the target NLC listed above, then improvements in building envelope performance are necessary to reduce heat loss.

2. Each unit area of glazing requires 3 unit areas of primary thermal mass for heat storage:

   (400 ft^2) (3) = 1200 ft^2 [112 m^2]

   This exceeds the floor area of the building. Assuming that 700 ft^2 [65 m^2] of the floor surface could be used as thermal storage, then (1200 − 700) or 500 ft^2 [47 m^2] of equivalent mass must be provided in walls, partitions, or other storage objects. Using a 2:1 multiplier to account for the fact that this is secondary thermal mass, this equates to 1000 ft^2 [93 m^2] of non-floor mass.

   Assuming building dimensions of 50 ft by 20 ft [15.3 by 6.1 m], the interior surface area of exterior walls in this building would be around: (8 ft) (20 + 50 + 20 + 50) = 1120 ft^2 [104 m^2]. Subtracting the 400 ft^2 [37 m^2] of solar glazing, 720 ft^2 [69 m^2] of secondary mass would be available just using these walls (if of high mass construction and well insulated on the exterior of the mass). Thermal mass is likely to be marginally adequate without the addition of dedicated mass elements.

   Again assuming a 50 ft [15.3 m] long south facade, the glazing would need to be (400 ft^2/50 ft) or 8 ft high [37/15.3 = 2.4 m]. Without a sloped ceiling/roof, the south facade would be all glass. This is possible, but will dramatically affect facade design and building appearance.

Examples

4.151 Concrete floors absorb solar radiation in the direct gain dining hall of Islandwood Campus on Bainbridge Island, Washington.

4.152 Classic example of solar apertures, solar control, and thermal mass in the Shaw residence in Taos, New Mexico.

3. The building has an estimated design heat loss of 3.5 Btu/ft^2 DDF [72 kJ/m^2 DDC]. Heating degree days = 7981 65 °F [4434 18 °C].
4. The estimated NLC of 3.5 [72] is below (although just barely) the target value of 3.6 [74] from Table 4.11.
5. This NLC is acceptable, and also suggests that the initial use of a high solar glazing ratio was reasonable.

Further Information

Balcomb, J.D. et al. 1980. *Passive Solar Design Handbook, Vol. 2, Passive Solar Design Analysis*. U.S. Department of Energy, Washington, DC.

Fosdick, J. 2010. *Whole Building Design Guide*: "Passive Solar Heating." National Institute of Building Sciences, Washington, DC. www.wbdg.org/resources/psheating.php

Grondzik, W. et al. 2010. *Mechanical and Electrical Equipment for Buildings*. 11th ed. John Wiley & Sons, Hoboken, NJ.

Mazria, E. 1979. *The Passive Solar Energy Book*, Rodale Press, Emmaus, PA.

Sustainable Sources. "Passive Solar Design." passivesolar.sustainablesources.com/

BEYOND SCHEMATIC DESIGN

Schematic design is the phase in which a direct gain system must pass proof-of-concept. The decisions regarding footprint, elevations, orientation, and spatial layout required for a successful system must be made as early as possible. During design development, these decisions will be adjusted to optimize system performance—but radical changes in the basic system elements will be hard to make as these elements are really the building itself.

An INDIRECT GAIN system is a passive solar heating system that collects and stores energy from the sun in an element that also acts to buffer the occupied spaces of the building from the solar collection process. Heating effect occurs as natural radiation, conduction, and/or convection redistributes the collected energy from the storage element to the building spaces. Conceptually speaking, occupants reside right *next to* an indirect gain system—whereas they reside *in* a direct gain system and *near* an isolated gain system. As is the case with most passive systems, an indirect gain system will exert substantial influence on the form of the building as a whole.

There are three basic types of indirect gain passive solar heating systems: thermal storage walls using masonry (also called Trombe walls), thermal storage walls using water (sometimes called water walls), and thermal storage roofs (roof ponds).

4.154 View of Trombe wall at Zion National Park Visitor's Center in Springdale, Utah. THOMAS WOOD, DOE/NREL

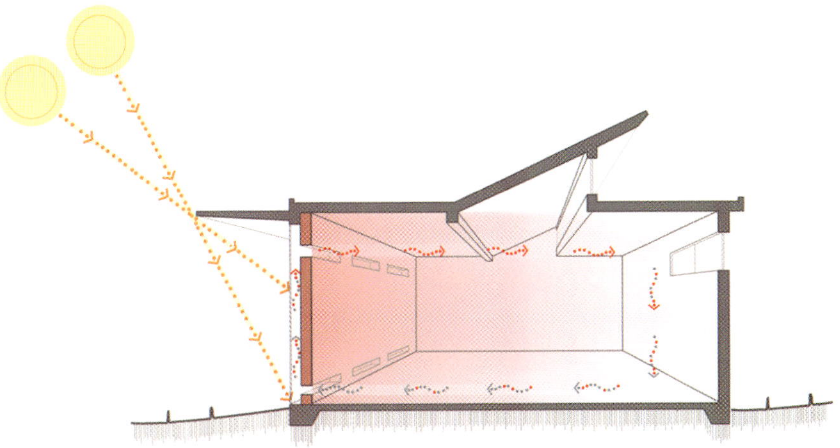

4.153 Schematic diagram of an indirect gain heating system showing the collection of solar energy in a south-facing thermal storage wall, which then transfers heat into the occupied space. JON THWAITES

INTENT
Climate control (heating), thermal comfort

EFFECT
Use of a renewable resource, passive heating, energy efficiency

OPTIONS
Thermal storage wall (masonry or water), thermal storage roof

COORDINATION ISSUES
Active heating, passive cooling, daylighting, interior furnishings, occupant controls

RELATED STRATEGIES
Site Analysis, Glazing, Night Ventilation of Mass, Direct Gain, Isolated Gain, Shading Devices

PREREQUISITES
Suitable climate, suitable site, suitable building type, appropriate design intent

A thermal storage wall is a south-facing glazed wall with an appropriate storage medium (such as heavy masonry or substantial water) located immediately behind the glass. Solar radiation passes through the glass and is absorbed by, and subsequently warms, the storage element. The collected heat is conducted slowly through the masonry or water to the interior face of the element and then into the occupied spaces. Vents are often placed in the top and bottom of a Trombe wall to permit additional heat transfer through convection (tapping into a mini stack effect). In water walls, convective currents in the water wall enable heat transfer to the interior, somewhat improving the efficiency of heat transfer into and through the storage element.

A thermal storage roof is similar in concept to a thermal storage wall, except that the storage mass is located on the roof. The thermal mass is either masonry (rare), water in bags, or a shallow pond of water. Movable insulation is opened and closed diurnally, exposing the storage mass to solar radiation during the day and insulating it at night to reduce heat losses. The same roof system can provide passive cooling during the summer by tapping into the radiant cooling potential of the night sky.

TABLE 4.12 Plan and section requirements and heating characteristics of indirect gain systems

SYSTEM TYPE	PLAN/SECTION REQUIREMENTS	HEATING CHARACTERISTICS
Masonry thermal storage wall (Trombe wall)	South-facing wall and glazing required. Storage wall should be within 25 ft [7.6 m] of all occupied spaces	System is slow to warm up and slow to cool in the evening, with small temperature swings
Water thermal storage wall (water wall)	South-facing wall and glazing required. Storage elements should be within 25 ft [7.6 m] of all occupied spaces	System is slow to warm up and slow to cool in the evening, with small temperature swings
Thermal storage roof (roof pond)	Flat or low slope (<3:12) roof required. Skylights are discouraged. Additional structural support required for the roof	Low temperature swings, can provide heating in winter and cooling in summer

Key Architectural Issues

The designer must consider site climate, building orientation, and solar access potential when considering a passive solar heating system. The form of a solar building will tend to strongly reflect its role as a solar collector and heat distributor. An indirect gain heating system must be integrated with plan and section decision making. The placement of glazing (solar apertures) and absorber/storage elements must be considered in concert with decisions regarding the building envelope.

There is no substantial performance penalty if the solar glazing faces within 5 ° of true south. Glazing facing 45 ° from true south, however, incurs a reduction in performance of more than 30%. Direct gain systems are sometimes intentionally shifted in orientation to give preference to morning or afternoon warm-up; such shifts make less sense in an isolated gain system where there is an inherent time delay built into the entry of solar heating effect into the conditioned space.

The design of solar glazing must include provision for shading as a means of seasonal performance control. The building design as a whole should consider ventilation in summer, both for general comfort cooling and for mitigation of potential overheating from the solar system. Design to provide for easy operations and maintenance, especially for the cleaning of glazing.

4.155 Thermal storage (Trombe) walls behind the glazed facades of this retail building in Ketchum, Idaho collect solar energy.
BRUCE HAGLUND

4.156 Circular inlet opening at the bottom of the Ketchum Trombe wall (above) brings warm air up through the cavity into a second story office via the circular outlet (see Fig. 4.157).
BRUCE HAGLUND

4.157 Interior view of Trombe wall inlet in the Ketchum building shown in Fig. 4.155.
BRUCE HAGLUND

Adequate space/volume and structural support must be provided for thermal mass (masonry or water). This is especially true for a roof-based indirect gain system. Structural solutions that minimize additional costs are ideal. A backup or auxiliary heating system will be required in many projects to meet design intent/criteria.

Implementation Considerations

Early in the design process, determine the most applicable system type (thermal storage wall, water wall, or thermal storage roof) and its general impact upon the plan and section of the building. An appropriate system type will match the climate, program, and schedule of use of the building. In addition, the system type will be seen as working with (even complementing) the intended form and aesthetic of the building.

Anticipated needs for daylighting and cooling should be coordinated with the selection of the passive solar heating system type. Consider the provision of adequate shading and ventilation to prevent and/or mitigate summertime overheating.

A backup heating system will be required in many climates. Space must be allocated for this equipment.

The following issues are worthy of consideration during schematic design:

- **Overheating.** Inadequate thermal storage capacity will cause overheating. Match thermal storage capacity with system type and the proposed collector area.
- **Lag time.** Excessive thermal storage capacity will cause overly long lag times in system response, impeding system performance. Appropriate lag time depends upon building type, diurnal weather patterns, and design intent.
- **Leakage/storage failure.** Absorber surfaces and storage media are subject to large, daily shifts in temperature, increasing opportunities for failure. Routine, preventive maintenance can prevent a catastrophic failure—especially critical when water is the storage medium. Provide adequate space and access for maintenance and repair during schematic design, including provisions for normal and emergency drainage.
- **Maintenance.** In addition to maintenance access for water storage elements, provide adequate space and access for periodic cleaning of glazing and absorber surfaces.

Design Procedure

The purpose of the procedure outlined herein is to establish the general sizes of system components during the schematic design phase of a project. These rough estimates will be refined and optimized during design development.

SAMPLE PROBLEM

The Not-Real-Big Competition House is a 640 ft^2 [60 m^2] home located in Lansing, New York.

1. Between 0.40 and 1.0 ft^2 [m^2] of south-facing Trombe wall

The first, and most important, step in the design of a passive solar heating system is to minimize the rate of heat loss through non-south-facing envelope components (including infiltration losses). This is a design concern that is typically addressed in later phases of design—as specific components are selected and specified. Some opportunities to minimize losses, however, will be missed if not made during schematic design—earth berming, building form, orientation, for example. The bottom line is that it makes little sense to attempt to heat a leaky or poorly insulated building with solar energy (or any form of energy for that matter). "Insulation before insolation" has been used to describe this step.

1. Estimate the required size of solar apertures (glazing). Use the ranges given below logically—a value toward the higher end being appropriate for a moderately well-insulated building, a colder climate, and/or a climate with limited solar resources.
   - For a Trombe wall (masonry storage) in a cold climate, use between 0.40 and 1.0 ft^2 [m^2] of south-facing, double-glazed aperture for each ft^2 [m^2] of heated floor area. In moderate climates, use between 0.20 and 0.60 ft^2 [m^2] of similar aperture for each ft^2 [m^2] of heated floor area.
   - For a water wall in a cold climate, use between 0.30 and 0.85 ft^2 [m^2] of south-facing, double-glazed aperture for each ft^2 [m^2] of floor area. In moderate climates, use between 0.15 and 0.45 ft^2 [m^2] of similar aperture for each ft^2 [m^2] of floor area.
   - Roof ponds are not recommended for cold climates. For a moderate climate, use between 0.6 and 0.9 ft^2 [m^2] of appropriately "glazed" pond with night insulation for each ft^2 [m^2] of floor area.
2. Estimate the required amount of thermal storage considering the proposed glazing area. General rules are as follows, with the presumption that these thicknesses are for storage elements that are the same area as the solar aperture. As with glazing area estimates, apply these ranges logically; thicker storage elements provide greater heat capacity, but also increase time lag:
   - For a Trombe wall (masonry mass) provide 8–12 in. [200–300 mm] of adobe (or similar earthen product), 10–14 in. [250–350 mm] of brick, or 12–18 in. [300–460 mm] of concrete.
   - For a water wall provide a minimum 6 in. [150 mm] "thickness" of water storage.
   - For a roof pond provide a water (thermal storage) depth of between 6 and 12 in. [150–300 mm].
3. Estimate the "non-south" building envelope (excluding conduction/convection losses through solar apertures) and overall infiltration heat loss rate—per degree of temperature difference. Multiply this hourly unit heat loss by 24 to obtain the total heat loss per day (essentially heat loss per 24-hour period per degree day); this value is called the net load coefficient (NLC).

aperture is recommended for each unit of floor area. Therefore, 260 to 640 ft^2 [24–60 m^2] of aperture would be required. Because of Lansing's rather dreary winter climate, a value near the high end is most appropriate—say 600 ft^2 [56 m^2].

For a water wall, between 0.30 and 0.85 ft^2 [m^2] of south-facing aperture is required for each unit of floor area. Therefore, 200 to 545 ft^2 [20–50 m^2] of aperture would be required. Again, considering climate, a value of around 500 ft^2 [46 m^2] is considered appropriate.

A roof pond would not be a reasonable option for the cold Lansing climate.

2. A concrete storage wall would be most appropriate for this building context, with a 16 in. [400 mm] thickness used as a starting point for design. If using water storage, an 8 in. [200 mm] thick element would be a good starting point.
3. U-factors for all of the non-south-aperture envelope elements are estimated, along with anticipated infiltration. The estimated total (less south-facing glazing) heat loss for the house is 90 Btu/h °F [48 W/°C].

   The Net Load Coefficient is (24) (90) = 2160 Btu/DDF [4102 kJ/DDC].
4. Normalizing this loss for building floor area, 2160/640 ft^2 = 3.38 Btu/DDFft^2 [68 kJ/DDC m^2].

TABLE 4.13 Overall heat loss criteria for a passive solar heated building. BALCOMB, J.D. ET AL. *PASSIVE SOLAR DESIGN HANDBOOK*, VOL. 2

ANNUAL HEATING DEGREE DAYS Base 65°F [18°C]	TARGET NLC Btu/DDF ft^2 [kJ/DDC m^2]
Less than 1000 [556]	7.6 [155]
1000–3000 [556–1667]	6.6 [135]
3000–5000 [1667–2778]	5.6 [115]
5000–7000 [2778–3889]	4.6 [94]
Over 7000 [3889]	3.6 [74]

4. Divide the overall NLC by the total floor area, and check the unit NLC against the data presented in Table 4.13.
5. If the estimated NLC is greater than the target NLC listed above, improvements in building envelope performance are necessary to reduce heat loss.

Examples

4.158 South-facing, sawtooth Trombe wall, Blue Ridge Parkway Destination Center (Asheville, NC)—externally shaded to prevent overheating in summer. LORD, AECK & SARGENT

Lansing, New York, experiences 7182 65 °F [3990 18 °C] annual heating degree days; therefore a reasonable NLC target is 3.6 Btu/DDF ft^2 [74 kJ/DDC m^2].

5. The Not-Real-Big Competition House envelope is thus adequate (it does not exceed the target heat loss).

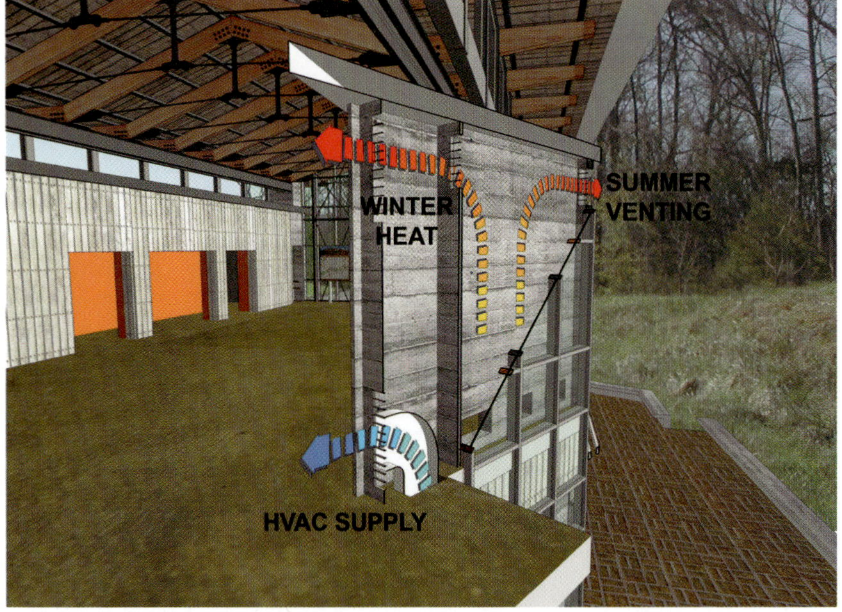

4.159 Blue Ridge Parkway Destination Center Trombe wall acts as an integrating element for structure, passive heating and ventilation, and supplemental HVAC. LORD, AECK & SARGENT

4.161 Side view of Trombe wall segments, Blue Ridge Parkway Destination Center—showing daylighting apertures. LORD, AECK & SARGENT

4.160 Zion National Park Visitor's Center in Springdale, Utah, showing a Trombe wall and clerestory (direct gain) windows. ROBB WILLIAMSON, DOE | NREL

Further Information

Balcomb, J.D. et al. 1980. *Passive Solar Design Handbook, Vol. 2, Passive Solar Design Analysis*. U.S. Department of Energy, Washington, DC.

Brown, G.Z. and M. DeKay. 2001. *Sun, Wind & Light: Architectural Design Strategies*, 2nd ed. John Wiley & Sons, New York.

Grondzik, W. et al. 2010. *Mechanical and Electrical Equipment for Buildings*. 11th ed. John Wiley & Sons, Hoboken, NJ.

Mazria, E. 1979. *The Passive Solar Energy Book*, Rodale Press, Emmaus, PA.

BEYOND SCHEMATIC DESIGN

More accurate (and complex) analysis methods will validate the decisions made in schematic design. Numerous energy modeling programs are available to assist in better understanding building energy demands, integrating passive systems, and reducing annual energy use. These programs (EnergyPlus, for example) can be of great assistance in "right-sizing" solar apertures versus thermal storage.

A User's Manual should be developed to provide occupants with an outline of their role in the operation and performance of a passive heating system and to give them a sense of what conditions should be anticipated in a passive building.

NOTES

An ISOLATED GAIN system is a passive solar heating system that collects and stores energy from the sun in a building element that is thermally separated from the occupied spaces of the building. A sunspace (attached "greenhouse") is the most common example, although there are other configurations, including convective loops. Heating effect occurs as solar energy captured in the collector element is redistributed from a storage component to the occupied building spaces through natural radiation, conduction, and/or convection. As opposed to a direct or indirect gain system, where occupants reside in or right next to the passive heating system, an isolated gain system provides thermal and spatial separation between the occupancy and heat collection functions. An isolated gain system will substantially influence the form of the building.

4.163 Sunspace in a residence in Dublin, New Hampshire. ALAN FORD, DOE | NREL

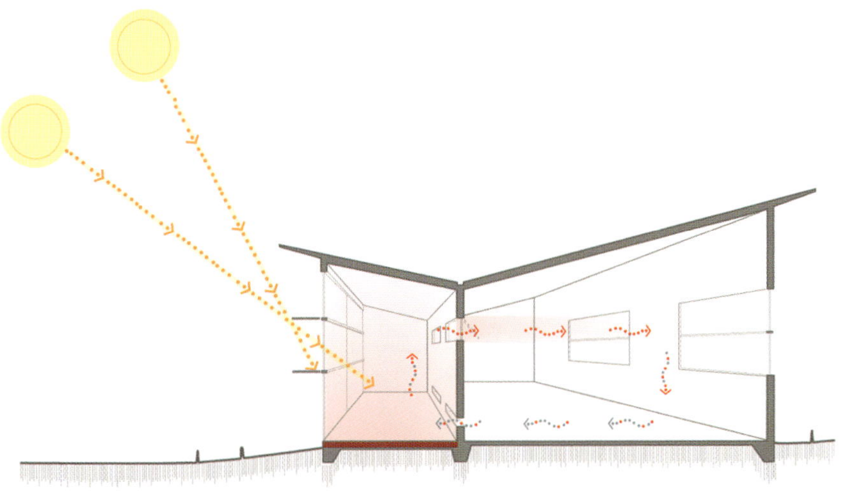

4.162 Conceptual diagram of an isolated gain passive solar heating system. JON THWAITES

A sunspace can fit into the overall building floor plan in many ways—including adjacency with the main building along one side of the sunspace, adjacency with the main building along two sides, or adjacency along three sides (where the building embraces the sunspace). A sunspace could also be an internal element, such as an atrium, but solar access and heat distribution would be difficult in such a configuration. Convective loop systems employ a collector element located below the elevation of the building proper; heat flows to the occupied building by air circulating in a convective loop via the stack effect. Thermal storage components of an isolated gain system include masonry floors and/or walls, water tubes or barrels, or a rock bed when using a convective loop.

INTENT
Climate control (heating), thermal comfort

EFFECT
Use of a renewable resource, passive heating, energy efficiency

OPTIONS
Sunspace, convective loop

COORDINATION ISSUES
Active heating, passive cooling, daylighting, interior furnishings, occupant controls, secondary use of space

RELATED STRATEGIES
Site Analysis, Glazing, Night Ventilation of Mass, Direct Gain, Indirect Gain, Shading Devices

PREREQUISITES
Suitable climate, suitable site, suitable building type, appropriate design intent

Key Architectural Issues

A key issue to consider relative to sunspace systems is that thermal collection/distribution functions dictate the conditions of the space; functioning as a comfortably occupiable space is a secondary role. During the course of heat collection and discharge, a sunspace will likely reach temperatures substantially above and below the comfort zone. This is both natural and necessary. Use of the space (for people or plants) must accommodate these temperature swings. A working sunspace will often make a bad dining room or conservatory.

The designer must consider site climate, building orientation, and solar access potential when considering a passive solar heating system. The form of a passive solar building will tend to reflect strongly its role as a solar collector and heat distributor. This is especially true of isolated gain systems, which involve substantial areas of glazing that are not quite part of the building proper.

Solar glazing should generally face within 5 ° of true south. Glazing facing 45 ° from true south incurs a substantial reduction in performance. As with direct gain systems, isolated gain apertures can be intentionally oriented to give preference to morning or afternoon warm-up—although the time lag provided by storage and thermal isolation make "time-tuning" of these systems less simple.

The design of solar glazing must include provision for shading as a means of seasonal performance control. This is especially true for sunspaces, which tend to include substantial glazing, often tilted from the vertical. Shading is fundamental to system success on a year-round basis. Natural ventilation can be used to mitigate summer overheating in a sunspace. Design to provide for easy operation and maintenance, especially for the cleaning of sloped glazing.

Implementation Considerations

Determine the most applicable system type (sunspace or convective loop) early in the design process. Convective loop systems work best when there is a natural elevation change on site that can be used to advantage. Establish how the collector element will integrate with the main building. An isolated gain heating system can drive the aesthetics of a small building.

The distribution of heat from the isolated gain collector area to the occupied spaces is a major design challenge. By its very nature an isolated gain system removes the heating function from the vicinity of the occupied spaces. Natural heat transfer must convey the heat from its collection point to where it is needed.

Two fundamental options exist with an attached sunspace system: (1) the connecting wall between the collector and the occupied building is insulated and all heat transfer occurs by convection (this is a truly isolated gain system), or (2) the connecting wall is uninsulated and provides both heat storage and transfer functions (like an oversized Trombe wall arrangement). This is a decision that can be deferred until design development and analysis involving detailed simulations.

A backup heating system for the occupied building will be required in most climates. It is important to allocate space for this equipment.

Design Procedure

The purpose of this procedure is to establish general sizes of components during the schematic design phase of a project (see the Indirect Gain strategy for notes and commentary regarding this procedure). This procedure applies only to sunspace systems; convective loop systems are too specialized to generalize (although similar thermal principles apply).

1. Estimate the required size of solar apertures (glazing). Use the ranges given below—a value toward the higher end being appropriate for a moderately well-insulated building and/or a climate with limited solar resources.
   - In a cold climate, use between 0.65 and 1.5 ft^2 [m^2] of south-facing, double-glazed aperture for each ft^2 [m^2] of heated floor area.
   - In moderate climates, use between 0.30 and 0.90 ft^2 [m^2] of similar aperture for each ft^2 [m^2] of heated floor area.
2. Estimate the required amount of thermal storage needed considering the proposed glazing area. General rules for sunspaces follow, with the presumption that these thicknesses are for storage elements that are collectively roughly the same area as the solar aperture. As with glazing area estimates, apply these ranges logically; thicker storage elements provide greater heat capacity, but also increase time lag.
   - Provide 8–12 in. [200–300 mm] of adobe (or similar earthen product), 10–14 in. [250–350 mm] of brick, or 12–18 in. [300–460 mm] of concrete.
   - For water-based storage, provide a minimum of 8 in. [150 mm] "thickness" of water storage.
3. Estimate the "non-solar" building envelope (excluding conduction/convection losses through solar apertures) and overall infiltration heat loss rate—per degree of temperature difference. Multiply this hourly unit heat loss by 24 to obtain the total heat loss per day (essentially heat loss per day per degree day); this value is called the net load coefficient (NLC).
4. Divide the overall NLC by the total floor area, and check the unit NLC against the data presented in Table 4.14.
5. If the estimated NLC is greater than the target NLC listed above, then improvements in building envelope performance are necessary to reduce heat loss.

SAMPLE PROBLEM

A 2500 ft^2 [230 m^2] homeless shelter is proposed for Vancouver, British Columbia.

1. For a temperate climate, use 0.30 to 0.90 ft^2 [m^2] of south-facing sunspace aperture for each unit of floor area. Thus, 750 to 2250 ft^2 [70–210 m^2] of aperture would be required. A value nearer the high end seems appropriate (considering a desire to minimize the use of active heating and the cloudy climate)—leading to say 2000 ft^2 [186 m^2] of aperture. This is too much glazing for this size building. Select a different passive heating system or reduce performance expectations.
2. Assuming a smaller system would be acceptable, a concrete storage wall is considered for this building context, with a 16 in. [400 mm] thickness used as a starting point. The floor of the sunspace would also be used for thermal storage (at a lesser thickness), which would reduce the required area of storage wall proportionately.
3. U-factors for all of the non-solar envelope elements were established, along with anticipated infiltration. The estimated total (less solar glazing) heat loss for the shelter is 385 Btu/h °F [205 W/°C].

   The Net Load Coefficient is (24) (385) = 9240 Btu/DDF [17,548 kJ/DDC].

Examples

4.164 An adobe residence with an attached sunspace in Santa Fe, New Mexico.

4.165 Sunspaces in the residential units of Beddington Zero Energy Development (Wallington, England) provide solar gain and extended living space when the weather permits. GRAHAMGAUNT.COM

4. Normalizing this loss for building floor area, 9240/2500 ft^2 = 3.7 Btu/DDF ft^2 [76 kJ/DDC m^2].
5. Vancouver experiences around 3000 65°F [1667 18 °C] annual heating degree days; from Table 4.14 a reasonable NLC target is 5.6 Btu/DDF ft^2 [115 kJ/DDC m^2]. The proposed shelter is thus adequately insulated (i.e., it does not exceed the target heat loss).

4.166 Dining and outdoor-ish activities in a residential sunspace in the Beddington Zero Energy Development near London. GRAHAMGAUNT.COM

4.167 Ecohouse in Oxford, England integrates a number of strategies including an attached sunspace, roof integrated photovoltaic panels, and flat plate collectors for solar water heating.

4.168 The sunspace of the Ecohouse opens to a sitting area and English garden beyond.

TABLE 4.14 Overall heat loss criteria for a passive solar heated building. BALCOMB, J.D. ET AL. *PASSIVE SOLAR DESIGN HANDBOOK*, VOL. 2.

ANNUAL HEATING DEGREE DAYS Base 65°F [18°C]	TARGET NLC Btu/DDF ft^2 [kJ/DDC m^2]
Less than 1000 [556]	7.6 [155]
1000–3000 [556–1667]	6.6 [135]
3000–5000 [1667–2778]	5.6 [115]
5000–7000 [2778–3889]	4.6 [94]
Over 7000 [3889]	3.6 [74]

Further Information

Balcomb, J.D. et al. 1980. *Passive Solar Design Handbook, Vol. 2, Passive Solar Design Analysis*. U.S. Department of Energy, Washington, DC.

Brown, G.Z. and M. DeKay. 2001. *Sun, Wind & Light: Architectural Design Strategies*, 2nd ed. John Wiley & Sons, New York.

Grondzik, W. et al. 2006. *Mechanical and Electrical Equipment for Buildings*. 11th ed. John Wiley & Sons, Hoboken, NJ.

Mazria, E. 1979. *The Passive Solar Energy Book*, Rodale Press, Emmaus, PA.

U.S. Department of Energy, Energy Efficiency and Renewable Energy, "Isolated Gain (Sunspaces)." www.energysavers.gov/your_home/designing_remodeling/index.cfm/mytopic=10310

BEYOND SCHEMATIC DESIGN

More accurate (and complex) analysis methods (see Further Information) will validate, and help to optimize, early design decisions. Energy modeling programs, such as EnergyPlus, can be of great assistance in "right-sizing" solar apertures versus thermal storage.

A User's Manual should be developed to provide occupants with an outline of their role in the operation and performance of the passive system—and give them a sense of what conditions should be anticipated in a passive building.

ACTIVE SOLAR THERMAL ENERGY SYSTEMS

ACTIVE SOLAR THERMAL ENERGY SYSTEMS utilize energy from the sun for domestic water heating, pool heating, preheating of ventilation air, and/or space heating. The most common application for active solar thermal energy systems is heating water for domestic use. The major components of an active solar thermal system include a collector, a circulation system that moves a fluid (water or air) from the collectors to storage, a storage tank (or equivalent), and a control system. A backup heating system is typically included.

The focus of this strategy is domestic hot water heating systems using water-based collectors. Air systems and space heating applications are mentioned only peripherally. In this context, there are four basic types of active solar thermal systems: thermosiphon systems, direct circulation systems, indirect circulation systems, and air–water systems.

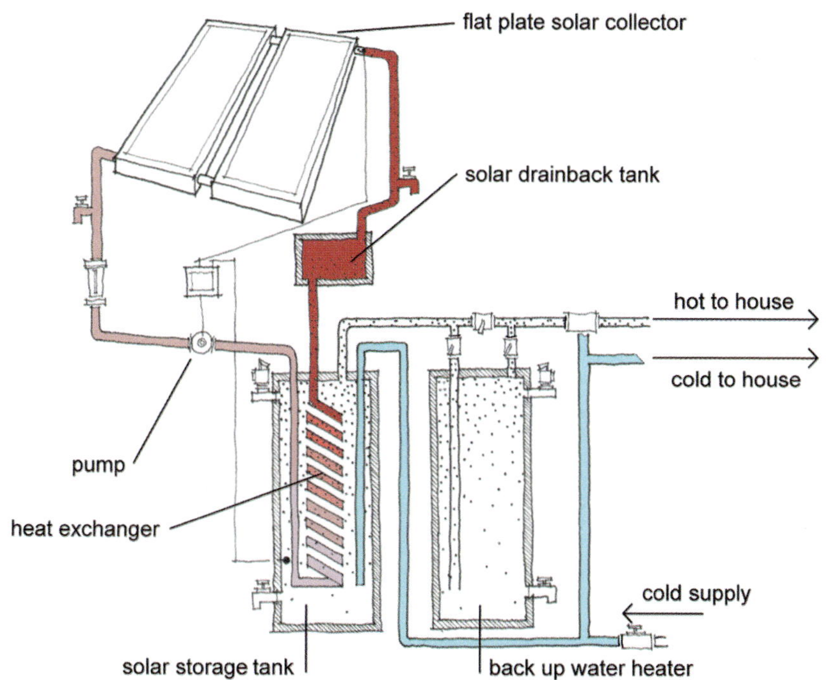

4.169 Solar thermal system components and their general arrangement in a drain-back configuration. JONATHAN MEENDERING

In a thermosiphon system, the collector heats water (or a freeze-resistant fluid), which causes the fluid to rise by convection to a storage tank. Pumping is not required, but fluid movement and heat transfer are dependent upon the temperature of the fluid. A thermosiphon system is a good option for climates with good solar radiation resources and little chance of low outdoor air temperatures.

A direct circulation system pumps water from a storage tank to collectors during hours of adequate solar radiation. Freeze protection is addressed either by recirculating hot water from the storage tank through the collectors or by draining the water from the collectors when freezing conditions occur.

4.170 Evacuated tube solar collectors at the 2005 University of Texas-Austin Solar Decathlon House.

INTENT
Energy efficiency

EFFECT
Reduced use of purchased energy resources, water heating, space heating

OPTIONS
Thermosiphon, direct circulation, indirect circulation, air–water configurations

COORDINATION ISSUES
Active heating and cooling systems, plumbing system, orientation and tilt of potential collector mounting surfaces, provision for mechanical space

RELATED STRATEGIES
Site Analysis, Energy Recovery Systems

PREREQUISITES
Building heating and cooling requirements, domestic hot water requirements, design heating and cooling data, site climate data

An indirect circulation system circulates a freeze-resistant fluid through a closed loop. A heat exchanger transfers heat from this closed collector loop to an open potable water circuit. Freeze protection is achieved by specification of an appropriate antifreeze fluid. Glycol-based solutions are commonly used for closed loop freeze protection.

The collector in an air–water system heats air. A fan moves the heated air through an air-to-water heat exchanger. The efficiency of an air-to-water heat exchanger is generally in the range of 50–60%. Air-based solar systems, while not as efficient as water systems, are an option if the inherent freeze protection provided by air is a key point of interest. Solar heated air can also directly heat a space, with heat storage occurring in a rock-bed storage bin.

4.171 Typical batch solar thermal collector. FLORIDA SOLAR ENERGY CENTER

There are four common types of solar collectors: batch collectors, flat plate collectors, evacuated tube collectors, and transpired collectors.

A batch (or breadbox) collector includes an insulated storage tank, lined with glass on the inside and painted black on the outside. The collector is mounted on a roof (or on the ground) in a sunny location. Cold inlet water comes from the building's potable water system. The breadbox is the collector, absorbing and retaining heat from the sun. An outlet at the top of the insulated storage tank supplies the building with heated water. Direct and thermosiphon systems often employ batch collectors.

4.172 Flat plate solar thermal collectors at the Woods Hole Research Center in Falmouth, Massachusetts.

The flat plate collector is the most common collector type. A flat plate collector is a thin, rectangular box with a transparent or translucent cover, usually installed on a building's roof. Small tubes run through the box carrying either potable water or a water-antifreeze mixture to a black absorber plate. The lightweight plate absorbs solar radiation and quickly heats up; the heat is transferred to the circulating fluid. A small pump (or gravity) moves the fluid into the building. Direct, indirect, and thermosiphon systems commonly use flat plate collectors.

Evacuated tube collectors consist of parallel rows of transparent glass tubes each containing an absorber tube with a selective surface coating (providing high absorbtivity and low emissivity). Solar radiation enters the tube, strikes the absorber, and heats a freeze-protected liquid flowing through the absorber. The tubes are vacuum-sealed, which helps them achieve extremely high temperatures with reasonably high efficiencies (due to reduced heat losses). Such collectors can provide solar heat on days with limited amounts of solar radiation. Evacuated tube collectors are generally used with indirect circulation systems.

A transpired collector is a south-facing exterior wall covered by a dark sheetmetal collector. The collector heats outdoor air, which is drawn into the building through perforations in the collector. The heated air can heat a space or be used to precondition ventilation air.

Key Architectural Issues

The designer must consider climate, orientation, solar access, and the loads being served when integrating an active solar thermal system into a project. Consider collector location in the context of the overall design of the building envelope, although the optimum location is usually on a south-facing wall or roof. Placement of collectors should include provisions for operations and maintenance access, especially for cleaning of collector surfaces and checking for leaks.

System components located inside the building (typically circulation, storage, and control components) require adequate space, including room for maintenance and repair.

Implementation Considerations

Freeze protection is a critical component of all water-based solar systems. When designing for a climate where freezing is possible, three basic methods can be employed to avoid damage:

- Design an indirect system using an antifreeze solution that will not freeze at the lowest temperature likely to occur at the site.
- Design an indirect system with a drainback mode, to drain the fluid from the collectors when freezing conditions are expected.
- Design a drain-down system so that water can be drained from the collectors when freezing temperatures occur. This type of freeze protection should only be used in climates where freezing temperatures are infrequent.

Determine if a low-temperature or high-temperature domestic water heating system is necessary by reviewing project needs, climate data, and groundwater temperatures. A low-temperature solar water heating system can preheat water in locations with low groundwater temperatures; when hot water is needed, the preheated water is boosted to full temperature with a conventional hot water system.

A high-temperature solar domestic hot water system can provide ready-to-use hot water. A conventional gas or electric backup system is operated only when there is limited solar radiation for an extended period of time. A high-temperature system can provide greater energy savings than a low-temperature system—but the tradeoff is a more expensive system. A life-cycle cost analysis can provide guidance for this decision.

In addition to freeze protection, consider the following for systems using water as the distribution medium:

- **Overheating.** If water stagnates in a solar collector, very high temperatures result, which can rupture the system from overpressure. Pressure venting or continuous circulation of fresh fluid through the collector will reduce overpressure problems.
- **Hard water.** In areas with hard water, calcium deposits can clog passages or corrode seals in collectors. Direct circulation systems are especially vulnerable. A water softener, the use of buffering chemicals, or an indirect system should be considered in such areas.
- **Leakage.** Seals, piping, and storage media will at some point leak. Routine, preventive maintenance can prevent a catastrophic failure, but well-placed drains are a good idea.

- **Pumping.** Electric pumps can use a significant amount of parasitic energy, and each pump requires a controller that increases the cost of the system. Failure of a pump (often difficult to detect) can result in stagnation or freezing damage to an entire system.

Design Procedure

1. Select an appropriate system type for the climate and projected loads from among the thermosiphon, direct circulation, indirect circulation, and air-based options. Select an appropriate collector type for the system chosen.
2. Estimate the required solar collector area according to the following design guidelines:
   - Domestic hot water systems using flat plate collectors; collector area per person being served by the system:
     high latitudes: 20 ft^2 [1.8 m^2]
     temperate latitudes: 16 [1.5 m^2]
     tropics: 8 [0.7 m^2]
   - Domestic hot water systems using evacuated tube collectors; collector area per person being served by the system:
     high latitudes: 14 ft^2 [1.3 m^2]
     temperate latitudes: 10 [0.9 m^2]
     tropics: use flat plate collector
   - Pool heating systems: 0.6 to 1.1 ft^2 [m^2] of collector area per ft^2 [m^2] of pool surface area. Use a higher value for year-round pool heating.
   - Space heating systems: as a very rough estimate, consider a solar collector area equal to 30–50% of the heated floor area.

   Use the lower value in the above estimates in warm climates and/or areas with good (and reliable) solar radiation resources. Use the higher value in the opposite situation.
3. Estimate an appropriate storage tank size based upon load and needs. The tank must be large enough to meet the peak hourly hot water demands of a domestic water system or to assist meaningfully with space heating loads. For domestic water heating, a 60-gallon [230-L] storage tank is reasonable for one or two people. An 80-gallon [300-L] storage tank is recommended for three to four people. Consider a larger tank for more than four people. Providing adequate storage capacity reduces overheating on good collection days. (An alternative estimating guideline suggests 1.5–2.0 gallons [61–82 L] of storage for each square foot [square meter] of collector area—generally applicable to both space heating and domestic water systems.)
4. Select a backup approach or system to provide hot water/space heating when adequate solar radiation is not available.

Solar thermal systems can also provide space cooling via connection to an absorption chiller. Although intriguing from an energy perspective, this solar application is rare—impeded not by technology, but by

SAMPLE PROBLEM

A small, off-grid residence in Massena, New York will heat domestic hot water using active solar thermal collectors.

1. Because of extended periods of overcast sky and extremely cold winter conditions, an indirect circulation system using evacuated tube solar collectors is chosen.
2. With four occupants, and 10 ft^2 [0.9 m^2] per occupant with evacuated tube collectors, the estimated collector area is 40 ft^2 [3.6 m^2].
3. An 80-gal [300 L] storage tank is recommended by one guideline and (1.5) (40) = 60 gal [227 L] is recommended by another guideline. The larger capacity is considered more appropriate due to the off-grid nature of the building (demanding greater self-sufficiency).
4. Because the building is off-grid, does not have access to a natural gas line, and propane is not acceptable to the client, a wood stove backup water heating system is selected.

equipment availability at the residential scale and first costs at all scales. No general sizing guidelines exist for active solar cooling systems.

Examples

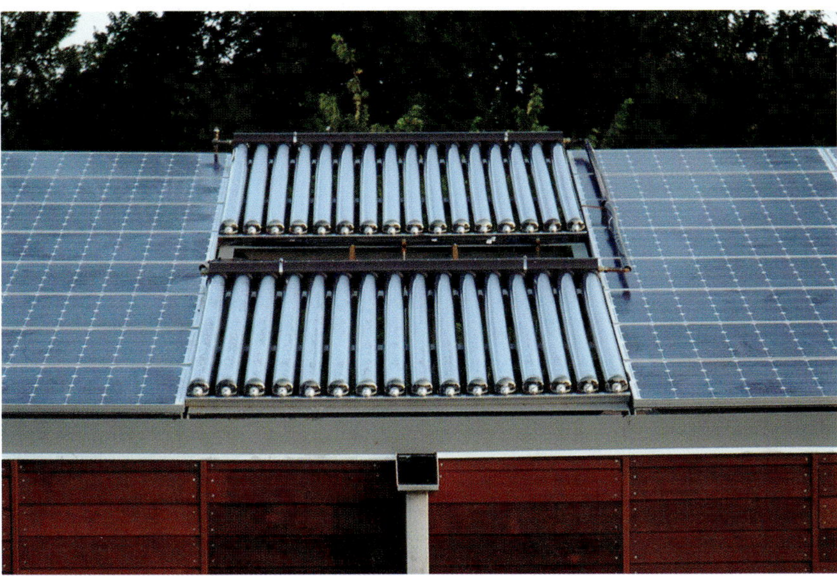

4.173 Evacuated tube solar thermal collectors (surrounded by photovoltaic panels) mounted on the roof of the 2005 Cornell University Solar Decathlon competition entry. NICHOLAS RAJKOVICH

4.174 Evacuated tube solar thermal collectors mounted vertically on walls of the 2009 Cornell University Solar Decathlon house. PV panels are mounted horizontally on the roof. JIM TETRO PHOTOGRAPHY, FOR U.S. DOE.

4.175 Active solar thermal collector arrays provide domestic hot water for the Kindergarten of the 2008 Olympic Village, Beijing, China. BEIJING SUNDA SOLAR TECHNOLOGY CO., LTD

Further Information

ASHRAE 2006. *ASHRAE GreenGuide*, 2nd ed. Butterworth-Heinemann and American Society of Heating, Refrigerating and Air-Conditioning Engineers, Atlanta, GA.

Brown, G.Z. et al. 1992. *Inside Out: Design Procedures for Passive Environmental Technologies*. 2nd ed. John Wiley & Sons, New York.

U.S. Department of Energy, A Consumer's Guide to Energy Efficiency and Renewable Energy, "Water Heating." www.eere.energy.gov/consumer/your_home/water_heating/index.cfm/mytopic=12760

U.S. Department of Energy, Solar Hot Water Resources and Technologies www1.eere.energy.gov/femp/technologies/renewable_shw.html

BEYOND SCHEMATIC DESIGN

Detailed design of an active solar thermal system requires the expertise of a qualified mechanical engineer or solar consultant—who will be involved during design development to verify preliminary system sizing decisions and develop the final design of the system, including equipment selection and specification and consideration of controls and systems integration. Skillful detailing of collector supports and piping penetrations through the building envelope is critical to long-term owner satisfaction.

All solar thermal systems should be commissioned and a User's Manual prepared to assist the owner with system operations and maintenance.

GROUND SOURCE HEAT PUMPS

GROUND SOURCE HEAT PUMPS use the mass of the earth to improve the performance of a vapor compression refrigeration cycle—which can heat a building in winter and cool it in summer. Ground temperature fluctuates less than air temperature. The enormous mass of soil at even moderate depths also contributes to a seasonal temperature lag, such that when air temperatures are extreme (summer and winter), the ground temperature is comparatively mild. The price of the improved efficiency of a ground source heat pump is higher equipment cost.

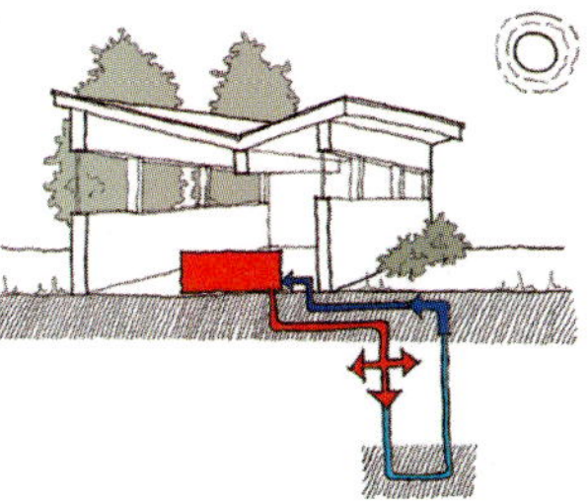

4.177 Ground source heat pump using a vertical ground loop. KATE BECKLEY

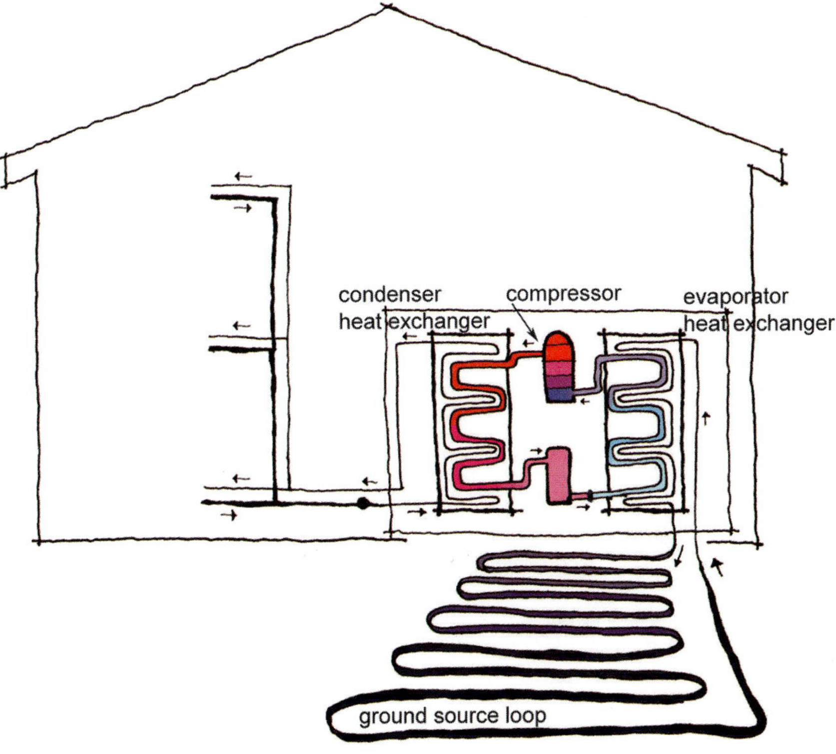

4.176 Schematic diagram of a water heating ground source heat pump. The majority of the components are conventional vapor compression system components (except for the ground source tubing and heat exchanger). The hot water produced may be used for a radiator/baseboard convector, for radiant heating, and/or domestic hot water heating. KATE BECKLEY

A basic ground source heat pump system includes a vapor compression cycle that produces the basic heating/cooling effect, an air or water loop to distribute the heating/cooling effect, and a pump/tubing subsystem to obtain or reject heat from/to the soil or groundwater. The heat exchange fluid in the tubing (usually water) is circulated through a pipe field (or well) that is located outside of the building. The tubes—usually made of high-density 3/4-in. [20 mm] polyethylene—allow the fluid to absorb heat from the surrounding soil during winter months, or dump heat to the soil during summer months. The amount/length of tubing depends upon the configuration of the system, the soil conditions, and the heating/cooling capacity required. A heat exchanger is used to transfer heat from the

INTENT
Energy-efficient heating and cooling, thermal comfort

EFFECT
Reduced energy consumption, lower utility bills

OPTIONS
Open loop versus closed loop, horizontal versus vertical loop, air or water delivery

COORDINATION ISSUES
Site planning, water heater integration, mechanical spaces and location

RELATED STRATEGIES
Site Analysis, various passive heating and cooling strategies

PREREQUISITES
Site area that is large enough for desired configuration and capacity, an annual average ground temperature of 55–65 °F [13–18 °C]

refrigerant in the heat pump cycle to air or water that is then circulated throughout the building for climate control. A deep well may substitute for horizontally buried tubing.

Because of the thermal advantage provided by the more benign below-ground environment, this strategy presents an energy-efficient alternative to conventional heat pumps—and a great advantage over electric resistance heating systems.

Ground source heat pumps can be used in many types of buildings in virtually any climatic condition. The cost of a ground source heat pump system is influenced by the depth of the frost line; the deeper the frost line, the deeper the tubing needs to be buried to benefit from a buffered ground temperature.

Various configurations have been used for the ground source component: closed horizontal loops are very common (these involve pipe fields running parallel to the plane of the ground a few feet below the surface and require minimum excavation); closed vertical loops (similar to an enclosed well) can overcome deep frost lines and the constraints of small sites; open loop systems (such as an open well) can reduce costs in areas where groundwater is plentiful and connection to the aquifer is permitted by code.

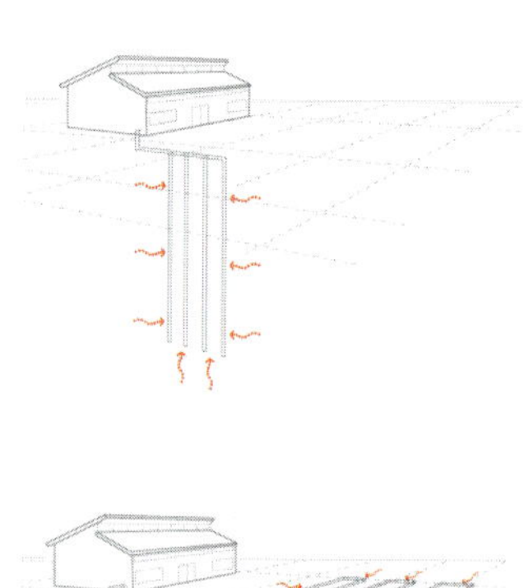

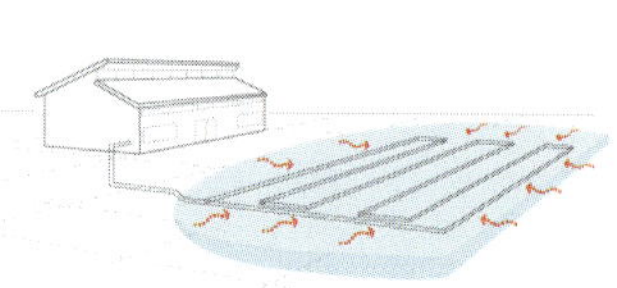

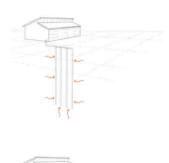

4.178 Typical configurations of ground source heat pumps (vertical field, horizontal field, water body). JON THWAITES

Key Architectural Issues

Ground source heat pumps are a virtually invisible technology. The ground elements are underground (or underwater) and the associated mechanical equipment is practically identical in size to conventional active heating/cooling equipment. As a result, site planning is the most important factor when considering a ground source heat pump. Landscaping and paving may need to be designed to provide access to or protection for the tubing system. Landscaping can be used to provide soil shading, shielding the ground from solar gains (if this is climatically desirable). Landscaping may also be planned to highlight or illustrate the loop system hidden underground.

Implementation Considerations

- **Excavation.** Not only is excavation expensive, it can also be difficult and/or dangerous, with utilities (electric, cable, telephone, sewer, and water lines) often running below ground. A thorough analysis of the site and existing infrastructure will indicate how difficult (costly) excavation will be. If other systems require excavation at the same time, however, this can reduce the combined expense of the systems through a common burial.
- **Future site planning.** Because the ground components of a heat pump system can last between 35 and 50 years, planning for the future development of a site is critical. Depending upon site constraints, installation of a horizontal ground loop may make future development difficult or impractical. System sizing should take into account expected future loads due to expansion or change of function that may occur during the life of the system.

- **Frost depth/ground temperature.** The economics of a ground source heat pump are seriously affected by prevailing ground temperatures—as this variable affects required excavation depth and the thermal efficiency of the system.

Design Procedure

The sizing of a ground source heat pump is a specialized and technical issue. For schematic design purposes, however, here are some guidelines for estimating the extent of the exterior "source" components that will be required.

Guideline for horizontal loops. Assume a loop capacity of 400–650 ft/ton of heating or cooling [35–60 m/kWh]. Trenches are normally 4–6 ft [1.2–1.9 m] deep and up to 400 ft [120 m] long, depending upon how many pipes are in a trench. Most horizontal loop installations use trenches about 6 in. [150 mm] wide.

A well-insulated 2000 ft^2 [185 m^2] home would need about a 3-ton [10.5 kW] system with 1500–1800 ft [460–550 m] of pipe. Non-residential building loads can be estimated using appropriate guidelines.

Guideline for vertical loops. The typical vertical loop will be 150–450 ft [45–140 m] deep. About 100–200 ft^2 of contact area will supply about 1 ton [3.5 kW] of heating/cooling capacity.

Guideline for flow rates. Average ground loop flow rates should be about 2–3 gal per min/ton of heating or cooling [0.36–0.54 L/s per kW].

SAMPLE PROBLEM

What size horizontal ground loop will be required for a small office building in a temperate climate with an estimated cooling load of 10 tons [35 kW]?

For a horizontal loop, using 500 ft per ton [45 m per kW] as a guide (toward the low end of the range considering the temperate climate), the horizontal loop would be $500 \times 10 = 5000$ ft [$45 \times 35 = 1575$ m] in length. Remembering that the purpose of the loop is to exchange heat with the soil, this length must be developed without too much crowding or overlapping of tubes.

Examples

4.179 Eight miles [12.9 km] of piping, staged for placement in a river—in a water-based ground source application. HYDRO-TEMP CORPORATION

4.180 Installation of a large-scale horizontal ground loop in Arkansas. HYDRO-TEMP CORPORATION

4.181 Ground source loops being installed in a 3-ft [0.9 m] deep trench at a school in Mississippi. HYDRO-TEMP CORPORATION

4.182 Installation of vertical well field for the ground source heat pump system at the Armour Academic Center, Westminster School, Simsbury, CT. GUND PARTNERSHIP

4.183 Staging of tubing for the vertical well field at the Armour Academic Center. GUND PARTNERSHIP

4.184 Armour Academic Center Mechanical room. Supply piping from the ground source heat pump loops enters the room at the right. ROBERT BENSON PHOTOGRAPHY

4.185 Construction photo showing mechanical room entry point for ground source loop supply pipes at Armour Academic Center. GUND PARTNERSHIP

Further Information

ASHRAE 1997. *Ground Source Heat Pumps: Design of Geothermal Systems for Commercial & Institutional Buildings*, American Society of Heating, Refrigerating and Air-Conditioning Engineers, Atlanta, GA.

Econar Energy Systems. 1993. *GeoSource Heat Pump Handbook*. Available at: artikel-software.com/file/geo.pdf

Geothermal Exchange Organization. www.geoexchange.org/

Grondzik, W. et al. 2010. *Mechanical and Electrical Equipment for Buildings*. 11th ed. John Wiley & Sons, Hoboken, NJ.

Hydro-Temp Corporation. www.hydro-temp.com/

International Ground Source Heat Pump Association. www.igshpa.okstate.edu/

Water Furnace International. www.wfiglobal.com/

BEYOND SCHEMATIC DESIGN

During design development, detailed calculations of heating and cooling loads will be undertaken. These loads will be used to select appropriate equipment and distribution components. Similarly detailed calculations of required loop capacity and capability would be undertaken to finalize design of the below-ground system components. Commissioning of the heat pump system is critical.

NOTES

COOLING

The most effective means of reducing energy use for mechanical cooling is to eliminate the need for it through climate-adapted design. While this is not always possible, climate-based design strategies can reduce the run-time and/or the size of mechanical cooling systems. Identifying an appropriate cooling strategy for a particular building during schematic design requires an understanding of three things: climate, building type, and pattern of operation.

Monthly climate data, plotted on a bioclimatic chart, provides a visual indication of possible cooling strategies. In a hot desert climate, high thermal mass with night ventilation can provide comfort even with high daytime temperatures because of the low relative humidity and large diurnal temperature swings. No amount of direct ventilation, however, can produce comfort under such daytime conditions. Similarly, no amount of thermal mass or airflow can produce comfort under a combination of high air temperature and high relative humidity. The first design requirement is to match the cooling strategy to the climate.

Buildings can be broadly grouped into two thermal types: skin-load dominated and internal-load dominated. Skin-load dominated buildings (most residences and small commercial buildings) do not generate much internal heat. Their cooling requirements are largely determined by exterior climate and design of the building envelope. Internal-load dominated buildings (such as large office buildings) have occupant, lighting, and equipment heat loads that are not driven by exterior conditions. The second design requirement is to match the cooling strategy to the building type.

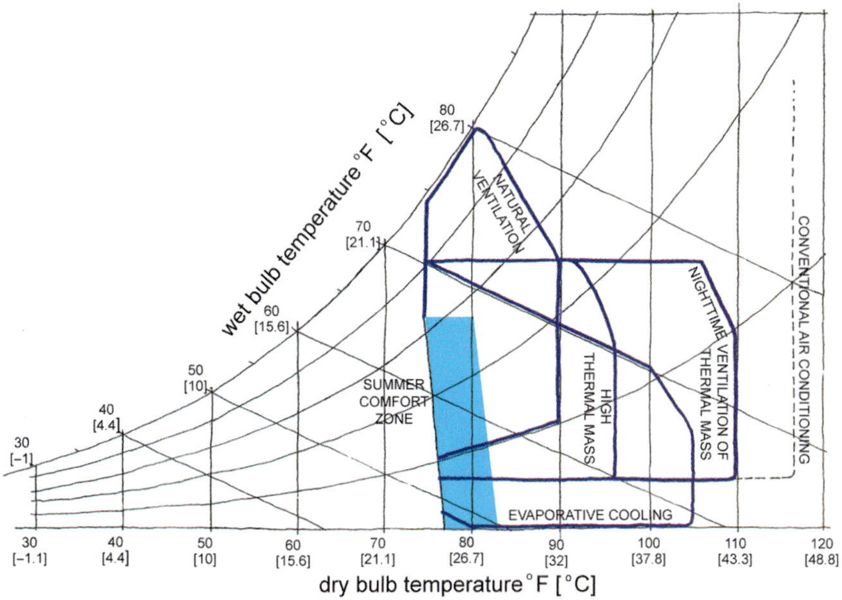

4.186 Applicability of building cooling strategies. ADAPTED FROM *ENERGY CONSERVATION THROUGH BUILDING DESIGN*

STRATEGIES

Cross Ventilation
Stack Ventilation
Evaporative Cool Towers
Night Ventilation of Thermal Mass
Earth Cooling Tubes
Earth Sheltering
Absorption Chillers

ENVELOPE LIGHTING HEATING COOLING ENERGY PRODUCTION WATER & WASTE

A designer must also understand patterns of building operation. A facility that is not open during the hottest time of the day or year needn't be designed to provide comfort during those periods. For example, an elementary school that closes during summer months need not provide comfort under early August conditions. Additionally, if a school closes at 2:30 P.M., window shading and cooling requirements may be very different than for a school that closes at 4:30 P.M. The third design requirement is to understand the patterns of building usage.

Several passive cooling strategies that may be able to contribute to development of a greener project are presented. One active cooling strategy—absorption refrigeration—is also presented as a possible alternative to vapor compression refrigeration.

CROSS VENTILATION

CROSS VENTILATION establishes a flow of cooler outdoor air through a space; this flow carries heat out of a building. Cross ventilation is a viable and energy-efficient alternative to mechanical cooling under appropriate climate conditions. The design objective may be direct cooling of occupants, as a result of increased air speed and lowered air temperature, or the cooling of building surfaces (as with night-time flushing) to provide indirect comfort cooling. The effectiveness of this cooling strategy is a function of the size of the inlets, outlets, wind speed, and outdoor air temperature. Air speed is critical to direct comfort cooling; airflow rate is critical to structural cooling.

4.188 A café in Bang Bao, Koh Chang, Thailand utilizes high ceilings and windows for cross ventilation combined with thatched overhangs for shading. KATE BECKLEY

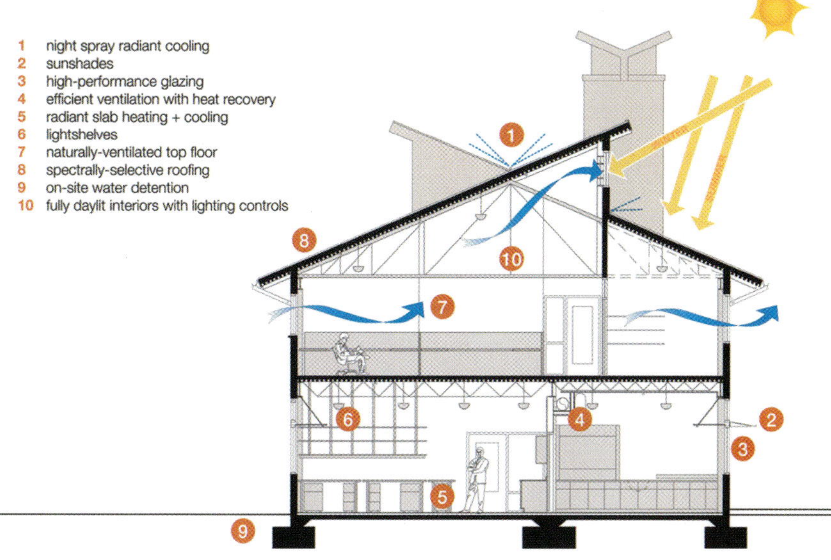

4.187 Schematic section of the Global Ecology Research Center at Stanford University, Palo Alto, California showing the integration of several strategies, including orientation to the prevailing winds to maximize cross ventilation potential on the second floor. EHDD ARCHITECTURE

Cross ventilation cooling capacity is fundamentally dependent upon the temperature difference between the indoor air and outdoor air. Cross ventilation cooling is only viable when the outdoor air is at least 3 °F [1.7 °C] cooler than the indoor air. Lesser temperature differences provide only marginal cooling effect (circulating air at room temperature, for example, cannot remove space heat or reduce space temperature). Outdoor airflow rate is another key capacity determinant—the greater the airflow, the greater the cooling capacity.

Wind pressure is the driving force behind cross ventilation. The greater the wind speed, the greater the cross ventilation cooling potential. Prevailing wind direction often changes with the seasons, and may shift throughout the day. Wind speed is usually variable daily and seasonally—and typically very weak at night in the

INTENT
Climate control (cooling), thermal comfort

EFFECT
Passive cooling

OPTIONS
Comfort cooling, structural cooling

COORDINATION ISSUES
Active heating and cooling, security, acoustics, air quality, orientation, footprint, internal partitions

RELATED STRATEGIES
Site Analysis, Glazing, Sidelighting, Stack Ventilation

PREREQUISITES
Prevailing wind direction and design average wind speed (monthly), outdoor air temperatures (monthly, hourly), estimated design cooling load, desired indoor air temperature

absence of solar heating of the ground. If no air enters the inlet of a cross ventilation system the system does not work.

Buildings are typically best naturally ventilated when they are very open to the breezes yet shaded from direct solar radiation. Building materials in a cross ventilated building may be light in weight, unless night ventilation of mass is intended—in which case thermally massive materials are necessary.

Key Architectural Issues

Successful cross ventilation requires a building form that maximizes exposure to the prevailing wind direction, provides for adequate inlet area, minimizes internal obstructions (between inlet and outlet), and provides for adequate outlet area. An ideal footprint is an elongated rectangle with no internal divisions. Siting should avoid external obstructions to wind flow (such as trees, bushes, or other buildings). On the other hand, proper placement of vegetation, berms, or wing walls can channel and enhance airflow at windward (inlet) openings.

Implementation Considerations

Cross ventilation for occupant comfort may direct airflow through any part of a space if the outdoor air temperature is low enough to provide for heat removal. At high outdoor air temperatures, cross ventilation may still be a viable comfort strategy if airflow is directed across the occupants (so they experience higher air speeds). Cross ventilation for night-time structural cooling (when adequate wind speed exists) should be directed to maximize contact with thermally massive surfaces. A design caution: High outdoor relative humidity may compromise occupant comfort even when adequate sensible cooling capacity is available.

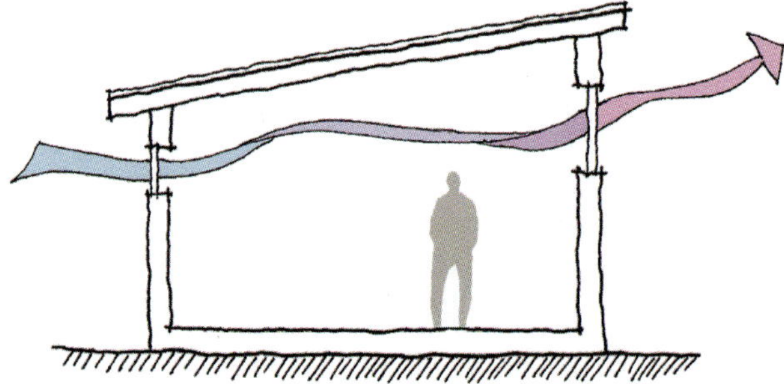

4.189 High inlets and outlets provide structural cooling but no air movement at occupant level. KATE BECKLEY

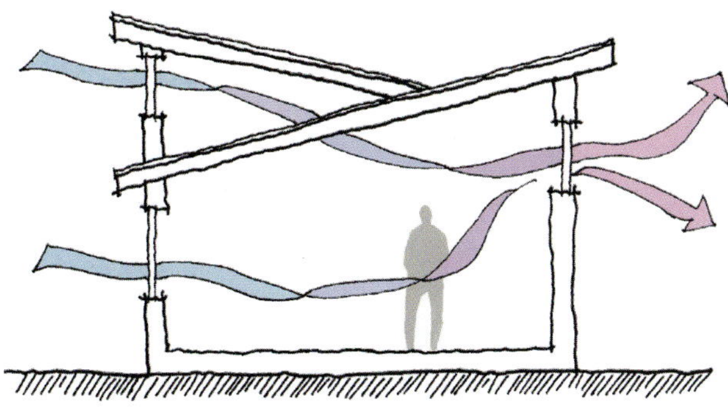

4.190 Clerestories do not assist in occupant level air movement. Cross ventilation through lower inlets provides occupant level air movement. Orientation of the building to the prevailing winds will maximize airflow. KATE BECKLEY

Cross ventilation flushes outside air through a building to provide cooling, allowing anything in the air to be introduced to the building. For this reason, careful consideration of the location of intake openings and ambient air quality is important. Cross ventilation can also easily introduce noise into a building through inlets and outlets. Attention should be paid to nearby noise sources. Openings can sometimes be located to minimize the effect of noise on occupied spaces.

Design Procedure

Cross ventilation should normally be analyzed on a space-by-space basis. An exit opening equal in size to the inlet opening is necessary. This procedure considers only sensible loads and calculates the size of the inlet (assuming an equal or larger outlet).

1. Arrange spaces to account for the fact that building occupants will find spaces near inlets (incoming outdoor air) to be cooler than spaces near outlets (exiting warmed air). Substantial heat sources should be placed near outlets, not near inlets.
2. Estimate design sensible cooling load (heat gain) for the space(s)—including all envelope and internal loads (but excluding ventilation/infiltration loads). *Btu/h* or *W*
3. State the design cooling load on a unit floor area basis. *Btu/h* ft^2 or W/m^2
4. Establish the ventilation inlet area (this is free area, adjusted for the actual area of window that can be opened and the estimated impact of insect screens, mullions, shading devices). Determine the floor area of the space that will be cooled. The inlet area may be based upon other design decisions (such as view) or be a trial-and-error start to cooling system analysis. ft^2 or m^2
5. Determine the inlet area as a *percentage* of the floor area: (inlet area/floor area) × 100.
6. Using Figure 4.191, find the intersection of the inlet area percentage (Step 5) and the design wind speed (from local climate data). This intersection gives the estimated cross ventilation cooling capacity—assuming a 3 °F [1.7 °C] indoor–outdoor air

SAMPLE PROBLEM

Assume a 4500 ft^2 [418 m^2] small commercial building located in a temperate European climate.

1. A spatial layout anticipated to maximize cooling effectiveness for the occupants is established.
2. The design cooling load is estimated to be 120,000 Btu/h [35,170 W].
3. Given the 4500 ft^2 [418 m^2] floor area:

   20,000/4500 = 26.7 Btu/h ft^2

   [35,170/418 = 84.1 W/m^2].
4. Assume 250 ft^2 [23 m^2] of free inlet area as an initial trial.
5. Inlet area as a percentage of floor area is found to be:

   (250/4500) × 100 = 5.6%

   [(23/418) × 100 = 5.6%].
6. With a design wind speed of 7 mph [3.1 m/s] Figure 4.191 gives the estimated cooling

temperature difference. Design wind speed should represent a wind speed that is likely to actually be available during the time of design cooling load.

7. Compare the estimated ventilation cooling capacity (Step 6) with the required cooling capacity (Step 3).
8. Increase the proposed inlet area as required to achieve the necessary capacity; decrease the proposed inlet area as required to reduce excess cooling capacity.

This design procedure addresses "worst case" design conditions when outdoor air temperatures are usually high. Extrapolation beyond the values in Figure 4.191 for a greater Δt is not recommended as a means of sizing openings. On the other hand, greater temperature differences will exist during the cooling season permitting a reduction in inlet and outlet size under such conditions. Extrapolation for higher wind speeds is not recommended due to potential discomfort from too-high indoor air speeds. Remember, wind speeds at airport locations (a typical source of climate data) can be very different than at the city center or in suburban areas, depending upon the terrain. During schematic design, adjustments can be made to account for the variation by comparing "local" and airport wind speed data. As a rough estimate, urban wind speeds are often only a third of airport wind speeds; and suburban wind speeds two-thirds of airport speeds.

capacity as 45 Btu/h ft^2 [142 W/m^2].

7. The available cooling capacity is greater than the required cooling capacity (45 > 26.7) [142 > 84.1].
8. The inlet area could be reduced to

   $(26.7/45) \times 250 = 148$ ft^2

   $[(84.1/142) \times 23 = 13.6$ m$^2]$

   and still provide adequate cross ventilation capacity.

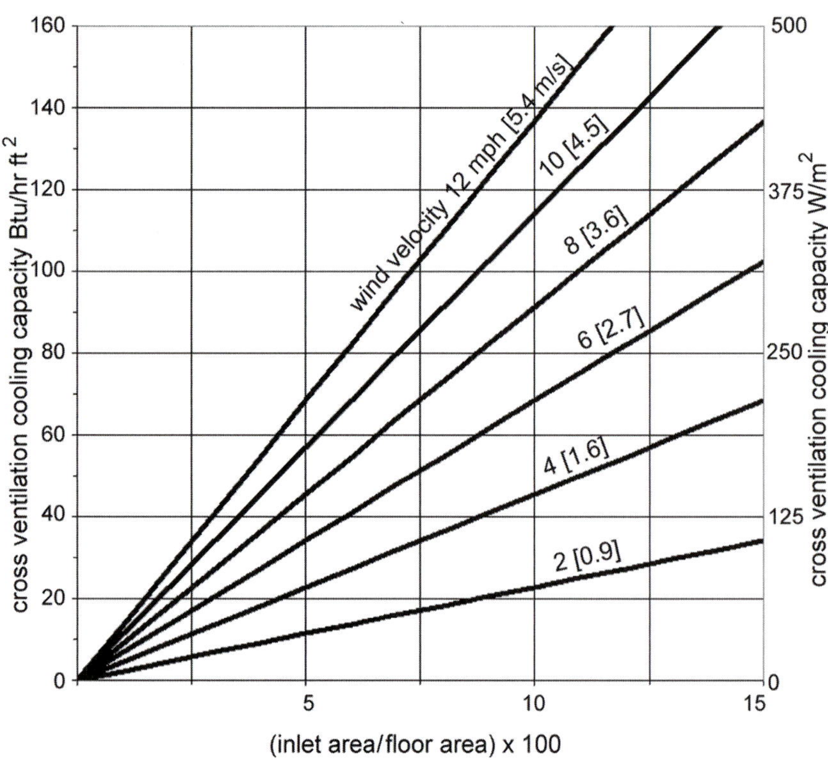

4.191 Cross ventilation cooling capacity. Heat removed per unit floor area (based upon a 3 °F [1.7 °C] temperature difference) as a function of size of inlet openings and wind speed. KATHY BEVERS; DERIVED FROM EQUATIONS IN *MECHANICAL AND ELECTRICAL EQUIPMENT FOR BUILDINGS*, 10TH ED.

Examples

4.192 Operable windows along a corridor (left) allow air movement through a classroom building at Islandwood Campus, Bainbridge Island, Washington. Dog-trot house on Kauai, Hawaii (right) with cross ventilation through wrap-around porches used for indoor and outdoor living.

4.193 Café at the Honolulu Academy of Arts, Honolulu, Hawaii uses floor-to-ceiling sliding doors and ceiling fans to enhance air movement.

4.194 Open plan office space with cross ventilation, Habitat Research and Development Centre, Windhoek, Namibia. NINA MARITZ

Further Information

Brown, G.Z. and M. DeKay. 2001. *Sun, Wind & Light: Architectural Design Strategies*, 2nd ed. John Wiley & Sons, New York.

Grondzik, W. et al. 2010. *Mechanical and Electrical Equipment for Buildings*. 11th ed. John Wiley & Sons, Hoboken, NJ.

National Climatic Data Center. www.ncdc.noaa.gov/oa/ncdc.html

Olgyay, V. 1963. *Design with Climate*, Princeton University Press, Princeton, NJ.

Royle, K. and C. Terry. 1990. *Hawaiian Design: Strategies for Energy Efficient Architecture*, Diane Publishing Co., Collingdale, PA.

Square One. "Passive Cooling, Natural Ventilation." www.squ1.com/archive/

BEYOND SCHEMATIC DESIGN

Validation of cross ventilation effectiveness during design development requires the use of sophisticated computer simulation or physical modeling tools. Computational fluid dynamics (CFD) is sometimes used for numerical simulations. Wind tunnel tests are typically used for physical simulations. Both involve steep learning curves, considerable technical expertise, and appropriate software/laboratory facilities.

Be sure to inform users how the ventilation system is intended to operate and the thermal conditions likely to be encountered.

STACK VENTILATION

STACK VENTILATION is a passive cooling strategy that takes advantage of temperature stratification. It relies on two basic principles: (1) as air warms, it becomes less dense and rises; (2) ambient (hopefully cooler) air replaces the air that has risen. This system of natural convection creates its own air current, where warmer air is evacuated at a high point, and cooler outdoor air is brought in at a lower level. Stack ventilation will only work for thermal comfort conditioning when the outside air temperature is cooler than the desired inside temperature. In order to function effectively (i.e., generate a substantial airflow), the difference between ambient indoor and outdoor air temperatures needs to be at least 3 °F [1.7 °C]. A greater temperature difference can provide more effective air circulation and cooling. Because it creates its own air current, stack ventilation is only minimally affected by building orientation. Air won't flow properly, however, if an outlet faces the windward direction.

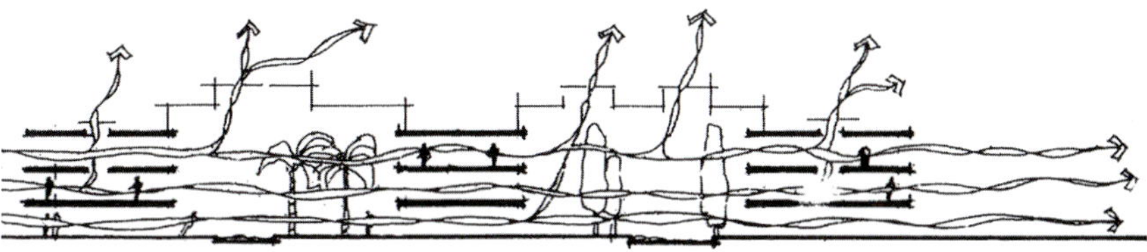

4.195 Schematic competition entry for the IBN-DLO Institute for Forestry and Nature Research in Wageningen, The Netherlands. Cooler outdoor air enters at the building perimeter, is warmed as it moves through the building, and then rises and exits through openings in the roof. BROOK MULLER

One way to encourage a greater temperature difference is to increase the height of a stack—the higher the stack, the greater the potential for vertical stratification of temperatures. Because of the need for height to achieve effective air stratification, stack ventilation is often designed in section. See Figure 4.197 for a few common stack ventilation design strategies.

Another way to increase the temperature difference between entering and exiting air is to use solar energy to heat the air. In the BRE building (Figure 4.201) in the UK, ventilation stacks are located along the southern face of the building. These stacks are glazed with a translucent material so that solar radiation heats the air in the stack, causing an increase in airflow within the building.

As seen in the projects illustrating this strategy, the use of stack ventilation brings with it some interesting architectural possibilities. For example, in the BRE building the stacks are given greater height than the rest of the building, providing an architectural feature that highlights the significance of these devices to the functioning of the building.

Key Architectural Issues

To work well, a stack needs to generate a large temperature difference between exhaust air and incoming air. This can be done in several ways, including increasing stack height. A typical stack will provide effective ventilation for areas within the lower half of its total

4.196 Solar chimneys at the Building Research Establishment offices, Garston, Herfordshire, UK. THERESE PEFFER

INTENT
Climate control (cooling), indoor air quality, thermal comfort

EFFECT
Reduced energy usage/costs, improved indoor air quality

OPTIONS
Central versus distributed stacks, stack height, number of stacks

COORDINATION ISSUES
Active heating and cooling, security, acoustics, air quality, orientation, footprint, internal partitions, fire and smoke control

RELATED STRATEGIES
Site Analysis, Cross Ventilation, Night Ventilation of Mass, Evaporative Cool Towers, Double Envelope

PREREQUISITES
Substantial height available for stack, potential for properly sized and located air inlets and outlets, solar access (for solar-assisted stacks only)

height. This implies that stacks be double the height of the building if they are to serve all floors of a building, or that they only serve a portion of the total floor area.

Stacks may be integrated or exposed. This is a question of expression: Placing a stack on the building perimeter for solar access or integrating it into an atrium represent very different architectural solutions. This decision will hinge not only upon aesthetics, but also upon climate conditions, cooling loads, and zoning and building codes. Exterior finishes and landscaping (plants, misting, and ground covers) can lower the incoming air temperature. Inlet (and outlet) sizing is critical to system performance. Inlet location, quantity, and size can affect building security, building facade appearance, and the quality of the incoming air (inlets should not be located near loading docks or in parking garages).

Implementation Considerations

Stacks tend to "blur" thermal zones—favoring spaces lower on the "ventilation chain;" in other words, providing more air movement (ventilation) at lower levels of a multi-entry stack. Modular and separated stacks can address this problem, but multiple stacks are costly and require more openings, which may not be possible for a variety of reasons: security, location, adjacencies, etc. Zoning by function and occupancy needs (both in plan and section) should be a primary schematic design consideration. Additionally, vertical stacks may need to be integrated with HVAC and structural systems to ensure effective utilization of space. Although stack ventilation will generally work in most climates, climates with large diurnal temperature ranges are ideal.

Stack ventilation brings outside air into a building to provide cooling, allowing anything in the air to be introduced to the building. For this reason, careful consideration regarding the location of intake openings and ambient air quality is important. Stack ventilation can easily introduce noise into a building. Attention should be paid to nearby noise sources. Openings can be located to minimize the effect of noise on occupied spaces.

Design Procedure

A trial-and-error process will typically be required to zero-in on a workable design that balances system capabilities with cooling requirements.

1. Establish a workable stack height for the project. An effective stack will usually be twice as tall as the height of the tallest space it is ventilating. It is common to zone buildings such that only the lower floors are served by a stack (allowing for partial stack ventilation without exceptionally tall stack protrusions).
2. Size the stack openings (inlet, outlet, and throat area). The smallest of the following areas will define system performance: the total free area of inlet openings, the total free area of outlet openings, or the horizontal cross-sectional area (the "throat area") of the stack.

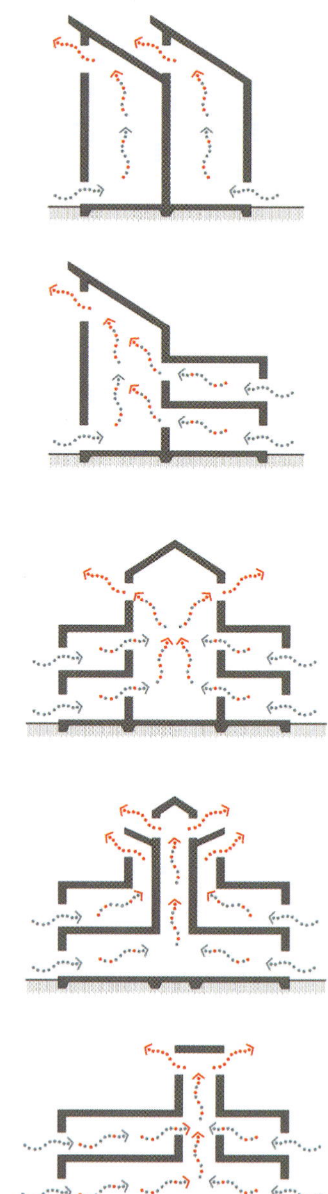

4.197 Various stack ventilation configurations. JON THWAITES

SAMPLE PROBLEM

A two-story building has a large atrium, which is 30 ft [9.1 m] tall.

1. The first floor of the building will be ventilated using the atrium as a stack, providing an effective stack height of around 20 ft [6.1 m].
2. The openings at ground level and the top of the stack

3. **Using Figure 4.198, estimate the cooling capacity of the stack ventilation system on the basis of stack height and stack-to-floor area ratio (where floor area is the area served by the stack or stacks).**

4. **Adjust stack openings and/or height as necessary to obtain desired cooling capacity.**

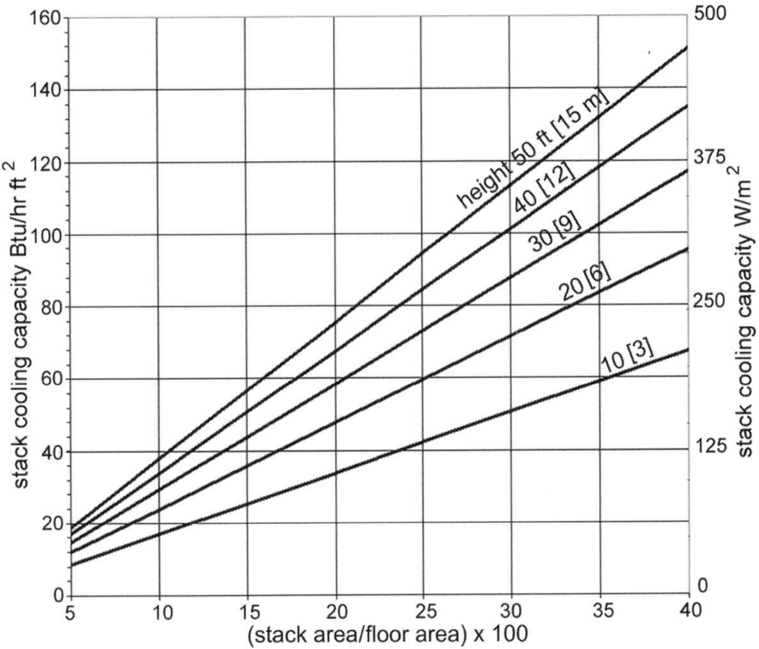

4.198 Stack ventilation capacity. Heat removed per unit floor area (based upon a 3 °F [1.7 °C] temperature difference) relative to stack size and height. KATHY BEVERS; DERIVED FROM EQUATIONS IN *MECHANICAL AND ELECTRICAL EQUIPMENT FOR BUILDINGS*, 10TH ED.

Examples

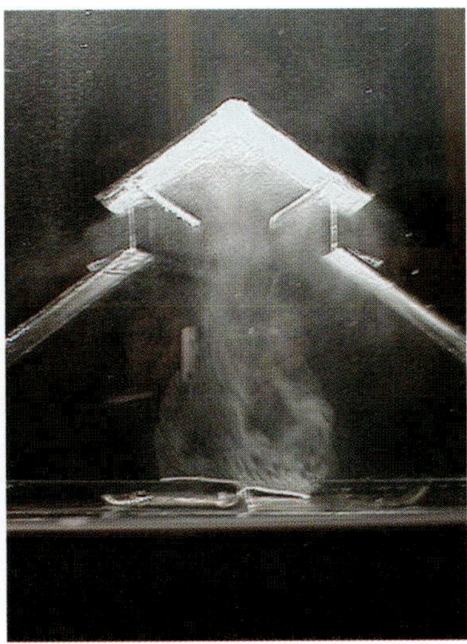

4.199 The Logan House (left), Tampa, FL, a well-studied example of stack effect ventilation. Bubble-testing a model of the Logan House (right) to determine stack performance and examine alternative window configurations. ALISON KWOK | CHRISTINA BOLLO

(atrium) are 200 ft^2 [18.6 m^2] each; throat area is not a limiting factor.

3. The floor area to be ventilated via the stack is 2000 ft^2 [186 m^2]. The stack-to-floor area percentage is: (200/2000) × (100) = 10. From Figure 4.198, the estimated cooling capacity of a 20-ft [6.1 m] tall stack with a ratio of 10 is about 24 Btu/h ft^2 [76 W/m^2]. This capacity assumes a 3 °F [1.7 °C] temperature difference between indoor and outdoor air (likely possible on some summer days).

4. This cooling capacity would be compared with the estimated cooling load of the spaces being ventilated to determine whether it is adequate. As seen in Figure 4.198, capacity can be increased by increasing stack height (unlikely in this example) or by increasing stack opening area.

4.200 Model of the Logan House (cross and stack ventilation) in wind tunnel for performance testing.

4.201 South-facade features photovoltaic panels, solar chimneys (with glass block to assist) and a stack ventilated top floor at the Building Research Establishment offices, Garston, Herfordshire, UK. THERESE PEFFER

4.203 Windows open into the solar stack in an office space at the Building Research Establishment. The undulating ceiling provides a channel for cross ventilation across the building for night ventilation of thermal mass. THERESE PEFFER

4.202 Stack ventilation towers exhaust warm air at Lanchester Library at Coventry University, Coventry, UK.

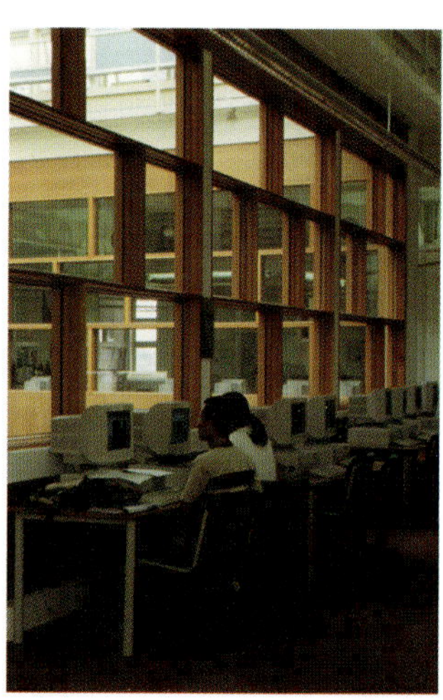

4.204 Lanchester Library features a large central vertical well that provides air supply and exhaust.

4.205 The atrium of the Lillis Business Complex (Eugene, Oregon) serves as an entry, circulation, and social space. Balconies surrounding a circular stair provide study areas where students (and authors) gather. The atrium also exhausts air from the classroom wings via stack effect.

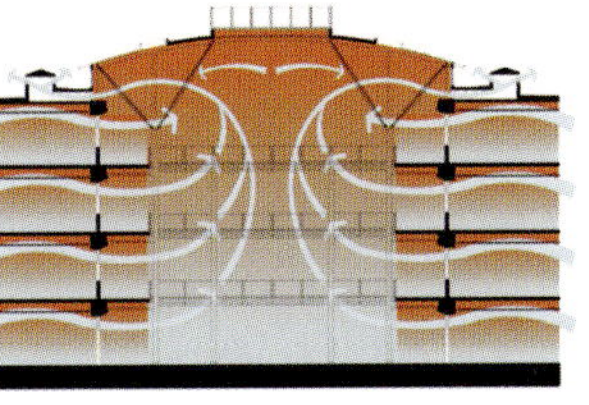

4.206 Lillis Business Complex natural ventilation strategy—air enters through inlets in the classrooms and exits through outlets at the sides of the atrium. SRG PARTNERSHIP

Further Information

Grondzik, W. et al. 2002. "The Logan House: Signing Off," *Proceedings of 27th National Passive Solar Conference—Solar 2002* (Reno, NV). American Solar Energy Society, Boulder, CO.

Grondzik, W. et al. 2010. *Mechanical and Electrical Equipment for Buildings*. 11th ed. John Wiley & Sons, Hoboken, NJ.

Walker, A. 2010. Whole Building Design Guide, "Natural Ventilation." www.wbdg.org/resources/naturalventilation.php

BEYOND SCHEMATIC DESIGN

The estimate of stack ventilation sizing and performance made during schematic design will be verified during design development. Such validation is not easy, and might include the use of computer simulation tools or physical models to optimize the effectiveness of potential design configurations.

Clearly convey requirements and expectations for system operation to occupants via a User's Manual.

NOTES

EVAPORATIVE COOL TOWERS

EVAPORATIVE COOL TOWERS use the principles of direct evaporative cooling and cool-air down-draft to passively cool hot dry outdoor air and circulate it through a building. The resulting cooler and more humid air can be distributed through a building using the inertia inherent in the falling air. Cool towers are sometimes referred to as reverse chimneys.

Hot dry air is exposed to water at the top of the tower. As water evaporates into the air inside the tower, the air temperature drops and the moisture content of the air increases; the resulting denser air drops down the tower and exits through an opening at the base. The air movement down the tower creates a negative (suction) pressure at the top of the tower and a positive pressure at the base. Air leaving the base of the tower enters the space or spaces requiring cooling.

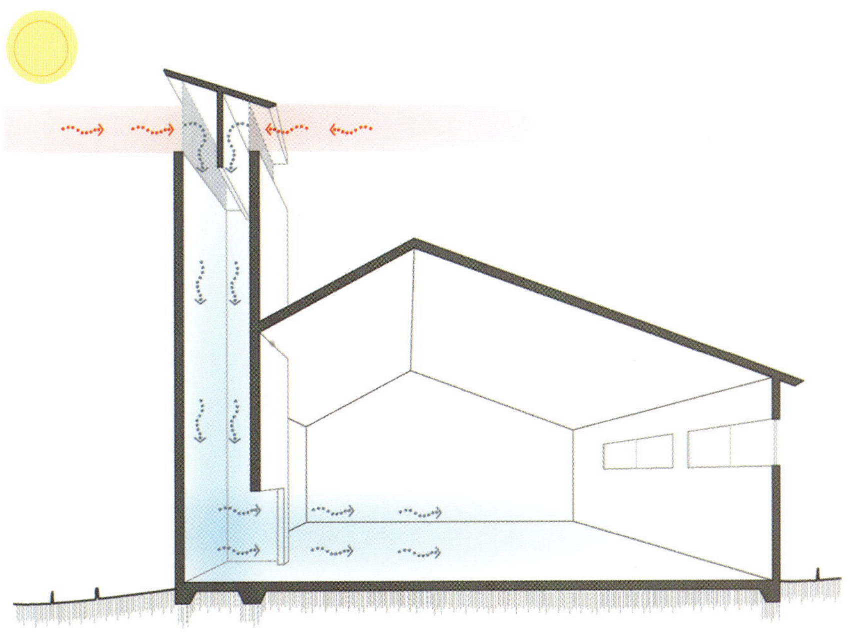

4.207 Warm dry air enters the top of a cool tower, passes through moist pads, and exits the base of the tower as cooler and more humid air. JON THWAITES

An evaporative cool tower can provide a very low-energy alternative to active (mechanical) cooling for a building in a hot and dry climate. The sole energy input (required only in low water pressure situations) is for a pump to raise water to the top of the tower. A cool tower does, however, consume water—which may be an environmental concern in an arid climate.

In theory (and generally in practice) an evaporative cooling process exchanges sensible cooling for latent heating along a constant enthalpy (heat content) line. As the process proceeds, dry bulb and wet bulb air temperatures converge. Theoretically the air emerging from the evaporation process would have a dry bulb temperature

4.208 Evaporative cool tower at the Center for Global Ecology, Stanford University, California.

INTENT
Climate control (cooling), thermal comfort

EFFECT
Passive cooling, humidification

OPTIONS
Number and location of towers

COORDINATION ISSUES
Effective thermal envelope, spatial layout, generally unimpeded interior airflow

RELATED STRATEGIES
Site Analysis, Night Ventilation of Mass, Water Reuse/Recycling, Water Catchment Systems

PREREQUISITES
Hot dry climate, available height for towers, water source

equal to the wet bulb temperature. In practical applications the process results in a dry bulb temperature that is about 20 to 40% higher than the wet bulb.

Evaporative cool tower performance is dependent upon the wet bulb depression (the difference between dry and wet bulb air temperatures) of the outside air. The greater the wet bulb depression, the greater the potential difference between the outdoor air temperature and the temperature of the cooled air exiting the tower. The airflow rate from the base of the cool tower is dependent upon the wet bulb depression and the design of the tower—specifically the height of the tower and the area of the wetted pads at the top of the tower.

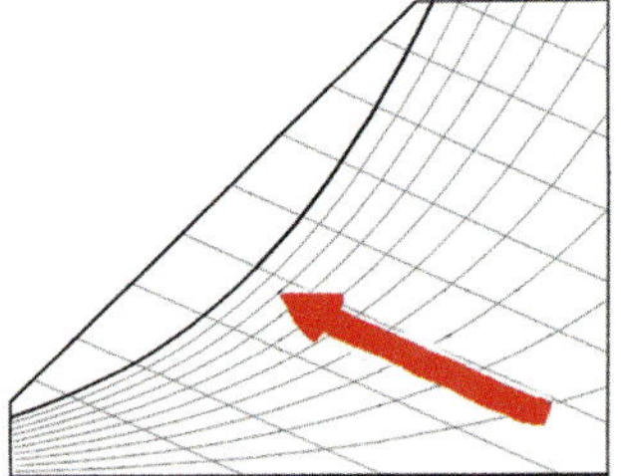

4.209 The evaporative cooling process plotted on a psychrometric chart.

Key Architectural Issues

Cool towers can add architectural interest to a building. The cool tower at the Visitor Center in Zion National Park in Utah was designed to echo the form of the dramatic high canyon walls along the river in the park. The base of the tower in the Visitor Center's interior invokes the feeling of a massive hearth.

4.210 Wind catcher, Qeshm Island, Iran—a hot, humid climate. IMAN REJAIE

Evaporative cool towers work best in buildings with open floor plans that permit the cooled air to circulate freely without being impeded by walls or partitions. Cool towers do not rely upon wind for air circulation and require minimal energy input. Cool towers do require continuously wetted evaporative pads. Cool towers also involve fairly large airflow volumes that must be accommodated through building design. This above-normal airflow can be a plus relative to indoor air quality and occupant satisfaction with the thermal environment.

Because a cool tower involves wetted pads (or misting) and regions of high relative humidity, biological growth (mold) is a potential problem. Ready access for inspection and maintenance of the wetted areas should be provided.

Consideration of a dual-function tower may be warranted in some climates—operating as an evaporative cool tower during the day and a stack ventilator during the night.

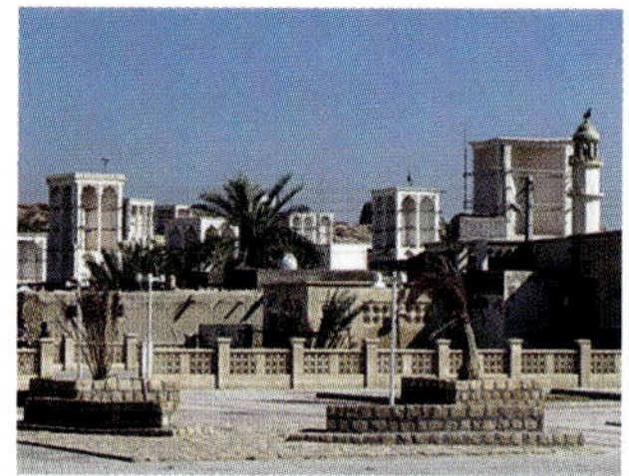

4.211 Wind catchers in a hot, arid climate—Semnan, Iran. IMAN REJAIE

Implementation Considerations

Evaporative cool towers work best under dry, hot conditions. In an arid climate the wet bulb depression is normally high so the evaporative cooling effect is maximized. The resulting increase in relative humidity of the exiting air is not a problem (and should be a comfort benefit). The effectiveness of a cool tower does not depend upon wind, so cool towers can be used in areas with little or no wind resources and on sites with limited or no wind access.

In *Passive and Low Energy Cooling of Buildings*, Givoni developed formulas for estimating the effectiveness of an evaporative cool tower based upon exit temperature and airflow. He found that wind speed had little impact on exit temperature. His formulas are based upon a limited amount of data for towers with wetted pads at the top, but are considered appropriate for schematic design.

Design Procedure

1. Establish design conditions. Find the design ambient dry bulb (DB) and mean coincident wet bulb (WB) temperatures for the hottest time of the year for the building site. The wet bulb depression is the difference between the dry bulb and wet bulb temperatures.

2. Find the approximate exiting air temperature to determine feasibility. Using the wet bulb depression and the ambient outdoor dry bulb temperature, estimate the exiting air temperature using Figure 4.212. If this temperature is low enough to provide useful cooling, continue to Step 3.

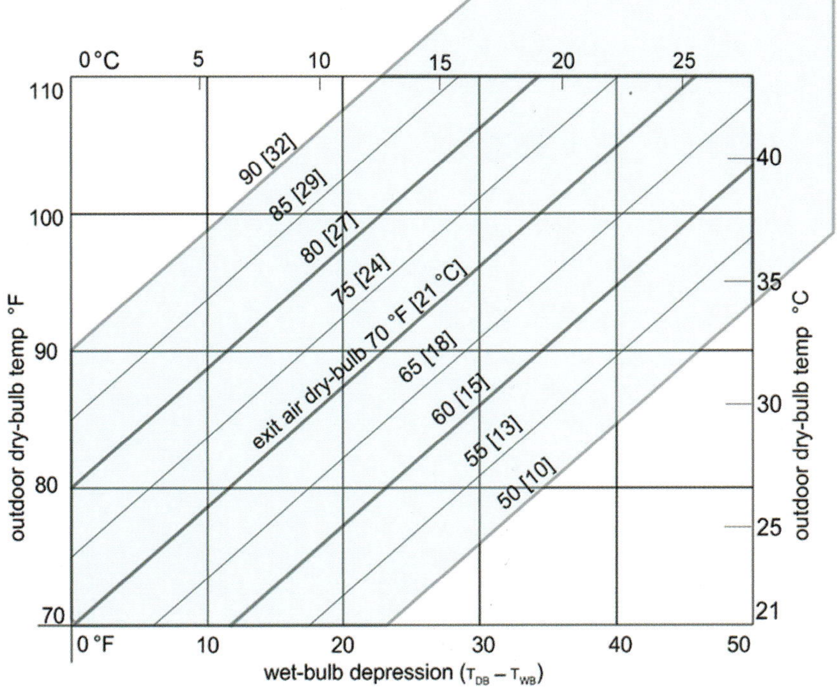

4.212 Exiting evaporative cool tower air temperature as a function of wet bulb depression and outdoor dry bulb air temperature. KATHLEEN BEVERS; DERIVED FROM *MECHANICAL AND ELECTRICAL EQUIPMENT FOR BUILDINGS*, 10TH ED.

3. Determine the necessary airflow rate by establishing the exiting airflow quantity (at the leaving dry bulb temperature) required to offset the space/building sensible cooling load.

$$Q = q/(F)(\Delta t)$$

where,
Q = airflow rate, cfm [L/s]
q = design sensible cooling load, Btu/h [W]
Δt = temperature difference between supply (cool tower exiting) air and room air, °F [°C]
F = conversion factor, 1.1 [1.2]

SAMPLE PROBLEM

Determine if an evaporative cool tower would adequately cool a 4000 ft^2 [372 m^2] office building in Boulder, Colorado with an estimated cooling load of 15 Btu/h ft^2 [47.3 W/m^2].

1. Boulder has a design DB of 91 °F [32.8 °C] and a mean coincident WB of 59 °F [15 °C]—giving a wet bulb depression of (91 – 59) = 32 °F [17.8 °C]. Figure 4.212 confirms that this falls well within the conditions appropriate for evaporative cooling.

2. The wet bulb depression is (91 – 59 °F) = 32 °F [17.8 °C]. From Figure 4.212, an exiting air temperature of about 65 °F [18.3 °C] is predicted.

3. Determine the amount of supply air at T_{exit} required to offset the building cooling load.

   $Q = q/(1.1)(\Delta t)$

   $q = (15 \text{ Btu/h ft}^2)\ (4000 \text{ ft}^2)$

   $= 60{,}000 \text{ Btu/h}$

   $\Delta t = (78 - 65) = 13\ °F$

   $Q = 60{,}000/(1.1)(13)$

   $Q = 4195$ cfm [1980 L/s]

   A flow rate of about 4200 cfm [1980 L/s] of 65 °F [18.3 °C] exiting tower air will offset the cooling load of 15 Btu/hft^2 [47.3 W/m^2].

4. From Figure 4.213, a wet bulb depression of 32°F [17.8 °C] and a flow rate of 4200 cfm [1980 L/s] suggest that a 35-ft [10.7 m] tower with a 48-ft^2 [4.5 m^2] total pad size will cool the office building with an exiting temperature of 65 °F [18.3 °C].

4. **Determine tower height and area of wetted pads. Based upon the required airflow rate, use the graph in Figure 4.213 to determine an appropriate tower height and wetted pad area.**

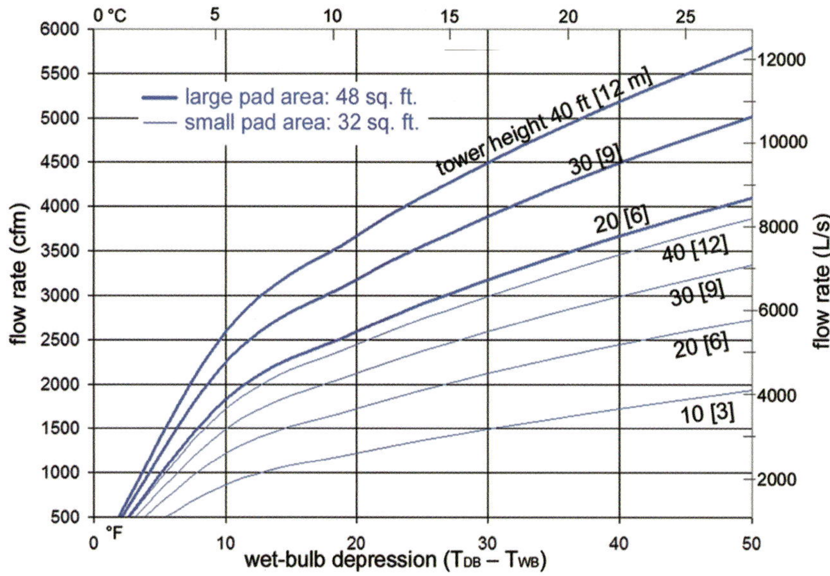

4.213 Recommended cool tower height and wetted pad area as a function of required airflow rate and wet bulb depression. KATHLEEN BEVERS; DERIVED FROM *MECHANICAL AND ELECTRICAL EQUIPMENT FOR BUILDINGS*, 10TH ED.

Examples

4.214 Evaporative cool towers at Zion National Park Visitor's Center, Zion, Utah. HARVEY BRYAN

4.215 Exceptionally tall wind catcher in Dolat Abad garden in Yazd, Iran. IMAN REJAIE

4.216 Historic wind catcher in Yazd, Iran. IMAN REJAIE

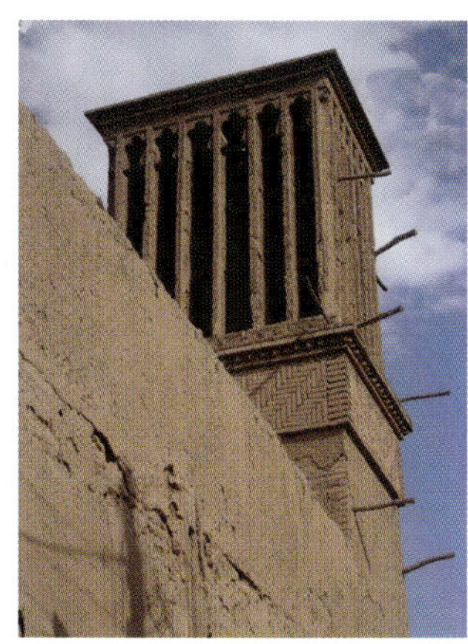

4.217 Four-sided wind catcher in Yadz, Iran. IMAN REJAIE

4.218 Evaporative cool tower at the Global Ecology Research Center at Stanford University, Menlo Park, California

4.219 Evaporative cool tower at the Habitat Research and Development Centre, Windhoek, Namibia. Prosopis (mesquite) branches are used to shade the elevated water storage tanks. NINA MARITZ

4.220 Looking up into the mister (the equivalent of a wetted pad) at the top of the cool tower of the Global Ecology Research Center. ROBERT MARCIAL

4.221 Discharge opening from Global Ecology Research Center cool tower is located in the lobby.

4.222 Cool towers define roof line of the Habitat Research and Development Centre.
HEIDI SPALY

4.223 Cool tower at the Springs Preserve, Las Vegas, Nevada.

4.224 Discharge of cool tower, Springs Preserve.

Further Information

Chalfoun, N. 1997. "Design and Application of Natural Down-Draft Evaporative Cooling Devices," *Proceedings 1997 Conference of ASES*. American Solar Energy Society, Boulder, CO.

Givoni, B. 1994. *Passive and Low Energy Cooling of Buildings*, Van Nostrand Reinhold, New York.

Givoni, B. 1998. *Climate Considerations in Building and Urban Design*, Van Nostrand Reinhold, New York.

Global Ecology Research Center, Stanford University. globalecology.stanford.edu/DGE/CIWDGE/CIWDGE.HTML (select "About" and "Our Green Building")

Thompson, T., N. Chalfoun and M. Yoklic. 1994. "Estimating the Thermal Performance of Natural Draft Evaporative Coolers." *Energy Conversion and Management*, vol. 35, No. 11, pp. 909–915.

U.S. Department of Energy, Office of Energy Efficiency and Renewable Energy, High Performance Buildings, Zion National Park Visitor Center. eere.buildinggreen.com/overview.cfm?projectid = 16

BEYOND SCHEMATIC DESIGN

If shown to be feasible during schematic design, architectural and technical detailing of the cool tower(s) would occur during design development. At that time the use of alternative sources of water (perhaps a cistern) or pumping energy (perhaps PV) can be solidified.

Performance of the cool tower should be verified through building commissioning and a User's Manual describing operation and maintenance prepared.

NOTES

NIGHT VENTILATION OF THERMAL MASS

NIGHT VENTILATION OF THERMAL MASS takes advantage of the heat storage properties of massive materials to maintain comfortable space temperatures. The mass materials moderate air temperature, reducing extreme swings of alternating hot and cold temperatures. During the day, when temperatures are warmer and solar radiation and internal loads act to increase interior space temperatures, the building mass absorbs and stores heat. At night, when outdoor air temperatures are cooler, outdoor air is circulated through the building. The heat that was absorbed during the day is released from the mass to the cooler air circulated through the space and then discharged outdoors. This cycle allows the mass to discharge, renewing its potential to absorb more heat the following day. During colder months the same mass may be used to help passively heat the space (see the Related Strategies sidebar entry).

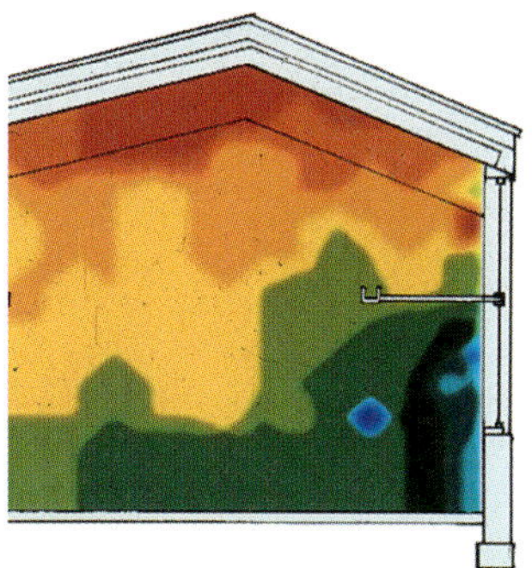

4.226 Isothermal rendering of a thermally massive partition wall.
WENDY FUJINAKA

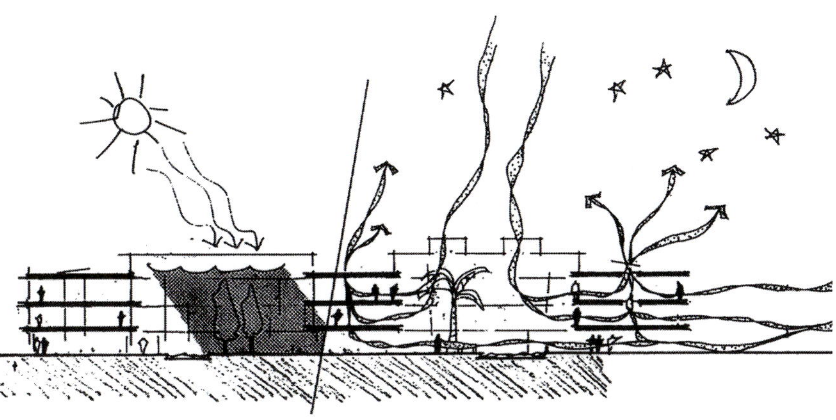

4.225 Schematic competition entry for the IBN-DLO Institute for Forestry and Nature Research in Wageningen, The Netherlands. During the day, heat is absorbed by interior mass; at night that heat is released into cool outdoor air circulated through the space.
BROOK MULLER

The success of this strategy is highly dependent upon the local climate. The diurnal temperature difference must be large (around 20 °F [11 °C]). High daytime temperatures (and/or solar loads and internal heat gains) produce cooling loads. Low night-time temperatures can provide a heat sink (a source of coolth) to mitigate these loads. The thermal mass connects these two non-coincident conditions across time.

Key Architectural Issues

Because this strategy relies upon the extensive flow of outdoor air throughout a building, the arrangement of building spaces is critical to its success—especially if natural ventilation will provide the airflow. The use of stack ventilation as the airflow driver is encouraged, since in many climates adequate night-time cross ventilation may be difficult due to the relatively low wind speeds that tend to prevail on summer nights.

INTENT
Climate control (cooling), thermal comfort

EFFECT
Passive cooling, natural ventilation, reduced energy consumption

OPTIONS
Location and type of mass, cross ventilation and/or stack ventilation, mechanically assisted ventilation

COORDINATION ISSUES
Building orientation, massing, internal spatial layout, security

RELATED STRATEGIES
Site Analysis, Cross Ventilation, Stack Ventilation, Shading Devices, Direct Gain, Indirect Gain

PREREQUISITES
Reasonable diurnal temperature swing, acceptable night-time relative humidities, ability to ventilate at night, adequate mass (spread over a large surface area)

ENVELOPE LIGHTING HEATING COOLING ENERGY PRODUCTION WATER & WASTE

The structural loads associated with mass will affect the spacing and sizing of load-bearing members (of particular concern in a multistory building). Concrete is often used to provide mass for this strategy, as well as the structural strength to overcome the added loads. Exposed structural systems are a logical means of providing thermal mass. Any material with substantial mass will work as thermal storage, however, including masonry units and water containers.

For this strategy to work effectively, the thermal mass needs to be exposed to the ventilation airflow. The surface area of exposed thermal mass is usually one to three times that of the conditioned (passively cooled) floor area—which will clearly have a large impact upon the design of a building.

It is critical to reduce thermal loads as much as possible through the use of appropriate microclimate and envelope design techniques before attempting to passively cool a building.

Implementation Considerations

For effective night ventilation, the thermal mass must be thoroughly washed by a flow of outdoor air. This is a critical implementation issue.

Because the hours of heat gain (in most climates) exceed the hours of cooling potential during the summer, openings need to be large to move a lot of air in a short time period. This strategy relies upon the ability to close a building during the day, and open it up substantially at night. Security, therefore, is an issue. Adequate daytime ventilation will need to be provided (either passively or mechanically) to ensure indoor air quality during occupied hours.

Outside air is flushed through the building to provide cooling, allowing anything (such as dust, odors, or small insects) in the air to be introduced to the building. For this reason, careful consideration to the location of intake openings and ambient air quality is important. This strategy can introduce noise into a building (although this may be less of a concern at night than with daytime ventilation strategies). Attention should be paid to occupancy schedules and nearby noise sources. If necessary, openings can be located to minimize the effect of noise on occupied spaces.

Design Procedure

During schematic design, the designer needs to establish the potential of this strategy in a given site/building context, the storage capacity of the mass, and the ventilation strategy to be used to cool the mass. Adapted from guidelines in *Mechanical and Electrical Equipment for Buildings*, 11th ed., this procedure is based upon a "high" mass building—for example, a passive solar-heated, direct gain building with an exposed concrete structure. Buildings with less mass will perform differently and the designer must consider this.

SAMPLE PROBLEM

An 1800 ft^2 [167 m^2] office in Bozeman, Montana is to be constructed with lightweight, exposed concrete floors and walls with approximately 3800 ft^2 [350 m^2] of exposed surface. Average daily cooling load is estimated to be 170 Btu/ft^2 [510 Wh/m^2], based upon a 9-hour working day.

1. Determine the potential of night ventilation of thermal mass for the given location. Climates with a large diurnal swing in temperature are ideal candidates for this strategy. Applicable climate data are available from many sources for populated locales—and can be estimated for more rural/remote sites.

2. Obtain climate data and calculate the lowest possible indoor air temperature. The lowest DB temperature depends upon the highest summer design dry bulb air temperature (DBT) and the mean daily temperature range for the project site. It is calculated as:

$$\text{lowest DBT} = (\text{highest DBT} - \text{mean daily range})$$

3. Approximate the lowest mass temperature. This estimate is important because the objective is to cool the mass at night so its temperature is close to the lowest DBT. To approximate the lowest mass temperature for high daily range climates (greater than 30 °F [16.7 °C]), add 1/4 of the mean daily temperature range to the lowest DBT. For low daily range climates (less than 30 °F [16.7 °C]), add 1/5 of the mean daily range to the lowest DBT.

4. Calculate the storage capacity of the thermal mass. From Figure 4.227, use the summer design outdoor dry bulb temperature and the mean daily range of temperatures to determine the thermal mass storage capacity. Coordinated with the operational hours (open or closed mode) of daily heat gain, the thermal mass should be shown to have enough capacity to perform satisfactorily under this cooling strategy.

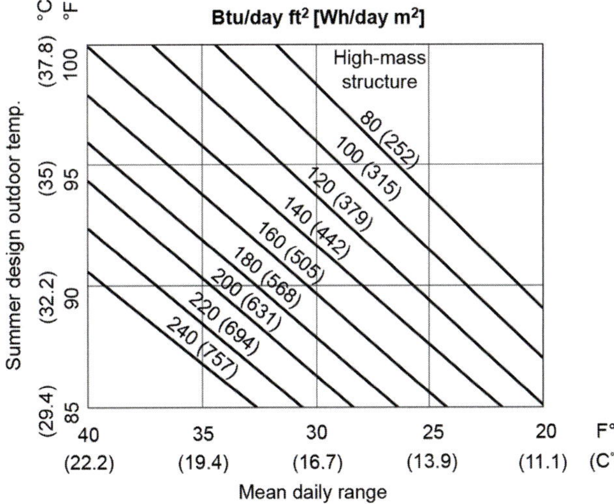

4.227 Estimated storage capacity of high thermal mass buildings. The graph assumes a mass-area to floor-area ratio of 2:1—roughly equivalent to a 3-in. thick [75 mm] concrete slab (or both sides of a 6-in. [150 mm] thick slab or wall) providing thermal storage capacity. *MECHANICAL AND ELECTRICAL EQUIPMENT FOR BUILDINGS*, 10TH ED.

5. Determine the percentage of stored heat that can be removed at night. The most heat can be removed from the mass when the Δt, the temperature difference between the mass and the outside air,

1. Climate data suggest that night ventilation of mass is possible during July and August.

2. The design summer temperature in Bozeman is 87 °F [30.6 °C], and the mean daily range is 32 °F [18 °C]. The lowest indoor air temperature that can be achieved, then, is (87 − 32) = 55 °F [12.8 °C], which would be very acceptable (at least from a cooling perspective).

3. The lowest mass temperature is estimated as per the following: (1/4)(32 °F) = 8 °F [4.4 °C], and 8 °F + 55 °F = 63 °F [17.2 °C].

4. From Figure 4.227, a building with high mass (and an 87 °F design temperature and 32 °F daily range) will absorb about 210 Btu per ft^2 per day [662 Wh per m^2 per day]. The average daily cooling load of 170 Btu/ft^2 per day [510 Wh/m^2 day] is less than this potential capacity.

5. By extrapolation within Figure 4.228 (for the defined design conditions), approximately 12% of the heat stored each day can be removed by night ventilation during the "best" cooling hour. This represents (0.12) (210 Btu/ft^2 day = 25.2 Btu/ft^2 day [79.5 Wh/m^2 day].

6. From Figure 4.229 the maximum hourly difference in temperature is about 15 °F [8.3 °C].

Refer to the Cross Ventilation strategy to determine if it is possible to remove excess heat at night using that strategy. If not, consider stack ventilation. If neither is feasible, consider mechanical circulation of ventilation air.

is the greatest. From Figure 4.228, using the mean daily range and the summer design outdoor temperature, determine the percentage of heat gains that can be removed.

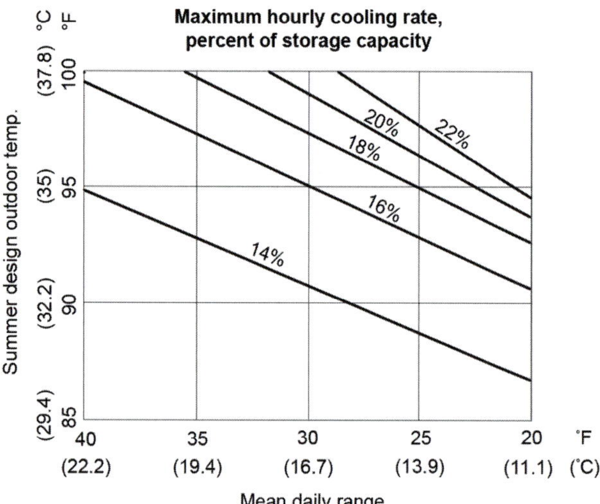

4.228 Percentage of heat gains stored in the thermal mass that can be removed during the "best" hour of night ventilation cooling. MECHANICAL AND ELECTRICAL EQUIPMENT FOR BUILDINGS, 10TH ED.

6. Determine the ventilation rate necessary to night cool the thermal mass. If the building is completely passive, refer to the Cross Ventilation or Stack Ventilation strategies to determine if ventilation openings are adequately sized to remove stored heat during the hour of maximum cooling (using the Δt from Figure 4.229). Remember that night-time average wind speeds are often much lower than daytime speeds, hindering the effectiveness of cross ventilation. Forced ventilation may be used if necessary. The required ventilation rate during the hour of maximum cooling can be estimated from the following equation:

$$Q = q/(1.1)(\Delta t)$$

where,

Q = required air flow rate, cfm [L/s]

q = sensible cooling load, Btu/h [W]

F = conversion factor, 1.1 [1.2]

Δt = temperature difference, °F [°C]

7. Night ventilation of thermal mass is considered a viable strategy for this situation—assuming that adequate airflow can be provided (either passively or mechanically).

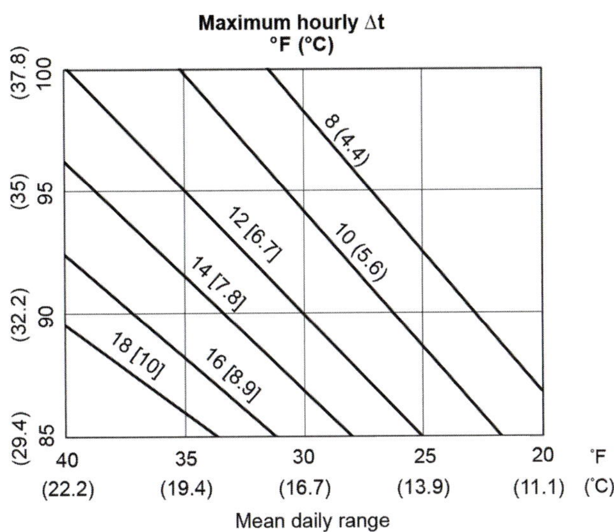

4.229 Temperature difference between interior mass and outdoor temperature for the "best" hour of night-time cooling. MECHANICAL AND ELECTRICAL EQUIPMENT FOR BUILDINGS, 10TH ED.

7. **Compare ventilation requirements with other design needs. Depending upon the ventilation strategy chosen, the inlet/outlet openings required may or may not work with other building needs. It is critical to double-check that the proposed cooling system is compatible with other building requirements (e.g., security, circulation, indoor air quality, and fire safety).**

Examples

4.230 The Emerald People's Utility District office building in Eugene, Oregon uses mass in the floor, roof/ceiling, and partition walls coupled with cross and mechanical ventilation to cool the building during the overheated season. JOHN REYNOLDS

4.231 Cored concrete slabs used as thermal storage and air circulation channels in a night ventilation system. JOHN REYNOLDS

Further Information

Brown, G.Z. and M. DeKay. 2001. *Sun, Wind & Light: Architectural Design Strategies*, 2nd ed. John Wiley & Sons, New York.

Grondzik, W. et al. 2010. *Mechanical and Electrical Equipment for Buildings*. 11th ed. John Wiley & Sons, Hoboken, NJ.

Haglund, B. "Thermal Mass In Passive Solar Buildings," a Vital Signs Resource Package. arch.ced.berkeley.edu/vitalsigns/res/downloads/rp/thermal_mass/mass-big.pdf

Kolokotroni, M. 1998. *Night Ventilation for Cooling Office Buildings*. BRE. See: products.ihs.com/cis/Doc.aspx?AuthCode=&DocNum=200687

Moore, F. 1993. *Environmental Control Systems: Heating, Cooling, Lighting*, McGraw-Hill, Inc., New York.

Santamouris, M. 2004. *Night Ventilation Strategies*, Air Infiltration and Ventilation Centre, Brussels.

BEYOND SCHEMATIC DESIGN

If night ventilation of thermal mass proves feasible during schematic design, all design decisions regarding location and quantity of mass and location and size of ventilation openings will be revisited during design development as more accurate information regarding building loads becomes available. Detailing of system elements to ensure that design intents and performance requirements are met is essential.

Initial system operation should be confirmed via building commissioning and a User's Manual detailing ongoing system operation be prepared.

EARTH COOLING TUBES

EARTH COOLING TUBES (cool tubes) are used to cool a space by bringing outdoor air into an interior space through underground pipes or tubes. The air is cooled (and possibly dehumidified) as it travels below ground. The cooling effect is dependent upon the existence of a reasonable temperature difference between the outdoor air and the soil at the depth of the tube. A cool tube can be used to temper incoming air when the soil temperature is below outdoor air temperature, or to provide actual space cooling effect if soil temperature is below the intended room temperature. A cool tube can also be used to temper outdoor air in the winter, but it will not provide any space heating effect.

4.233 Installation of earth cooling tubes for a residential application. TANG LEE

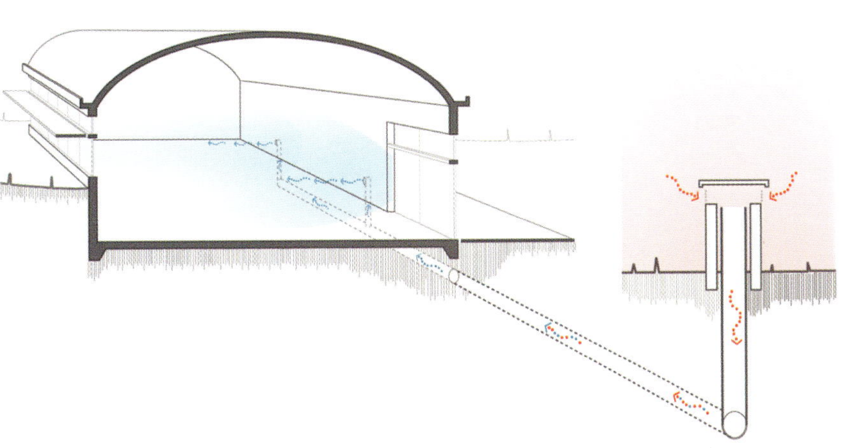

4.232 Schematic diagram showing an open loop cooling tube configuration, assisted by stack effect ventilation. The length of the cooling tube is greatly understated in this sketch. JON THWAITES

INTENT
Climate control (cooling), tempering of outdoor air

EFFECT
Passive cooling, tempering (cooling/warming) of outdoor air

OPTIONS
Closed-loop or open-loop configuration

COORDINATION ISSUES
Site planning, soil conditions, cooling loads, spatial layout (including partitions), indoor air quality

RELATED STRATEGIES
Site Analysis, Stack Ventilation, Cross Ventilation, Night Ventilation of Mass

PREREQUISITES
Estimated cooling loads, monthly climate data (temperature and relative humidity), basic soils information (type, approximate moisture content)

In an open-loop configuration outdoor air is introduced directly into an interior space (usually with the assistance of electric fans) after passing through a cool tube. In Figure 4.232 cross ventilation is used, likely in combination with a fan, to draw cool air from the earth tube into and through the interior space. The use of an electric fan makes this example a hybrid system (as opposed to a fully passive system). In a closed-loop configuration, room air is circulated through the tubes and back into the occupied spaces.

In either open- or closed-loop mode, the cooling effect of the earth tubes is commonly used to reduce overall space cooling load rather than attempting to cool a space solely with cool tubes. The cooling (or heating) contribution from a cool tube is often focused upon canceling the outdoor air (ventilation) load. Cooling a building exclusively using earth tubes is rarely cost-effective because of the large number of very long tubes required to do the job. Material and installation costs would likely be prohibitive—unless there is a mitigating factor such as easy or cheap excavation.

Key Architectural Issues

Earth cooling tubes need to be constructed from a durable, strong, corrosion-resistant, and cost-effective material such as aluminum or plastic. According to the U.S. Department of Energy (USDOE), the choice of material has little influence on thermal performance—although thermal conductivity is to be valued and thermal resistance avoided. While PVC or polypropylene tubes have been used, these materials may be more prone to bacterial growth than other materials.

The diameter of earth cooling tubes is typically between 6 and 20 in. [150–500 mm] depending upon tube length. Larger diameter tubes permit a greater airflow, but also place more of the air volume at a distance from the heat exchanging surface of the tube. The length of the tubes is a function of the required cooling capacity, tube diameter, and site factors that influence cooling performance such as:

- local soil conditions
- soil moisture
- tube depth
- other site-specific factors (such as vegetation or evaporative cooling).

To optimize cooling performance, tubes should be buried at least 6 ft [1.8 m] deep. When possible the tubes should be placed in shady locations.

According to the USDOE, the temperature of soil typically varies as follows:

- From 20 to 100 ft [6–30 m] deep, about 2–3 °F [1.1–1.7 °C] higher than the mean annual air temperature.
- Less than 10 ft [3 m] deep, soil temperatures are influenced by ambient air temperatures and vary throughout the year.
- Near the surface, soil temperatures closely correspond to air temperatures.

Implementation Considerations

Earth cooling tubes will not perform well as a source of space cooling unless the soil temperature is decidedly lower than the desired room air temperature. Tempering of outdoor air, however, simply requires that the soil temperature surrounding the earth tubes be reasonably lower (or warmer, in winter) than the outdoor air temperature. Over the course of the cooling season, the soil surrounding earth tubes will warm up from its normal temperature condition due to the transfer of heat from the tube to the soil. This tends to degrade performance over time during a cooling or warming season.

4.234 Non-perforated drainage pipes used as earth cooling tubes. TANG LEE

4.235 Inserting earth cooling tubes through a basement foundation wall. TANG LEE

4.236 Three earth cooling tubes enter a building and terminate in a header where an in-duct fan pulls air from the tubes and discharges it into a return air duct. TANG LEE

Although condensation in earth tubes is possible, substantial dehumidification of outdoor air is usually difficult and may require the use of mechanical dehumidifiers or passive desiccant systems.

A major concern with cooling tubes is that the tubes can become a breeding ground for mold, fungi, and/or bacteria. Condensation or groundwater seepage can cause water to accumulate in the tubes exacerbating the problem. If the tubes cannot be easily monitored and/or cleaned it might be wise to consider an indirect approach whereby cooling effect is transferred from "tube air" to another independent air stream prior to entry into the building. This will, however, decrease system capacity. Grilles and screens are advisable to keep insects and rodents from entering occupied spaces from the exterior through the tubes.

Design Procedure

1. Determine the summer soil temperature. The summer soil temperature at a depth of 6 ft [1.8 m] is roughly equal to the average summer dry bulb air temperature of the site. For a rough estimate of the cooling capacity of an earth tube installation calculate the average ambient temperature for the entire cooling season and use this value as an estimate for the ground temperature (T_{GROUND}) at the site.
2. Determine desired tube exiting air temperature ($T_{OUTFLOW}$). This will be the supply air temperature from the tube (which must be several degrees lower than room air temperature if the earth tube installation is handling the entire cooling load, which is not generally recommended). If the earth tube is simply precooling outdoor air then a higher exiting temperature would be acceptable. Exiting air temperature will likely be around 4 °F [2.2 °C] above the temperature of the soil surrounding the tube.
3. Determine the soil moisture characteristics. From on-site testing and observation, establish whether the soil surrounding the earth tube will normally be dry, average, or wet. Figure 4.237 is based upon average soil moisture—the cooling capacity in wet soil conditions would be approximately twice as high as for average soil; and for dry soil approximately half as great. Soil conditions play an important role in earth tube performance.
4. Estimate the cooling load to be handled by the earth tube installation. This may be the design cooling load for the building, based upon building type and size. For an air tempering installation, the earth tube load will be some portion of the full cooling load. For outdoor air tempering, simply neutralizing the outdoor air load is the objective. This load will be expressed in Btu/h [kW].
5. Use Figure 4.237 to estimate the required length of earth tube. The intersection of the $T_{OUTFLOW} - T_{GROUND}$ value (Steps 1 and 2) and the cooling load (Step 4) gives the required tube length. For wet or dry soil conditions use the adjustments noted in Step 3.

SAMPLE PROBLEM

Design an earth tube system to cool ventilation air for a 3000 ft^2 [279 m^2] office building in Michigan. The total hourly building heat gain is estimated to be 10.2 Btu/h ft^2 [32.2 W/m^2] of which 2.0 Btu/h ft^2 [6.3 W/m^2] is due to required outdoor ventilation air.

1. The average ambient air temperature during the cooling season in Michigan is estimated as 70 °F [21.1 °C], which is considered equal to T_{GROUND}.
2. The desired indoor temperature is 78 °F [25.6 °C]. Assuming that the cooling tube will be sized only to mitigate the outdoor air load, set the exiting temperature at 78 °F [25.6 °C], which is equal to $T_{OUTFLOW}$.
3. The soil on the site tests as neither damp nor dry; so the "average" soil values of Figure 4.237 are appropriate.
4. The cooling load to be handled by the earth tube is (2.0 Btu/h ft^2) (3000 ft^2) = 6000 Btu/h [(6.3)(279) = 1758 W].

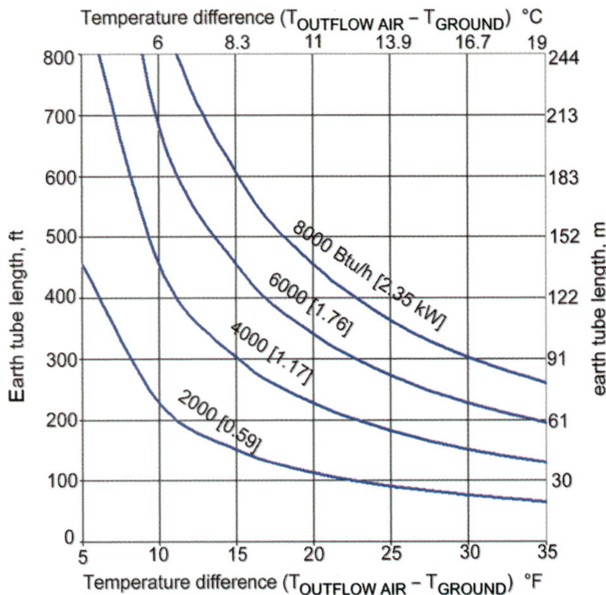

4.237 Estimating required cool tube length as a function of cooling capacity and temperature difference assuming average soil moisture content. The chart is based upon a tube diameter of 12 in. [300 mm] and a reasonably low flow rate. KATHY BEVERS ; DERIVED FROM EQUATIONS IN *MECHANICAL AND EQUIPMENT FOR BUILDINGS*, 10TH ED.

Examples

4.238 Air intake (left, under construction) as part of a driveway marker for the house in the distance, Calgary, Alberta, Canada. Air intake (right) designed as a bulletin board and bench. Note the three tubes rising out of the ground; an air filter is located behind the air intake grille. TANG LEE

5. $(T_{OUTFLOW} - T_{GROUND}) =$ (78 – 70 °F) = 8 °F [4.4 °C]. Using Figure 4.237, enter the horizontal axis at 8 and move up to the 6000 line (extrapolating ever so slightly). At this intersection, read the vertical axis value indicating about 800 ft [244 m] of tube length to accomplish the desired precooling of outdoor air.

4.239 Installation of earth tubes at the Aldo Leopold Legacy Center, Baraboo, Wisconsin. THE KUBALA WASHATKO ARCHITECTS

4.240 Post-construction photo of Aldo Leopold Legacy Center, showing ground cover typical of an earth tube field. THE KUBALA WASHATKO ARCHITECTS

4.241 Inlet to Aldo Leopold earth tube system. THE KUBALA WASHATKO ARCHITECTS

Further Information

Brown, G.Z. and M. DeKay. 2001. *Sun, Wind & Light: Architectural Design Strategies*, 2nd ed. John Wiley & Sons, New York.

Grondzik, W. et al. 2010. *Mechanical and Electrical Equipment for Buildings*. 11th ed. John Wiley & Sons, Hoboken, NJ.

Lee, T.G. 2004. "Preheating Ventilation Air Using Earth Tubes," *Proceedings of the 29th Passive Solar Conference* (Portland, OR). American Solar Energy Society, Boulder, CO.

Clean Energy Exhibition. Earth Tubes Exhibit. solar.world.org/solar/earthtubes.

BEYOND SCHEMATIC DESIGN

During design development the estimated performance of an earth cooling tube system will be verified (although there are, unfortunately, few readily available tools to do so), likely requiring the services of a thermal simulation specialist. Details regarding system components and installation would be finalized. Because of concerns about biological growth in earth tubes it would be wise to develop a User's Manual for the system that describes recommended operation and maintenance procedures.

EARTH SHELTERING

EARTH SHELTERING capitalizes upon the inherent climate control capabilities of the subterranean environment. Earth sheltering is essentially a passive implementation of the principle underlying ground source heat pumps, that is to say that deep soil provides a warmer environment in the winter and a cooler environment in the summer than the atmospheric environment above ground. Building in this environment can substantially reduce winter heat losses (although not actually heating a building) and reduce summer cooling loads (while perhaps also providing coolth). The magnitude of climate tempering provided by earth sheltering is a function of soil depth. At and beyond 6 ft [1.8 m] below grade, temperatures may vary only a few degrees throughout the course of a year. Near the surface, however, soil temperature is only slightly attenuated from air temperature. In addition to mitigating temperature extremes, soil cover can also produce substantial time lags—shifting the lowest temperatures out of mid winter and into spring and the highest temperatures out of summer and into fall.

4.243 Burying some or all of a building in order to capitalize upon stable subterranean soil temperatures. KATE BECKLEY

4.242 Section through a typical earth sheltered residential building configuration. MALCOLM WELLS

Earth sheltering improves the performance of building envelope assemblies by reducing the magnitude of conductive and convective heat losses and gains and by reducing infiltration. By providing a very stable exterior environment, building climate control becomes more energy-efficient and cost-effective—and the prospect for passive strategies is improved. Heating and cooling loads and costs may be reduced by 50% or more with effective earth sheltered design. The need for active backup climate control systems may be greatly reduced or eliminated.

Noise intrusion can be greatly reduced or eliminated by building below grade. Earth shelters are ideally suited for steeply sloped sites and the potential of small sites can be maximized by preservation of exterior space and views. Earth shelters may also reduce insurance premiums due to their ability to withstand fire and high winds.

INTENT
Climate control

EFFECT
Energy efficiency, potential for passive cooling, heat loss reduction

OPTIONS
Earth bermed or fully below-grade wall construction, earth covered or conventional roof

COORDINATION ISSUES
Orientation, ventilation, water runoff and/or catchment, air quality, daylighting, structural loads, soil conditions

RELATED STRATEGIES
Site Analysis, Cross Ventilation, Stack Ventilation, Night Ventilation of Mass, Green Roofs, Toplighting, Sidelighting, Direct Gain

PREREQUISITES
Site adequately above water table, appropriate soil conditions for excavation or berming

Key Architectural Issues

Earth sheltering can be implemented under a wide range of site situations. Underground structures may be constructed by building below grade on level sites, by "berming" or banking earth around the perimeter of a building, or by excavating into the side of a sloped site. Extensive rock at or near grade will usually restrict excavation. Perpetually moist clays can damage a structure and be prone to slides. Depending upon climate control intent and the need for other benefits (such as storm protection), the depth and extent of earth sheltering can be varied. All construction should occur above the water table to reduce the potential for leaks and structural damage via hydraulic uplift. Proper drainage design is integral to the viability of an earth shelter. Appropriate building materials and systems should be used to ensure structural strength and resistance to water damage and leaking. Reinforced concrete and/or masonry are typically utilized.

Orientation is important to the success of an earth sheltered design. With one or more walls covered with earth, daylighting and ventilation become important concerns to be addressed during schematic design. Siting an earth shelter with south-facing glazing will aid in the utilization of solar radiation for passive space heating, especially as adequate thermal mass is usually easily provided. Skylights or light pipes can be used to bring daylight into interior spaces. Natural ventilation can be utilized with an earth shelter if consideration is given to inlet/outlet location. Allowing some portion of the building structure to remain above ground makes cross ventilation more feasible. Courtyards and attached sunspaces can also provide additional ventilation opportunities. Mechanical cooling systems or package dehumidifiers are often used to assist with dehumidification in humid climates.

Implementation Considerations

The appropriate use of multiple green design strategies can improve the performance of an earth sheltered building. Each site is different (with varying resources and detriments) and each client has different project requirements. The designer must assess the appropriateness of other strategies outlined in this book in that context. Orientation, glazing ratios, thermal storage, and ventilation strategies must be considered early in the design process.

Two key questions—how much earth shelter is enough and where and how much thermal insulation to use on below-ground or bermed elements—are fundamental decisions that are not terribly amenable to rational analysis, especially in schematic design. Earth covered roofs become "green roofs" and can provide shading to reduce summer cooling loads, thermal mass to shift loads across time, and evaporative cooling potential to also reduce cooling loads.

Design Procedure

The design procedure for an earth sheltered building is as complex as the design process for any other building—but with additional considerations related to structure, waterproofing, earth cover, and insulation design. Several key areas are presented below to guide the designer through schematic design.

1. Analyze the site, considering natural drainage patterns, existing vegetation, solar access, wind flow patterns, microclimates, and subsurface conditions. Select a building location that is most amenable to meeting the project's design intents.

2. Select a structural system. Many systems (both conventional and otherwise) can be successfully used with an earth sheltered building. Poured-in-place reinforced concrete is often chosen as it provides appropriate structural capacity and a generally monolithic construction that can enhance waterproofing efforts. This does not preclude other properly engineered structural systems. Load-bearing partitions can be used to reduce structural spans. Misplaced partitions, however, can divide the floor plan into front (with access to sun and daylight) and rear (darker and cooler) zones (see Figure 4.242 for workarounds).

3. The extent of earth cover (both on the roof and along the walls) is a function of design intent coordinated with site conditions. The minimum viable depth of soil on an earth sheltered roof is in the order of 24 in. [600 mm]. This minimum depth is more for viability of vegetation than thermal effect. See the Green Roofs strategy for further information on roof plantings. In most climates a 2 ft [0.6 m] soil cover will still require the use of thermal insulation at the roof plane. Fire egress must be considered in conjunction with earth covering/berming decisions, such that earth sheltering does not preclude the provision of required exit routes.

4. Waterproofing will be addressed during design development, but site decisions (slopes, swales, elevations) should enhance the flow of water away from and around an earth sheltered building. No element of an earth shelter should act as a dam to water flow.

5. Determine what other green strategies will be included in the building. Passive heating, passive cooling, and daylighting are particularly suitable to an earth sheltered building with inherent thermal mass, reduced thermal loads, and a need for a connection to the outdoor environment.

The schematic plans and sections of an earth sheltered building will show clear provisions for water diversion, adequate egress, an appropriate orientation to support passive heating or cooling strategies, consideration of daylighting, adequate structure (12-in. [300 mm] walls, 12–24-in. [300–600 mm] roof structure depth with reasonable spans), and reasonable soil cover.

SAMPLE PROBLEM

The design of an earth sheltered building involves the design of a complete (if unconventional) building. This many-stepped and complex process cannot be captured in a sample problem.

The adjacent Design Procedure describes several key characteristics of a successful earth sheltered building that should be evident during schematic design.

Examples

4.244 Vineyards farmed with sustainable practices surround an earth sheltered building serving as a wine processing and storage facility at the Sokol Blosser Winery in Dundee, Oregon. A green roof is integral with the earth sheltering.

4.245 The earth sheltered Pinot Noir facility of Domaine Carneros Winery in Napa, California, begins to disappear into the soil of the vineyards. The roofscape also features 120 kW of building integrated photovoltaic panels to reduce the winery's annual energy consumption and carbon dioxide emissions. POWERLIGHT, INC.

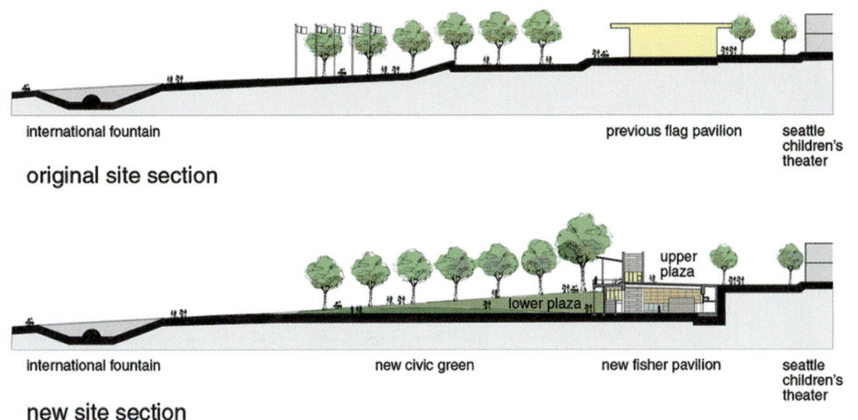

4.246 Site section showing the earth sheltered Fisher Pavilion situated within the landscape in Seattle, Washington. MILLER/HULL PARTNERSHIP

4.247 Tower plaza entry (in the foreground) to the Fisher Pavilion during construction shows the grade change to the top of the building via the stairway. MILLER/HULL PARTNERSHIP

4.248 Cradle-to-cradle earth-sheltered design. MALCOLM WELLS

Further Information

Baum, G. 1980. *Earth Shelter Handbook*, Technical Data Publications, Peoria, AZ.

Boyer, L. and W. Grondzik. 1987. *Earth Shelter Technology*, Texas A&M University Press, College Station, TX.

Carmody, J. and R. Sterling. 1983. *Underground Building Design: Commercial and Institutional Structures*, Van Nostrand Reinhold, New York.

Sokol Blosser Winery. www.sokolblosser.com/

Sterling, R., W. Farnan and J. Carmody. 1982. *Earth Sheltered Residential Design Manual*, Van Nostrand Reinhold, New York.

Underground Buildings: Architecture & Environment. www.subsurfacebuildings.com/

BEYOND SCHEMATIC DESIGN

Many key design decisions for an earth sheltered building will be made during design development—such as waterproofing details, insulation specification and detailing, structural system sizing, and the integration of mechanical systems. Much of the effort for an earth sheltered building lies beyond schematic design.

ABSORPTION CHILLERS

4.250 A single-stage, direct-fired absorption chiller. TRANE

ABSORPTION CHILLERS, while an active design solution, can have a fairly low environmental impact when compared with other refrigeration devices. Absorption chillers produce a refrigeration effect through use of a heat source, as opposed to the more commonly encountered compressor-driven machines that use electric motors and consume electricity. Absorption chillers consume substantially less electricity than a vapor compression chiller, and they do not require chlorofluorocarbon (CFC) or hydrochlorofluorocarbon (HCFC) refrigerants. Absorption chillers are best-suited to situations where there is a plentiful, low-cost heat source (such as waste heat or perhaps solar thermal), and mesh nicely with other green design strategies, such as hot water heated by industrial-process waste heat or a fuel cell.

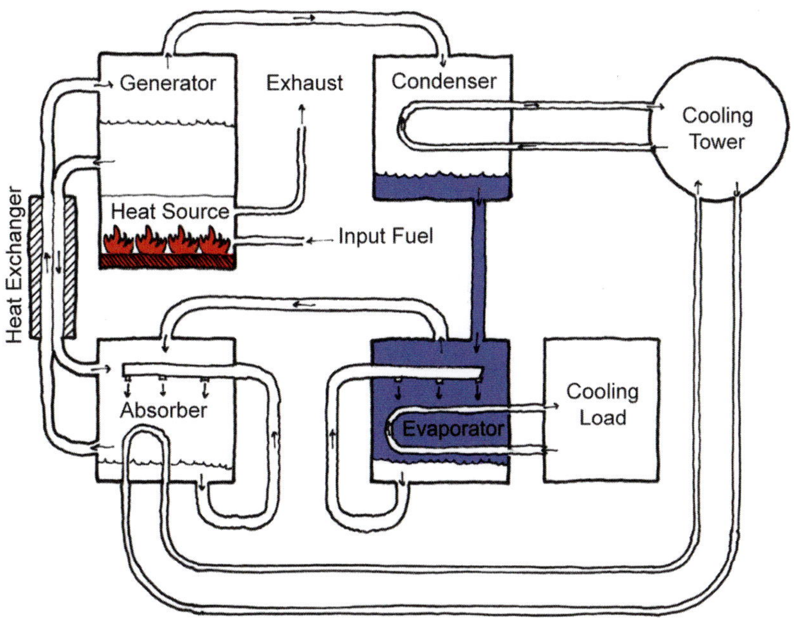

4.249 Schematic diagram of the absorption refrigeration cycle. NICHOLAS RAJKOVICH

There are two general types of absorption chillers. "Indirect-fired" chillers use steam, hot water, or hot gas as energy input. "Direct-fired" chillers utilize a dedicated combustion-based heat source. Both types work via the absorption cycle, whereby a refrigerant (typically lithium bromide and water) absorbs and discharges heat as it changes state. Water flows through a four-stage process of evaporation, condensation, evaporation, absorption—moving heat as an integral part of the process. The lithium bromide undergoes a two-stage process of dilution and concentration—attracting or releasing water at various locations in the loop.

An absorption machine consists of four interconnected chambers. In the generator chamber, heat is used to evaporate water from the lithium bromide/water solution. The concentrated lithium bromide is transferred to the absorber chamber, while the freed water vapor is condensed in the condenser chamber. The liquid water flows to the evaporator chamber to continue the cycle. In the evaporator

INTENT
Active cooling, energy cost savings, beneficial use of waste heat

EFFECT
Refrigeration

OPTIONS
Indirect-fired or direct-fired

COORDINATION ISSUES
Active heating and cooling systems, HVAC sizing

RELATED STRATEGIES
Combined Heat and Power Systems, Active Solar Thermal Systems

PREREQUISITES
Basic information on utility availability and rates, preliminary floor plans, information on process loads (if applicable)

chamber, water again changes state as it draws heat from chilled water circulating through the chamber. The resulting water vapor passes into the absorber chamber, where it is attracted by the lithium bromide solution. The vapor pressure in the chamber is reduced by the absorption of water, allowing more water vapor to evaporate as it is chemically attracted to the absorber chamber. The process continues as water and lithium bromide loop through the system.

Using a free (or low-cost) heat source, and with fewer moving parts to maintain, absorption chillers are more cost-effective than mechanical/electrical compressor-driven systems. Their overall coefficient of performance (COP) can be as low as 0.7 (versus 3.0 and higher for a vapor-compression machine), however, and they generate nearly twice as much waste heat as compressive refrigeration machines. This affects overall energy consumption and cooling tower sizing: for each unit of refrigeration, an absorption system must reject around 2.5 units of heat versus approximately 1.3 units for a vapor compression machine.

Key Architectural Issues

Spatial organization relative to required floor area, the structural grid, cooling tower location, and maintenance and access are of key concern when selecting mechanical systems. Chiller(s) and cooling tower(s) can be separated by substantial distance as necessitated by site/building conditions.

Absorption chillers can provide between 200 and 1000 tons [703–3517 kW] of cooling capacity. During schematic design, chiller footprint is a primary architectural design consideration. See Figure 4.251 for mechanical (chiller) room sizing information.

The cooling towers used with absorption chillers tend to be larger than those used with comparable capacity vapor-compression systems. External space for the cooling towers must be considered during schematic design. An on-site water source, such as a lake or well, can be used as a heat sink instead of a cooling tower—if available and permitted by local regulations.

Implementation Considerations

Using an absorption chiller instead of a vapor-compression chiller should be considered if one or more of the following conditions applies:

- the building or facility uses a combined heat and power (CHP) unit and cannot use all of the heat generated;
- waste heat (from a process of some sort) is available;
- low-cost combustion fuel (typically natural gas) is available;
- low boiler efficiency is projected due to a poor load factor (and this could be improved by adding thermal load);
- the project site has electrical load limit restrictions;

- the project team has concerns about the use of conventional refrigerants;
- noise and vibration from a vapor-compression chiller are likely to be objectionable.

Depending upon the size of the chiller, good practice recommends allowing 40–60 in. [1.0–1.5 m] of space around a chiller for maintenance. Chiller room temperature should not drop below 35 °F [2 °C]. Direct-fired chillers require a supply of combustion air. In general 12 ft^3 [0.4 m^3] of air is needed for every 1000 Btu [0.29 kWh] of heat consumed. It is wise to leave space for additional chillers, which may be required as a building expands or new building loads come online.

Design Procedure

The procedure for selecting an absorption chiller is complex and beyond the scope of schematic design efforts. Building cooling load, however, can be estimated early in the design process, allowing for a reasonable estimate of space requirements.

1. Establish conditioned (cooled) area of building under design.
2. Estimate cooling load using Table 4.15.
3. Obtain approximate chiller space requirements from Figure 4.251.
4. Integrate these space requirements into development of building floor plans and sections, considering appropriate locations for the mechanical room relative to building loads, adjacent spaces, maintenance access, and access for future equipment replacement.

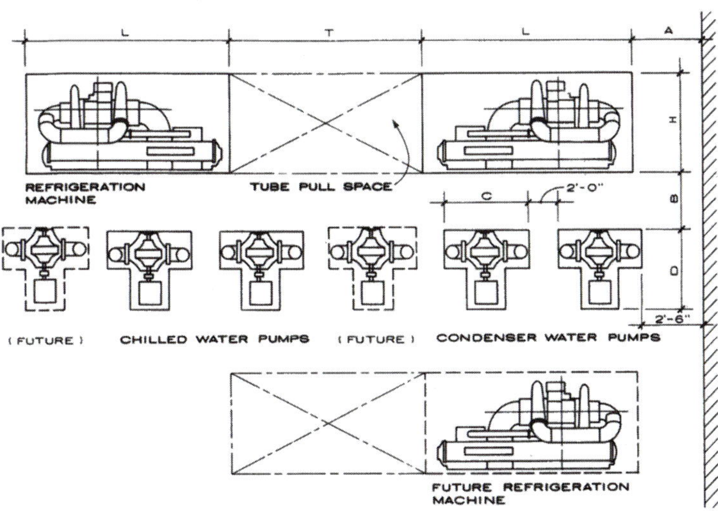

REFRIGERATION EQUIPMENT ROOM SPACE REQUIREMENTS

L = 18 - 30 ft [5.6 - 9 m]	A, B = 3.6 ft [1 m]
T = 18 - 29 ft [5.6 8.9 m]	C = 4.6 7 ft [1.4 - 2 m]
W = 9 - 11 ft [2.7 - 3.4 m]	D = 4 - 6 ft [1.2 - 1.8 m]
H approx.= 14 ft [4.3 m]	Minimum room height: approx. 17 ft [5 m]

4.251 Mechanical (chiller) room sizing requirements. *ARCHITECTURAL GRAPHIC STANDARDS*, 10TH ED. DATA SUMMARIZED BY AUTHORS

SAMPLE PROBLEM

Estimate the floor area requirements for absorption chillers to serve a 50,000 ft^2 [4650 m^2] office building in a hot, humid climate.

1. The building area is given as 50,000 ft^2 [4650 m^2]. Conservatively assume all of this area is cooled.
2. The estimated cooling load is (50,0000 ft^2/350 ft^2/ton) = 145 tons [500 kW]. This estimate assumes this to be a "medium" office and further assumes that a load value near the lower end of the range in Table 4.15 is appropriate considering the climate conditions.
3. From Figure 4.251, it is estimated that a 150-ton absorption chiller will require about (20 + 20 + 4) (10 + 4 + 4) = 790 ft^2 [74 m^2] of floor area (including access and tube pull space). This estimate is based upon length and width values near the lower end of the dimension ranges—as this is a small capacity chiller. In addition, space for pumps and accessories (roughly the same area as for the chiller) must be allocated along with an exterior location for a cooling tower.
4. An appropriate location for the main mechanical (chiller) room will be selected.

TABLE 4.15 Cooling load estimates by building type. ADAPTED FROM *GUIDELINE: ABSORPTION CHILLERS*, SOUTHERN CALIFORNIA GAS, NEW BUILDINGS INSTITUTE.

BUILDING TYPE	COOLING CAPACITY ft^2 per ton	COOLING CAPACITY m^2 per kw
Medium office	340–490	9–13
Large office	280–390	7–10
Hospital	520–710	14–19
Hotel	350–490	9–13
Outpatient clinic	440–545	12–14
Secondary school	240–555	6–15
Large retail	420–1000	11–26

Examples

4.252 One of six two-stage, direct-fired absorption chillers located in a mechanical room with high bays near the top of Four Times Square in New York, New York. TRANE

Further Information

Allen, E. and J. Iano. 2006. *The Architect's Studio Companion*, 4th ed. John Wiley & Sons, Hoboken, NJ.

ASHRAE 2010. *ASHRAE Handbook—Refrigeration*, American Society of Heating, Refrigerating and Air-Conditioning Engineers, Atlanta, GA.

CIBSE 2008. *Refrigeration*, The Chartered Institution of Building Services Engineers, London.

Pressman, A. ed. 2007. *Ramsey/Sleeper: Architectural Graphic Standards*, 11th ed. John Wiley & Sons, New York.

Southern California Gas Co. 1998. *Guideline: Absorption Chillers*. www.stanford.edu/group/narratives/classes/08-09/CEE215/ReferenceLibrary/Chillers/AbsorptionChillerGuideline.pdf

USDOE. 2003. *Energy Matters Newsletter* (How Does It Work? Absorption Chillers, Fall 2003). U.S. Department of Energy, Washington, DC. www.nrel.gov/docs/fy04osti/34705.pdf

BEYOND SCHEMATIC DESIGN

The selection of a chiller and its integration into an HVAC system requires the expertise of a mechanical engineer. Much of the detailed effort in this regard will occur during design development—but that work will follow upon decisions made during schematic design. Commissioning of refrigeration systems is highly recommended.

NOTES

STRATEGIES

ENERGY PRODUCTION

Consideration of on-site energy production should begin with a review of proposed energy-efficiency strategies. Every effort should first be made to reduce demand. Reducing demand reduces the size of an on-site generation system and/or permits a system of a given size to offset a greater percentage of building energy load. At a recent net-zero-energy conference it was repeatedly emphasized that a high-performance building is all about reduced loads.

Given an efficient building, on-site energy production can further reduce environmental impacts. Selecting the best strategy for on-site generation involves consideration of factors such as type and location of the project, macro- and microclimates, utility rates, and possible tax and financial incentives for clean and/or renewable energy.

Cogeneration, also known as combined heat and power (CHP), is the production of electricity and useful heat in a single process. To be cost-effective, a CHP facility must have a significant heat load. Cogeneration is common in many industrial facilities. At the individual building scale, it is best suited to projects such as restaurants, retirement homes, hotels, large condominium projects, swimming pools, and office buildings with absorption cooling or dehumidification systems.

The cost of electricity generated from wind power has fallen considerably and rivals that of fossil fuel generation. The intermittency of wind resources means that battery storage or a utility grid connection with net metering is necessary to assure continuous power at an individual building site.

At the individual building scale, the most common on-site electrical production method has been photovoltaics. Photovoltaics may be building integrated—replacing traditional building materials in curtain wall, skylight, or roofing systems. Because photovoltaics generate electricity only during daylight hours, battery storage or a utility grid connection with net metering is necessary to assure continuous power. Photovoltaics are attractive at the building scale because they are silent, relatively easily installed, and can be either hidden from view on the roof or prominently featured, depending upon the desires of the building owner and designer.

Fuel cells, while holding considerable promise, are not readily applicable for residential or small commercial buildings at the present time. They are most appropriate for large projects where high-quality, uninterruptable power is required.

Whatever type of on-site generation is selected, it will be most effective when integrated with energy-efficiency strategies. A dual-focus approach will lead to the greatest reduction in environmental impact. Put simply, it's usually a lot cheaper to save energy than to generate it.

NOTES

PLUG LOADS represent the electrical consumption potential of all the appliances and smaller (not hardwired) equipment in a building. They account for a fair percentage of the total energy needs of many building types (see Figure 4.253). Plug loads are an important green design consideration for several reasons: (1) their inherent impact on building energy consumption, (2) their secondary impact on building cooling loads, and (3) the fact that these loads are amenable to being met by reasonably small on-site power generating systems (such as PV, wind, microhydro, or fuel cells).

Because plug loads are by their very nature portable and easily changeable—and also often the result of occupant decisions and preferences (even in non-residential buildings)—they are often established not by the design team but rather by the building owner and users (after occupancy commences). Evaluation of projected plug loads, however, is absolutely necessary to size an on-site electrical generation system. In addition, greening of plug loads should be part of the design process for every building.

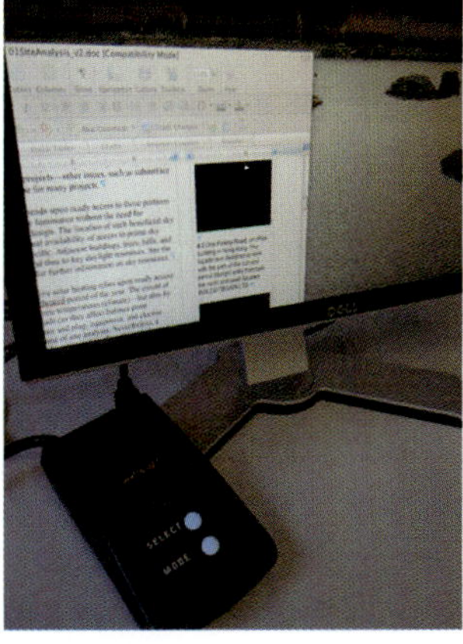

4.254 A Watt meter tracking desktop computer monitor energy use—in this case 32 watts in active mode.

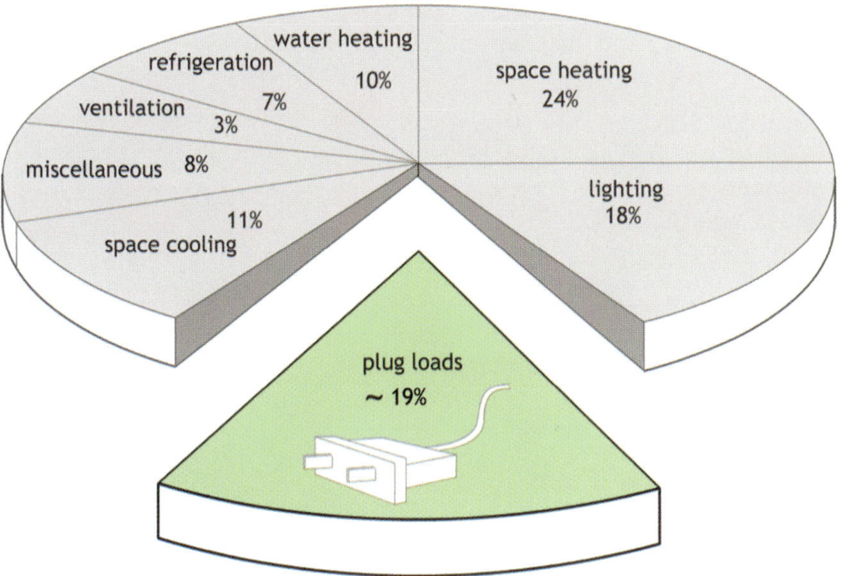

4.253 Contribution of plug loads to overall building energy usage. JON THWAITES adapted from U.S. Department of Energy, *Buildings Energy Databook*

Each watt of plug load contributes a watt [3.41 Btu/h] of cooling load that will need to be removed by an active or passive cooling system. In a passively cooled building, plug loads add to what (in many building types and climates) is an already difficult job of matching available natural cooling resources to building cooling demands. In an actively cooled building, plug loads increase system size and energy consumption. Potential plug load (what could be connected) is less of a concern than actual plug load (what is actually being used and for how long).

In most non-residential buildings, plug loads will be a contributor to peak building electrical demands and resulting demand charges.

INTENT
Energy efficiency

EFFECT
Reduced electricity consumption, reduced electrical demand, reduced cooling loads

OPTIONS
Efficient equipment, alternative equipment, demand control

COORDINATION ISSUES
Building function, client preferences, occupancy schedules

RELATED STRATEGIES
Cooling strategies, energy production strategies, electric lighting

PREREQUISITES
A clear picture of building function and usage

Where demand charges are a major component of the monthly electric bill, aggressive demand control strategies are often undertaken to reduce peak demands and their effects on overall electric bills. Such control strategies typically involve the automatic shedding of unnecessary loads.

Key Architectural Issues

Plug loads have little direct effect on the architectural design of a building—electrical wiring is easily coordinated and concealed. The energy demands resulting from plug loads, however, will affect building energy efficiency and consumption, the sizing of cooling systems, and the sizing of on-site power generation systems. The greater the plug loads, the larger the supporting electrical system must be.

Implementation Considerations

The design of on-site power and passive and active cooling systems demands that the nature of plug loads be accurately estimated during schematic design. The direction of design should be toward green (energy-efficient) management of plug loads.

Incorporating programmable timers into selected equipment/appliance circuits can help shift some electrical load to non-peak hours, likely lowering heat gains and demand charges (a bulk ice maker working at night rather than at noon is an example).

Many items of electrical equipment such as televisions, stereos, computers, and kitchen appliances have "phantom loads"—such appliances continue to draw a small amount of power even when they are switched off. Phantom loads will increase an appliance's energy consumption by a few watt-hours above what might otherwise be expected and can collectively account for a lot of "wasted" energy.

Design Procedure

The following procedure represents a general approach toward greening plug loads for a building.

1. Develop a list of equipment/appliances likely to be used in the building and determine their respective wattages. Wattage information may come from the nameplate of a specific appliance or from a generic reference (such as Table 4.16).
2. Estimate the number of hours each unit will be used during the course of a typical day.
3. For those devices that are not in continuous use, estimate the dormant or sleep mode power draw and the number of hours per day that the equipment/appliance would operate in that condition.
4. Estimate the total power consumption of plug loads by multiplying the operating wattage of each item (Step 1) by the number of

SAMPLE PROBLEM

A small writer's retreat (cabin) near Gulf Hammock, Florida will be powered solely by on-site generation of electricity.

1. The appliances expected to be in the cabin include: clock radio, coffee maker, clothes washer, clothes dryer, computer and monitor, ink jet printer, fax machine, microwave oven, stereo, refrigerator, and small water heater. (Apparently, it's a nice cabin.)
2. Operating hours for each appliance are estimated using best judgment (see Step 4). For some appliances, the operating hours are

hours of operation (Step 2). Also include the estimated dormant power consumption (as described in Step 3). For equipment where wattage is not readily available:

a. Find the voltage (*V*) and amperage (*A*) of the equipment. This information can usually be obtained from a manufacturer or from online resources.
b. Calculate the watts (*W*) of power draw by:

$$W = V \times A \text{ (for single phase loads)}$$

5. Sort the plug loads in decreasing order of magnitude of daily energy consumption. For the most energy-consuming equipment, investigate energy-efficient options (Energy Star equipment, alternative equipment that can provide equivalent service, etc.).
6. Prepare a list of recommended equipment/appliance options for consideration by the client/owner. Include a cost–benefit analysis that demonstrates the effect of inefficient equipment on energy bills, cooling system capacity and cost, and life-cycle costs. Such an analysis can be easily adapted as a template for use on future projects.

TABLE 4.16 Typical wattages of various appliances. ADAPTED FROM THE U.S. DEPARTMENT OF ENERGY, ENERGY EFFICIENCY AND RENEWABLE ENERGY

APPLIANCE	WATTAGE
Aquarium	50–1210
Clock radio	10
Coffee maker	900–1200
Clothes washer	350–500
Clothes dryer	1800–5000
Computer (personal)	CPU: awake, 120; asleep 30 or less
Computer monitor	30–150
Computer (laptop)	50
Dishwasher	1200–2400
Dehumidifier	785
Drinking fountain	500–800
Fax machine	60
Fans (ceiling)	65–175
Heater (portable)	750–1500
Microwave oven	1000–1800
Photocopiers	200–1800 during photocopying
Printers	10–20
Stereo	70–400
Refrigerator (frost-free, 16 ft^3 [0.45 m^3])	725
Vending machine refrigerated	3500
Water heater (40 gal [150 L])	4500–5500

based upon estimated full-load hours per 24-hour day.

3. Dormant mode use is also estimated (see Step 4).
4. Power consumption is estimated as follows, using values from Table 4.16:

   Clock: (10 W)(24 h) = 240 Wh

   Coffee maker: (1000 W) (2 h) = 2000 Wh

   Washer: (400 W)(0.5 h) = 200 Wh

   Dryer: (2200 W)(0.5 h) = 1100 Wh

   Computer: (120 W)(9 h) = 1080 Wh (active use)

   Computer: (30 W)(15 h) = 450 Wh (standby)

   Monitor: (35 W)(24 h) = 840 Wh

   Printer: (20 W)(9 h) = 180 Wh

   Fax: (60 W)(24 h) = 1440 Wh

   Microwave: (1400 W)(1 h) = 1400 Wh

   Stereo: (100 W)(10 h) = 1000 Wh

   Refrigerator: (725 W)(6 h) = 4350 Wh

   Water heater: (5000 W) (4 h) = 20,000 Wh.

5. The three largest power consumers are the water heater, the refrigerator, and the coffee maker.
6. The owner will be advised to upgrade these to more energy-efficient devices—in particular, a solar hot water heater is recommended. The fax machine consumption will be investigated to see if a "sleep" mode load has been overlooked. A broader discussion about the need for all these appliances will take place.

Further Information

Oxford Brookes University, Electronic Appliances & Energy Labels. www.brookes.ac.uk/eie/ecolabels.htm#3

Suozzo, M. et al. 2000. *Guide to Energy-Efficient Commercial Equipment*. 2nd ed. American Council for an Energy-Efficient Economy, Washington, DC. Now available in an online version (dated 2004) at: www.aceee.org/ogeece/ch1_index.htm

U.S. Department of Energy 2005. *Buildings Energy Databook*, U.S. Department of Energy, Office of Energy Efficiency and Renewable Energy, Washington, DC. buildingsdatabook.eren.doe.gov/.

U.S. Environmental Protection Agency, Energy Star program. www.energystar.gov/

BEYOND SCHEMATIC DESIGN

Implementation of plug load mitigation strategies will occur beyond schematic design—during building occupancy in many cases. A means of transferring thinking about plug loads from schematic design to occupancy must be developed by the design team. Educating building operators and occupants about ongoing management of plug loads is also critical.

AIR-TO-AIR HEAT EXCHANGERS

AIR-TO-AIR HEAT EXCHANGERS are mechanical devices designed to effectively transfer heat from one airflow stream to another. The prototypical application is an air-to-air heat exchanger that transfers heat (or coolth) from exhaust air to incoming outdoor air, reducing the significant waste of energy normally inherent in the process of providing ventilation air to a building (for control of indoor air quality). The resulting increase in process efficiency translates to energy savings and often to reduced heating and cooling equipment sizes since loads are reduced.

Photograph of air-to-air heat exchanger installed in a high-performance residence.

In residential and light commercial applications, an air-to-air heat exchanger may be packaged with a fan as a unitary product. For larger applications, there are numerous air-to-air heat exchanger configurations that provide flexibility for HVAC system design efforts and for locating building air intakes and exhausts.

4.256 Energy recovery ventilator works as an integral part of the total building HVAC system.
NICHOLAS RAJKOVICH

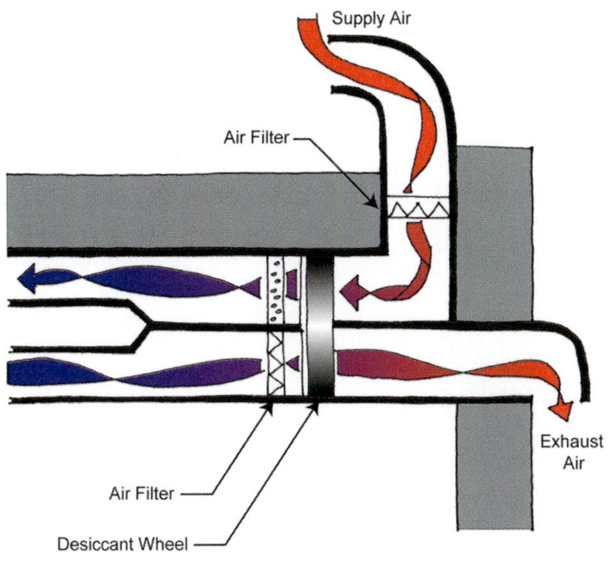

4.255 Typical arrangement of heat exchanger and ductwork for a commercial building.
NICHOLAS RAJKOVICH

INTENT
Energy efficiency, indoor air quality

EFFECT
Reduced energy use for active ventilation

OPTIONS
Sensible versus sensible and latent exchange, various heat exchanger types and configurations

COORDINATION ISSUES
HVAC system type, exhaust and intake locations, ductwork design

RELATED STRATEGIES
Energy Recovery Systems

PREREQUISITES
Preliminary floor plans, a general estimate of minimum required outdoor airflow, preliminary heating/cooling loads

Two types of air-to-air heat exchangers manufactured specifically for residential and small commercial applications are the heat recovery ventilator (HRV) and the energy recovery ventilator (ERV). An HRV exchanges only sensible heat, while an ERV transfers both heat and moisture (sensible and latent heat). An HRV or ERV unit typically includes a fan for air circulation and a filter to remove contaminants from incoming air. Manufacturers offer an array of additional options such as automatic defrosting (a critical feature in cold climates) and moisture control for HRVs.

Air-to-air heat exchange devices and systems for larger buildings cover a range of types and include packaged devices as well as custom built-up installations of components. The following discussion highlights key points regarding the most common types of air-to-air heat exchangers.

Plate heat exchangers (Figure 4.258): Numerous channels for intake and exhaust air are separated by heat-conducting plates that allow for sensible heat transfer. A plate heat exchanger with a permeable separation medium can transfer moisture as well as heat.

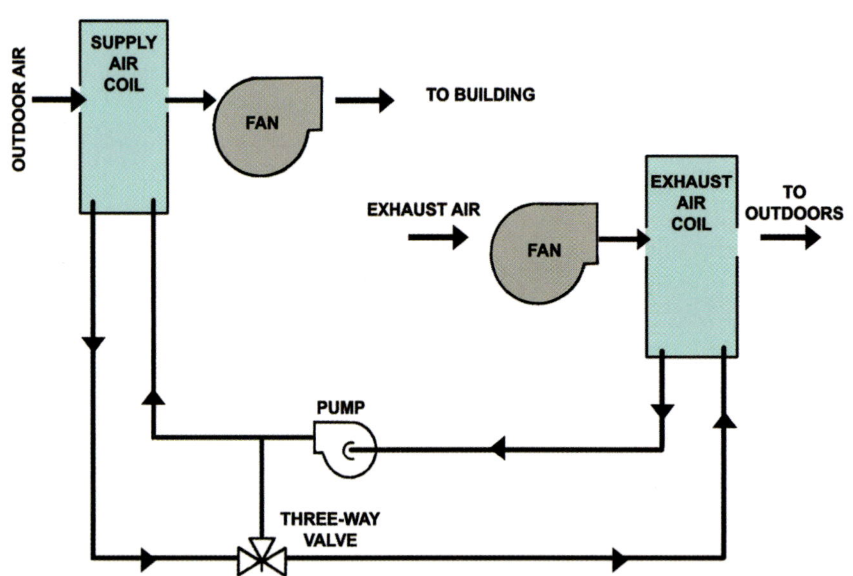

4.257 Runaround coil (or runaround loop). ADAPTED FROM 2004 *ASHRAE HANDBOOK—HVAC SYSTEMS AND EQUIPMENT*

Rotary heat exchangers (Figure 4.259): A cylindrical wheel transfers heat from the exhaust air stream to the supply air stream as the wheel turns. This type of heat exchanger is potentially more likely than the other types to permit exhaust air contaminants into the inflow air stream. Some products, however, provide rigorous protection against cross-contamination. The heat transfer medium in an energy (latent) wheel allows for the exchange of moisture as well as heat. Latent heat wheels are more common than sensible heat wheels.

Heat pipe heat exchangers (Figure 4.260): When one end of a heat pipe grows warmer, an enclosed liquid (often a refrigerant) evaporates. The resulting change in pressure and temperature sends the vapor to the opposite end of the pipe where a cooler temperature causes it to condense on the pipe walls. Heat released by this change of state is transferred through the walls to air flowing around the pipe; the condensed refrigerant then returns to the other end of the pipe via a wick. A typical unit consists of a packaged assembly of multiple heat pipes.

Runaround coils (Figure 4.257): A closed loop connects finned-tube water coils placed in the incoming and outgoing air streams. Heat is

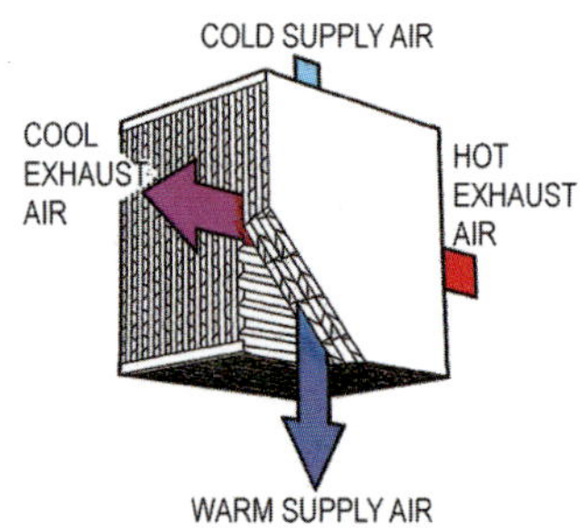

4.258 Plate heat exchanger.
ADAPTED FROM 2004 *ASHRAE HANDBOOK—HVAC SYSTEMS AND EQUIPMENT*

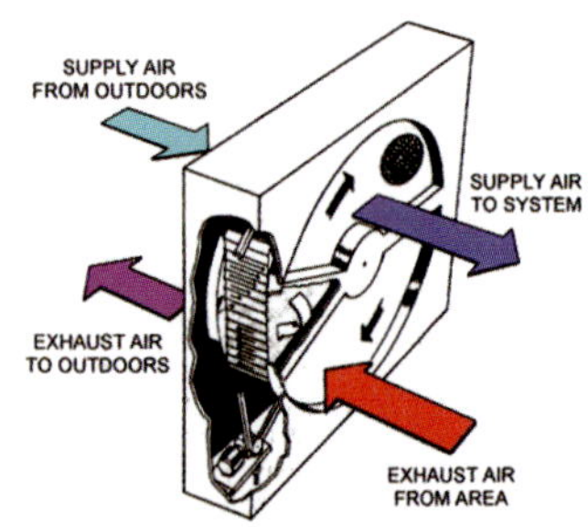

4.259 Rotary heat exchanger.
ADAPTED FROM 2004 *ASHRAE HANDBOOK—HVAC SYSTEMS AND EQUIPMENT*

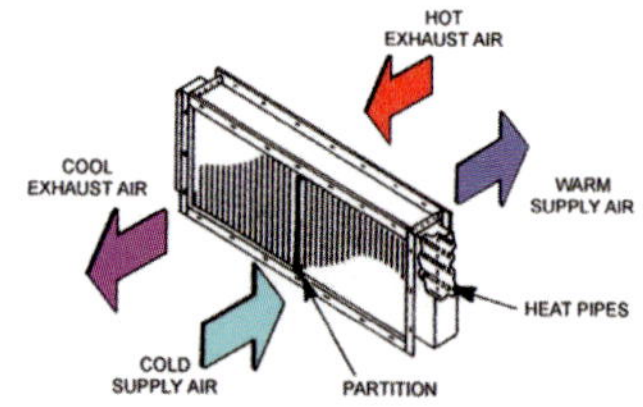

4.260 Heat pipe heat exchanger.
ADAPTED FROM 2004 *ASHRAE HANDBOOK—HVAC SYSTEMS AND EQUIPMENT*

exchanged via the heat transfer fluid in this loop, which allows the air streams to be located a good distance apart (if needed). Various techniques can be used to protect against freezing of the heat transfer fluid.

Key Architectural Issues

Equipment location and size are the two most critical architectural design concerns related to use of air-to-air heat exchangers. The basic idea in most applications is to run two air streams adjacent to each other so that connections to the heat exchanger are easy to make. Once adjacency of air streams is established, adequate space for the selected device must be provided (along with ready access for maintenance). Adjacency of exhaust and intake air streams will usually influence the location of intakes (louvers/hoods) and exhausts (louvers/hoods) on the building envelope. Since an air-to-air heat exchanger by definition taps into airflows transported within ductwork, the availability of adequate volume for co-located ducts is important.

4.261 An industrial grade energy recovery wheel designed to handle air flow volumes from 15,000 to 150,000 cfm [7080–70,785 L/s] with a total effectiveness of up to 90%. Wheel diameters range from 6 to 20 ft [1.8–6.1 m]. THERMOTECH ENTERPRISES, INC.

Implementation Considerations

Grease and lint, which may be found in some exhaust air streams, are potential fire hazards. Such airflows should not be fed directly to a heat exchanger unless appropriate filters are used. Maintenance is critical to the efficient operation of a heat exchanger. This may involve a filter change several times a year or regular manual cleaning of surfaces/components. Maintenance is particularly important as a means of lengthening the life of latent heat exchangers. Easy access to the heat exchanger unit will increase the likelihood and frequency of proper maintenance and, consequently, have a direct impact on its efficiency. Some types of heat exchangers are designed to handle a high number of air volume exchanges in environments with high contaminant levels—where standard heat wheels or permeable-plate heat exchangers cannot adequately prevent cross-contamination.

4.262 Close up of energy recovery wheel medium with a 4A desiccant coating on an aluminum substrate to provide for total enthalpy recovery. The medium has approximately 13 openings per inch [0.5 per mm] and is designed to provide laminar flow. THERMOTECH ENTERPRISES, INC.

To reduce airflow-related noise and increase energy efficiency, ductwork leading to a heat exchanger should be appropriately sized and reasonably routed (not squeezed and contorted).

For residential applications, the choice between an HRV unit and an ERV unit is determined primarily by climate and the resulting economics of cost-effectiveness. In some cold and some hot, humid climates, a heat exchanger may be required by code. If the intended site is in a mild climate where the temperature differential between indoor and outdoor air is minimal, the savings potential of an air-to-air heat exchanger may be too small to make its inclusion cost-effective.

Design Procedure

Residential

1. Estimate the minimum outdoor airflow required by the local building code, good design practice (in the absence of code requirements), and/or to offset infiltration. This airflow is very much influenced by building location (jurisdiction) and/or building design (air tightness) and is difficult to generalize. It should, however, be relatively easy to estimate this value in the context of a particular project. The airflow rate will be in cfm [L/s].
2. Refer to online product information readily provided by many manufacturers to obtain information on an appropriate unit—including capacity, physical size, and installation requirements.
3. Provide an appropriate location for the selected device, with adequate space/volume and accessibility.

Non-residential

There are many variables and equipment types involved with non-residential applications. Nevertheless, it is possible to quickly estimate minimum building outdoor airflow on the basis of prevailing code requirements and obtain rough equipment sizing and configuration information from manufacturers based upon this flow rate. Several equipment options should be reviewed such that no reasonable approach is precluded by early design decisions.

Examples

4.263 The mechanical closet for the 2005 Cal Poly San Luis Obispo entry for the USDOE Solar Decathlon competition. An energy recovery ventilator is located at the top left corner of the closet. NICHOLAS RAJKOVICH

SAMPLE PROBLEM

A new, 4-bedroom residence with 3100 ft^2 [288 m^2] of conditioned floor space is being designed for Presque Isle, Maine.

1. Per ASHRAE Standard 62.2, this type of building would have a minimum ventilation rate of around 75 cfm [35 L/s]. Using intermittent exhaust, however, an exhaust airflow of 100 cfm [47 L/s] for the kitchen and 50 cfm [24 L/s] for each bathroom would be required, for a total airflow of 200 cfm [94 L/s]. The air-to-air heat exchanger should be able to handle this volume.
2. From an online manufacturer's catalog, an ERV with dimensions of 31 × 18 × 15 in. [788 × 458 × 380 mm] with 6 in. [150 mm] round duct connections appears to meet the airflow requirements.
3. This is a fairly large house, so using two smaller ERVs may require less connecting ductwork and be easier to coordinate.

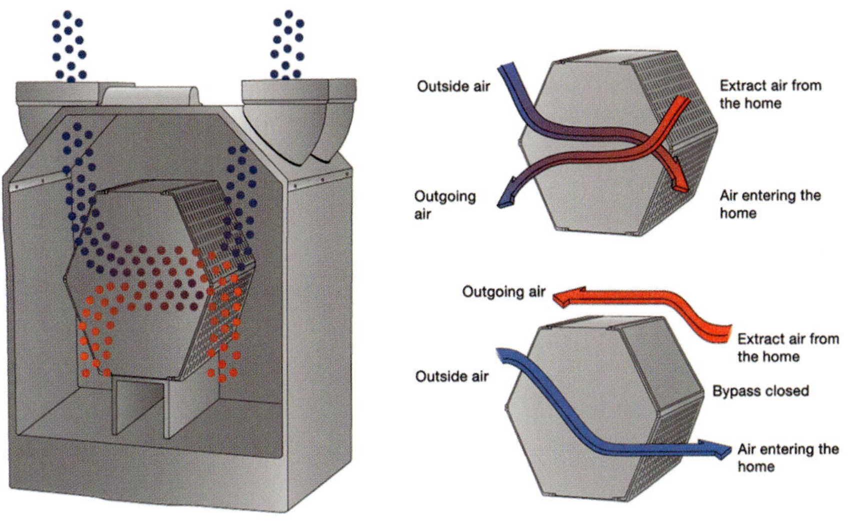

4.264 Diagram of air-to-air heat exchanger operation; these devices are commonly installed in PassivHaus projects. ZEHNDER AMERICA INC.

4.265 Photograph of air-to-air heat exchanger installed in a high-performance residence.

Further Information

ASHRAE 2010. Standard 62.2-2010: "Ventilation and Acceptable Indoor Air Quality in Low-Rise Residential Buildings, American Society of Heating, Refrigerating and Air-Conditioning Engineers, Atlanta, GA.

Dausch, M., D. Pinnix and J. Fischer. "Labs for the 21st Century: Applying 3Å Molecular Sieve Total Energy Recovery Wheels to Laboratory Environments." labs21.lbl.gov/DPM/Assets/a3_fischer.pdf

ASHRAE 2006. *ASHRAE GreenGuide*, 2nd ed. American Society of Heating, Refrigerating and Air-Conditioning Engineers, Atlanta, GA.

Stipe, M. 2003. "Demand-Controlled Ventilation: A Design Guide." Oregon Office of Energy. egov.oregon.gov/ENERGY/CONS/BUS/DCV/docs/DCVGuide.pdf

BEYOND SCHEMATIC DESIGN

Estimates of equipment sizes made during schematic design will be validated during design development. Specific equipment will be selected and connections detailed. Air-to-air heat exchangers should be commissioned (mal-performance will not be obvious) and a User's Manual prepared to assist the owner/operator with maintenance.

NOTES

ENERGY RECOVERY SYSTEMS

ENERGY RECOVERY SYSTEMS are of two basic types: general energy recovery systems (covered in this strategy) and air-to-air heat exchanger systems (covered in the previous strategy). An energy recovery system transfers sensible heat from one fluid to another fluid through an impermeable wall. In this type of system, the fluids (air and/or water) do not mix. Energy recovery systems have many applications, including industrial and production processes, and can recover heat from fluid streams as diverse as exhaust air ducts, boiler stacks, or waste water piping. An informed designer can often discover applications for harnessing waste heat using heat exchangers that are unique to a particular project.

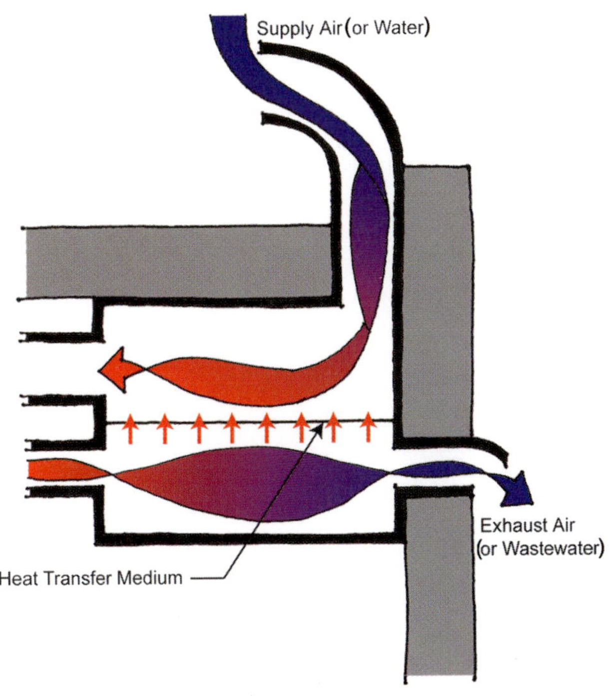

4.266 A simple counter-flow heat recovery system. NICHOLAS RAJKOVICH

An energy recovery system is an integral part of all combined heat and power (CHP) systems, in which "waste" heat from the electricity generation process is recovered for use in another application (such as heating domestic hot water, space heating, or space cooling). Opportunities for heat reclaim exist in most large building projects, not just those with CHP systems.

Key Architectural Issues

The heat exchange equipment associated with this strategy requires adequate space/volume. All energy recovery systems include a heat exchange component, one or more fans or pumps to move the fluids through the heat exchanger, and controls to manage the flow rates. The size of the heat exchanging elements is a function of the capacity and efficiency of the equipment—it is often rather large.

4.267 Air-to-water heat exchanger (above and to the rear of the oven) transfers heat from a pizza oven exhaust to a hot water supply.

INTENT
Energy efficiency

EFFECT
Reduced consumption of energy resources

OPTIONS
Various fluid streams (usually air or water) and arrangements (parallel-flow, cross-flow, counter-flow)

COORDINATION ISSUES
Active heating and cooling systems, additional space/volume requirements, air/water stream routing, intake/exhaust locations

RELATED STRATEGIES
Air-to-Air Heat Exchangers, Combined Heat and Power

PREREQUISITES
Climate data for site, estimated ventilation requirements, estimated hot water requirements, estimated building heating and cooling loads

In addition to providing adequate space for equipment, the designer must consider the location of supply and exhaust ducts and/or piping to and from equipment with recoverable heat potential—the details of which vary depending upon the building, its systems, and their configurations.

Energy recovery systems are categorized by how the fluids enter and exit the system. In a parallel-flow arrangement, the fluids enter the system at the same end and travel in parallel with one another until they exit the system. In a cross-flow arrangement, the fluids travel roughly perpendicular to one another. In a counter-flow arrangement, the fluids enter from opposite ends and flow in opposite directions. In general, the counter-flow arrangement is the most efficient (due to beneficial temperature differences throughout the heat exchanger), but often requires the largest area/volume for the heat exchanging equipment and for the navigation of ductwork/piping.

Implementation Considerations

Virtually every building discharges energy into the surrounding environment. The design question is: Can the energy embodied in the various building waste streams be economically recovered? In general, simplicity is the key to cost-effective installation of an energy recovery system. An energy simulation and life-cycle cost analysis can determine if a heat reclaim system will provide a favorable payback on investment for a proposed facility and its climate conditions. For most buildings, attempting to recover all of the energy from wastewater or exhaust air will not be worth the incremental cost to get to that level of extraction.

Design Procedure

A review of the following issues during schematic design will help to establish whether an energy recovery system is an appropriate strategy to pursue.

1. Consider demand for hot water and need for outdoor air. Energy recovery systems make economic sense in facilities that require large amounts of hot water and/or outdoor air for control of indoor air quality or process. Such facilities include laundries, restaurants, laboratories, and hospitals.
2. Evaluate available temperature differentials. Heat recovery makes economic sense in applications where there is a large temperature difference (roughly 20 °F [11 °C] or greater) between the supply and exhaust (or waste) streams.
3. Consider cleanliness of the waste/exhaust stream. Systems with relatively clean exhaust air and/or wastewater are the best candidates for an energy recovery system. Contaminants in exhaust air or wastewater can clog or damage heat exchange equipment.
4. Consider the type of heating/cooling system. Generally, it is less expensive to install centralized heat exchange equipment in a

SAMPLE PROBLEM

The adjacent design procedure is conceptual. As such, elaboration using a sample problem is not appropriate.

facility than to install numerous smaller, distributed heat exchangers. Large buildings with central heating and cooling plants, such as laboratories and medical facilities, are prime candidates for heat recovery systems.

5. Consider space requirements. Adequate space must be available for the inclusion of an energy recovery system and its equipment. Due to the wide range of potential equipment and systems, it is difficult to generalize these requirements. As a rule, a building with equipment that is not crammed into place can probably accommodate a heat recovery system. In most large buildings, the routing of fluids (air and water) to the energy recovery equipment will present more of a design challenge than the space requirements for the equipment itself.

Examples

4.268 Heat exchangers are an integral part of the energy-efficient HVAC system at Four Times Square in New York, New York. TRANE

4.269 A water-to-water heat recovery system taps into heat in the wastewater from showers at the Goodlife Fitness Club in Toronto, Canada. WATERFILM ENERGY INC.

Further Information

ASHRAE 2008. *ASHRAE Handbook—2008 Systems and Equipment*, American Society of Heating, Refrigerating and Air-Conditioning Engineers, Atlanta, GA.

ASHRAE 2006. *ASHRAE GreenGuide*, 2nd ed. American Society of Heating, Refrigerating and Air-Conditioning Engineers, Atlanta, GA.

Goldstick, R. 1983. *The Waste Heat Recovery Handbook*, Fairmont Press, Atlanta, GA.

Goldstick, R. and A. Thumann. 1986. *Principles of Waste Heat Recovery*, Fairmont Press, Atlanta, GA.

BEYOND SCHEMATIC DESIGN

Detailed design of an energy recovery system requires the expertise of a mechanical engineer. Energy simulations will typically be undertaken to ensure the selection of optimized equipment and associated control strategies. Most of this effort will occur during design development. An energy recovery system should be commissioned to ensure that it performs as intended.

PHOTOVOLTAICS are systems that produce electricity through the direct conversion of incident solar radiation. A photovoltaic (PV) cell provides direct current (DC) output. This DC output can be used directly to power DC loads, can be stored in a battery system, or can be converted (inverted) to alternating current (AC) to power AC loads or be fed into an electrical grid. Stand-alone PV systems have no grid interconnection; grid-connected systems typically use the local electrical grid both as a backup electrical supply and a place to "store" excess generation capacity.

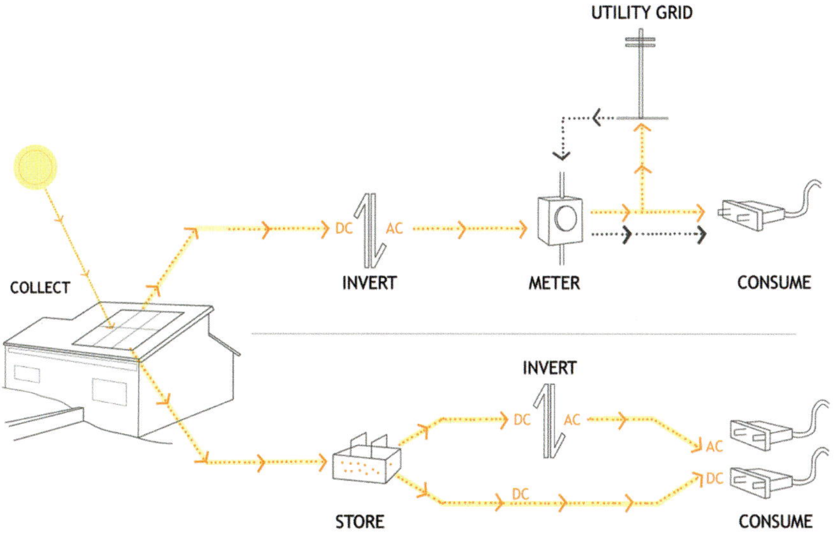

4.270 Schematic diagram of photovoltaic systems; grid-connected (top) and stand-alone (bottom). JON THWAITES

There are currently three basic types of PV modules:

1. **Mono-crystalline panels.** These PV modules often look like a series of circles assembled in a frame. This is the original PV design, typically somewhat more efficient than other panels—but also more expensive. Peak power density (based on overall module area) is typically around 11–12 W/ft^2 [118–129 W/m^2].
2. **Poly-crystalline panels.** These modules appear grainy or crystalline, the PV elements cover the entire panel, and they contain no glass (so are almost unbreakable). This design is typically a bit less efficient than mono-crystalline PVs, but peak power densities (based upon overall module area) are similar to those of mono-crystalline panels.
3. **Thin-film panels.** These modules have a more uniform surface appearance, the PV elements cover the entire panel, and they contain no glass (so are almost unbreakable). Thin-film PV panels have lower efficiencies than mono- or poly-crystalline panels, but lose less power under high temperature conditions than crystalline panels. Rigid thin-film peak power densities are in the order of 5–6 W/ft^2 [54–65 W/m^2]; flexible (bendable) thin-film power densities are around 3 W/ft^2 [32 W/m^2].

4.271 Atrium facade glazing—PV cells are laminated within a glass curtain wall.

INTENT
On-site generation of electricity

EFFECT
Reduced demand on the electrical grid, increased use of renewable energy resources

OPTIONS
Stand-alone or grid-connected system, integration with building envelope, fixed or tracking installation

COORDINATION ISSUES
PV orientation and tilt, integration with other architectural elements (shading devices, building enclosure), structural requirements, energy storage (battery system), grid system connection

RELATED STRATEGIES
Site Analysis, Wind Turbines, Microhydro Turbines, Hydrogen Fuel Cells, Combined Heat and Power, Shading Devices

PREREQUISITES
Clear design intent, a defined budget, local climate data, knowledge of site characteristics and obstructions, information on building electrical loads and usage profiles

Other notable types of PV modules include colored PVs (designers may no longer be limited to blue/black) and tubular PV modules, with a peak power density of around 7–8 W/ft^2 [75–86 W/m^2]—both opening up new opportunities for module installation.

Photovoltaic panels are generally available in capacities ranging from 5 W up to 200 W peak output. Lower wattage panels are typically 12 V, while most high-wattage panels are available only in 24-V configurations. PVs are a manufactured product, and current information about available module options is best found in manufacturers' literature. Manufacturers produce modules, which are assembled on site into arrays. Module output is established by the manufacturer; array output (system capacity) is determined by the building design team. Various module interconnection schemes can be used to vary the output voltage and/or amperage of a PV array.

4.272 Installation of lightweight, interlocking photovoltaic panels.
POWERLIGHT, INC.

Key Architectural Issues

Photovoltaic systems can be installed essentially as an add-on system with little integration with other building elements or with project aesthetics—or as building integrated photovoltaics (BIPV). A BIPV approach involves more consideration of multifunctional uses (such as PV modules used as shading devices) and/or the complete integration of PV with another technology (such as glazing or roofing products). Exciting developments (such as flexible PV panels and colored modules) suggest that greater opportunities for BIPV lie ahead.

4.273 Monocrystalline silicon roof modules (peak power output of 63 W) designed to replace composition shingles for residential buildings.
POWERLIGHT, INC.

As is the case with any alternative energy system (and as should be the case with conventional systems as well) an aggressive implementation of energy-efficiency strategies should precede consideration of a PV system. As PV is rarely cost-effectively used to heat or cool a building, such efficiency efforts will usually entail reducing building plug loads that would be served by the PV system.

A grid-connected system will require less equipment (typically no batteries, saving a fair amount of space), but requires a connection to (and dealings with) the local utility provider. Net metering is a common option with grid-connected systems. Stand-alone systems almost always involve battery storage (requiring more space) and may involve the use of DC equipment and appliances.

The tilt and orientation of PV panels will have an impact on system efficiency. PV modules should generally be oriented to the south (or nearly so) to maximize daily solar radiation reception. Deviations from south are acceptable (within reason), but will usually incur a penalty on system output—quirky daily patterns of fog or cloudiness may change this general rule. PV panels should be tilted such that the greatest PV output matches periods of greatest load (or so that PV output is optimized). Due to their high first cost, PV modules should be installed in a manner that maximizes their useful output (and increases return on investment).

4.274 PV embedded in prototype louvers on the 2007 Solar Decathlon house from Germany.

Depending upon site constraints (and proposed building design intentions), it may be advantageous to locate a PV array on the roof of a building, on the south facade, or on the ground somewhere near the building. PV location will have an impact on landscaping, the appearance of the facade/roof, and perhaps security measures necessary to prevent theft of or vandalism to the array.

PV arrays that track the sun across the sky can increase insolation (accessible solar radiation) by 35–50%, thus increasing power production of the array. The price of this improved output will be the greater expense and maintenance needs of a reasonably complex mounting system. Tracking arrays are most effective at lower latitudes, where the angle of the sun changes significantly throughout the day.

Only 10–20% of the solar radiation striking a PV module is converted to electricity; the majority of the remaining radiation is converted to heat. This heat tends to degrade the performance of a PV module—at the same time, it might have some useful application in a building. Applications where a synergy of electricity and heat production are possible should be considered.

4.275 The Natural Energy Laboratory in Hawaii integrates numerous green strategies—including a substantial PV array. FERRARO CHOI AND ASSOCIATES LTD.

Implementation Considerations

PV systems with meaningful capacities require a substantial initial investment. They will be most cost-effective where there are subsidies (tax credits, utility rebates, etc.) to minimize system first cost. Depending upon competing energy costs, it can take anywhere from 10 to 30 years to reach payback on a typical non-subsidized system. Design intent and client resources may, however, make this consideration moot. Recent studies suggest that the energy payback (about 3 to 4 years) of a typical PV system is much less than the monetary payback period.

Although PV modules are designed for exposed installations and are electronic (versus mechanical) devices, they do require some maintenance to produce design energy output over the long term. Provision for regular cleaning and access to the panels is advisable.

Design Procedure

A really rough estimate. Assuming a 4% PV module efficiency (pretty low, see below* for adjustments) the required area of PV module necessary to obtain a given output capacity can be estimated as follows:

$$A = C/3.3$$

where,
A = required area of PV module in ft^2 [divide by 10 for m^2]
C = desired PV system output in W

*divide the above-estimated area by 2 for 8% efficiency modules, by 3 for 12% efficiency, or by 4 for 16% efficiency

SAMPLE PROBLEM

Rough estimate: Starting with a general target of providing a 1-kW capacity system for a single family residence, a rough estimate of required array size (assuming 8% efficient modules) gives:

$(1000\,W/3.3)/2 = 150\,ft^2\,[14\,m^2]$.

Stand-alone system:

1. An 1800 ft^2 [167 m^2] conventional residence on

Sizing a stand-alone PV system. With a stand-alone PV system no power is transferred to or from a utility grid. The PV system generates and stores enough electricity to meet building needs. System size will depend upon electrical loads, peak generation capacity, off-peak generation, storage, and desired safety factor.

1. Estimate average daily building electricity use.

$$\text{ADEU} = \sum((\text{P})(\text{U}))$$

where,

ADEU = average daily energy use (Wh)
P = average power draw of each load to be supplied by the PV system (W)
U = average number of hours each load is used per day (h)

This estimate should consider how loads are served; any AC loads served through an inverter must be adjusted to account for the efficiency of the inverter and associated controls equipment (an overall efficiency of 75% is typically appropriate).

2. Establish required storage capacity. Based upon a sense of how many days without usable solar radiation the system should be able to span or float (a function of climate, design intent, and alternative backup generator capacity—if any). Estimate required battery storage capacity as follows:

$$\text{S} = (\text{ADEU})\,(\text{Days})$$

where,

S = storage capacity (Wh)
ADEU = average daily electricity use (Wh)
Days = desired days of storage

The number of batteries required can be estimated by converting the storage capacity in Wh to Ampere-hours by dividing by the battery (system) voltage and then dividing that value by the unit storage capacity of the intended battery type.

3. Estimate required daily PV system output. PV system output must be able to provide for the current day's electricity needs, as well as provide some extra output that can go into storage to recharge batteries. The longer the time allowed for recharge (primarily a function of weather patterns), the smaller the system capacity can be. Note where this discussion leads: In a stand-alone PV system any charging capacity (output in excess of daily needs) will be wasted capacity whenever batteries are fully charged. Note also that "rainy-day" storage capacity is above and beyond the daily storage capacity required to provide electricity during nighttime hours.

Guam is estimated to use 10,500 kWh/year, while an energy-efficient home of the same floor area would use 8000 kWh/year. This gives an average daily electricity usage of about 28 kWh (or 22 kWh for the energy-efficient option). (If this type of annual usage information is available, it is possible to bypass the load-by-load approach to estimating system capacity outlined in the design procedure.)

2. The design intent and climate data suggest that 2 days of storage is a reasonable goal. This equates to:

(28 kWh/day)(2 days) = 56 kWh (44 kWh for the efficient alternative).

Assume standard 12-V deep-cycle batteries with a capacity of 850 Ah connected in series to provide a 24-V system. Convert kWh to Ah: 56,000 Wh/24 V = 2333 Ah—or, for the more efficient residence, 44,000/24 = 1833 Ah. Thus, 2333/850 = 2.7 (say 4) batteries are needed—in a parallel/series arrangement—although the efficient building (requiring 2.2 batteries) might be able to make do with just 2 batteries.

3. The required system capacity (assuming that battery recharge can occur over a 4-day period) is:
((2 days of storage/4 days for recharge) + 1) (28 kWh) = 42 kWh—or, for the energy-efficient alternative, 33 kWh.

4. Array capacity is estimated as follows:
(28 kWh per day)/(say 5 kWh per day for a bountiful climate) = 5.6 kW peak

The required system size (capacity) can be estimated as:

$$C = ((RDS/RD) + 1)(DL)$$

where,
C = system capacity (kWh)
RDS = required days of storage—which represents the desired system float (see Step 2 above)
RD = recharge days—which represents the number of days over which storage can be charged
DL = daily load—which is the average daily PV-generated electric load

4. Determine required PV array capacity. PV production is primarily a function of available solar insolation—which varies with latitude, climate, module orientation, and module tilt. Rough estimates of annual PV production (per kW of system capacity) range from about 2000 kWh/year for very sunny, low latitude climates to 1000 kWh per year for generally cloudy, high latitude climates. This corresponds to an approximate daily production of 5.5 to 2.7 kWh—per kW of system output capacity. These values assume south-facing modules installed at a tilt equal to site latitude. The required array capacity can be estimated as follows:

$$AC = (RADC)/(ADP)$$

where,
AC = array capacity (peak kW)
RADC = required average daily capacity (kWh)
ADP = average daily production (kWh per peak kW)

5. Estimate size of array required to provide indicated capacity. For schematic design, assume a PV array area of 0.015–0.08 ft^2 [0.0014–0.007 m^2] per W of peak output. The lower values correspond to higher efficiency PV modules.

Sizing a grid-connected array. Sizing a grid-connected system is simpler than a stand-alone system, as there is no need to deal with storage devices or additional output capacity to charge storage. The utility grid provides a place to "store" excess generation capacity and a source of electricity (backup) when the on-site PV system cannot provide adequate output.

The sizing method described above (minus the storage elements) can be used to obtain a preliminary estimate of PV system size for a grid-connected system. The limiting constraints are usually budget (how much PV can be afforded) and PV mounting location space availability. As a starting point, an array that provides about 40% of a building's non-climate control electrical needs (for small to mid-sized buildings) is often reasonable. The U.S. National Renewable Energy Laboratory's *PVWatts* online system sizing program is recommended as a fast way of estimating grid-connected PV system performance.

capacity—or 4.4 kW for the efficient alternative.

5. Array size is estimated (using the lower end of the sizing range because the system capacity is fairly large) as: (5600 W) (0.1 ft^2 per W) = 560 ft^2 [52 m^2].

For the energy-efficient residence, the array size is estimated as:
(4400 W) (0.1) = 440 ft^2 [41 m^2].
The point of looking at an energy-efficient alternative in this example is to illustrate that an investment in reducing electric loads pays off in reduced need for PV capacity. In most cases, the efficiency can be obtained at much lower cost than the PV.

A life-cycle cost analysis can be used to determine the most cost-effective PV system size for any given building situation. Although this type of analysis will require computer simulations for any reasonable degree of accuracy, this is a viable schematic design activity due to the substantial architectural impact of PV modules. Required input information will include local climate data, detailed utility tariffs (including information on time of day and demand rates), a reasonable estimate of building electrical loads and usage profiles, equipment costs, and some estimate of system maintenance and repair costs.

4.276 The rooftop photovoltaic array on the Martin Luther King Jr. Student Union at the University of California Berkeley generates 59 kW during peak conditions. POWERLIGHT, INC.

TABLE 4.17 Estimated Annual Production for PV Systems*

SOUTH-FACING PV, TILT = LATITUDE	
Low solar resource:	9 [97] kWh
Moderate solar resource:	13 [140] kWh
High solar resource:	17 [183] kWh

* Assuming a grid-connected system using poly-crystalline silicon PV modules; per square foot [m^2] of PV

4.277 Photovoltaic panels incorporated into the roof form of the Ridge Winery, California. POWERLIGHT, INC.

TABLE 4.18 Approximate Derating Factors for Table 4.17 Estimates

TILT = LATITUDE	TILT = HORIZONTAL	TILT = VERTICAL
E or W facing: 0.7	Low latitude, S facing: 0.9	Low latitude, S facing: 0.55
SE or SW facing: 0.9	Mid latitude, S facing: 0.85	Mid latitude, S facing: 0.65
	High latitude, S facing: 0.78	High latitude, S facing: 0.75

4.278 Photovoltaic panels shade parking areas while producing 67 kW of electricity at the Patagonia Headquarters, Ventura, California. MILLER HULL PARTNERSHIP

Examples

4.279 Penn State's "Natural Fusion" 2009 Solar Decathlon house featured tubular PV collectors installed over a green roof. GRETCHEN MILLER

4.280 Single-axis tracking PVs over tensioned fabric panels shading a parking lot provide over 400 kW of peak capacity at The Springs Preserve in Las Vegas, Nevada.

Further Information

Capehart, B. 2010. Distributed Energy Resources (DER) in *Whole Building Design Guide*. www.wbdg.org/resources/der.php

Florida Solar Energy Center. 2007. Solar Electricity. www.fsec.ucf.edu/en/consumer/solar_electricity/index.htm

Hankins, M. 2010. *Stand-alone Solar Electric Systems*, Earthscan Publications Ltd, London.

IEA Photovoltaic Power Systems Programme. www.iea-pvps.org/

NREL. PVWatts (online PV system estimator). www.nrel.gov/rredc/pvwatts/

NREL. Solar Resource Information. www.nrel.gov/rredc/solar_resource.html

Strong, S. 2010. Building Integrated Photovoltaics (BIPV) in *Whole Building Design Guide*. www.wbdg.org/design/bipv.php

U.S. Department of Energy, National Center for Photovoltaics. www.nrel.gov/pv/ncpv.html

BEYOND SCHEMATIC DESIGN

The size of a PV system estimated for proof-of-concept during schematic design is just that—an estimate. During design development more detailed simulations and analyses will be run to confirm these early estimates and optimize the investment in PV terms of life-cycle cost. Specific PV equipment and associated controls will be selected, detailed, and specified during design development. Without question, a PV system should be commissioned to ensure that it delivers to its full potential. A User's Manual should be provided to the client.

NOTES

WIND TURBINES produce electrical energy from an ever-renewable resource—the wind. Wind energy is an indirect implementation of solar energy. The sun's radiation warms the earth's surface at different rates in different places and the various surfaces absorb and reflect radiation at different rates. This causes the air above these surfaces to warm differentially. Wind is produced as hot air rises and cooler air is drawn in to replace it. According to the American Wind Energy Association, a large wind project can produce electricity at lower cost than a new power plant using any other fuel source. Wind farms are cropping up in Europe and the U.S.

Wind turbines change the kinetic energy of the wind into electric energy in much the same way that hydroelectric generators do. A wind turbine captures wind with its blades; the rotating blades (called rotors) turn a drive shaft connected to a generator which converts the rotational movement into electricity. The wind speed determines the amount of energy available for harvest, while the turbine size determines how much of that resource is actually harvested.

A small wind electric system includes a rotor (the blades), a tail, a generator or alternator mounted on a frame, a tower, wiring, and other system components (called the balance-of-system in photovoltaic systems) including controllers, inverters, and/or batteries.

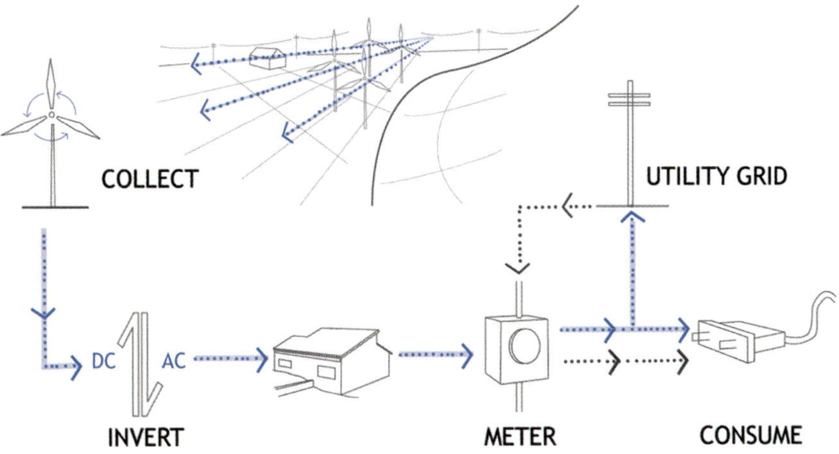

4.281 Schematic diagram showing major components of a grid-tied wind energy system. JON THWAITES

Horizontal upwind turbines, the most common type of wind machine, have two or three blades. The swept area is the area of the circle created by the turning blades, which determines the quantity of wind intercepted by the turbine. The larger the swept area, the greater the amount of power a turbine can produce. The frame of the turbine holds the rotor and generator and supports the tail, which keeps the turbine facing into the wind.

Wind turbines are rated by power output. Small turbine capacities range from 20 W to 100 kW. The smallest turbines, called "micro" turbines, range from 20 to 500 W and are commonly used to charge batteries for recreational vehicles and sailboats. Turbines of 1 to

4.282 Three wind turbines on a mid-rise mixed use building in downtown Portland, Oregon.

INTENT
On-site electricity production

EFFECT
Reduces use of electricity generated from non-renewable resources

OPTIONS
Various products, capacities ranging from small-scale residential to commercial to large-scale wind farms

COORDINATION ISSUES
Site zoning restrictions, site topography, building electrical loads and profiles, space for balance-of-system components, aesthetics

RELATED STRATEGIES
Site Analysis, Plug Loads, Photovoltaics, Hydrogen Fuel Cells

PREREQUISITES
Site zoning restrictions, site wind data, building electrical load profiles

10 kW are often used to pump water. Those ranging from 400 W to 100 kW are typically used to generate electricity for residential and small commercial applications.

A residential or homestead-sized turbine—with a rotor up to 50 ft [15 m] in diameter and a tower up to 120 ft [35 m] tall—may be used to supply electricity to a home or business. A small wind turbine can be one of the most cost-effective home-based renewable energy systems and may lower a residential electric bill by 50 to 90%.

Key Architectural Issues

The aesthetics of a wind turbine (including the height and profile) should be considered relative to its impact on the overall project. Towers are a necessary part of a wind system because wind speeds increase with height—the higher the tower the more power a turbine can produce.

The power generated by a wind turbine is a function of the cube of the wind speed, so building a higher tower can be cost-effective. For example, raising a 10-kW wind turbine from a 60-ft [18 m] tower height to a 100-ft [30 m] tower can produce 29% more power and cost just 10% more to construct.

It might be tempting to mount a turbine on a rooftop but this is not recommended. Vibrations from the turbine can cause structural problems as well as irritate building occupants and users. A rooftop turbine would also be subject to turbulence caused by the building form. The noise produced by early wind turbines was an issue in residential neighborhoods, but newer turbines produce less noise. The ambient noise level of most small turbines is about 55 decibels (dBA)—no noisier than an average refrigerator.

Implementation Considerations

According to the U.S. Department of Energy's Energy Efficiency and Renewable Energy program, a wind turbine might be reasonably considered for any location where most of the following conditions exist:

- The site has a good-to-acceptable wind resource (an average annual wind speed of at least 9 mph [4 m/s]). Many parts of the world have adequate wind resources to power a small turbine.
- The site is at least 1 acre [0.4 ha] in size.
- Local zoning ordinances allow wind turbines.
- A wind turbine could produce a sizable amount of the electricity required by the building—"sizable" is relative, but a function of design intent.
- A wind turbine represents an acceptable life-cycle investment for the client.

- The site is in a remote location that does not have ready access to the electric grid or is served by a very high-cost electric utility.

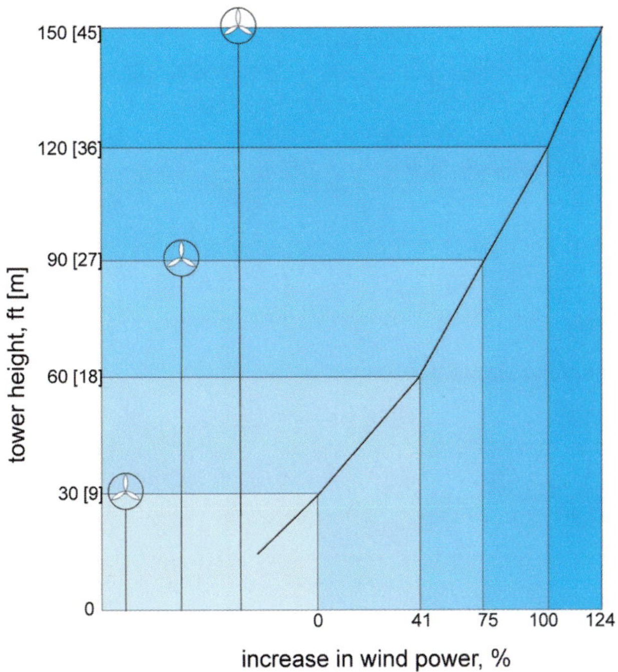

4.283 Wind speeds increase with height above the ground. KATHY BEVERS ADAPTED FROM DOE/EERE

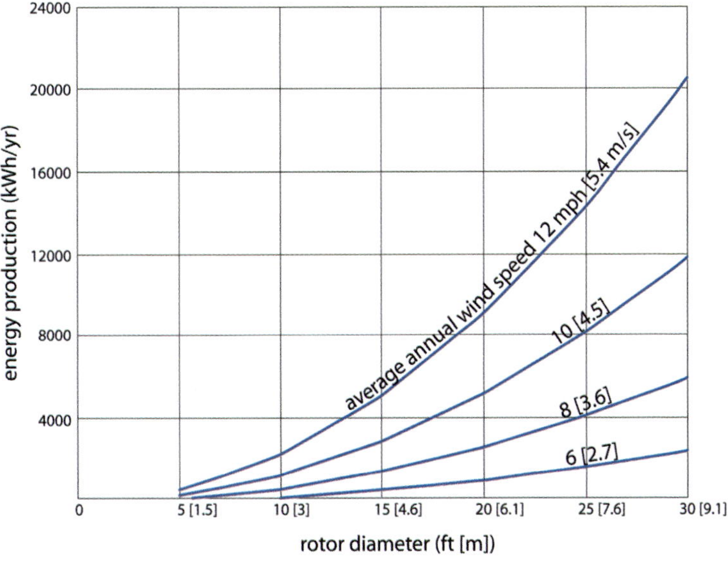

4.284 Estimated annual energy production of a horizontal axis wind machine as a function of rotor diameter and average annual wind speed (based upon the equation $AEO = 0.01328\ D^2V^3$). MATT HOGAN

A grid-connected system uses an inverter that converts the direct current (DC) produced by the wind generator to alternating current (AC) to make the system electrically compatible with the utility grid and conventional appliances. This allows power from the wind system to be used in a building or sold to the utility company as is most economically appropriate at any given time. Batteries are not normally required for a grid-connected system.

A grid-connected system is a good choice when:

- The site has an average annual wind speed of at least 10 mph [4.5 m/s].
- Utility-supplied electricity is relatively expensive.
- Connecting a wind system to the utility grid is not prohibited or overly burdened with bureaucratic roadblocks.
- There are incentives available for the sale of excess electric generation and/or for the purchase of the wind turbine.

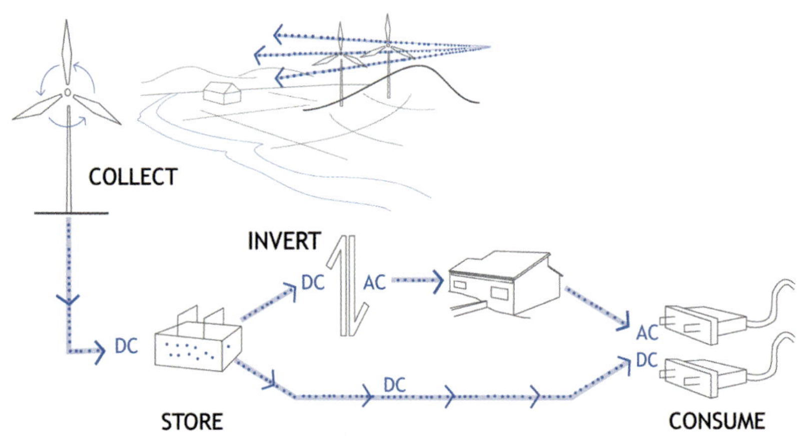

4.285 Schematic diagram of a hybrid stand-alone wind power system. JON THWAITES

4.286 Nine Canyon Wind Project in Benton County, Washington was completed in 2002. Each of the 37 wind turbines has a rating of 1300 kW, yielding a project capacity of 48 MW. ENERGY NORTHWEST, DOE/NREL

4.287 Utility scale wind turbine in Boone, North Carolina—the precursor of wind machines now appearing on wind farms.

A stand-alone system is not connected to the utility grid. This type of system can provide power in remote locations where access to power lines is difficult or very expensive. With no utility backup, this system configuration requires batteries to store energy that can be used when there is no wind. A charge controller keeps the batteries from overcharging. An inverter is required to convert DC output to alternating current (AC)—unless all loads (including appliances) are DC. DC versions of most residential appliance are, in fact, readily available.

A hybrid system combines wind and photovoltaic (or other site-based) technologies to produce energy. This can be an optimal combination if wind speed is low in summer when solar radiation for the PVs is plentiful and wind is stronger in winter when there is less radiation available to the PVs.

A stand-alone or hybrid system is a good choice when:

- The site is in an area with average annual wind speed of at least 9 mph [4.0 m/s].
- A grid connection is either unavailable or prohibitively expensive.
- Independence from purchased energy resources is a major design intent.
- The use of renewable energy resources is a major design intent.

Design Procedure

1. Research land use issues for the proposed site. Determine if a wind turbine would be in compliance with local zoning ordinances. Typical issues addressed by local ordinances include:
   - minimum parcel size (often 1 acre [0.4 ha]);
   - maximum allowable tower height;
   - setback requirements.
2. Evaluate the wind resource. Wind speed and direction are changing all the time; wind speed can change significantly between daytime and night-time and seasonally. Evaluating the distribution of wind speeds throughout the year is the best way of accurately estimating the energy that a wind turbine will produce on a given site. For preliminary estimates an average wind speed can be used (refer to a wind resource map—such as the *Wind Energy Resource Atlas of United States*). The specific terrain of the site must also be taken into account because local conditions may alter wind speeds. Other methods for evaluating the wind resource for a site include obtaining wind data from a nearby airport, using portable wind measurement equipment (especially to gauge local effects) and obtaining information from existing wind turbine owners (or wind surfers) in the area.
3. Estimate building electrical energy requirements in kWh per year. Estimates of daily and seasonal distribution of this annual consumption will be useful during design development. According to the U.S. Department of Energy, a typical (not green) U.S. home uses approximately 10,000 kWh of electricity per year. Commercial building electricity consumption can be estimated or correlated from available data sources (typically on a per unit floor area basis).
4. Estimate wind turbine size using Figure 4.284. Compare the estimated annual energy output (for a given diameter wind turbine at the site's annual average wind speed) with the energy requirement estimate derived from Step 3 to see how a particular turbine proposal matches needs. The equation can also be rearranged to solve for the rotor diameter required to provide the necessary electrical output.

SAMPLE PROBLEM

Investigate the feasibility of using a wind turbine to produce electricity for a small, two-story medical office building to be located on an unobstructed site in the Midwestern United States.

1. A check of local ordinances suggests there are no legal impediments to the installation of a wind turbine on the chosen site.
2. The average wind speed at the site is estimated to be 12 mph [19 km/h]—based upon wind speed maps and the absence of site obstructions.
3. The annual electrical energy needs of the office building are estimated to be 20,000 kWh.
4. Estimate the required diameter of a wind turbine rotor using Figure 4.284:

   For 20,000 kWh with a 12-mph wind, the necessary diameter is around 29 ft [9 m].

   A wind turbine with a 30-ft [9-m] diameter rotor could, potentially, produce all of the electricity needed to power the office throughout the year.

5. **Determine where the turbine will be located on site and establish tower height. The bottom of the rotor blades should be at least 30 ft [9 m] above any obstacle that is within 300 ft [90 m] of the tower. Choose a placement for the turbine that considers prevailing wind direction and obstructions.**

5. Because this two-story office would be about 25 ft [7.6 m] tall, a 55-ft [16.8-m] tower would provide reasonable access to winds above the influence of the building wind shadow.

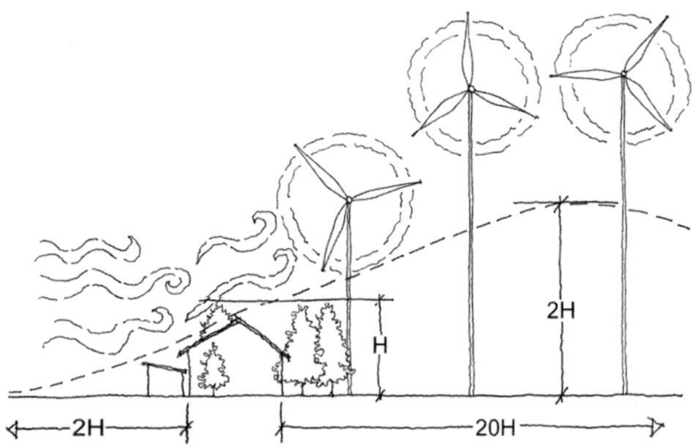

4.288 Turbulent airflow zone (to be avoided) caused by ground level obstructions. KATE BECKLEY

Examples

4.289 Micro-wind turbines at the 2007 Texas A&M Solar Decathlon House.

4.290 Horizontal axis micro-wind turbines on Yale University's Becton Engineering and Applied Science Center.

Further Information

American Wind Energy Association. Wind energy fact sheets. www.awea.org/

NREL. *Wind Resource Assessment*, includes State Wind Maps and International Wind Resource Maps. National Renewable Energy Laboratory. www.nrel.gov/wind/resource_assessment.html

U.S. Department of Energy, Energy Efficiency and Renewable Energy. *Installing and Maintaining a Small Electric Wind System*. www.energysavers.gov/your_home/electricity/index.cfm/mytopic=10990

BEYOND SCHEMATIC DESIGN

During design development the nuts-and-bolts details of a wind turbine system will be refined. Analyses will be conducted to ensure that system performance is acceptable throughout the year, to size system accessory components (such as a battery bank or inverter), and to develop an estimate of system life-cycle cost. Equipment will be specified. A User's Manual is recommended—and commissioning of the wind power system is highly recommended.

NOTES

MICROHYDRO TURBINES

MICROHYDRO TURBINES generate electricity by tapping into a flow of water. Microhydro electric systems, when thoughtfully designed, can produce low impact, environmentally-friendly power by harnessing the renewable kinetic energy in moving water.

The power available from a microhydro turbine system is derived from a combination of water "head" and "flow." Head is the vertical distance between the water intake and the turbine exhaust. This distance determines the available water pressure. Head distances of less than 3 ft [0.9 m] will usually prove ineffective. A low-head system typically involves 3 to 10 ft [0.9 to 3.1 m] of head. Flow is the volume of water that passes through the system per unit of time—usually expressed in gpm [L/s].

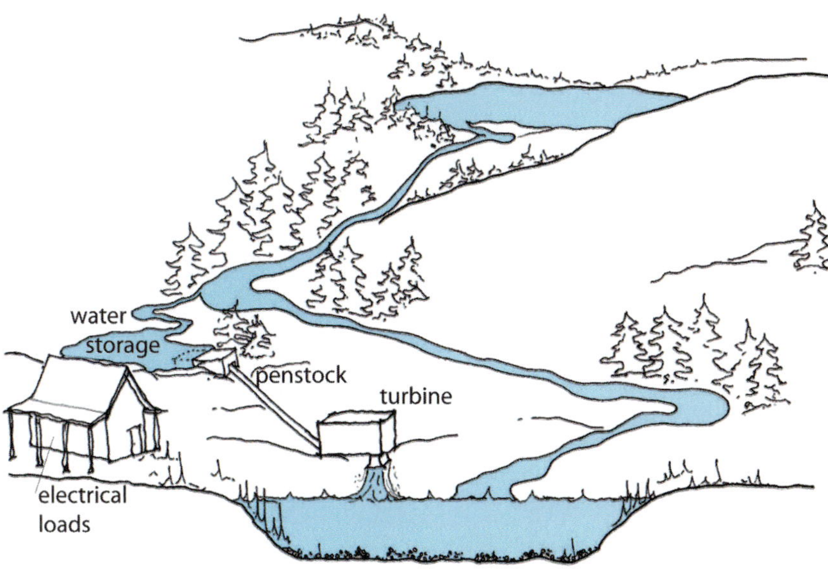

4.291 Components of a microhydro turbine electrical generating system. KATE BECKLEY

Water is delivered to a turbine through a pipe or penstock from a source (usually a pond or lake) that provides storage capacity for the system. The turbine, in turn, powers a generator. A turbine is a rotary engine that derives its power from the force exerted by moving water. Hydroelectric turbines are categorized as impulse, reaction, or propeller types. While power generation from a PV or wind system will vary throughout the day, microhydro power generation is stable on a daily basis (but may vary seasonally).

The feasibility of a microhydro turbine system is dependent upon governing regulations dealing with water rights and usage, water availability and reliability, the potential power available from that source, and system economics.

4.292 Water inlet to the penstock of a residential microhydro installation. JASON ZOOK

INTENT
On-site electricity generation

EFFECT
Reduced use of fossil fuel-generated electricity

OPTIONS
Reaction turbines, impulse turbines, propeller turbines

COORDINATION
Site selection, environmental impacts, storage pond location (if applicable), building electrical loads and usage profile

RELATED STRATEGIES
Site Analysis, Wind Turbines, Photovoltaics, Hydrogen Fuel Cells, Plug Loads

PREREQUISITES
Consistently flowing water source, available head of at least 3 ft [0.9 m], regulatory approval

Key Architectural Issues

Site analysis is essential to the success of a microhydro turbine power system. The site must have a reliable water source that can provide adequate water flow. The site must also have adequate slope to provide a minimum of 3 ft [0.9 m] of head for water delivery (greater slope is better).

Water is diverted from a stream, river, or lake into a penstock. An intake is placed at the highest convenient point of the water source. The intake penstock may be sited within a dam or diversion pool to increase head (pressure) and create a smooth, air-free inlet to the delivery components. Screens are positioned at the mouth of the penstock to filter debris that could damage the turbine.

A housing of some sort is constructed to protect the turbine and generator from the elements and/or tampering. This "powerhouse" should be located in an area safe from floodwaters. Housing for a battery bank (if used) must also be provided.

A "transmission line" runs from the generator to the point of use. The shortest possible route between generator and point of use should be utilized to minimize voltage losses due to resistance in this line—this is particularly true if DC power is distributed (versus AC from an inverter).

Implementation Considerations

A generator converts the rotational force of the turbine shaft into electricity. Generators produce direct current (DC) that may be used directly by DC appliances, used to charge a battery bank, or run through an inverter to produce AC power (alternating current) to supply conventional plug loads. Typical residential generator units produce 120/240 VAC power that is appropriate for most appliances, lighting, and heating equipment. Generators operate at a frequency determined by the rotational speed of the generator shaft; higher RPM produces a higher frequency.

An emergency system shutdown control can prevent overloading or underloading of the system in the event of a malfunction or accident. If connected to a public grid, an emergency system shutdown will be required.

Impulse turbines operate in an open-air environment in which high velocity jets of water are directed onto "blades" to facilitate shaft rotation. Impulse turbines are best suited for "high" head (and often low-flow) situations. Reaction turbines operate fully immersed in water. The pressure and flow of water against the runner facilitates turbine rotation (much like a pin-wheel). Reaction turbines are best suited for "low" head (and often high-flow) applications. Propeller turbines are typically used in high-flow, no-head situations (they act much as a boat propeller, but in reverse). Residential microhydro turbine systems may produce up to 100 kW, while larger (but still small-scale) systems can produce up to 15 MW.

Design Procedure

1. Determine whether it is legally acceptable to divert water from the intended source.
2. Determine the available head. There are a number of ways to do so, including a formal engineering survey or an informal survey using level lines and tape measures. The gross head is the vertical distance from the water surface at the intake point to the exhaust of the turbine. Net (available) head is gross head minus friction loss in the penstock (due to pipe, fittings, and valves). For schematic design purposes, assume that net head will be 80–90% of gross head.
3. Determine flow. If not available from local regulatory agencies, flow rate may be estimated using several simple methods. There are at least two flows of primary interest—the anticipated lowest flow (required to match loads to output and for design of backup power supplies) and the average flow (which will give a sense of the annual energy production available from the turbine system).
4. Estimate turbine power output using the equation:

$$P = ((\text{flow})(\text{head}))/F$$

   where,
   P = power output (W)
   flow = water flow rate (gpm) [L/s]
   head = net head (ft) [m]
   F = 10 [0.192], a conversion factor (that includes a typical efficiency for the turbine)

5. Compare the projected microhydro turbine output with the building's electrical power needs (estimated on the basis of appliances anticipated to be installed in a residential building or unit power density values for larger buildings) to determine whether this strategy can reasonably contribute to the project's electricity needs.
6. If the microhydro turbine is to be located some distance from the building(s) being served, determine the transmission line length and estimate line losses (input from an electrical consultant is advised).
7. Determine where the turbine and associated equipment will be located. Space demands for the turbine/generator are not great (perhaps 100–200 ft^2 [9–18 m^2] depending upon system capacity); space for batteries (if used) will be more substantial. Location of the turbine is an acoustical concern; the equipment can be somewhat noisy.

SAMPLE PROBLEM

A small environmental research station will be built in the foothills of the Rocky Mountains in Canada.

1. Permission to install a microhydro system was readily given by Provincial authorities, considering the pollution and noise that would be produced by a diesel generator power source (the most likely alternative).
2. Available head on the site (from the mean elevation of an existing storage pond to the turbine axis) is 45 ft [13.7 m].
3. Average annual flow is estimated to be 200 gpm [12.6 L/s].
4. Estimated instantaneous power output is: ((200)(45)/10) = 900 W.
5. The building electrical load is estimated to be 2.5 W/ft^2 [26.9 W/m^2] (including efficient lighting and substantial equipment loads—but excluding heating loads). For the 2000 ft^2 [186 m^2] building this equates to 5000 W—substantially more than the 900 W output. The building will operate 8 hours a day, however, whereas power generation will occur over a 24-hour period. Comparing daily usage with output: (8)(5000) = 40,000 Wh versus (24)(900) = 21,600 Wh.

   The proposed microhydro system provides roughly half of the daily electric needs of the research station—assuming substantial battery capacity is provided to match output to loads. A wind, PV, or fuel cell system might be

Examples

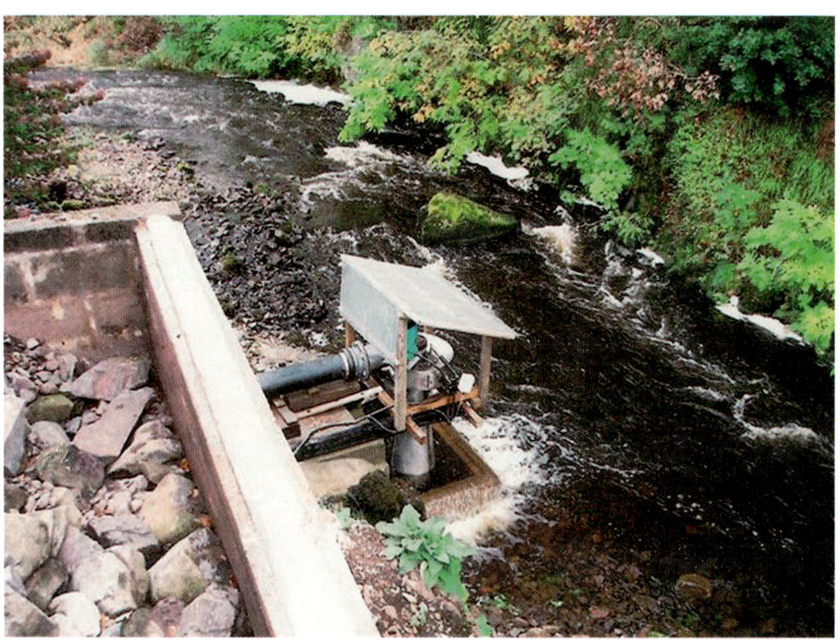

4.293 Microhydro turbine at the Ironmacannie Mill in Scotland which operates on 18 ft [5.5 m] of head creating 2.2 kW of power. NAUTILUS WATER TURBINE, INC.

4.294 Looking downstream from two microhydro turbines at the Tanfield Mill in Yorkshire, England. The installation is part of an ongoing development in renewable energy projects focusing upon microhydro applications. NAUTILUS WATER TURBINE, INC.

considered—or the building loads reduced by a factor of 50% (perhaps through aggressive daylighting).

6. The turbine and generator will be located about 300 ft [91 m] from the research station. The effect of transmission losses across this distance will be addressed in design development.
7. A remote outbuilding will house and protect the turbine, generator, and batteries. Noise is not an issue at this distance from the occupied building (although it might disrupt the tranquility of the site, but less than a diesel generator would).

4.295 The 400-year-old Tanfield Mill now uses one 30-kW Francis turbine and two smaller 3-kW turbines (shown above), with an operating head of 9 ft [2.7 m]. Water flow is 23,760 gpm [1501 L/s] for the large turbine and 2376 gpm [150 L/s] for the smaller units. The turbines are combined with conventional battery storage and inverter technology.
NAUTILUS WATER TURBINE, INC.

Further Information

ABS Alaskan. 2010. Micro Hydroelectric Power. www.absak.com/library/micro-hydro-power-systems

Harvey, A. et al. 1993. *Micro-Hydro Design Manual: A Guide to Small-Scale Water Power Schemes.* ITDG Publishing, Rugby, Warwickshire, UK.

Masters, G. 2004. *Renewable and Efficient Electric Power Systems.* Wiley-IEEE Press, New York.

U.S. Department of Energy, Microhydropower Systems. www.eere.energy.gov/consumer/your_home/electricity/index.cfm/mytopic=11050

BEYOND SCHEMATIC DESIGN

Assuming that a microhydro turbine system proves feasible during schematic design, the system will be further analyzed, detailed, and integrated during design development. Specific equipment (turbine, batteries, inverter, etc.) will be selected, coordinated, and specified.

Commissioning of this type of unconventional system is essential. A User's Manual should be prepared to assist the client/user with training, operations, and maintenance activities.

Examples

4.298 Fuel cells do not need to be drab and grey. A colorful 200-kW fuel cell provides electricity for the Los Angeles Zoo in Los Angeles, California. UTC POWER

4.299 A 200-kW fuel cell provides electricity and heats domestic hot water at Richard Stockton College, Pomona, New Jersey. UTC POWER

4.300 A 200-kW fuel cell provides electricity and heats domestic hot water for the Ford Premier Automotive Group Headquarters in Irvine, California. UTC POWER

Further Information

Fuel Cells 2000. www.fuelcells.org/

Hoogers, G. 2002. *Fuel Cell Technology Handbook*, CRC Press, Boca Raton, FL.

U.S. Department of Energy, Hydrogen Program. www.hydrogen.energy.gov/fuel_cells.html

UTC Power. www.utcfuelcells.com/fs/com/bin/fs_com_Page/0,11491,0229,00.html

Walsh, B. and R. Wichert. 2010. Fuel Cell Technology in *Whole Building Design Guide*. www.wbdg.org/resources/fuelcell.php

BEYOND SCHEMATIC DESIGN

Once a decision to use a fuel cell has been made and validated during schematic design, much of the actual design work on the system (including final sizing and equipment selection) will occur during design development. Efforts at that time will include refinement of electrical load estimates, matching of load profiles to fuel cell control and operation strategies, optimization of waste heat usage strategies and equipment, specification of all components, and development of a User's Manual for the fuel cell system. Commissioning the fuel cell system is critical.

Key Architectural Issues

In addition to adequate space for the CHP equipment, space is required for maintenance and replacement operations. If installed near an occupied space, appropriate noise and vibration control strategies must be implemented. Since CHP systems often involve on-site combustion, the location of exhaust stacks and combustion air inlets must be considered. Structural system elements must be sized to accommodate CHP equipment loads.

4.303 A microturbine CHP system provides up to 120 kW of electricity and heat at Floyd Bennett Field in Brooklyn, New York. DENNIS R. LANDSBERG, LANDSBERG ENGINEERING

Implementation Considerations

There are five basic types of combined heat and power systems: gas turbines, microturbines, reciprocating engine-driven generators, steam turbines, and fuel cells.

4.304 The Ritz-Carlton Hotel in San Francisco, California combines four 60-kW microturbines and a double-effect absorption chiller to provide 240 kW of electricity and refrigeration to a 336-room hotel. UTC POWER

TABLE 4.19 Advantages, disadvantages, and electrical capacities of typical CHP systems.
ADAPTED FROM U.S. EPA CATALOGUE OF CHP TECHNOLOGIES

CHP SYSTEM	ADVANTAGES	DISADVANTAGES	CAPACITY
Gas turbine	High reliability Low emissions High grade heat available No cooling required	Requires high-pressure gas or gas compressor	500 kW–250 MW
Microturbine	Small number of moving parts Compact and lightweight Low emissions No cooling required	High first cost Relatively low efficiency Limited to lower temperature cogeneration applications Cooling required High emissions High noise levels	30–350 kW
Reciprocating engine	High power efficiency Fast start-up Low first cost	High maintenance costs Limited to low temperature cogeneration applications Cooling required High emissions High noise levels	4–65 MW
Steam turbine	High overall efficiency Multiple fuel options High reliability	Slow start-up Low power to heat ratio	50 kW–250 MW
Fuel cell	Low emissions High efficiency Modular design	High first cost Fuels require special processing unless pure hydrogen is used	200–250 kW

Gas turbines use a fuel to turn a high-speed rotor connected to an electrical generator. High temperature exhaust from the combustion process generates steam at conditions as high as 1200 psig [8270 kPa] and 900 °F [480 °C]. Gas turbines are generally available in electrical capacities ranging from 500 kW to 250 MW and can operate on a variety of fuels such as natural gas, synthetic gas, landfill gas, and fuel oils. Large CHP systems that maximize power production for sale to the electrical grid constitute much of the current gas turbine-based CHP capacity.

Microturbines also burn fuel to turn a high-speed rotor and are similar to gas turbines in construction, but smaller in scale. Microturbines can use a variety of fuels including natural gas, gasoline, kerosene, and diesel fuel/heating oil. In a microturbine CHP application, a heat exchanger transfers heat from the exhaust to a hot water system. This heat is useful for various building applications, including domestic hot water and space heating, to power an absorption chiller, or to recharge desiccant dehumidification equipment. Microturbines have been on the market since 2000 and are generally available in the 30–350 kW range.

A third system type uses a reciprocating engine to drive an electrical generator. Natural gas is the preferred fuel (because of lower emissions); however, propane, gasoline, diesel fuel, and landfill gas can also be used. Reciprocating engines start quickly, are able to throttle up or down to follow changing electrical loads, have good part-load efficiencies, and are generally highly reliable. Reciprocating engines are well suited for applications that require a quick start-up and hot water or low-pressure steam as the thermal output.

Steam turbines generate electricity as high-pressure steam from a boiler rotates a turbine and generator. Steam turbines can utilize a variety of fuels including natural gas, solid waste, coal, wood, wood waste, and agricultural by-products. The capacity of commercially available steam turbines typically ranges from 50 kW to over 250 MW.

TABLE 4.20 A Comparison of Common CHP Systems

CHP SYSTEM TYPE	INSTALLATION COST (per KW)	GREENHOUSE GAS EMISSIONS	POWER EFFICIENCY	OVERALL EFFICIENCY	RELATIVE NOISE
Gas turbine	Low	Moderate	22–36%	70–75%	Moderate
Microturbine	Moderate	Moderate	18–27%	65–75%	Moderate
Engine-driven generator	Moderate	High	22–45%	70–80%	High
Steam turbine	Low	Moderate	15–38%	80%	High
Fuel cell	High	Low	30–63%	65–80%	High

ADAPTED FROM THE U.S. EPA *CATALOGUE OF CHP TECHNOLOGIES*

Ideal applications for steam turbine-based CHP systems include medium- and large-scale industrial or institutional facilities with high thermal loads and/or where solid or waste fuels are readily available for use in the steam boiler.

The fifth system type—fuel cells—is an emerging technology that has the potential to meet power and thermal needs with little or no greenhouse gas emissions. Fuel cells use an electrochemical process to convert the chemical energy of hydrogen into water and electricity. Fuel cells use hydrogen, processed from natural gas, coal gas, methanol, or other hydrocarbon fuels.

Design Procedure

Review the following steps to determine if a CHP system is appropriate for the intended building/facility context. Specifying and designing a CHP system will require the expertise of a qualified electrical/mechanical engineer, and will usually involve a detailed energy simulation to establish peak (and partial) electrical and thermal loads for the facility.

1. Consider electrical and thermal loads: As the smallest CHP capacity is around 30 kW, facilities with relatively high electrical loads—and with coincident (and substantial) thermal loads—are best suited for CHP applications.
2. Consider load schedules: Most successful applications of CHP systems involve facilities where demands for electricity and heat are generally in sync (avoiding a need for thermal storage or substantial operation of an independent heating boiler). Continuous use facilities often fit this condition.
3. Consider infrastructure: Facilities with central heating and cooling capabilities, such as a college campus, provide a good match for CHP systems because an infrastructure for distributing heating and cooling already exists, and there is generally a continuous or large demand for electricity and heat.
4. Consider power quality and required reliability: A facility requiring high-quality or uninterruptible power, such as a data center or hospital, typically requires standby electrical generation equipment. As a significant part of the cost of a CHP system resides in the purchase, installation, and interconnection of the electrical generation system to the grid, if a generator is required anyway, it is often easier to justify the first cost of a CHP system.
5. Consider electrical demand charges: CHP systems are often financially viable when the peak electrical and thermal loads of a facility coincide with times of high utility rates or cause high

SAMPLE PROBLEM

The adjacent design procedure is more conceptual than physical; thus a sample problem is not provided.

demand charges. A CHP system can help to "shave" energy usage during peak demand hours.

6. Consider fuel availability: Fuel (such as natural gas, diesel, or biofuel) used to power a CHP system must be readily available at the project site. Depending upon the type of system selected, auxiliary equipment such as compressors or storage tanks may be required. Such accessories require space and affect the economic viability of a CHP system.

7. Consider space requirements: Adequate space must be provided for CHP system components. It is hard to generalize about these requirements. In many cases, CHP system elements (boilers, chillers, perhaps even a generator) would be required even without the CHP system. The designer must deal with system aesthetics, as well as spatial integration.

If, after reviewing the above issues, a facility appears to be a good match for a CHP system, planning for such a system should be included in schematic design decisions.

Examples

4.305 Four 60-kW gas microturbines at the University of Toronto, Canada, are integrated with a 110-ton, double-effect absorption chiller. In the winter, waste heat from the microturbines helps to heat the campus. In the summer, waste heat drives the absorption chiller, reducing both the peak cooling and electrical loads for the campus. UTC POWER

4.306 The A&P Fresh Market in Mount Kisco, New York, uses four 60-kW microturbines with a double-effect absorption chiller to provide electricity, summertime cooling, winter heating, sub-cooling for the process refrigeration system, and desiccant regeneration. UTC POWER

4.307 Biogas reactor at Stahlbush Island Farms, Corvallis, Oregon, produces enough electricity from fruit and vegetable byproducts to power 1100 homes. STAHLBUSH ISLAND FARMS

Further Information

Case study profiles on CHP systems from UTC Power. www.utcpower.com/ (search on CHP)

ASHRAE 2006. *ASHRAE GreenGuide*, 2nd ed. American Society of Heating, Refrigerating and Air-Conditioning Engineers, Atlanta, GA.

(UK) Combined Heat and Power Association. www.chpa.co.uk/

U.S. Clean Heat & Power Association. www.uschpa.org/i4a/pages/index.cfm?pageid=1

U.S. Environmental Protection Agency, Combined Heat and Power Partnership. www.epa.gov/chp/

U.S. Environmental Protection Agency 2008. *Catalogue of CHP Technologies*, United States Environmental Protection Agency, Combined Heat and Power Partnership, Washington, DC. www.epa.gov/chp/basic/catalog.html

BEYOND SCHEMATIC DESIGN

The design of a CHP system is highly technical and requires the early input of mechanical and electrical engineering consultants, and simulations of load patterns and coincidences (which are the basis for a successful system). Some of this detailed analysis will occur during schematic design. During design development, system components, interconnections, and controls are selected and detailed. A CHP system should be commissioned and the client provided with a User's Manual to assist with operator training for ongoing operations and maintenance requirements.

NOTES

WATER AND WASTE

Reducing water use requires the implementation of strategies at both the building and site scales. Many water-efficiency strategies, such as low-flow fixtures and automatic controls, involve little or no additional first cost and/or very short payback periods. Other measures—such as greywater recycling or rainwater harvesting at the building scale, and constructed wetlands or bioremediation at the site scale—have significant cost impacts.

Low-flow plumbing fixtures have been the norm for more than a decade. To move beyond these now common standards, consider ultra-low-flow toilets, dual-flush toilets, waterless urinals, composting toilets, and automatic lavatory controls. Further reductions in building water use can be achieved by separately plumbing potable and greywater systems. Waterless urinals, composting toilets, and greywater recycling are not acceptable in all jurisdictions. Confirm local requirements before proceeding with these systems. In a small number of projects, on-site water treatment (such as a Living Machine) may be appropriate.

At the site scale, water use reductions can be achieved by using greywater or harvested rainwater for landscape irrigation. Reduced water runoff and increased groundwater recharge can be achieved through reductions in paved surface areas, the use of pervious materials where paving is required, bioswales, water retention areas, and constructed wetlands.

Green features such as waterless urinals and composting toilets may require special training or instructions for building occupants. These features, and others such as pervious pavement and bioswales, also require revised maintenance procedures. Designers and building owners should educate operations personnel about the environmental intent, as well as the operation and maintenance requirements, of these systems.

WATER AND WASTE

STRATEGIES

Composting Toilets
Water Reuse/Recycling
Living Machines
Water Catchment Systems
Pervious Surfaces
Bioswales
Retention Ponds

NOTES

COMPOSTING TOILETS

COMPOSTING TOILETS (sometimes called biological toilets, dry toilets, or waterless toilets) manage the chemical breakdown of human excrement, paper products, food wastes, and other carbon-based materials. Oxygenated waste is converted into "humus," a soil-like product that can be used as a fertilizer for non-edible agricultural crops.

The benefits of composting toilets include reduced potable water usage (especially for a low-grade task such as waste removal) and reduced loads on central sewer or local septic systems. Composting toilets have been used with success in both residential and commercial/institutional buildings. Waterless urinals are often used in conjunction with composting toilets in commercial/institutional buildings.

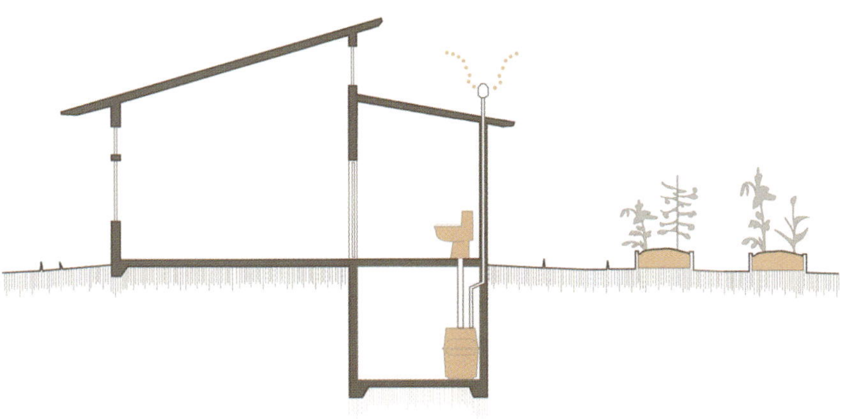

4.308 Schematic diagram of a composting toilet system—with input, digestion, and disposal components. JON THWAITES

Composting toilets rely upon aerobic bacteria and fungi to break down wastes—the same process that occurs in yard waste composting. Proper sizing and aeration enable the waste to be broken down to 10–30% of its original volume. Some composting toilet systems require "turning" the pile or raking to allow surface areas to receive regular oxygen exposure. Other systems maintain adequate air spaces and facilitate oxygenation through the introduction of high-carbon materials like sawdust, straw, or bark.

Composting toilet systems may utilize self-contained (local) water closets (toilets) or centralized units with a "destination" catchment area. Self-contained units are more labor intensive, utilizing relatively small pans or trays for removal of the humus. Centralized systems reduce the need for operator/user attention and are available in both batch and continuous systems. A batch unit uses a compost receptacle that is emptied as the container reaches capacity. Continuous systems rely on "raking" and removal of finished humus to assist the composting process. Both systems need only infrequent attention, often as little as once or twice per year. Some regular maintenance will be necessary with any composting toilet system.

4.309 Composting toilet in the classroom building on the Islandwood Campus, Bainbridge Island, Washington.

INTENT
Reduce the use of potable water

EFFECT
Water conservation, reduced load on central or local sewage disposal systems

OPTIONS
Self-contained equipment, remote composting equipment—in batch or continuous operation configurations

COORDINATION ISSUES
Local plumbing regulations, spatial organization, humus disposal area

RELATED STRATEGIES
Water Reuse/Recycling

PREREQUISITES
Local plumbing regulations, building occupancy information, information on client maintenance practices

Key Architectural Issues

Ventilation of catchment spaces, as well as direct system ventilation, is necessary. Ventilation systems should exhaust at least 2 ft [0.6 m] above the building roof peak—typically using 4-in. [100 mm] PVC or other code-approved pipe. Effective composting requires a minimum ambient temperature of 65 °F [18 °C]; lower temperatures slow the composting process.

Water closets must be placed vertically above a catchment tank to permit proper transport of solid waste materials. (Low water-flow models are available that permit offset installations—if absolutely required by design constraints.) Pipes or chutes that connect fixtures to tanks generally have a diameter of 14 in. [355 mm] and must connect to the highest point at the rear of the tank to ensure that the composting process is continuous. A maximum of two water closets per catchment tank is generally advised.

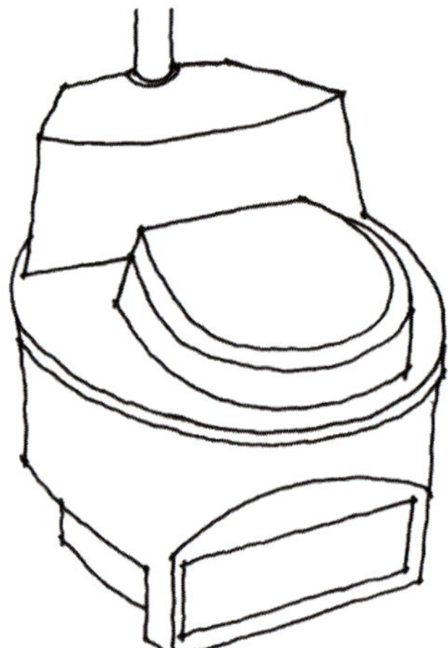

4.310 Self-contained residential composting toilet. AMANDA HILLS

Catchment tanks require a minimum of 1 ft [0.3 m] of overhead clearance for pipe connections and 4 ft [1.2 m] of clearance in front of tanks for removal of composted material. Direct access to the exterior of the building from the catchment tank area is suggested. The area housing the catchment tank should be properly drained and free of flood risk.

Sizing of composting toilet units or systems is dependent upon building occupancy and anticipated usage. Tank sizes vary from manufacturer to manufacturer. Table 4.21 provides a sense of the dimensions of common equipment. Multiple tanks are common in high-use (commercial/institutional) situations to obtain the required capacity. The public face of a composting toilet is similar in appearance and footprint to conventional water closets, but looks a bit "clunkier" or "chubbier."

TABLE 4.21 Typical composting toilet dimensions

TYPE	USES/DAY	LENGTH in. [cm]	WIDTH in. [cm]	HEIGHT in. [cm]
Self-contained	6	25 [64]	33 [84]	25 [64]
Remote tank	9	44 [112]	26 [66]	27 [68]
Remote tank	12	69 [175]	26 [66]	30 [76]
Remote tank	80	115 [292]	62 [158]	64 [162]
Remote tank	100	115 [292]	62 [158]	89 [226]

Dimensions for remote tank units include the catchment tank, but not the toilet (which is a separate component).

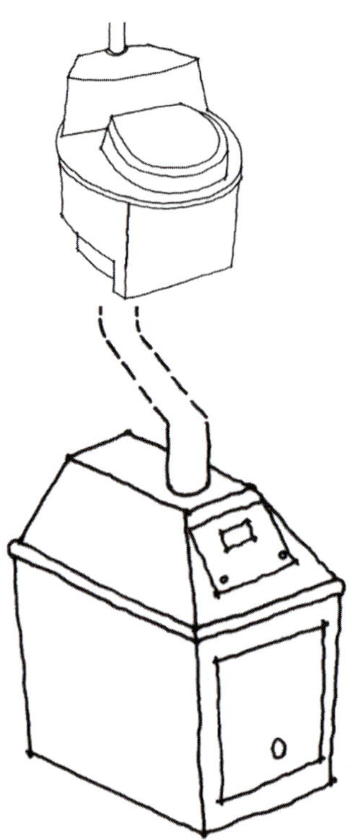

4.311 Composting toilet with remote, continuous composting tank. AMANDA HILLS

Implementation Considerations

How humus will be disposed of should be considered during schematic design. Adequate garden or other planted area should be available if humus is to be used as fertilizer (the most logical and ecological means of disposal). For planning purposes, assume that every 25 uses will produce 1 gal [3.8 L] of humus. Humus/fertilizer should not be used near water wells or edible crops. Local codes should be checked for specific requirements.

Maintenance of adequate temperatures in catchment areas is a design concern to be addressed early on—and is a good application for a passive solar heating system.

Design Procedure

1. Estimate the daily composting toilet usage by establishing a building occupancy count and assuming 3 uses per person per 8-hour stay.
2. Choose a self-contained or central system on the basis of required capacity, design intent, and a sense of how the building will be operated and maintained. A central system is recommended for most public, high-use facilities.
3. Allocate space for a remote tank(s) as required by the selected system type and required capacity.
4. Allocate space for access and maintenance around the remote tank(s). Ensure that plan layout and building structure will permit connection of the water closet to the remote tank (if that option is selected).

Examples

4.312 Remote, continuous composter tanks receive waste from toilets located on the floor directly above.

SAMPLE PROBLEM

A small research lab with a daily occupancy of a dozen people will be equipped with composting toilets.

1. The toilet capacity is estimated as: (12 occupants) (3 uses per day) = 36 daily uses.
2. A remote tank system is considered appropriate for this commercial application.
3. From Table 4.21, an 80-use per day system is selected with a tank footprint of roughly 10 ft [3 m] by 5 ft [1.5 m].
4. An additional 100% of this footprint will be allocated for access and maintenance.

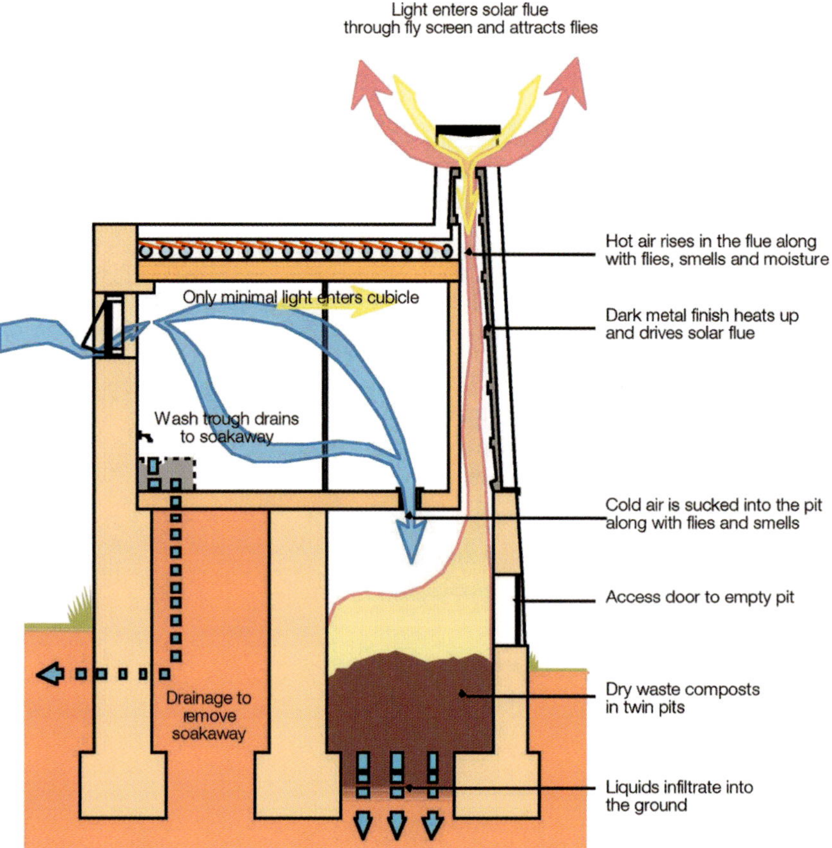
Light enters solar flue
through fly screen and attracts flies
Hot air rises in the flue along
with flies, smells and moisture
Only minimal light enters cubicle
Dark metal finish heats up
and drives solar flue
Wash trough drains
to soakaway
Cold air is sucked into the pit
along with flies and smells
Access door to empty pit
Drainage to
remove
soakaway
Dry waste composts
in twin pits
Liquids infiltrate into
the ground

4.313 The composting "VIP" latrine at the Druk White Lotus School (Ladakh, India) uses solar assisted stack ventilation for drying and odor control. ARUP + ARUP ASSOCIATES

4.314 Solar collector on latrine facility at Druk White Lotus School (Ladakh, India). CAROLINE SOHIE, ARUP + ARUP ASSOCIATES

Further Information

Del Porto, D. and C. Steinfeld. 2000. *Composting Toilet System Book: A Practical Guide to Choosing, Planning and Maintaining Composting Toilet Systems*, The Center for Ecological Pollution Prevention, Concord, MA.

Jenkins, J. 2005. *The Humanure Handbook: A Guide to Composting Human Manure*, 3rd ed. Jenkins Publishing, Grove City, PA.

Oikos, Green Building Source, "What is a Composting Toilet System and How Does it Compost?" oikos.com/library/compostingtoilet/

Reed, R., J. Pickford and R. Franceys. 1992. *A Guide to the Development of On-Site Sanitation*, World Health Organization, Geneva.

BEYOND SCHEMATIC DESIGN

Decisions regarding system capacity and toilet type made during schematic design will be validated during design development using more detailed information. Specific equipment will be sized, selected, detailed, and specified. Commissioning of the system might be prudent—but it is absolutely critical that a User's Manual be provided to the client. Signage informing users of composting toilet etiquette are commonly employed to educate occasional users.

WATER REUSE/ RECYCLING

WATER REUSE/RECYCLING conserves water by using a given volume of water more than once on the same building site. Water reuse is the reutilization of water for any application other than the original use—greywater systems are perhaps the most well-known example of this approach. Water recycling is the reutilization of water in the same application for which it was originally used. These two terms, however, are often used loosely and interchangeably.

Successful application of a water reuse strategy requires evaluating the degree of potability required for each water use. For example, the flushing of water closets and urinals can be accomplished using non-potable water, whereas cooking can only be done using potable water. Design for water reuse involves the integration of "effluent" from one system into the supply stream for another system. Success involves balancing the entering water quality needs for one usage with the quality of water leaving another usage. Intermediate treatment may be necessary for some reuses.

4.315 Schematic diagram of a greywater system, showing greywater sources, storage and treatment, and usage components. JONATHAN MEENDERING

Greywater consists of wastewater (from lavatories, showers, washing machines, and other plumbing fixtures) that does not include food wastes or human waste. Wastewater containing food and human wastes is termed "blackwater." Greywater is relatively easy to reuse, whereas blackwater is not. Greywater contains less nitrogen and fewer pathogens, and thus decomposes faster than blackwater. Reusing greywater can be an economical and efficient strategy to reduce a building's overall water consumption by directing appropriate wastewater not to the sewage system, but instead to other uses (such as irrigation). Reusing greywater in a building can reduce the load on a building's sewage system, lower a building's overall contribution to energy and chemical use, and create new landscaping opportunities. The extent of potential greywater reusage depends upon a building's potable water usage, distributions of that water usage across time, and the ability to conveniently collect and use greywater on site.

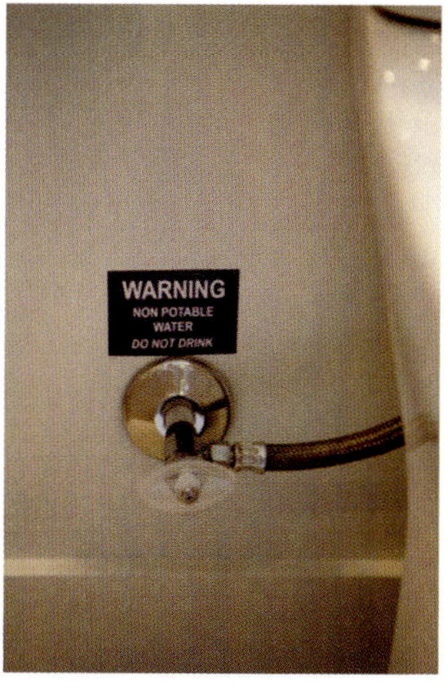

4.316 Don't drink the—recycled—water at Dockside Green, Victoria, British Columbia. BUSBY PERKINS + WILL

INTENT
Water conservation

EFFECT
Reduced demand on potable water supplies, reduced energy use for water treatment and distribution

OPTIONS
Scale, applications (sources and uses), treatment levels, heat recovery

COORDINATION ISSUES
Landscaping and irrigation, sewage treatment and disposal system, HVAC and plumbing systems (for heat reclaim), space for storage, local codes

RELATED STRATEGIES
Living Machines, Water Catchment Systems, Retention Ponds, Bioswales

PREREQUISITES
Site information, inventory of water uses/consumptions, local regulatory requirements

Key Architectural Issues

Water reuse strategies can have as much (or as little) effect on the feel and aesthetics of a building as a designer wishes. Water reuse can be celebrated as a visual learning tool, or treated as just another background building support system. Water storage and treatment systems can serve as beautiful organizing elements (wetlands or cisterns) in a design—but they require space.

See Figure 4.317 for examples of water treatment levels for potential water reuses. Rain catchment water, in most areas of the United States, needs to be treated at a tertiary level before being used in water closets/urinals (see, for example, U.S. Environmental Protection Agency Region 9 water reuse guidelines). Several states in the U.S. (including California, Oregon, Montana, Texas, Utah, Arizona, and New Mexico) have developed policies allowing for the beneficial use of greywater within and external to a building. Above and beyond such policies, the perceptions of building occupants must be considered when employing any water reuse/recycling strategy.

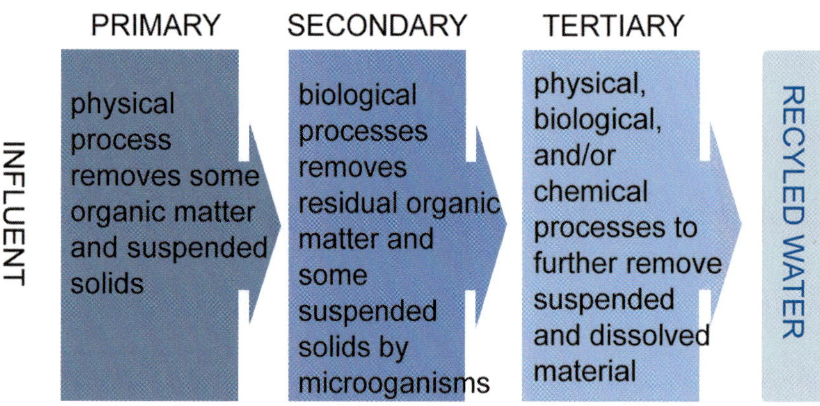
PRIMARY
SECONDARY
TERTIARY
INFLUENT
physical process removes some organic matter and suspended solids
biological processes removes residual organic matter and some suspended solids by microoganisms
physical, biological, and/or chemical processes to further remove suspended and dissolved material
RECYLED WATER

4.317 Treatment levels for recycled water. Disinfection to kill pathogens after secondary and tertiary treatment allows controlled uses of effluent. ADAPTED FROM *GRAYWATER GUIDE: USING GRAYWATER IN YOUR HOME LANDSCAPE*, STATE OF CALIFORNIA, OFFICE OF WATER USE RESOURCES

Implementation Considerations

Perhaps more than any other green building strategy, water reuse and recycling strategies are likely to incur close supervision from local code authorities as a result of health and safety concerns. Be prepared to address any such issues directly and early in the design process. Do the necessary research to understand potential concerns and be able to provide support for proposed strategies (by citing other building codes or via case studies of successful applications).

Implementing a workable greywater reuse strategy requires a building with sufficient potable water usage to generate adequate greywater and appropriate uses for the greywater that is generated. The building must also have space available to accommodate the infrastructure of a greywater system: Additional piping to carry greywater (with a separate blackwater system) along with storage and treatment tanks to prepare the greywater for reuse. The ideal building for greywater reuse is a high-occupancy residential building (or a similar occupancy) that generates significant greywater. For a greywater system to be technically viable and economically feasible, a building must produce significantly more greywater than blackwater.

Design Procedure—Greywater

1. Conduct a water-use inventory for the proposed building. The inventory will include an estimate of the types of water usage and their respective amounts for a typical time frame. Table 4.22 can be used as a starting point for such an inventory for residential applications.

TABLE 4.22 Estimating greywater resources in residential occupancies. ADAPTED FROM WWW.GREYWATER.COM/PLANNING.HTM AND *MECHANICAL AND ELECTRICAL EQUIPMENT FOR BUILDINGS*, 10TH ED.

WATER USAGE	WATER OUTFLOW	OUTFLOW QUALITY
Clothes washing machine	Top loader: 30–50 gal/load [115–190 L] Front loader: 10 gal/load [38 L] @ 1.5 loads/week/adult @ 2.5 loads/week/child	Greywater
Dishwasher	5–10 gal/load [19–38 L]	Greywater
Shower	Low-flow: 20 gal/day/person [75 L] High-flow: 40 gal/day/person [150 L]	Greywater
Kitchen sink	5–15 gal/day/person [19–56 L]	Greywater

2. Establish appropriate applications for greywater usage and estimate the greywater quantity needed. Estimating techniques will vary depending upon the anticipated usage—an inquiry to a local agricultural extension agent or landscape professional is suggested for potential external uses.
3. Decide if greywater reuse is appropriate based upon the available greywater capacity, architectural and site considerations, and the quantity of water that could be utilized by potential greywater applications.
4. Decide if treatment/storage or immediate reuse should be employed based upon design considerations and the relationship between greywater production and consumption over a representative period of time.
5. Determine whether filtration will be employed based upon the nature of the reuse application and storage needs.
6. Incorporate the greywater collection/storage elements into the project design.

SAMPLE PROBLEM

A 10-unit apartment complex in Moab, Utah, will use greywater for landscape irrigation. Estimate the weekly quantity of greywater produced.

1. Each apartment unit will be occupied by 4 people and will contain 1 kitchen sink, 2 lavatories, 2 water closets, 2 showers, 1 dishwasher, and 1 washing machine. Weekly greywater production is estimated as follows (making assumptions regarding flows and usage from Tables 4.22 and 4.24):

   Showers:
   (2 units)(30 gal)(2 users) = (120 gal/day)(7 days/week) = 840 gal [3180 L]/week

   Kitchen sink (included as a greywater resource since food waste management is addressed in green tenant guidelines):
   (1 unit) (10 gal) (4 users) = (40 gal/day) (7 days/week) = 280 gal [1060 L]/week

   Dishwasher:
   (1 unit) (10 gal) (say 0.5 load/day) = (5 gal/day) (7 days/week) = 35 gal [135 L]/week

   Washing machine:
   (1 unit) (40 gal) (6 loads/week) = 240 gal [910 L] / week

   Total weekly greywater production = 1395 gal [5280 L]

   The effluent from water closets and lavatories is not included as it is considered blackwater.

2. The estimated irrigation water requirements for 4000 ft^2 [372 m^2] of mixed use garden in Moab are as follows (assuming a 1-in. [25 mm] weekly watering requirement): (4000 ft^2)(1 in.

Examples

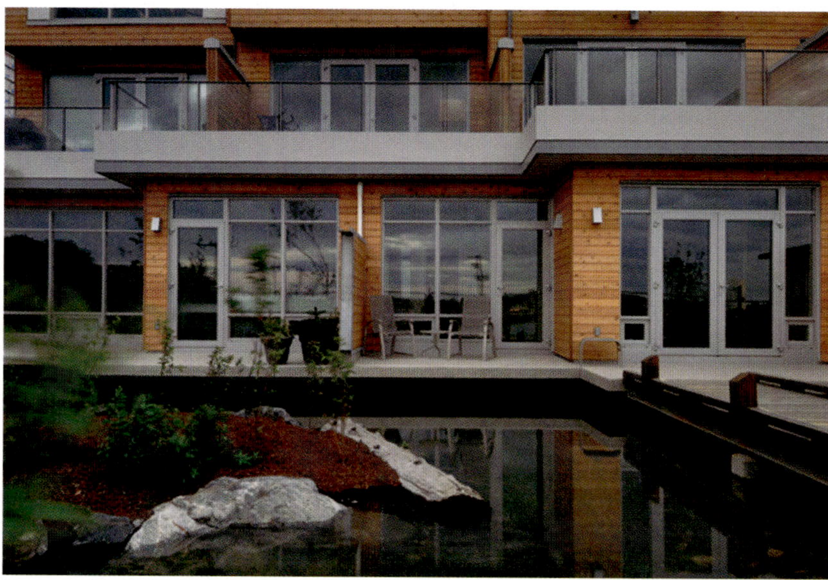

4.318 View of townhouses at Dockside Green, Victoria, British Columbia. On-site wastewater treatment (not seen) and stormwater ponds provide an integrated water management plan for the development. BUSBY PERKINS + WILL

4.319 All wastewater is treated on site, with processed water being recycled to replenish water features and flush toilets. BUSBY PERKINS + WILL

water /wk) = (4000)(1/12) = 333 ft^3/wk 333 ft^3 = 2490 gal [9425 L]. Thus, the greywater system should be able to provide for roughly 1395/ 2490 = 55% of the garden's water needs.

3. This application of greywater is considered appropriate (even though it only partially meets the needs) because of its water conservation potential.
4. A continuous irrigation system will be used to mitigate the need for greywater storage.
5. Sand filtration will be used to improve water quality for this public use and to minimize the deposition and collection of sediments over time.
6. No storage elements are required for this application.

4.320 The amenities of recycling water. BUSBY PERKINS + WILL

4.321 Green roofs, stormwater ponds, and aggressive water management helped Dockside Green obtain a LEED Platinum rating. BUSBY PERKINS + WILL

4.322 Waterway feature at Dockside Green, which is replenished by recycled water. BUSBY PERKINS + WILL

Further Information

The Chartered Institution of Water and Environmental Management. Water Reuse. http://www.ciwem.org/resources/water/reuse.asp

"Greywater: What it is . . . how to treat it . . . how to use it." www.greywater.com/

Ludwig, A. 2006. *Create an Oasis with Greywater*, 5th ed. Oasis Design, Santa Barbara, CA.

Oasis Design. Greywater Information Central. www.greywater.net/

State of Florida, Department of Environmental Protection. 2003. "Water reuse resources." www.dep.state.fl.us/water/reuse/techdocs.htm

U.S. Environmental Protection Agency (Region 9). "Water Recycling and Reuse: The Environmental Benefits." www.epa.gov/region9/water/recycling/

BEYOND SCHEMATIC DESIGN

The nuts and bolts of water reuse and recycling will be worked out during the design development phase as treatment equipment, storage facilities, and piping interconnections are selected and/or designed. The success of this strategy, however, will lie in the schematic design analysis of feasibility and connections between effluent and influent. Commissioning of these systems is imperative—as is development of a User's Manual.

NOTES

LIVING MACHINES are a proprietary, engineered waste treatment system designed to process a building's sanitary drainage on site. The treatment is accomplished via a series of anaerobic and aerobic tanks that house bacteria that consume pathogens, carbon, and other nutrients in the wastewater thereby making it clean and safe for reuse/recycling (for selected applications) or reintroduction into the local landscape.

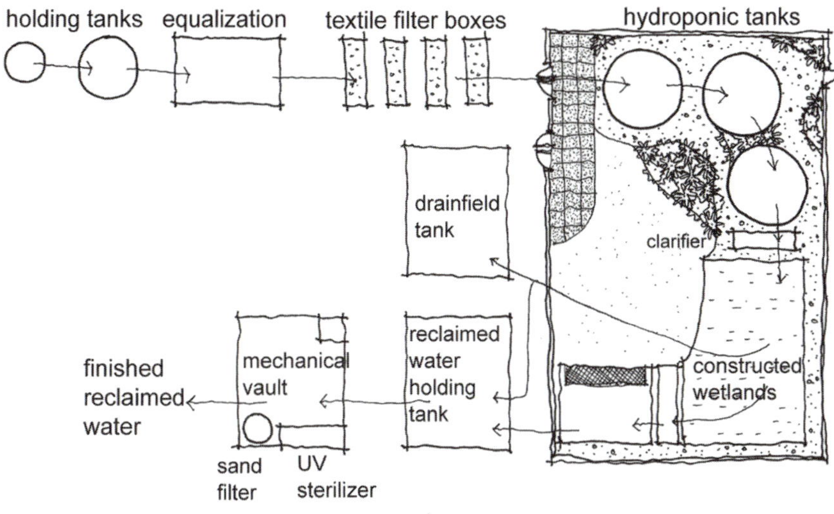

4.323 Diagram showing the typical components and sequence of flows in a Living Machine. KATE BECKLEY

4.324 One of three hydroponic reactors that treat and recycle waste water at Islandwood Campus, Bainbridge Island, Washington.

The most common type of Living Machine is the hydroponic system that relies on bacteria, plants, and an overflow wetland to clean wastewater. More specifically, it consists of two anaerobic tanks, a closed aerobic tank, three open aerobic (hydroponic) tanks, a clarifier, an artificial wetland, and a UV filter.

Water is a precious resource that is essential for life, yet human impacts on freshwater reserves—salinization, acidification, and pollution, to name a few—jeopardize its availability for many. Institutional buildings typically use 75–125 gallons [285–475 L] per person per day. Most of this consumption then becomes wastewater that flows, usually many miles, to a treatment center where it is cleaned and dumped into a river, lake, ocean, or perhaps aquifer. A Living Machine can provide an alternative to this centralized disposal paradigm or to less-effective or less-desirable on-site sewage disposal methods. In either case, water is retained on site, which can be ecologically desirable.

Key Architectural Issues

Living Machines are large objects with a substantial footprint—accommodating their spatial and volumetric demands will be a key architectural design concern.

INTENT
On-site wastewater treatment

EFFECT
Treats sanitary drainage for recycling/reuse or on-site disposal

OPTIONS
Approach to housing the aerobic digesters, water "disposal" approach (constructed wetland or other technique)

COORDINATION ISSUES
Building wastewater loads, local jurisdiction approval, location on site, footprint

RELATED STRATEGIES
Site Analysis, Water Reuse/Recycling, Water Catchment Systems, Composting Toilets, Bioswales

PREREQUISITES
Sufficient area on site, amenable client and design intent, local jurisdiction approval, estimated wastewater loadings

Living Machines require ongoing care for proper operation. This maintenance must be within the capabilities of the client and be addressed during design.

Living Machines produce liquid output generally equal in volume to the potable water intake of the building. This water discharge must be accommodated on site. A fair amount of vegetation is also produced and harvested and this should be beneficially used on site.

There are landscape design implications for an on-site wetland and aesthetic possibilities for the various processing tanks and their enclosure.

4.325 Healthy and flourishing plants in a Living Machine hydroponic reactor.

Implementation Considerations

Living Machines require exterior space, preferably adjacent to the building being served, where the closed aerobic tanks can be buried. These tanks should be located where they are accessible to maintenance workers and machinery.

The Living Machine treatment cycle relies upon metabolic processes that occur best within a specific range of temperatures. Nitrification, which occurs in the open aerobic tanks, has an optimal temperature range of 67–86 °F [19–30 °C]. Therefore, these particular tanks must be housed within a temperature-controlled facility for optimal performance. A solar greenhouse (or sunspace) has worked well in some climates and can reduce the use of purchased energy to support wastewater treatment.

Living Machines are functioning wastewater treatment systems and should be treated as such. Separation (at least from the thermal, airflow, and occupant circulation perspectives) of the Living Machine from the building being served by the system is recommended. This does not preclude tours through the system or observation through view elements.

Design Procedure

As a proprietary technology, there is no general guideline available for the sizing of a Living Machine. Living Machine design for a specific project will involve consulting with a system design specialist. For schematic design purposes the following information should permit allocation of appropriate spaces. The values are based upon information from several existing Living Machine installations.

1. Determine the building wastewater load in gallons per day (gpd) [L/d]. Building design handbooks can provide values in support of this estimation.

2. Estimate the approximate sizes of aerobic tank and clarifier from Table 4.23. If an on-site wetland will be used to facilitate the flow of processed water back into the ecosystem, estimate its size (also from Table 4.23).

SAMPLE PROBLEM

A proposed renewable energy museum on Prince Edward Island, Canada will include two bathrooms, a small kitchen space, and a small classroom/lab with several sinks. Approximately 100 people visit and work at the museum each day.

1. An institutional building of this type is estimated to produce 87 gal [330 L] per person/day of wastewater. (100 users) (87 gdp) = 8700 gdp [32,930 L/d].

3. Lay out a conditioned space for the aerobic digesters so that there is enough space for maintenance workers to walk around the tanks, prune plants, and conduct water quality tests. Allow space (10% additional is suggested) for supporting equipment including pumps, meters, piping, and a UV filter. If Living Machine tours are anticipated as part of the project design intent, provide for adequate circulation and "stop and look" spaces.
4. Provide space nearby for a supplemental equipment room: 6 × 10 ft [1.8 × 3 m] should suffice for a medium capacity system.
5. The exterior space required for the anaerobic tanks is roughly equal to the space needed for the aerobic tanks.

TABLE 4.23 Approximate dimensions of Living Machine components for three system sizes (capacities)

SYSTEM CAPACITY	AEROBIC TANK DIMENSIONS	CLARIFIER DIMENSIONS	WETLAND DIMENSIONS
Small: 2500 gpd [9460 L/d], use 3 aerobic tanks			
	diameter 6 ft [1.8 m]	diameter 8 ft [2.4 m]	15 × 30 ft [4.6 × 9.1 m]
	height 3 ft [0.9 m]	height 3 ft [0.9 m]	depth 3 ft [0.9 m]
	1500 gal [5680 L]	700 gal [2650 L]	
Medium: 10,000 gpd [37,850 L/d], use 6 aerobic tanks			
	diameter 8 ft [2.4 m]	diameter 8 ft [2.4 m]	20 × 20 ft [6.1 × 6.1 m]
	height 4 ft [1.2 m]	height 4 ft [1.2 m]	depth 4 ft [1.2 m]
	depth 8 ft [2.4 m]	depth 8 ft [2.4 m]	
	3000 gal [11,360 L]	3000 gal [11,360 L]	
Large: 35,000 gpd [132,475 L/d], use 4 aerobic tanks			
	diameter 14 ft [4.3 m]	diameter14 ft [4.3 m]	custom sizing required
	height 3 ft [0.9 m]	height 3 ft [0.9 m]	
	depth 10 ft [3 m]	depth 10 ft [3 m]	
	10,000 gal [37,850 L]	10,000 gal [37,850 L]	

2. From Table 4.23, a Living Machine for this "medium" load would require 3 at 8-ft [2.4 m] diameter aerobic tanks, a clarifier tank with the same dimensions, and a wetland that is about 20 × 20 ft [6.1 × 6.1 m]. Due to the site's reasonably cold winter climate the aerobic tanks should be housed in a heated enclosure (a solar greenhouse is suggested).
3. An 800 ft^2 [75 m^2] greenhouse space is proposed to house the aerobic tanks, supplemental equipment, and provide access for a limited number of visitors.
4. Space for a 100 ft^2 [9 m^2] equipment room will be allocated.
5. About 400 ft^2 [37 m^2] of exterior space adjacent to the greenhouse and wetlands will be required for the anaerobic tanks.

Examples

4.326 The Living Machine system at Islandwood Campus on Bainbridge Island, Washington is designed to treat and recycle an average flow of 3000 gallons per day [11360 L/d], approximately 70–80% of potable drinking water flow.

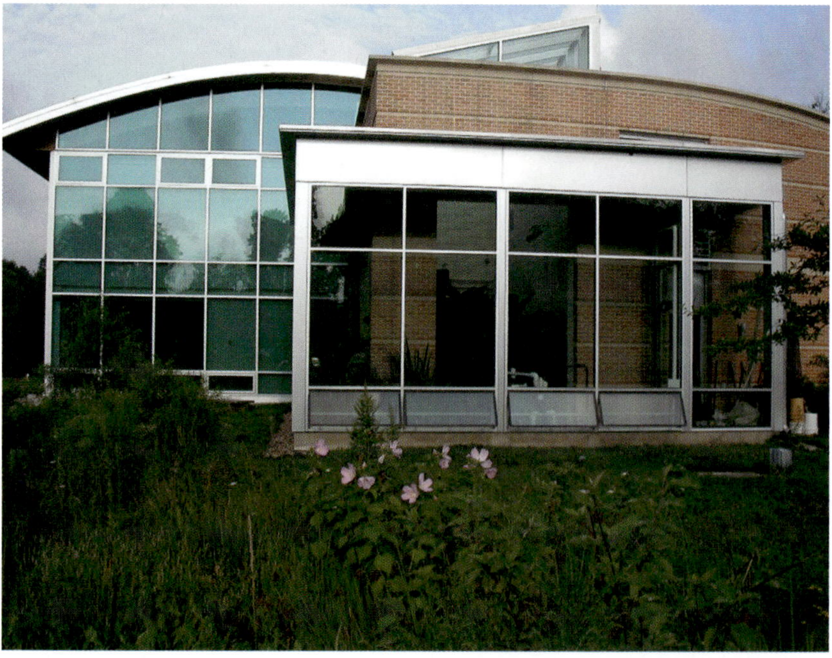

4.327 The Living Machine (foreground enclosure) at the Adam J. Lewis Center for Environmental Studies, Oberlin College, Oberlin, Ohio. System performance may be viewed online (see Further Information).

Further Information

Corkskrew Swamp Sanctuary Living Machine. www.audubon.org/local/sanctuary/corkscrew/Information/LivingMachine.html

Oberlin College. Adam Joseph Lewis Center, "Living Machine and Water Use." www.oberlin.edu/ajlc/systems_lm_1.html

Todd, J. and B. Josephson. 1994. "Living Machines: Theoretical Foundations and Design Precepts." *Annals of Earth*, 12, No. 1, pp. 16–24.

Todd, N.J. and J. Todd. 1994. *From Eco-Cities to Living Machines: Principles of Ecological Design*, North Atlantic Books, Berkeley, CA.

USEPA 2001. *The "Living Machine" Wastewater Treatment Technology: An Evaluation of Performance and System Cost*, U.S. Environmental Protection Agency, Washington, DC. EPA 832-R-01-004.

USEPA. 2002. Wastewater Technology Fact Sheet: The Living Machine®. U.S. Environmental Protection Agency, Washington, DC.

Worrell Water Technologies. (Living Machine). www.livingmachines.com/

BEYOND SCHEMATIC DESIGN

As a proprietary technology, a Living Machine will be designed by the manufacturer to suit the needs of a given facility. Detailed information regarding building usage and operation should be provided to the manufacturer as soon as possible to ensure that actual system requirements match those estimated during schematic design. Living Machines often require special certification and testing from local code authorities. Commissioning and development of a detailed User's Manual are strongly recommended.

NOTES

WATER CATCHMENT SYSTEMS

WATER CATCHMENT SYSTEMS have historically been used to collect water for potable uses, irrigation, laundry, and passive cooling. Also known as rainwater harvesting, this is a simple strategy with numerous benefits.

Wise use of water resources should be an inherent element of green building design. This strategy can be used to reduce the consumption of potable water derived from other sources or to supplement such sources to permit an application (such as gardening) that might otherwise be resource expensive. Rainwater stored in cisterns can provide a standby water source in times of emergency, or a supplemental source in times of increased need or reduced resources. Collecting and storing rainwater that runs off roofs and other impervious surfaces helps reduce stormwater flows and possible downstream flooding. Economically, water catchment can result in lower water supply costs.

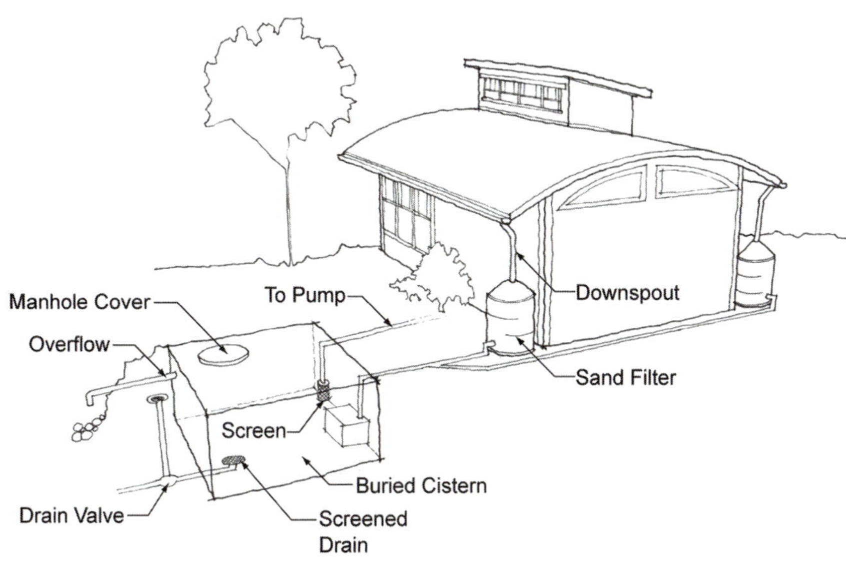

4.328 Schematic layout of a rainwater catchment and storage system for a residential building. JONATHAN MEENDERING

There are two commonly used scales of rainwater harvesting systems:

- smaller systems that collect roof runoff for domestic uses, and
- larger systems that use land forms as catchment areas to provide supplemental irrigation for agriculture.

The scale of a domestic system can be increased to encompass larger projects. On a building site scale, water catchment systems can incorporate bioswales and retention ponds. In general, components in a rainwater collection system serve one or more of the following functions: catchment, conveyance, purification, storage, and distribution.

4.329 A concrete cistern fed by a large gutter at Islandwood Campus on Bainbridge Island, Washington.

INTENT
Water conservation

EFFECT
Reduced use of purchased water supplies, increased availability of water resources

OPTIONS
Collector location and surface (roof, field, etc.); type, location, and capacity of storage

COORDINATION ISSUES
Site coordination, roof planes and materials, storage location, plumbing systems, landscaping design

RELATED STRATEGIES
Site Analysis, Water Reuse/Recycling, Bioswales, Retention Ponds, Green Roofs, Pervious Surfaces

PREREQUISITES
Local code requirements, information on water demands, local rainfall data

Key Architectural Issues

A design approach based upon water conservation reserves high-quality water for high-grade (potable) tasks and lower-quality water for lower-grade (non-potable) tasks. Such an approach emphasizes water recycling as a means of reducing the use of potable water resources, as well as reducing overall water usage. Water storage will require a substantial "tank" volume that can either be concealed or celebrated as a visible aspect of the project design. In either approach, the storage volume must be squarely addressed during schematic design.

Implementation Considerations

For most residential/commercial scale systems, roof design is the key consideration relative to catchment. The design process must address roofing materials as their selection will affect water quality. Factory-enameled (baked) galvanized steel or uncoated stainless steel are good roofing choices. Metal finishes must be lead- and heavy-metal-free. Asphalt shingles, wood shakes, and concrete/clay tiles are more likely to support the growth of mold, algae, and moss than are metal surfaces. Treated wood shingles may leach preservatives; asphalt shingles may leach petroleum compounds. A rough or porous roofing material will retain some water that might otherwise run off and be collected. Water purification is primarily a design development consideration, but must be considered if the collected water is to be used for potable purposes.

Water storage typically involves a cistern. Cistern materials include cast-in-place reinforced concrete, sealed concrete masonry units, brick or stone set with mortar and plastered with cement on the inside, ready-made steel tanks, precast concrete tanks, redwood tanks, and glass fiber tanks. Cisterns must be upslope of on-site sewage facilities. Avoid low places where flooding may occur. Cisterns can be incorporated into building structure, in basements, or under porches. An underground system can prevent freezing of stored water and keep water cool in the summer.

TABLE 4.24 Estimated daily per capita water needs (residential)

	GALLONS PER CAPITA DAY	LITERS PER CAPITA DAY
Recommended sustainable minimum	13	50
Developing countries	13–26	50–100
European countries	65–92	250–350
Australia (50% for exterior uses; 25% for toilets)	92	350
United Kingdom	89	335
United States (75% for interior uses; 25% for toilets)	106–145	400–550

Notes: Consumption estimates vary greatly from source to source (the above represents the consensus of several public sources); daily consumption is substantially affected by the use of water-efficient fixtures (the above values are based upon conventional fixtures).

Design Procedure

This procedure provides representative values for preliminary estimation purposes for domestic (potable) water systems. Actual water quantities may vary widely from project to project and are highly project dependent.

1. Plan for the use of low-flow plumbing devices. It makes no sense to embark on a water collection strategy without first reducing demand through appropriate selection of fixtures. Reduced flow fixtures can cut water demand by 25–50% (compared with conventional fixtures).
2. Estimate the water needs of the building. Interior water needs typically include water closets/urinals, showers, dishwashing, laundry, and drinking/cooking water. Water consumption is expressed in gpd [L/d] (gallons [liters] per day); a per capita consumption would be multiplied by building occupancy. Annual water needs can be estimated by multiplying gpd [L/d] by 365 days. For typical daily water needs see Table 4.24.

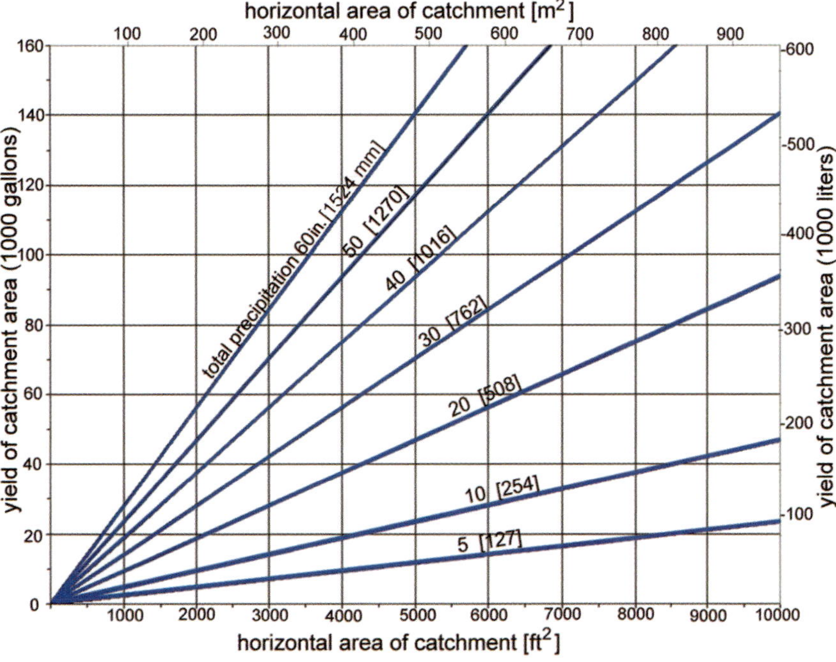

4.330 Sizing rainwater catchment areas. KATHY BEVERS ADAPTED FROM U.S. EPA OFFICE OF WASTE WATER MANAGEMENT

3. Determine available rainfall for the building site. Data are often available from government-source annual summaries. For rainfall collection purposes, assume that a "dry" year will produce 2/3 the precipitation of an average year. Therefore, (design precipitation) = (2/3) (average annual precipitation).
4. Determine required catchment area. From Figure 4.330, determine the catchment area required to provide for the annual water

SAMPLE PROBLEM

A 5000 ft^2 [465 m^2] single-story addition to an existing library in Allegheny River Valley, Pennsylvania will provide rainwater to supply water closets in the existing building.

1. Conventional water closets are used in the existing building.
2. Water usage is estimated to be 72 gpd [273 L/d] as follows: (1.6 gal/flush [10.6 L] × 3 flushes/day × 15 employees).
3. The design precipitation for the site locale is (2/3) (41 in.) = 27.3 in. [(2/3) (1041 mm) = 694 mm].

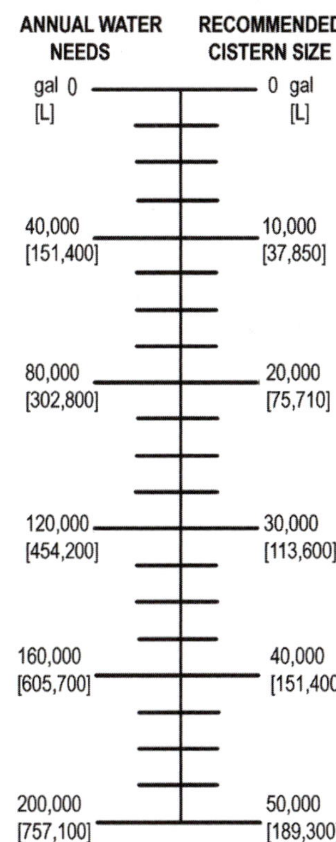

4.331 Estimating cistern size—assuming a storage capacity equal to ¼ of annual water needs. ADAPTED FROM *PRIVATE WATER SYSTEMS HANDBOOK*, 4TH ED. MIDWEST PLAN SERVICE

needs of the project (considering design annual rainfall). The roof area used for catchment calculations should be the projected horizontal area of the roof—not the actual surface area. In general, only 75% of average annual rainfall is actually going to be available for cistern storage (due to unavoidable losses due to evaporation, snow, ice, and roof-debris-washing cycles).

5. Calculate cistern volume. The estimated capacity should be based upon the length of the most extensive rainless period obtained from local climatological data. Cistern capacity = (gpd [L/d] of usage) (number of days in rainless period). The volume can be calculated as follows: 1 ft^3 = 7.48 gal of water [1 m^3 = 1000 L]. Alternatively, a rough estimate of cistern size can be found using Figure 4.331.
6. Establish cistern location. A cistern placed close to water usage locations is most logical and can reduce required pump capacity. An underground location can reduce visual impact and provide stability of water temperature. An above-ground location can provide an opportunity for visual impact and story telling.
7. Select or design the cistern. This will involve consideration of the required volume, desired material, maintenance procedures, and site considerations.

Examples

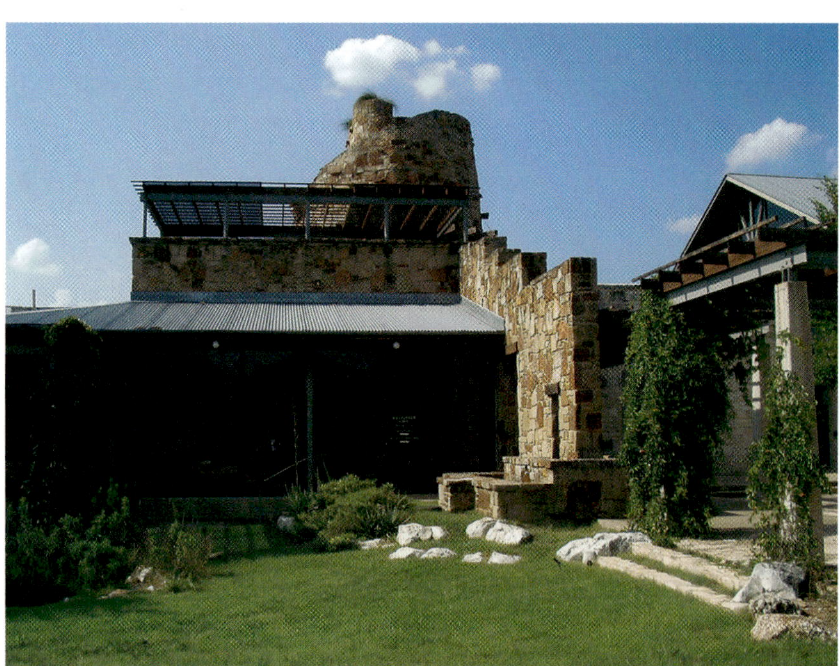

4.332 Observation tower and 5000-gal [18,930 L] cistern collect rainwater from the visitor's gallery and administration buildings at Lady Bird Johnson Wildflower Center in Austin, Texas.

4. Calculating annual water needs:

   72 gpd [273 L/d] × 365 days = 26,280 gal [99,645 L].

   From Figure 4.330, the catchment area needed for 26,280 gal [99,645 L] of water with 27 in. [694 mm] of design precipitation is approximately 2600 ft^2 [242 m^2].

   This represents about 50% of the library addition's roof area—which is quite feasible.

5. From climate data, the dry period for this area is estimated to be 90 days.

   Cistern capacity = 72 gpd [273 L/d] × 90 days = 6480 gal [24,525 L]. A quick check of Figure 4.331 shows that this estimation is reasonable.

   Cistern volume = 6480 gal/ 7.48 gal/ft^3 = 866 ft^3 [25 m^3].

4.333 A large cistern at the entry to the Lady Bird Johnson Wildflower Center in Austin, Texas is constructed with native rock and is part of the extensive rainwater harvesting system at the Center.

4.334 Cisterns assembled from recycled pickle barrels from a nearby factory are part of the highly visible rainwater catchment system at the Chesapeake Bay Foundation in Annapolis, Maryland.

Further Information

Grondzik, W. et al. 2010. *Mechanical and Electrical Equipment for Buildings*. 11th ed. John Wiley & Sons, Hoboken, NJ.

Iowa State University 2009. *Private Water Systems Handbook*, 5th ed. Midwest Plan Service, Ames, IA. www.mwpshq.org/

Rupp, G. 2006. "Rainwater Harvesting Systems for Montana." Montana State University Extension Service. msuextension.org/publications/agandnaturalresources/mt199707ag.pdf

USEPA. 1991. Manual of Individual and Non-Public Water Supply Systems (570991004). U.S. Environmental Protection Agency, Washington, DC.

WaterAid International, Rainwater Harvesting. www.wateraid.org/documents/plugin_documents/rainwater_harvesting.pdf

Young. E. 1989. "Rainwater Cisterns: Design, Construction and Water Treatment" (Circular 277). Pennsylvania State University, Agriculture Cooperative Extension, University Park, PA.

BEYOND SCHEMATIC DESIGN

The feasibility and approximate size of a water catchment system will be established during schematic design. Further analysis during design development will validate these early estimates. Specific system equipment and components will be sized, selected, and detailed. Non-residential water catchment systems should be commissioned; any scale of system should include a User's Manual that outlines the designer's assumptions and expectations, and provides maintenance and operations information.

PERVIOUS SURFACES

PERVIOUS SURFACES are ground covers (softscape or hardscape) that allow rainwater to infiltrate and reach subsurface layers. Pervious paving materials are of particular interest to green building design as a means of mitigating urban stormwater runoff and reducing the flow of pollutants from a site. Pervious paving surfaces can be used at a variety of scales (from patios to parking lots) and are available in a range of composition and construction options. The effectiveness of this strategy depends upon the type of pervious surface selected and its intended use (i.e., for parking, roadway, walkway, etc.). Pervious surfaces are amenable to use in most climates.

4.336 Pervious surfaces can play a significant role in the development of green sites.

4.335 Cross-section through a typical porous pavement installation. The components include a porous asphalt top course, a filter course of fine aggregate, a reservoir course of rough stone, and the subsurface ground layer. JON THWAITES

INTENT
Reduce stormwater runoff

EFFECT
Increases on-site percolation of stormwater, decreases off-site runoff

OPTIONS
Several manufactured products and generic materials are available

COORDINATION ISSUES
Site coordination, landscaping design and soil grading, accessibility

RELATED STRATEGIES
Site Analysis, Water Catchment Systems, Water Reuse/Recycling, Bioswales, Retention Ponds

PREREQUISITES
Rainfall data for site, information regarding surface/subsurface drainage conditions, local code requirements

Pervious surface options include plastic grid systems, porous asphalt pavements, porous block pavement systems, porous Portland cement concrete, and a range of granular materials (such as gravel or bark mulch)—as well as many types of vegetation. Vehicle or pedestrian circulation requirements and loads will dictate surface appropriateness.

Plastic grid systems are designed to support pedestrian or light traffic loads. These prefabricated pavement elements consist of a plastic lattice structure that can be filled with rock aggregate, soil and grass, or ground cover. The lattice structure retains the fill material while the fill material reinforces the rigidity of the lattice structure.

Porous (or open-graded) **asphalt pavement** contains no small aggregate particles, which results in a pavement structure with substantial voids. This allows water to enter—and subsequently drain through—the pavement layer. Porous asphalt pavement is appropriate for roads and parking lots.

Porous block pavement systems are constructed from modular interlocking brick, stone, or concrete elements assembled on site into surfaces that provide channels through which water can flow to the underlying substrate. Block pavements come in a range of patterns and colors. They are usually installed over a conventional aggregate base with sand bedding. Porous block systems can be used for high-load conditions (as well as low-load, low-traffic applications such as sidewalks and driveways).

Porous Portland cement concrete differs from non-porous concrete in that fine particles such as sand and small aggregates are left out of the mix. This leaves voids between the large aggregate components and allows water to drain through the concrete. Porous concrete is appropriate for many paving applications, including parking lots and streets.

4.337 Pervious paving of 100% recycled plastic provides adequate strength for parking and driveways while protecting plant roots. INVISIBLE STRUCTURES, INC.

Key Architectural Issues

Pervious surfaces can be used for a variety of vehicular and foot traffic loadings. It is important, however, to ensure a match of material to anticipated loading. Suitability for foot traffic (providing an even walking surface) may hinge more upon quality of installation and stability over time than on the particular paving material selected.

4.338 Porous geotextile fabric sits atop an engineered porous base course, is anchored with galvanized anchors and filled with gravel, and supports substantial loads. INVISIBLE STRUCTURES, INC.

The consideration of pervious surfaces opens the door to a comprehensive look at site landscaping. Some pervious surface approaches will require the selection of an infill material (which might be organic); all pervious materials will be bounded by building or landscape surfaces with inherent opportunities for integration of hardscapes and softscapes.

Surface temperatures of paved areas can be mitigated by using pervious paving. The voids in the material trap moisture which (due to the high specific heat of water) reduces the temperature increase that accompanies the absorption of solar radiation. The soil captured by plastic grid pavers also tends to reduce surface temperatures (relative to other forms of paving). Providing a more reflective surface will also help to reduce paving temperatures and improve the microclimate (at least during the summer). Evapotranspiration from vegetation infill used with plastic grid pavers can also reduce surface temperatures.

4.339 This product is a three-dimensional reinforcement and stabilization matrix for steep vegetated slopes, channel banks, and vegetated swales. The system can withstand intense rainfall or water flow. INVISIBLE STRUCTURES, INC.

Implementation Considerations

The two most critical implementation considerations related to pervious paving are suitability to task and appearance. In general, the appearance of most pervious paving systems is identical to (or an improvement upon) comparable impervious paving materials. Pervious paving systems with infill vegetation, however, can look "ragged" and this should be addressed if believed to be important. Manufacturers/suppliers can provide detailed information regarding load capabilities. Design judgment should be exercised regarding the suitability of foot traffic on pervious paving products.

Design Procedure

The following procedure has been adapted from USEPA Document EPA 832-F-99-023 (Storm Water Technology Fact Sheet: Porous Pavement).

1. **Evaluate site conditions**

   a) Verify soil permeability and porosity, depth of the water table at its highest point (during the wet season), and depth to bedrock. This is usually done by on-site testing, and is often part of the site selection/analysis process.

   b) Check the slopes on the site. Most pervious surface treatments are not recommended for slopes greater than 5%.

   c) Verify soil drainage rates by on-site testing. Pervious paving requires a minimum infiltration rate of 0.5 in. [13 mm] per hour for at least 3 ft [0.9 m] below the bottom of the installed pervious layers.

   d) Verify soil depth. A minimum depth of 4 ft [1.2 m] to bedrock and/or the highest water table is recommended.

   e) Verify site conditions. A minimum setback from water supply wells of 100 ft [30 m] is recommended—to be confirmed with local code authorities. A minimum setback from building foundations of 10 ft [3 m] down gradient and 100 ft [30 m] up gradient is suggested (unless provision is made for appropriate foundation drainage).

   f) Consider the potential for clogging of pavement voids. Pervious asphalt and concrete are not recommended for use in areas where significant amounts of windblown (or vehicle-borne) sediment is expected.

2. **Evaluate traffic conditions**

   a) Evaluate vehicle loadings. Pervious pavements are most successfully used for low-volume automobile parking areas and lightly used access roads. High-traffic areas and significant truck traffic require detailed analysis of loads versus material capabilities.

   b) Consider seasonal conditions. Avoid use in areas requiring snow plow operations; avoid the use of sand, salt, and de-icing chemicals. Consider the ramifications of wind- or water-deposited sand in coastal areas.

3. **Design-storm storage volume**

   Most jurisdictions do not require pervious surfaces to provide for mitigation of a design-storm storage volume unless they entirely replace conventional storm runoff solutions. Consult local codes for specifics.

SAMPLE PROBLEM

The adjacent design procedure is conceptual and involves no calculations that would be further illustrated by a sample problem.

Examples

4.340 Garden pavers and grass (left) provide a permeable, green courtyard at the Chinese wing of the Honolulu Academy of Arts in Honolulu, Hawaii. A hierarchy of stone sizes and landscaping (right) provides a pervious entry path to a private house in Kanazawa, Japan.

4.341 A porous paving system at an apartment complex in Virginia. INVISIBLE STRUCTURES, INC.

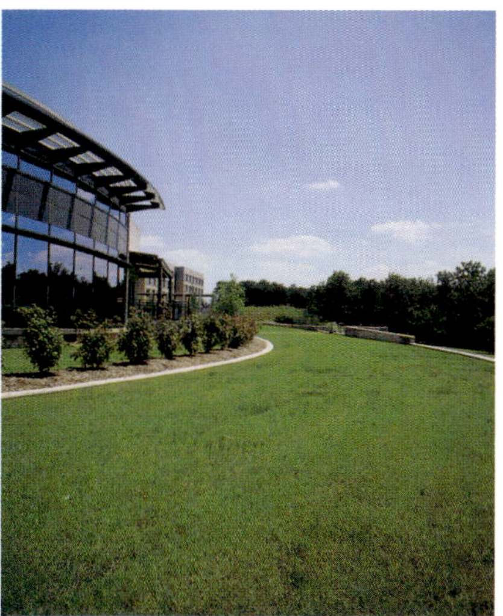

4.342 Installation of a pervious slope and erosion control system along a park path (left) and a porous grass pavement system (right) at the Sabre Holdings Headquarters in Southlake, Texas. INVISIBLE STRUCTURES, INC.

4.343 Pavers and tile artwork create a pervious patio near the dining hall of the Islandwood Campus on Bainbridge Island, Washington.

Further Information

Partnership for Advancing Technology in Housing, Toolbase, Permeable Pavement. www.toolbase.org/TechInventory/techDetails.aspx?ContentDetailID = 604

Sustainable Sources. 2004. "Pervious Paving Materials." perviouspaving.sustainablesources.com/

USEPA. 1980. Porous Pavement Phase I Design and Operational Criteria (EPA 600-2-80-135). United States Environmental Protection Agency, Urban Watershed Management Research, Washington, DC.

USEPA. 1999. Storm Water Technology Fact Sheet: Porous Pavement (EPA 832-F-99-023). United States Environmental Protection Agency, Office of Water, Washington, DC.

BEYOND SCHEMATIC DESIGN

The schematic design aspects of pervious surfaces are primarily related to proof of concept. Selection, design, detailing, and specification of a particular paving approach will occur during design development. This will include verification of traffic loading capabilities—as necessary and appropriate to project intents.

BIOSWALES are densely vegetated open channels designed to attenuate and treat stormwater runoff. These drainage ways have gentle slopes to allow runoff to be filtered by vegetation planted on the bottom and sides of the swale. Swales are shallow and standing water exposed to solar radiation heats up; such warming is detrimental to some ecosystems. Thus, a bioswale is not designed to hold water for an extended period of time.

Stormwater runoff has historically been dealt with through the use of drainage ditches that quickly routed stormwater to storm sewers. A site's stormwater problem was simply passed along to someone downstream. More ecologically-minded (and site-focused) stormwater management systems include bioswales and/or retention/detention ponds to cleanse stormwater before returning it to the local ecosystem.

4.345 Bioswale used in conjunction with expressive roof downspouts at the Water Pollution Control Laboratory in Portland, Oregon.

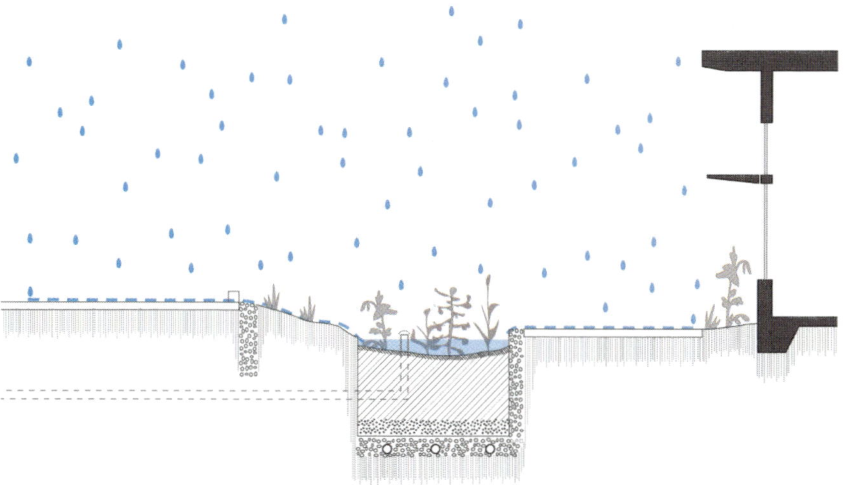

4.344 Section showing the general configuration of a bioswale at a parking lot. JON THWAITES

After stormwater traverses a bioswale, the filtered runoff can be managed in one of the following ways:

- infiltration into the soil;
- flow into a bioretention area or retention/detention pond;
- discharge to a storm sewer system;
- discharge to appropriate receiving waters.

There are several different kinds of swales, with varying arrangements and filtration mechanisms. Several common configurations are discussed below.

Grass channels are similar to conventional drainage ditches but with wide, flattened sides, providing greater surface area to slow down runoff. Such a channel provides preliminary treatment of stormwater as it flows to another stormwater management component such as a bioretention area.

INTENT
Stormwater management

EFFECT
Cleanses (via phytoremediation) and directs stormwater

OPTIONS
Wet, dry, and/or grassed swale

COORDINATION ISSUES
Site grading, placement of swales relative to drainage surfaces, integration of additional bioremediation features

RELATED STRATEGIES
Site Analysis, Retention Ponds, Water Catchment Systems, Water Reuse/Recycling

PREREQUISITES
Site plan, information on soil conditions, rainfall patterns, and storm sewer locations

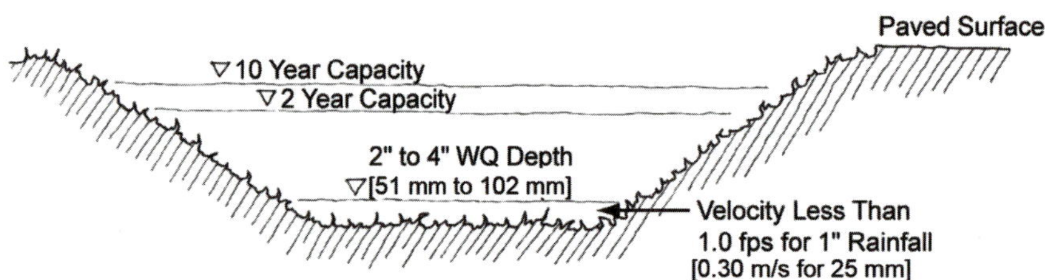

4.346 Section through grass channel bioswale, which slows stormwater runoff and passes it through grass. JONATHAN MEENDERING ADAPTED FROM *DESIGN OF STORM WATER FILTERING SYSTEMS*, CENTER FOR WATERSHED PROTECTION

Dry swales are similar in concept to a detention pond in that they have water-holding capacity and permit water to flow through the bottom of the swale—but are designed to leave the grassy top relatively dry. Dry swales include a large layer of soil fill inside a filter-fabric-lined channel with a perforated pipe system at the bottom of the swale—similar to a foundation perimeter drain. The perforated pipe constituting the underdrain usually directs treated stormwater to a storm drain system. Dry swales are a good strategy in residential areas (from a safety/usage perspective) and can be easily located along a roadway or at the edge of a property.

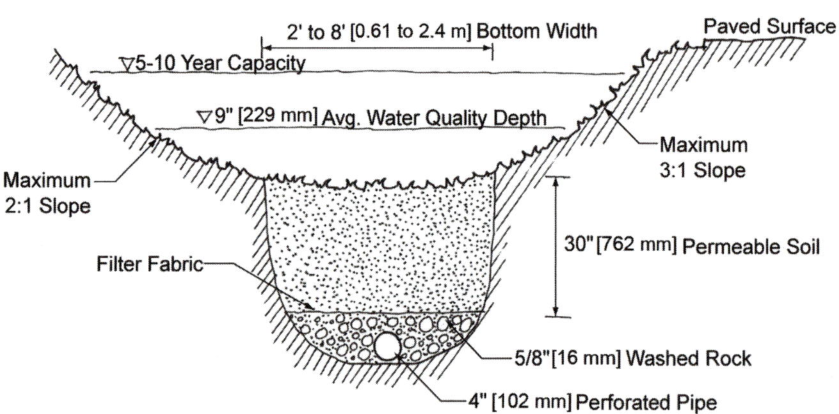

4.347 Section through a parabolic-shaped dry swale showing the various layers and their arrangement. JONATHAN MEENDERING ADAPTED FROM *DESIGN OF STORM WATER FILTERING SYSTEMS*, CENTER FOR WATERSHED PROTECTION

Wet swales are essentially long, linear wetlands, designed to temporarily store water in a shallow pool. Because it does not have a filtering bed of soil, a wet swale (similar to wetlands) treats stormwater by the slow settling of particles, infiltration of water, and bioremediation of pollutants. Vegetation can be purpose-planted or the swale can be allowed to naturally populate with emergent wetland plant species.

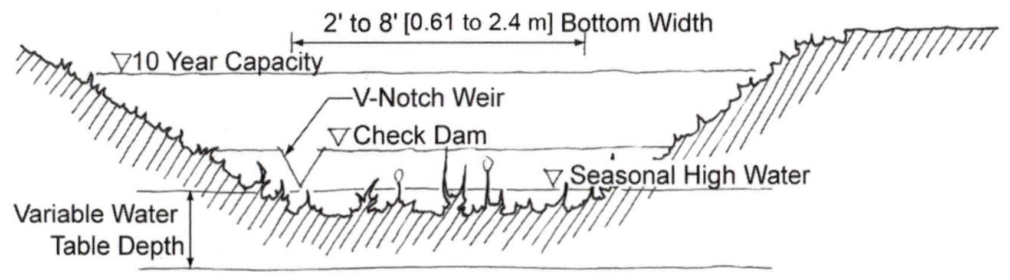

4.348 Section through a trapezoidal wet swale. Generally the bottom width is between 2 and 8 ft [0.6–2.4 m]. JONATHAN MEENDERING ADAPTED FROM *DESIGN OF STORM WATER FILTERING SYSTEMS*, CENTER FOR WATERSHED PROTECTION

Key Architectural Issues

The physical integration of swales relative to the locations of buildings, parking lots, and other water-shedding surfaces is a key consideration. The visual integration of swales into a site (including landscaping) is another concern.

Implementation Considerations

National and local stormwater management requirements should be understood. Some locales place restrictions on the use of grassed bioswales. In some locations, soil conditions (such as underlying bedrock or a high water table) would prevent the cost-effective or technically-effective use of this strategy. As a spatially extensive strategy, the availability of adequate site area and early integration into site planning is critical to the implementation of effective bioswale remediation strategies. The suitability and extent of bioswales for a given site will depend upon land use, size of the drainage areas, soil type, and slope. Many local jurisdictions have developed guidelines for the design of dry and wet swales; such guidelines should be consulted when available.

Design Procedure

The design process presented herein (extracted from *Design of Stormwater Filtering Systems*) has been simplified for the schematic design process. While other stormwater treatment practices are sized on the basis of volume of runoff water, bioswales are designed based upon flow rate and volume of water for surface storage. Dry swales are generally used in moderate- to large-lot residential settings. Wet swales are mainly used in high volume situations, such as to control runoff from highways, parking lots, rooftops, and other impervious surfaces. The dry and wet swale design procedure follows.

1. Determine water quality treatment volume (WQV) for the site.
    - Establish the runoff coefficient (R_v). For schematic design this is equal to the percentage of the site that is impervious (essentially the percentage of the site that is hard surfaced). This estimate can be finessed to include semi-pervious materials by using weighted average areas.
    - Use the following equation to estimate the required water "storage" volume (volume of swale):

SAMPLE PROBLEM

A green housing development in Virginia has site characteristics described below and approximately 300 ft [91 m] of length for a dry swale along an access road.

The development surfaces can be characterized as: Houses: 0.20 acres [0.08 ha] Lawns: 90.0 acres [36 ha] Pervious drives: 0.10 acres [0.04 ha] Asphalt street: 0.15 acres [0.06 ha]

1. Runoff coefficient, R_v: is estimated as the ratio of impervious surface area to total surface area
   $= (0.2 + 0.15) / 90.45$
   $= 0.0039$
   [$(0.08 + 0.06) / 36.18$
   $= 0.0039$].

$$WQV = (P)\ (R_v)$$

where,

P = design 24-hr rainfall (this value should be selected to allow the on-site detention of most common precipitation events; 1 in. [25 mm] is recommended for the mid-Atlantic United States, while 2 in. [50 mm] may be more appropriate for areas with more intense downpours)

R_v = the site runoff coefficient

- Convert WQV to swale volume as follows:
  swale volume in ft^3: (WQV) × (site area in acres) × (3629)
  swale volume in m^3: (WQV) × (site area in hectares) × (10).

2. Select the preferred shape of swale. Swales are generally trapezoidal or parabolic. In a trapezoidal section, 2–6 in. [50–150 mm] of soil/sand mix will be installed over approximately 5 in. [125 mm] of soil/gravel mix, which is placed over a perforated underdrain system. A parabolic section (see Figure 4.347) will have approximately 30 in. [760 mm] of permeable soil over 5 in. [125 mm] of gravel that surrounds a perforated underdrain pipe.
3. Establish bioswale dimensions. The dimensions should accommodate the swale volume calculated in Step 1.
   - Bottom width: typically 2–8 ft [0.6–2.4 m]
   - Side slopes: 2:1 maximum, with 3:1 or flatter preferred; the longitudinal slope is usually 1–2%
   - Length: as required to obtain necessary swale volume
   - Depth: A rough guideline is to use an average 12 in. [300 mm] depth for effective water treatment and another 6 in. [150 mm] to provide adequate capacity for a 10-year storm event
   - Underlying soil bed: below a dry swale, the soil bed should consist of moderately permeable soil, 30 in. [760 mm] deep, with a gravel/pipe underdrain system. Below a wet swale the soil bed may be wet for a long period of time and should consist of non-compacted (undisturbed) soils.
4. Verify slope and groundwater clearance. Stormwater moving too fast can cause erosion and may not be properly filtered by the vegetation in the swale. This is controlled by limiting the slope of the swale in the direction of flow. The bottom of a bioswale should be at least 2 ft [0.6 m] above the water table to prevent groundwater contamination via short-circuiting.
5. Select vegetation. The plant species in the swale should withstand flooding during runoff events and withstand drying between runoff events. Recommended plant species for bioretention are region-specific.

For a 1 in. [25 mm] rainfall,
WQV5(P) (R_v)
= (1) (0.0039)
= 0.0039
[(25) (0.0039) = 0.0967].

Swale volume in ft^3
= (0.0039) (90.45) (3629)
= 1280 ft^3

Swale volume in m^3
= (0.0967) (36.18) (10)
= 35 m^3.

2. A trapezoidal swale is selected.
3. A swale with a 6 ft [1.8 m] bottom width and a 9 in. [230 mm] depth is proposed. The area of this swale is: (6 ft) (0.75 ft) = 4.5 ft^2 [0.4 m^2].

   Swale volume at 300 ft [91 m] length = (300 ft) (4.5 ft^2) = 1350 ft^3 [(91 m) (0.4 m^2) = 36 m^3].

   Adequate swale volume to handle the projected runoff is available (1350 > 1280 [36 > 35]).
4. Swale slope is checked and found acceptable. The water table (during the wet season) is 4 ft [1.2 m] below the bottom of the swale.
5. Native grasses and herbaceous plant species are selected that are in keeping with the region's vegetation.

Examples

4.349 The City of Portland (Oregon) integrates vegetated areas to manage stormwater runoff, in what is referred to as a "green street" strategy.

4.350 A porous-pavement parking lot is surrounded by vegetated bioswales at the Jean Vollum Natural Capital Center (Ecotrust Building) in Portland, Oregon.

4.351 Close up of a "green street" stormwater management element.

4.352 Vegetated bioswale at the Jean Vollum Natural Capital Center in Portland, Oregon.

4.353 Rainwater from the roof (shown here) and parking lot of the RiverEast Center in Portland, Oregon—as well as from an adjacent street—is pretreated in this vegetated bioswale, then treated in a privately maintained facility before being allowed to flow into the Willamette River.

4.354 Vegetated bioswale on the campus of the University of Oregon, Eugene.

Further Information

California Stormwater Quality Association. 2003. "Vegetated Swale," in *New Development and Redevelopment Handbook*. www.cabmphandbooks.org/Development.asp

Center for Watershed Protection. 1996. *Design of Stormwater Filtering Systems*. Ellicott City, MD.

IFAS 2008. *Bioswales/Vegetated Swales*, Institute of Food and Agricultural Sciences, University of Florida, Gainesville, FL.

USEPA 2004. *Stormwater Best Management Practice Design Guide, Vol. 2, Vegetative Biofilters*, U.S. Environmental Protection Agency, Washington, DC. www.epa.gov/nrmrl/pubs/600r04121/600r04121a.pdf

BEYOND SCHEMATIC DESIGN

Prior to construction, the area where swales will be located should be protected from car and truck traffic to prevent compaction of the soil (which will reduce infiltration). During construction, equipment and tools should be cleaned off site to prevent polluting materials from contaminating the swales.

After construction is complete, optimum performance of a bioswale requires scheduled maintenance. Maintenance includes regular inspection twice a year, seasonal mowing and lawn care, removal of debris and litter, removal of sediment, grass reseeding, mulching, and the replacement or tilling of a new layer of topsoil into the existing surface. This information needs to be conveyed to the owner via a User's Manual.

RETENTION PONDS (also called detention ponds) are designed to control stormwater runoff on a site and, in some cases, to remove pollutants from the retained water. Stormwater control strategies include ditches, swales, ponds, tanks, and vaults. These generally function by capturing, storing, treating, and then slowly releasing stormwater downstream or allowing it to infiltrate into the ground. A retention (or infiltration) pond acts as a final storage destination for runoff, serving as the place where water is held until it either evaporates or infiltrates the soil. Detention ponds are designed to temporarily store accumulated water before it slowly drains off downstream. Since the primary purpose of both pond types is the same (reduced site runoff), the discussion here will focus on retention ponds.

4.356 Stormwater retention pond at the Water Pollution Control Laboratory in Portland, Oregon. TROY NOLAN PETERS

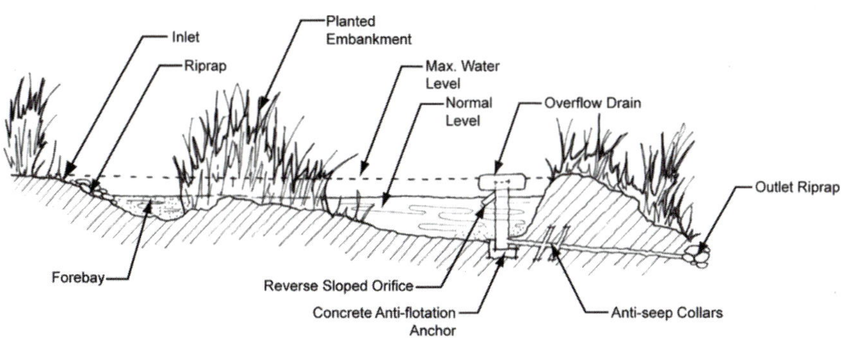

4.355 Section diagram of a retention pond. JONATHAN MEENDERING

Retention ponds are related to bioswales (see the Bioswale strategy). Bioswales, however, primarily direct the flow of moving water. Ponds are a destination for a quantity of water, which is held until it evaporates or infiltrates the soil. If water treatment is required, bioremediation methods can be included (thus the term "bioretention pond"). These methods involve the use of soil bacteria, fungi, and plants to remove pollutants. These organisms can rapidly break down the organic pollutants (e.g., oil) in stormwater. Bioretention areas are most beneficially employed near large impervious surfaces (such as parking lots), in street medians, and in the zones between buildings.

Key Architectural Issues

Principal areas of architectural concern with retention ponds are scale, site placement, and landscaping. Retention ponds can take up a fair amount of land, depending upon the amount of stormwater to be handled. The relationship between retention pond and buildings or other site structures (such as parking lots, driveways, outdoor areas) can be creatively addressed during the design process so that the pond functions well and integrates into a given site.

INTENT
Bioremediation, water recycling, reduced off-site stormwater flow

EFFECT
Reduces site runoff, cleanses and returns water to ecosystem

OPTIONS
Retention/detention or bioretention

COORDINATION ISSUES
Pond footprint relative to site, local code requirements, site grading

RELATED STRATEGIES
Site Analysis, Bioswales, Pervious Surfaces, Water Catchment Systems, Water Reuse/Recycling

PREREQUISITES
Information on soil conditions, average monthly rainfall on site, surface characteristics of the developed site

Implementation Considerations

Retention ponds are best suited to sites that will be graded or excavated, so the pond can be incorporated into the site plan without otherwise unnecessary environmental impact. They are generally ineffective in areas where the water table is within 6 ft [1.8 m] of the ground surface, where the soil is unstable, or where the slope of the adjacent areas is greater than 20% (which could lead to erosion). Sites with unstable soil conditions or poor permeability (more than 25% clay content) are not appropriate for bioretention. The U.S. Environmental Protection Agency (USEPA) recommends an infiltration rate of 0.5 in. [12 mm] per hour and soil pH between 5.5 and 6.5. Ideally, the soil should have a 1.5–3% organic content and a maximum 500-ppm concentration of soluble salts for good bioremediation of pollutants.

TABLE 4.25 Typical performance of bioretention areas. U.S. EPA OFFICE OF WASTE WATER MANAGEMENT

POLLUTANT	REMOVAL RATES
Phosphorus	70–83%
Metals (Cu, Zn, Pb)	93–98%
TKN*	68–80%
Suspended solids	90%
Organics	90%
Bacteria	90%

* Total Kjeldahl Nitrogen

For high performance, the soil surface (bottom of the retention pond) and the pollutants must be in contact for adequate periods of time. The infiltration rate of water through the soil must not exceed the rate specified above. Metals, phosphorus, and some hydrocarbons can be removed via adsorption. Further filtration occurs as runoff passes through the sand bed and vegetation surrounding the area. The filtering effectiveness of a retention area can decrease over time, unless it is maintained by removing debris and repairing the active components.

Design Procedure

There are a number of design methods for stormwater runoff—ranging from simple, intuitively designed systems of swales and ponds (developed with minimal calculations) to software programs that define and calculate drainage areas. The following procedure is adapted from the USEPA's "Factsheet on Bioretention." The size of the bioretention area is a function of the volume of rainfall and the drainage area of the site. The calculation of runoff is complex, so the

SAMPLE PROBLEM

A new elementary school in Chicago, Illinois will include a small parking lot. The client wants to provide a bioretention pond adjacent to and on the downhill side of the parking lot.

1. A rough plan of the site shows an asphalt parking lot

following procedure provides very rough guidelines for preliminary sizing during schematic design.

1. Develop a preliminary site plan showing the relative areas of various surface types and the potential location(s) for a retention/detention pond.
2. Calculate the size of the drainage areas. Estimate the areas of pavement, grass, and other surfaces from which runoff will occur.
3. Determine the runoff coefficients "c" for the site elements. The runoff coefficient is a unitless number that accounts for soil type and drainage basin slope. Coefficients for various exterior surfaces are shown in Table 4.26.
4. Calculate the bioretention area. Multiply the (rational method) runoff coefficient "c" by the drainage area for each surface type and sum the results. To estimate the required retention pond area, multiply the sum by 5% if a sand bed is used or by 7% without a sand bed. The USEPA recommends minimum dimensions of 15 ft [4.6 m] by 40 ft [12.2 m] to allow for a dense distribution of trees and shrubs. A rough guideline is to use a 25-ft [7.6 m] width, with a length at least twice the width. The recommended depth of the retention area is 6 in. [150 mm] to provide adequate water storage area, while avoiding a long-lasting pool of sitting water.

TABLE 4.26 Rational method runoff coefficients. LMNO ENGINEERING, RESEARCH AND SOFTWARE, LTD

	RUNOFF COEFFICIENT, c
Asphalt pavement	0.7–0.95
Brick pavement	0.7–0.85
Concrete pavement	0.7–0.95
Cultivated land	0.08–0.41
Forest	0.05–0.25
Lawns	0.05–0.35
Meadow	0.1–0.5
Parks, cemeteries	0.1–0.25
Pasture	0.12–0.62
Roofs	0.75–0.95
Business areas	0.5–0.95
Industrial areas	0.5–0.9
Residential areas	0.3–0.75
Unimproved areas	0.1–0.3

5. Develop a rough layout of the retention pond system. On a project site plan, develop a schematic layout showing approximate location and size of the drainage and bioretention areas. This should be done with due consideration to site parameters such as utilities, soil conditions, topography, existing vegetation, and drainage.

with interspersed grassy areas.

2. Drainage areas are estimated as: asphalt = 15,000 ft^2 [1394 m^2] and grass = 3000 ft^2 [279 m^2].
3. The "c" factors for these surfaces are assumed as asphalt: 0.9, and grass: 0.25.
4. Find the drainage area for each type of surface using the relationship (surface area)("c"). For asphalt this is (15,000 ft^2 [1394 m^2]) (0.9) = 13,500 ft^2 [1255 m^2]

   For grass this is (3000 ft^2)(0.25) = 750 ft^2 [279 m^2 × 0.25 = 70 m^2]

   Required retention pond area (with a sand bed): = (0.05)(13,500 ft^2 + 750 ft^2) = 712 ft^2 [66 m^2]

   Required retention pond area (without a sand bed) = (0.07) (13,500 ft^2 + 750 ft^2) = 998 ft^2 [93 m^2].
5. The required area of retention pond is included in a schematic layout of the site—and is placed in a location that permits gravity drainage into the pond.

Examples

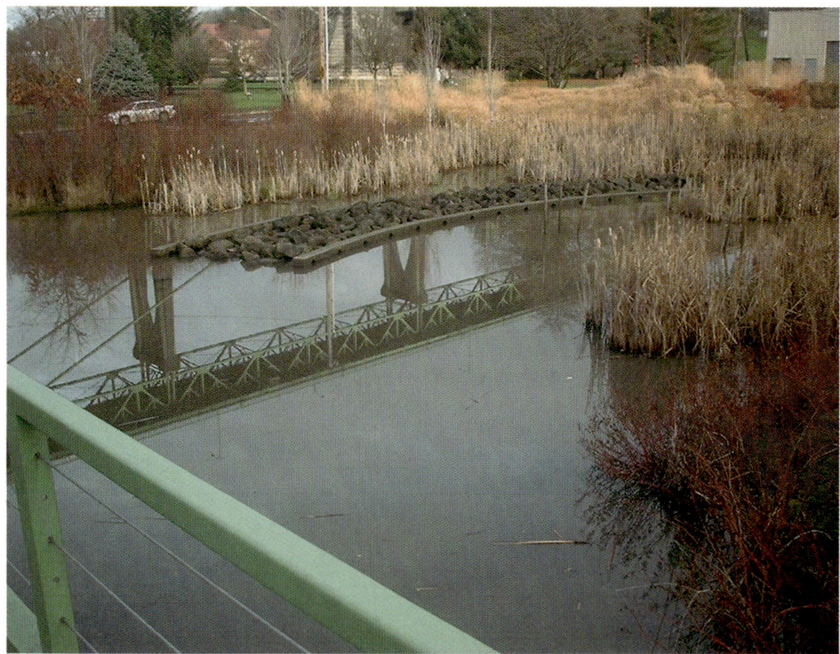

4.357 Native plants, shrubs, and grasses in the retention pond at the Water Pollution Control Laboratory in Portland, Oregon. TROY NOLAN PETERS

4.358 Wetland retention pond adjacent to a pervious-surface parking lot at the Chesapeake Bay Foundation in Annapolis, Maryland. The raised overflow component allows for the infiltration of water during most storm events before returning any site runoff directly to the Bay.

Further Information

Center for Watershed Protection. 1996. *Design of Stormwater Filtering Systems.* Ellicott City, MD.

LMNO Engineering, Research, and Software, Ltd. Rational Equation Calculator (an online tool to calculate drainage basin peak discharge rate). www.lmnoeng.com/Hydrology/rational.htm

USEPA 1999. *Storm Water Technology Fact Sheet: Bioretention (EPA 832-F-99-012)*, U.S. Environmental Protection Agency, Washington, DC.

USEPA 1999. *Storm Water Technology Fact Sheet: Wet Detention Ponds (EPA 832-F-99-048)*, U.S. Environmental Protection Agency, Washington, DC.

BEYOND SCHEMATIC DESIGN

The estimated sizes of retention ponds (or bioretention areas) established during schematic design will be verified during design development as more complete information about the site design is available and more detailed methods of analysis become appropriate.

Design details will be finalized during design development—including site landscaping, water collection elements, and the pond itself. A User's Manual should be developed to assist the owner with proper care and maintenance of the pond/bioremediation area.

NOTES

CHAPTER 5

CASE STUDIES

The case studies presented in this chapter include a range of buildings selected to provide a diversity of geographic locations, climates, building types, and green strategies. The design teams for these projects have made strong statements about green design intentions and have provided fertile ground for designers to learn from their projects. Each case study is organized as follows:

- a general description of the project;
- a sidebar "scorecard" with building, climate, client, and design team information;
- a statement of design intent and related design criteria;
- design validation methods that were employed (modeling, simulation, hand calculations, etc.);
- a description of the green strategies used;
- post-occupancy validation results (if available).

Each case study describes an outstanding project that integrated green strategies via an informed design process. All the projects offer informative lessons for future projects.

NOTES

A ROADMAP TO STRATEGIES AND CASE STUDIES

This matrix identifies which of the 42 green design strategies are incorporated in the 10 case studies that follow. The ● symbol indicates that a strategy is prominently featured; the ○ symbol indicates that a strategy is discussed; a blank space means the strategy is not discussed or not applicable.

Strategy	Bad Aibling Spa	Cambridge Public Library	John Hope Gateway at RBGE	Kenyon House	Offices for the KfW Banking Group, Frankfurt	Manitoba Hydro Place	Learning Resources Center at MCDS	One Brighton	Passive House U.S.	Yodakandiya Community Complex
1. Site Analysis	●	●	●	●	●	●	●	●		●
2. Insulation									●	
3. Straw Bale										
4. SIPs										
5. Glazing	○	●	●	○	●	●	○	●	●	
6. Double Envelope		●			●	●				
7. Green Roofs	○	○	○		○	○		○		
8. Daylight Factor	●	○	●		●	●	●	○		
9. Daylight Zoning	●	●	●	○	●	●	●			●
10. Toplighting	●	○	●				●			
11. Sidelighting	●	●	●	●	●	●	●	●	○	○
12. Light Shelves		●	○							
13. Internal Reflectance	○	●	○	●	○	○	○	○		
14. Shading Devices	○	●	○	○	●	●	●	○	○	●
15. Electric Lighting	○	○	○	○	○	○	○	○	○	
16. Direct Gain	○	○	○	○	●	●	●	●	●	○
17. Indirect Gain										○
18. Isolated Gain		○			○	●				
19. Active Solar Thermal			○				○		○	
20. Ground Source HP	●					●	●		○	
21. Cross Ventilation	●		●		●	●	●			●
22. Stack Ventilation	●	●	●		●	●	●			●
23. Evap Cool Tower					●		●			
24. Night Ventilation					●	●	●			○
25. Earth Cooling Tubes					●					
26. Earth Sheltering	○						○	○		
27. Absorption Chiller					○					
28. Plug Loads				○				○		
29. Air-to-Air Heat Exch									○	
30. Energy Recovery	○				●	●	●	●	●	
31. Photovoltaics			○				●	○	○	
32. Wind Turbines			○							
33. Microhydro										
34. Fuel Cells										
35. Combined Heat/Pwr					●					
36. Composting Toilets										
37. Water Reuse/Recycle	○	○	●	○	○	○	●	●		●
38. Living Machines										
39. Water Catchment		○	●		○		●	●		●
40. Pervious Surfaces	○	○	○	○	○		○	○		○
41. Bioswales							○			
42. Retention Ponds										

NOTES

Background and Context

Bad Aibling is a small town about 30 miles [48 km] southeast of Munich in the Bavarian region of southern Germany. The historic town has been a destination for mud and peat healing treatments since the mid nineteenth century. The discovery of thermal water in 2000 only added to the town's popularity as a destination for visitors.

Spa Baths Bad Aibling was the first commercial spa complex to open in the town and consisted of an indoor ice-skating rink and a sauna on a 9-acre [3.6 ha] site near the town center—along the Triftbach Stream with views of the Bavarian Alps to the south. Behnisch Architekten won 1st Prize in a 2003 design competition for the expansion of the spa complex.

From the very beginning, the client insisted that the new building should not be a large, noisy, indoor swimming hall. The desire was for a more relaxing and contemplative spa experience with both indoor and outdoor program elements. The 116,788 ft^2 [10,850 m^2] building includes space for bathing, saunas, beauty and wellness treatments, and eating.

5.1 A view of the spa baths at night from the Triftbach stream showing the domed "cabinet" baths in relation to the winter garden lounge and circulation space. ADAM MØRK – TORBEN ESKEROD

Design Intent and Validation

The design intent for the building was to create a variety of unique and ethereal spa experiences within individual domed, or "cabinet," spaces connected by a luminous winter garden providing circulation, lounge/lobby areas, and uninterrupted views through the space. The structural system is deliberately simple: round concrete columns, wood laminated beams with wood decking, and concrete shell domes.

The semi-enclosed configuration of spaces also allowed separation of wet, humid areas from the dry areas for thermal zoning and

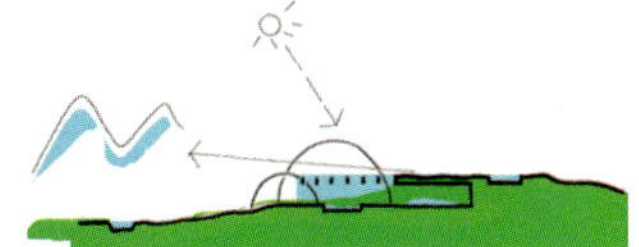

5.2 Diagrammatic sketch showing the solar and geographic orientation on the site. BEHNISCH ARCHITEKTEN

LOCATION
Bad Aibling, Bavaria, Germany
Latitude 47.9 °N
Longitude 12.0 °E

HEATING DEGREE DAYS
6006 base 65 °F
[3337 base 18.3 °C]
Munich, Germany data

COOLING DEGREE DAYS
2067 base 50 °F
[1148 base 10 °C]
Munich, Germany data

DESIGN DRY-BULB WINTER (99%)
15.5 °F [−9.2 °C]
Munich, Germany data

DESIGN DRY-BULB & MEAN COINCIDENT WET-BULB SUMMER (1%)
81.8/64.6 °F [27.7/18.1 °C]
Munich, Germany data

SOLAR RADIATION
Jan 441 Btu/ft^2/day
[1.39 kWh/m^2/day]
Jun 1613 Btu/ft^2/day
[5.09 kWh/m^2/day]

ANNUAL PRECIPITATION
43 in. [1090 mm]

ventilation purposes. Some of the unique design themes in the eight domes include a perforated plexiglass dome for hot and cold bathing; a dome with underwater music and a glowing LED-lit lantern with walls that change color; and a marble-clad dome with basins, tubs, and lanterns hanging from a red ceiling, each evoking rich sensory experiences.

5.3 A conceptual east–west elevation collage. BEHNISCH ARCHITEKTEN

Programmatically, the building acts as a filter of light—with the most transparent and open spaces to the south and the most opaque and enclosed spaces to the north. The changing rooms, placed toward the north side of the structure, respond directly to the change in elevation from south to north across the site. These spaces are literally buried in the site. By contrast, the south facade is a long wall of glazing, which allows views deep into the building. The domes "float" between the south facade and the changing areas, modulating the degree of transparency across the floor plate. Ample sidelighting and toplighting in the winter garden space enhance the transparency concept.

Validation for the overall design intent came primarily from computer and physical daylight modeling and from computational fluid dynamics (CFD) modeling of air movement between the winter garden and the domed spa spaces. These analysis techniques allowed the design team to evaluate alternative approaches to conserve energy and ensure occupant comfort while simultaneously achieving the spatial qualities and effects inherent in the initial design concept.

Strategies

Design strategies were carefully selected and developed throughout the design process to ensure that the finished building remained true to the initial design concept—while providing a high degree of occupant comfort, efficient environmental control systems, and access to daylight.

Site. The long facades of the spa building were oriented south to take advantage of a view toward the Alps, easily controlled daylighting, and solar heat gain during winter months. The steel and glass facade opens directly to a series of outdoor swimming pools and allows access along a path to a series of detached sauna structures adjacent to the Triftbach stream. The topography of the site was extensively reworked to slope uphill from the south, along the stream, to the north, where a large outdoor swimming pool is at the same elevation as the roof of the spa bath building.

BUILDING TYPE
Spa Baths

AREA
116,788 ft^2 [10,850 m^2]

CLIENT
Stadtwerke Bad Aibling

DESIGN TEAM
Architect, Behnisch Architekten

Energy/Climate Engineer, Transsolar Energietechnik

Structural Engineer, Duwe, Mühlhausen

Building Physics, Bobran Ingenieure

Lighting Design, IB Bamberger

Construction Manager, HW Ingenieur Consult

COMPLETION
September 2007

PERFORMANCE METRICS
Energy Utilization Index (EUI): Not Available

Carbon Emissions: Not Available

Water Use: Not Available

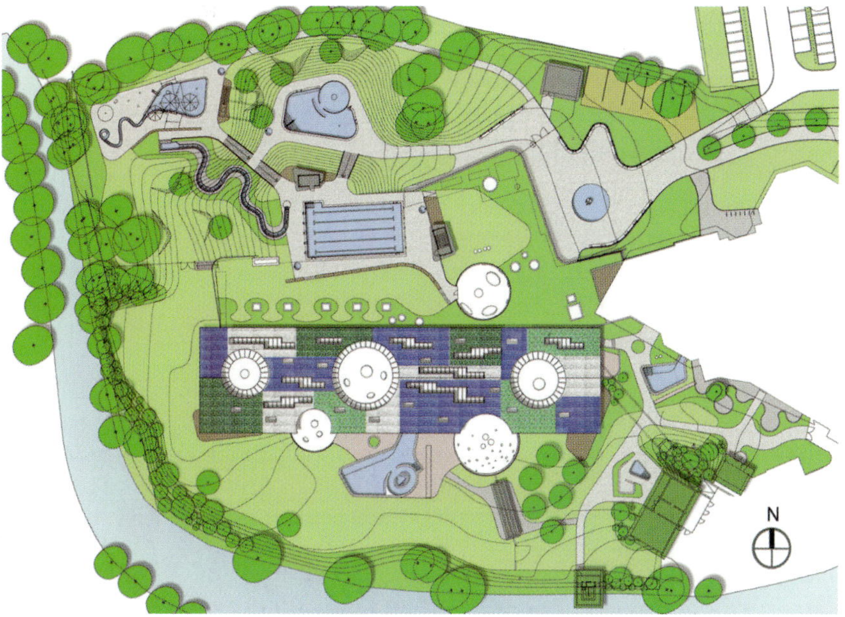

5.4 Site plan showing the south facade of spa bath oriented toward the Triftbach stream. BEHNISCH ARCHITEKTEN

Natural ventilation. The spa bath complex uses a mixed-mode ventilation regime whereby mechanical ventilation is provided in the winter and natural ventilation is provided in the spring, summer, and fall. Increasing outdoor temperatures and greater opportunities for harnessing direct solar heat gain make mechanical heating and ventilation unnecessary, which enables these systems to be turned off. Ventilation air is then naturally admitted into the building through doors in the south facade and exhausted through operable skylights or hatches in the roof of the winter garden space or at the top of the spa dome spaces. The use of natural ventilation for a significant portion of the year saves energy and satisfies patron thermal comfort.

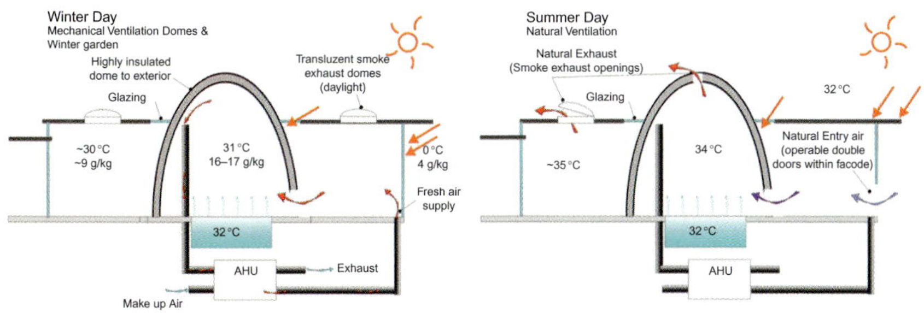

5.5 Diagrams showing the natural ventilation strategies for a winter day (left) and a summer day (right). TRANSSOLAR

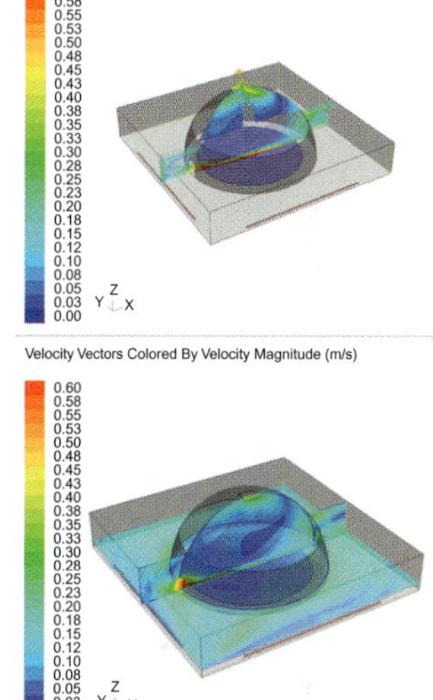

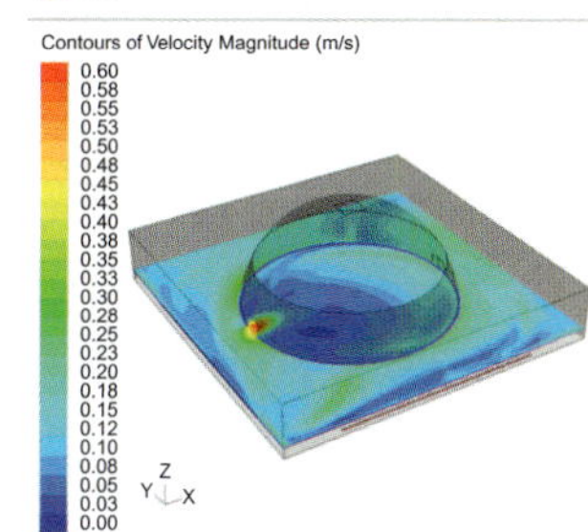

5.6 Compuational fluid dynamics (CFD) models of air movement through different sized doorways in the spa domes. TRANSSOLAR

Daylighting. The building was specifically sited and designed to take advantage of daylighting opportunities. A long, glazed facade is oriented south for solar access and views to the Alps. A roof overhang provides shading in the summer months, but allows the sun to penetrate deeply into the floor plan during the winter months. Initially, the design team envisioned a fully glazed winter garden space linking the eight domed spa spaces. A fully glazed roof, however, would have made it difficult to control solar heat gain, to control glare potential, and to provide thermally comfortable conditions for patrons. Extensive daylight modeling was conducted to determine the most appropriate extent of glazing, while still capturing the essence of the original design concept.

By the end of the schematic design phase, the glazed roof area had been reduced to 40%. The design analysis process continued, however, and the final building has a glazed roof area of 15%. Linear strip skylights were strategically positioned above lounge spaces to give the winter garden space a light-filled quality. Lighting focus was achieved by placing narrow skylights around the perimeter of the domes, which wash the exterior walls of the domes with sunlight.

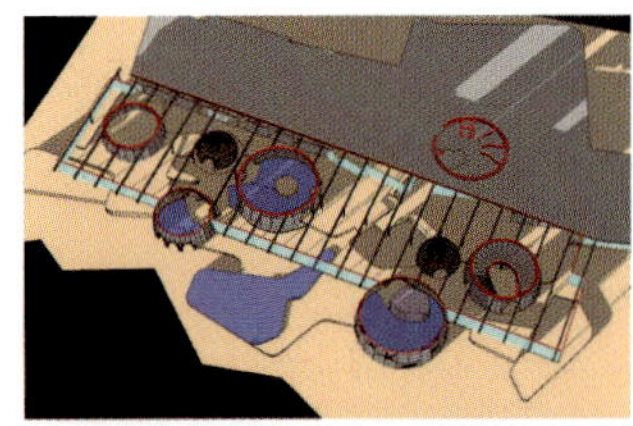

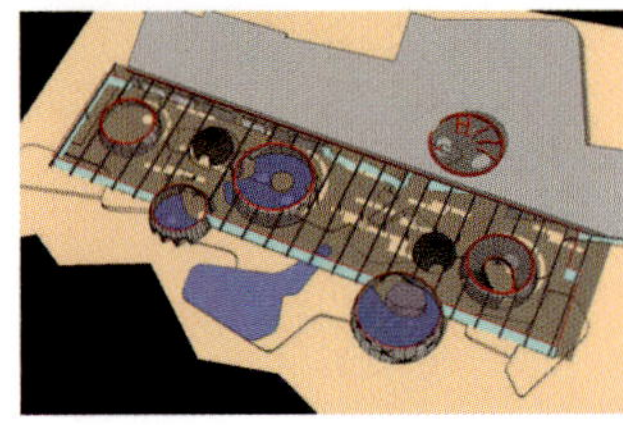

5.8 Daylighting models of winter (top) and summer (bottom) afternoon conditions resulting from optimized sidelighting and toplighting configurations. TRANSSOLAR

5.7 Winter garden lounge and circulation space showing spa domes and toplighting through skylight strips. ADAM MØRK — TORBEN ESKEROD

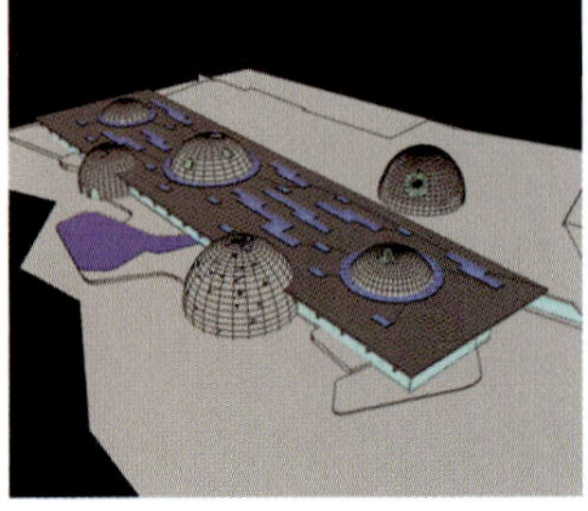

5.9 3D model of the final strip skylight design, which provides optimal daylighting within the winter garden while also addressing glare and occupant comfort issues. TRANSSOLAR

Electric lighting: An innovative light-emitting diode (LED) system was used for lighting effects within the spa domes and night-time lighting of pools and interior spaces. While LED lighting can be more expensive than traditional fluorescent or incandescent lighting, benefits include longer life, smaller size, and greater energy efficiency.

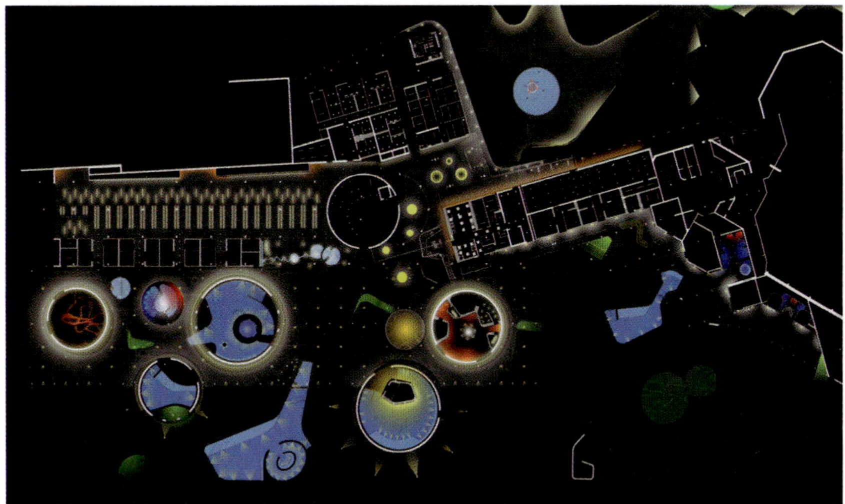

5.10 Rendering of electric lighting sources within the building. BEHNISCH ARCHITEKTEN

Passive solar heating. The glazed south facade was designed to provide passive solar heating in addition to providing ample daylighting as discussed above. The roof overhang shades the facade during the summer months when the sun is high in the sky, which prevents unwanted heat gain during the overheated months. In the winter, when the sun is lower in the sky, the roof overhang no longer shades the facade and solar radiation is allowed to warm the building during the underheated months. Thermal mass elements, such as concrete floor slabs, columns, and domes, absorb solar radiation during the winter daylight hours and the stored heat provides radiant warmth to interior spaces.

Thermal zones. While the individual domed areas appear to be a modern interpretation of traditional bath house architecture, they also serve an important climatic function within the building. Large indoor swimming pools are often energy intensive, uncomfortably humid, and prone to condensation. The heating demand in interior spaces with pools is directly related to the amount of water evaporation from those pools. As water temperature increases, the relative humidity of the indoor air decreases. This results in greater pool evaporation, which leads to an energy demand for dehumidifying the room air as well as replacing the heat lost in the evaporated water. Placing smaller spa pools within domed enclosures allows environmental conditions in the pool zones to be isolated from the lounge and circulation spaces located in the winter garden. By allowing higher humidity conditions within the spa domes only, the thermal comfort conditions for occupants can be optimized in the winter garden space and energy can be conserved. CFD modeling was used to study appropriate sizes for doorway openings into the domes. Air moves from the less humid winter garden zone to the more humid spa domes before being exhausted or conditioned.

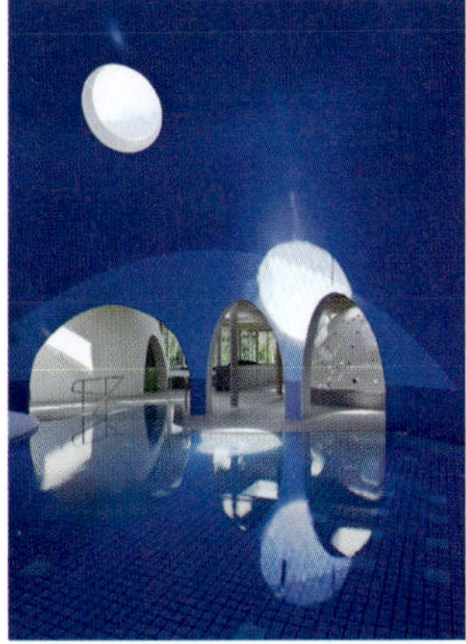

5.11 Spa domes were conceived as separate thermal zones with unique sensory themes. ADAM MØRK — TORBEN ESKEROD

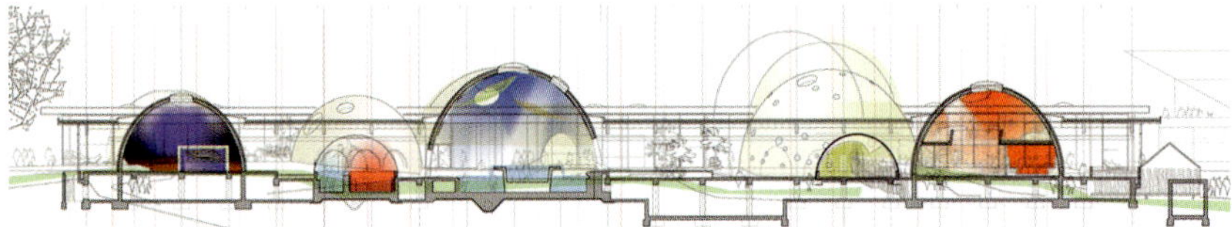

5.12 Building section showing the domed "cabinet" baths in relation to interstitial winter garden space. BEHNISCH ARCHITEKTEN

Materials. One of the detached saunas uses Finnish pine deadwood. Wet areas have granite flooring, while some dry areas have ash or smoked oak flooring. Sections of the flat roof are covered with recycled colored glass.

Green roofs. Large areas of green roof are used on the north side of the building adjacent to the outdoor swimming pool, which help to promote interactions between the building and the ambient landscape. The green roofs also protect the roofing membrane from UV degradation, act as a habitat for wildlife, and help insulate the building.

5.13 The winter garden is covered with a green roof on the north side of the building (left) and colored, recycled glass on the south side of the building (right). ADAM MØRK — TORBEN ESKEROD

Mechanical systems. Warm 102 °F [39 °C] mineral water is pumped from a 7546-ft [2300 m] deep well system, treated, and supplied to the pools within the complex. Gases accumulating within the well borehole are captured and used as fuel to heat the spa. Power and additional heating for the spa are provided by an existing district cogeneration plant on the site.

How Is It Working?

As one of the newest recreation destinations in Germany, the Spa Baths have been a popular attraction for visitors seeking healing treatments, relaxation, and stress-relief. Additional outdoor pools have been constructed since the opening of the building in 2007 and others are planned. Bad Aibling offers other recreational activities such as hot air balloon rides, nearby nature and forests, and the historic town center.

Further Information

Beautyman, M. 2008. "BUBBLE BATH–A spa by Behnisch Architekten bursts onto the scene in sleepy Bad Aibling, Germany," *Interior Design*, 79, No. 2, 180–187.

Behnisch Architekten. www.behnisch.com/site_files/pdf/190.pdf (A 7-page downloadable document that includes project information, a description, and color photographs of the interior and exterior.)

Jaeger, F. 2009. *Behnisch Architekten*, Jovis, Berlin. 116–123.

"Therme Bad Aibling–Behnisch Architekten." 2008. *L'Arca* (242): 74–80.

Therme (Spa) Bad Aibling. www.therme-bad-aibling.de (A webpage that includes project information, design team members, and a series of professional photographs of the interior and exterior.)

Transsolar Energietechnik. www.transsolar.com/download/e/pb_therme_bad_aibling_e.pdf (A concise, 1-page downloadable document that includes project information, descriptions of daylighting and climate control concepts used, and color images and diagrams. More descriptions of the design strategies are also available on the Transsolar website under "completed projects.")

Zacks, S. 2008. "Form Follows Performance: The German architect Stefan Behnisch pushes form and sustainable design into new energy-efficient directions," *Metropolis*, 28, No. 5, 74–81.

NOTES

CAMBRIDGE PUBLIC LIBRARY MAIN BRANCH

Background and Context

The Cambridge Public Library Main Branch is located in Cambridge, Massachusetts approximately 3 miles [4.8 km] from downtown Boston. Cambridge, a city of just over 100,000 people, is known for its prestigious universities (Harvard and MIT), its vibrant academic atmosphere, and its diverse population.

The library is located several blocks east of the Harvard University campus on a site bounded by two busy arterial roads—Broadway to the southwest and Cambridge Street to the north. The large Cambridge Rindge and Latin High School sits in close proximity to the complex on the north and west sides of the site, effectively screening the library from busy Cambridge Street. To the southwest, the Main Branch overlooks a 4-acre [1.6 ha] city park.

5.14 The historic "stone" and new "glass" buildings viewed side-by-side from Joan Lorentz Park. ROBERT BENSON PHOTOGRAPHY

The original library building, built in 1889 by Van Brunt and Howe, is an imposing Richardsonian Romanesque-style structure listed on the National Register of Historic Places. The interior of the building features Depression-era murals and extensive oak paneling. An addition was made to the original building in the 1960s.

By the 1990s, the library was in desperate need of renovation and additional space. The City of Cambridge undertook a 15-year planning and construction process that culminated in the demolition of the 1960s addition, a complete restoration of the 1889 historic building, a dramatic new addition that more than quadrupled the size of the library complex, and a newly landscaped city park. Community involvement, sensitivity to the existing building and site landscape, and a desire to welcome the public into the facility were hallmarks of the design process.

Design Intent and Validation

There were four main objectives for the Cambridge Public Library Main Branch project:

- Connecting the buildings to the surrounding site by creating a "library in the park."

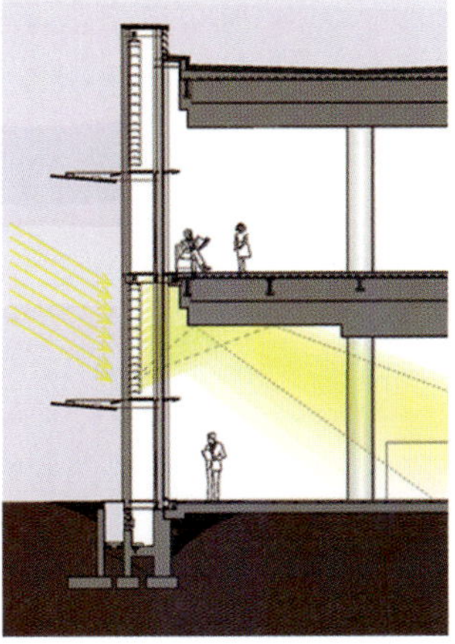

5.15 Section diagram showing daylighting through the double-skin facade of the new building. WILLIAM RAWN WITH ANN BEHA ARCHITECTS

LOCATION
Cambridge, MA, USA
Latitude 42.4 °N
Longitude 71.1 °W

HEATING DEGREE DAYS
5621 base 65 °F
[3123 base 18.3 °C]

COOLING DEGREE DAYS
2938 base 50 °F
[1632 base 10 °C]

DESIGN DRY-BULB WINTER (99%)
12.4 °F [−10.9 °C]

DESIGN DRY-BULB & MEAN COINCIDENT WET-BULB SUMMER (1%)
87.6/71.9 °F [30.9/22.2 °C]

SOLAR RADIATION
Jan 574 Btu/ft^2/day
[1.81 kWh/m^2/day]
Jun 1794 Btu/ft^2/day
[5.66 kWh/m^2/day]

ANNUAL PRECIPITATION
43 in. [1092 mm]

- Welcoming a diverse population of local citizens into the library.
- Seamlessly connecting the New Building to the Historic Library.
- Celebrating books and reading.

The historic library building was an important piece of the city's architectural heritage, but the library needed more space than the historic building provided. The design team responded to this challenge by preserving the historic library intact while adding a large new building that satisfied program requirements and fulfilled design goals for increased transparency with the community. The two wings differ dramatically in their architectural language. The new building does not attempt to mimic or duplicate the original structure, though it borrows key rhythms and regulating lines. It is a crisp and modern glass box, which acts as a counterpoint to the rustic, ornate, and volumetrically complex historic building. The two wings sit side-by-side defining the northern edge of the adjacent park.

A high degree of transparency and connection with the outdoors was achieved through the use of a double-skin curtainwall on the main, southwest-facing facade. The design team considered numerous North American and European buildings with double envelopes to determine the correct combination of features and components that would allow the facade to perform as many functions as possible. Ultimately, three characteristics—a deep cavity space, a multi-story cavity, and shading within the cavity—were identified as the most appropriate traits for daylighting, thermal comfort, thermal insulation, solar shading, passive solar heating, visual transparency, and natural ventilation. Validation for this approach came from observing buildings-in-use that employed similar facade systems as well as computational fluid dynamics (CFD) modeling by Arup during the design process.

5.16 Patron seating zone adjacent to the double envelope facade. ROBERT BENSON PHOTOGRAPHY

The connection between the new and old buildings was also critical for the design team. William Rawn Associates worked closely with Ann Beha Architects, the designers responsible for the restoration of

BUILDING TYPE
Library

AREA
27,200 ft^2 [2527 m^2] historic 1889 library restoration
76,700 ft^2 [7126 m^2] new library addition
103,900 ft^2 [9653 m^2] total library complex

CLIENT
City of Cambridge, Cambridge Public Library

DESIGN TEAM
Architect, William Rawn Associates

Associate Architect, Ann Beha Architects

Mechanical/Electrical/Plumbing/Fire Protection Engineer, Vanderweil Engineers

Structural Engineer, Le Messurier Consulting Engineers

Landscape Architect, Michael Van Valkenburgh Associates

Facade Engineer, Arup Facade Engineering, London

General Contractor, Consigli JF/White

Curtainwall Fabricator, Josef Gartner GmbH

COMPLETION
November 2009

PERFORMANCE METRICS
Energy Utilization Index (EUI): Not Available

Carbon Emissions: Not Available

Water Use: Not Available

the Historic Library building, to create a subtle physical connection between the old and new wings. A scheme was devised by which the floor plan for the new building was divided into four "bars," or programmatic zones. The first zone nearest the double-skin facade was for patron seating; the second zone was for book stacks; the third zone was for circulation, service desks, and connection to the old building; and the fourth zone was for offices and more-enclosed spaces. Teen areas and public computers were placed in the old building, which guaranteed that patrons would actively use the Historic Library. The program layout in the new building places the most open spaces closest to the double-skin facade on the south side of the building for optimal access to views and daylight. Indirect daylight is also introduced into the north-facing Archive Room and Children's Program Room.

From the very beginning of the planning and design process, the Director of the Library mandated that the renovation and addition "celebrate the book." Unlike some recent libraries that have focused on being community centers, the Main Branch was to be focused on reading. Books are visible everywhere in the buildings, which the library felt was appropriate given the intellectual and immigrant populations living in Cambridge.

5.17 Site plan showing the Main Branch in relation to the city park and the Cambridge Rindge and Latin High School. WILLIAM RAWN WITH ANN BEHA ARCHITECTS

5.18 The double-skin glass facade allows for a high degree of transparency between the library and the adjacent public park. WILLIAM RAWN WITH ANN BEHA ARCHITECTS

Strategies

The most prominent feature of the new building is the elaborate double envelope. This facade system is a key component in a complex environmental control strategy for the building that includes natural ventilation, passive solar heating, daylighting, thermal insulation, and optimized energy efficiency. This—combined with the adaptive reuse of the Historic Library and the site-sensitive belowground location of the garage and stormwater cistern—produced a library complex that carefully responds to its urban context and orientation.

Site. The relationship between the library and the adjacent city park was an important component of the design process. Wherever possible, the design team chose to lessen the impact of the construction on the landscape. A parking garage was buried beneath the park, which eliminated surface parking, reduced the heat island effect and stormwater runoff from paved surfaces, and protected two large European Beech trees and a large Weeping Willow tree. A large 350,000-gallon [1,324,900 L] cistern was also buried beneath the park. The tank is part of a stormwater catchment system that serves a 3-square mile [7.8 square km] section of Cambridge. The new building was carefully located in the northeast corner of the site, previously occupied by a parking lot, which allowed 4 acres [1.6 ha] of park space to be retained in front of the library complex.

Double envelope. The centerpiece of the new building is the 180-ft [55 m] long double-skin curtainwall on the southwest facade. This was the first application of a double wall facade system on a public library in the United States and the first to combine all three primary features of European double envelope technology: a 3-ft [0.9 m] cavity space; a 45-ft [13.7 m] height; and automated 12-in. [305 mm] deep microperforated, horizontal shading louvers within the cavity space. The facade provides a high degree of transparency, allowing views to the city park from the building and views deep into the building from the city park. Horizontal tinted glass "visors" provide shading for segments of the facade where mechanized shades would have negatively impacted views. Single-pane, low-iron glazing was used for the outer layer of the double-skin and double-pane; low-iron, low-emissivity (low-ε) coated insulated glazing units (IGU) were used for the inner layer of the double skin.

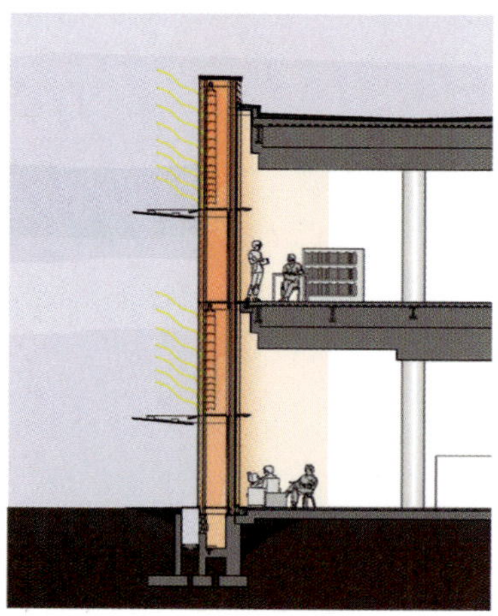

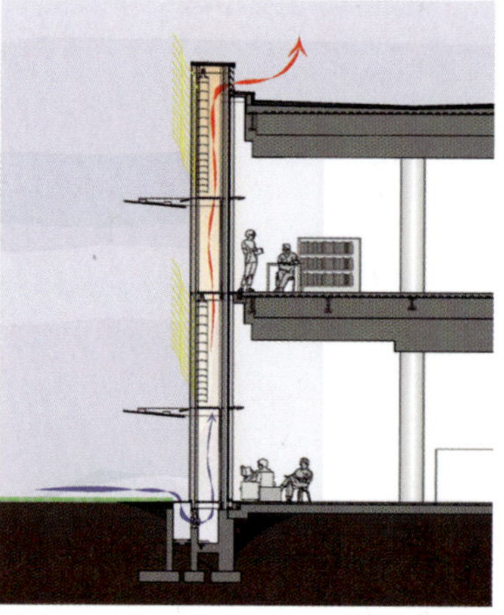

5.19 The double-skin facade shown in winter mode (left) and summer mode (right). WILLIAM RAWN WITH ANN BEHA ARCHITECTS

5.20 The double envelope showing the two facade shading devices: external horizontal "visors" and automated louvers within the cavity space. ROBERT BENSON PHOTOGRAPHY

Natural ventilation. Operable windows on the inner side of the double envelope facade allow occupants some personal control of thermal conditions. This configuration offered two key advantages to the design team: Insect screens were unnecessary (which had maintenance benefits) and tighter security to prevent book theft through windows was possible. In the historic building, existing window sashes were repaired, weatherstripped, and fitted with new storm windows, which improved thermal performance while still allowing for operable sashes for natural ventilation. In the stack wing of the historic building, existing windows were replaced with custom wood-framed, insulated glass units.

Solar control and passive solar heating. While the all-glass southwest elevation of the new building creates a high degree of transparency between the library and the city park and offers opportunities for passive solar heating in cold months, the design team had to find ways to limit excessive solar heat gain in warmer months and glare from changing daily sun angles. The double-skin facade system is intended to operate in two seasonal modes: Operable dampers at the bottom and top of the cavity are open in the summer to permit airflow (when temperatures can reach 90 °F [32 °C]) or closed in the winter to restrict airflow. The design assumes that air trapped within the cavity space in winter mode will act as a thermal buffer between the exterior and the interior of the building and that airflow within the cavity in summer mode will remove excess heat through stack ventilation to keep the inner layer of glazing cool. Two types of shading devices were incorporated into the facade: Fixed horizontal devices, or "visors," were attached to the exterior of the outer layer of glazing and automated horizontal louvers were installed within the cavity space. The fixed devices, placed approximately 8 ft [2.4 m] above floor level allow for unobstructed views through the facade. Louvers, which rotate once daily to respond to low sun angles, are placed between the fixed devices and the ceiling on each level.

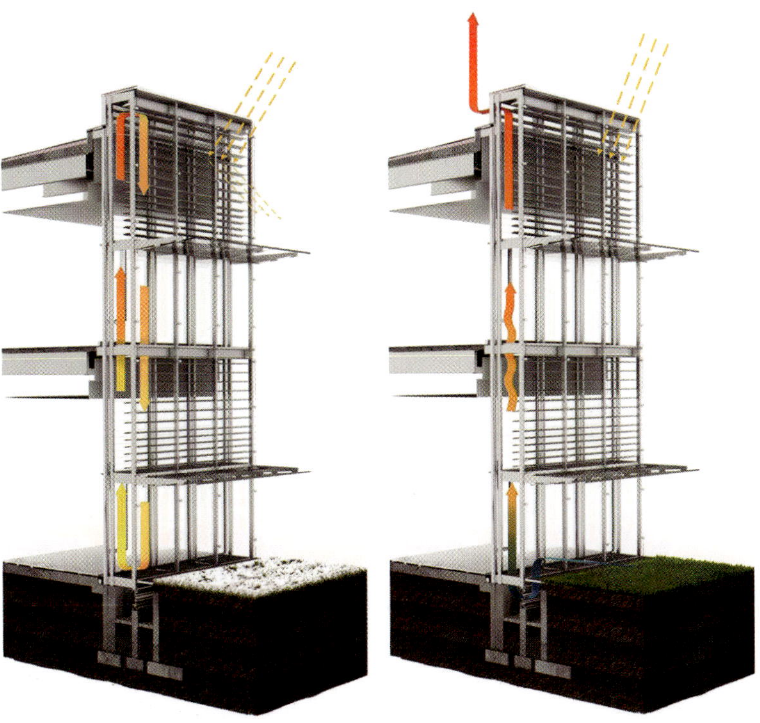

5.21 Axonometric model illustrating the movement of air within the double-skin facade cavity space in winter mode (left) and summer mode (right). WILLIAM RAWN WITH ANN BEHA ARCHITECTS

Daylighting. The design team was able to daylight 90% of the interior spaces at the Main Branch. In the Historic Library building, windows were repaired, replaced, and uncovered through the restoration process and the demolition of the 1960s addition. In the new building, windows on the north elevation, skylights above the circulation zone, and extensive glazing on the south elevation flood the interior with daylight. These daylighting strategies reduce the need for electric lighting and help to conserve energy. Fixed and operable shading devices were incorporated into the double-skin facade in an effort to control, modulate, and redirect daylight on the south side of the building. The fixed external "visors" consist of a sheet of white PVC laminated between two layers of glass. The result is a glass shading device that compliments the all-glass facade, yet is intended to block solar radiation from entering the interior spaces. In lieu of a sophisticated solar-tracking system to adjust the louvers within the cavity, the design team chose a simple system that rotates the position of the louvers once per day according to seasonal settings for sun angles. Microperforated blades are intended to allow some light transmission (reducing hard shadow lines) and to function as light shelves by redirecting light upward onto white interior ceilings.

Resource conservation. The Cambridge Public Library Main Branch incorporates a number of features to conserve resources. Low-flow plumbing fixtures were used throughout the facility to reduce water consumption. Enhanced building commissioning helped to ensure that building systems performed as intended. The double-skin facade is expected to lose 50% less heat per unit area than a conventional curtainwall facade system. Daylight sensors reduce electricity usage for interior lighting. A large cistern captures stormwater from the site and the surrounding Cambridge neighborhoods, which substantially reduces the burden on the municipal stormwater system during severe rain events and extends the positive environmental impact of the project beyond the site boundaries.

Green roofs. A 33,000 ft^2 [3066 m^2] intensive green roof covers the underground parking garage. The 4 ft [1.2 m] depth of cover medium allows for tree planting. The garage is essentially invisible beneath the park.

Adaptive reuse. The Historic Library building was restored and reused as part of the expanded library complex, which saved material resources but also protected an important historic landmark for the city. The overall approach was to remove any ad hoc additions and furnishings inside and outside the building and to incorporate modern services and systems as discretely and as invisibly as possible. On the exterior of the building, the brownstone masonry was cleaned and repointed, but the slate roof and copper flashing were replaced. The west facade was uncovered when the 1967 addition to the original building was demolished. Where possible, the design team cleaned and reused the existing materials. Some stone and wood trim had to be recreated. Because the stone quarries that provided the stone for the 1889 building were no longer in operation,

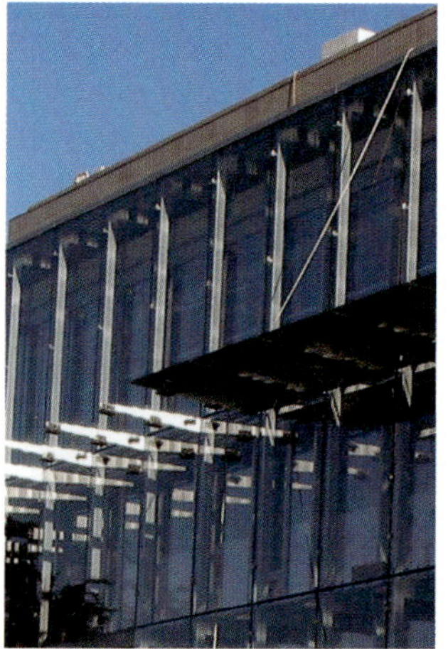

5.22 Installation of fixed horizontal shading "visors" on the exterior of the double-skin facade. WILLIAM RAWN WITH ANN BEHA ARCHITECTS

much of the new stone came from unlikely sources such as highway construction sites and from hidden stonework within the historic building. The main entrance to the library complex was moved to the new building and the original entry porch on the historic building was closed-in with glass to create a conference room and the stone steps were transformed into an outdoor seating area. Interior finishes, such as oak woodwork and lighting fixtures, were carefully restored or protected. Spaces within the old building were repurposed for a Young Adults Room and Lounge, a reading room, and a public internet access area. Wall murals painted in 1934 as part of the Works Progress Administration (WPA) and depicting the 10 divisions of knowledge that make up the Dewey Decimal System were carefully protected during the construction process and then restored.

Materials. Low VOC paints, carpets, and adhesives were used throughout the library. Bamboo flooring was used in the Young Adults Room and Lounge in the historic building. Materials were specified and sourced to pre-consumer and post-consumer recycled content. The combined recycled content as a percentage of the overall materials cost was nearly 21% as documented in LEED certification reports. Air-conditioning systems use CFC-free refrigerants. Vermont red slate, a historically accurate and durable local material sourced from within New England, was used for the reroofing of the historic building. During the construction process, 95% of waste was diverted from landfills.

Alternative transportation. The library has ample access to public transportation: Five bus routes run past the site and two subway stations are within a 2/3-mile [1 km] walk. The library encourages staff and patrons to ride bikes to the complex. A dedicated bicycle lane along Broadway provides easy bike access and the library has ample bike racks for secure storage. Staff has access to showers and locker space. The belowground garage (connected to the library via a tunnel) was kept as small as possible (70 spaces) and provides parking spaces for alternative fuel vehicles.

How Is It Working?

The Cambridge Public Library Main Branch has been a popular destination for citizens. An average of 2000 people visit the facility daily, of which 80 patrons come specifically to use the wireless internet. The library estimates that circulation is up 65%, computer use is up 55%, and library card registrations are up 63% in the 8 months since the building opened. Placing spaces for teens and computer use in the Historic Library has given the old building new life.

The City of Cambridge has a long-standing commitment to green and LEED-certified buildings. The Main Branch project is pursuing a LEED-NC 2.2 certification through the US Green Building Council. A post-occupancy evaluation (POE) of the building-in-use has not been performed to date.

Further Information

Ann Beha Architects. www.annbeha.com/ (The associate architect's website, which includes a photograph, a description of the project, and a list of awards received.)

The Cambridge Public Library. www.cambridgema.gov/cpl/announce.htm (The library website, which includes floor plans, photographs, and information about visiting and the green design features. There is also a link to a November 2009 article in the *Boston Globe* titled "What a posh hotel and a new library share.")

Gonchar, J. 2010. "More Than Skin Deep." *Architectural Record*. July 2010: 108–110. (A print article which describes the project and the double-skin facade system used.)

William Rawn Associates. www.rawnarch.com/civicrealm.html (The architect's website, which includes photographs, a description of the project, and a link to a double envelope case study.)

Background and Context

The new John Hope Gateway is the main entry to the Royal Botanic Garden Edinburgh (RBGE). RBGE was established in 1670, encompasses over 70 acres [28 ha], and is one of the most popular visitor destinations in Scotland with over 700,000 visitors annually. The gateway was named after John Hope who was the garden's Regius Keeper from 1761 to 1786. The building is a "threshold" to the gardens, underpinning the overall mission of the RBGE "to explore and explain the world of plants."

The architects were chosen through a competition held in 2003. The RBGE announced: "The purpose of the competition was to select an architect who understood the aspirations of the client and who could deliver a facility commensurate with the Garden's status as a visitor attraction and as an internationally renowned centre of excellence. We are sure that with Edward Cullinan Architects (ECA), RBGE have now found that architect." And, in fact, at that time an integrated design team was formed, including the architects, engineers, landscape architects, lighting designers, exhibition designers, project manager, contractor, and client.

5.24 Entry to the Gateway through a foyer that is alive with plants and bathed in light. MATT LAVER PHOTOGRAPHY

5.23 The front entrance to the John Hope Gateway. MATT LAVER PHOTOGRAPHY

To minimize loss of garden space, the new building was built over the site of several old buildings, including the former shop and bathrooms, which no longer met the Garden's needs. A new Biodiversity Garden runs right up to the curved glass wall of the exhibition space, helping to blur the distinction between the Garden and the building. Augmenting the theme of biodiversity, the building has a flat green

LOCATION
Edinburgh, Scotland, UK
Latitude 55.9 °N
Longitude 3.2 °W

HEATING DEGREE DAYS
6237 base 65 °F
[3465 base 18.3 °C]

COOLING DEGREE DAYS
979 base 50 °F
[544 base 10 °C]

DESIGN DRY-BULB WINTER (99%)
25.9 °F [−3.3 °C]

DESIGN DRY-BULB & MEAN COINCIDENT WET-BULB SUMMER (1%)
69.5/60.8 °F [20.8/16.0 °C]

SOLAR RADIATION
Jan 139 Btu/ft^2/day
[0.44 kWh/m^2/day]
Jun 1309 Btu/ft^2/day
[4.13 kWh/m^2/day]

ANNUAL PRECIPITATION
27 in. [677 mm]

roof planted with sedum. This has effectively increased the area of green space in the Garden and provides a swathe of natural color visible from the path to the top of a nearby hill. This green roof has the benefit of reducing heat gains in summer, slowing rain runoff to drains, and insulating the building.

The building organization is tripartite: a concrete public ground floor with entry, permanent and temporary exhibitions, a science studio where researchers will interact closely with the public, and indoor and outdoor shops; a semi-public wood-decked first floor with a public restaurant and terrace separated from the private offices by an atrium; and a restricted-access sedum-planted green roof also hosting photovoltaics, solar thermal panels, and the ETFE-glazed atrium lid (ethylene tetrafluoroethylene). The roof floats over the entire building as a single horizontal plane, creating a deep overhanging canopy that shelters the entrances and exits, the café, and access to the outdoor shop. An elegantly detailed, exposed timber roof structure on slender steel columns subdivides the open-plan space into a series of coffered bays.

BUILDING TYPE
Visitor Center

AREA
29,063 ft^2 [2700 m^2]

CLIENT
Royal Botanic Garden Edinburgh

DESIGN TEAM
Architect, Edward Cullinan Architects (ECA)

Structural, Civil, Facade, and Fire Protection Engineer, Buro Happold Ltd.

Environmental & Building Services Engineer, Max Fordham

General Contractor, Xircon Ltd.

Exhibition Designer, Navy Blue

Cost Consultant, David Langdon

Landscape Architect, Gross Max

COMPLETION
October 2009

PERFORMANCE METRICS
Energy Utilization Index (EUI):
Predicted
133,756 Btu/ft^2/yr
[422 kWh/m^2/yr]
(early estimate including catering and display lighting)

Predicted
42,789 Btu/ft^2/yr
[135 kWh/m^2/yr]
(modeled usage not including catering or display lighting)

Carbon Emissions:
Target
7 kg/CO_2/m^2/yr (excluding display lighting and plug loads)

Water Use:
Predicted
8.7 gal/ft^2/yr [344 L/m^2/yr]

Design Intent and Validation

> "One of the primary motivations for the John Hope Gateway was, quite simply, to take the lid off the Garden and reveal the research institute inside."
>
> *Stephen Blackmore, Regius Keeper*

The design intent was to minimize the impact on the landscape and to be sympathetic to the botanical garden site context. Edward Cullinan Architects affirmed: "The building will be a showcase for sustainable design and will include many demonstrable features such as a biomass boiler, rain water harvesting, a wind turbine, solar collectors and photovoltaic solar panels." The desire to provide natural ventilation and daylight strongly influenced the building form. Max Fordham Engineers assert: "The most overt sustainable design feature is the elegant roof-mounted 6 kW Quiet Revolution wind turbine which, in addition to providing some of the energy requirement for the Gateway building, is a potent symbol of the environmental ethos of the Gateway centre." At the onset, the environmental design brief for the building included:

- demonstrate/promote sustainable design;
- enthuse public with demos of practical sustainability;
- act as window to the world of nature and conservation;
- use energy-saving measures and on-site renewable energy;
- design, build, and operate as energy efficiently as possible.
- achieve best value with respect to cost, CO_2 savings, and demonstrability.

The team's approach was to engineer the building fabric and use on-site natural resources (daylight, air movement, heat, and water) to reduce base energy use as far as possible. With the RBGE's blessing the team chose to exceed the rating of BREEAM Excellent without actually going through the rating process. It now appears that the John Hope Gateway will eventually have to be BREEAM rated because it was a publicly funded project. In lieu of designing to the BREEAM checklist, Max Fordham Engineers set up a sustainability targets spreadsheet based on their *Edinburgh City Sustainability Guide*, written for the city council. The team steered the design to meet or exceed the spreadsheet's "best practices" criteria.

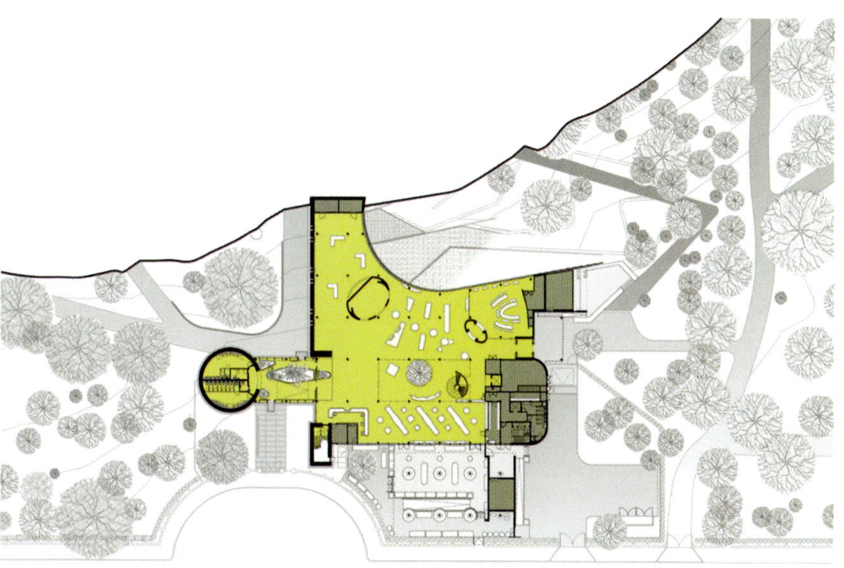

5.25 Ground floor plan of the John Hope Gateway showing how the building embraces the garden with protected and open outdoor spaces. EDWARD CULLINAN ARCHITECTS

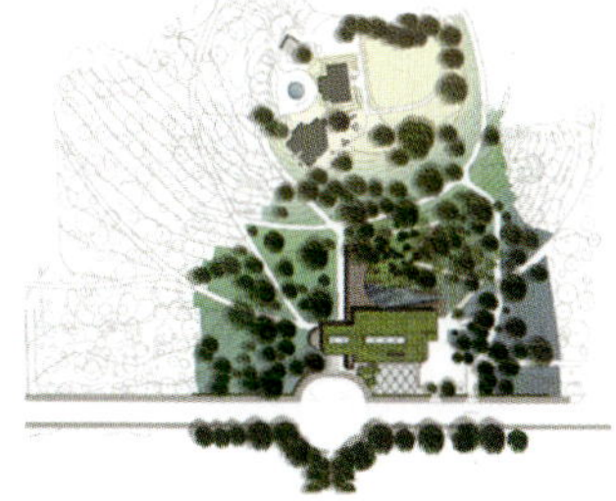

5.26 The John Hope Gateway is sited on the western perimeter of the Royal Botanic Garden Edinburgh at the foot of a hill that rises to the east. EDWARD CULLINAN ARCHITECTS

5.27 An early conceptual rendering stresses the integration of building and landscape. EDWARD CULLINAN ARCHITECTS

While the sustainability target spreadsheet kept the design on track, the team employed increasingly sophisticated modeling techniques from the onset to help make good design decisions. These tools ranged from basic spreadsheets to single room/zone models in TAS/VIZ/Ecotect, complex spreadsheets, and a full building model in IES (a 3D building and dynamic thermal modeling program). Along the way they were able to study daylighting in the atrium for human comfort and plant life and look at the conflict between daylighting and the need for external vertical shading for the west-facing offices. In the end the IES model allowed them to investigate energy consumption, thermal comfort, overheating and solar shading, CO_2 emissions, renewable energy feasibility, passive design strategies, ventilation airflow and air temperatures, material choice and envelope design, and energy performance compliance (for both Building Regulations Section 6 and Energy Performance Certificate (EPC)). Early modeling indicated an EPC rating of "A," but some of the lighting first considered as "display" (and therefore exempt) may have to be classified as "general." If so, an EPC rating of "C" should be attained, which is still quite good for such a highly used public building.

5.28 The modular structural system is elegantly detailed so that structure becomes interior finish. BRUCE HAGLUND

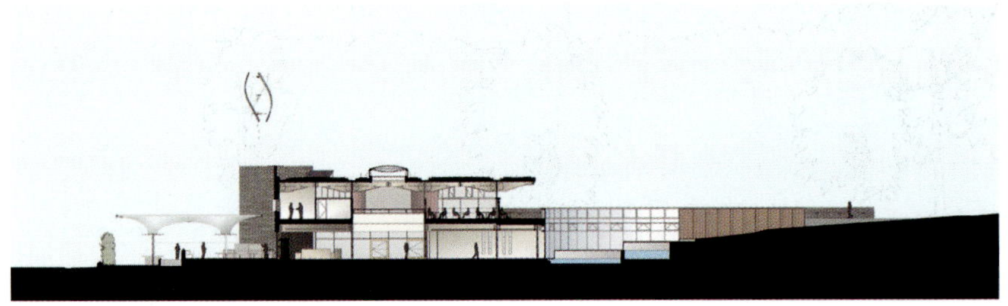

5.29 The west–east section illustrates the tripartite organization of the building as well as its integration with the sloped site. EDWARD CULLINAN ARCHITECTS

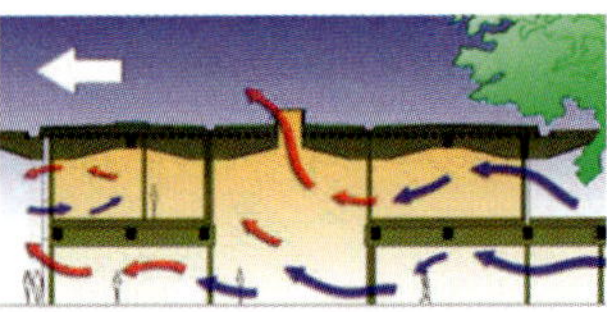

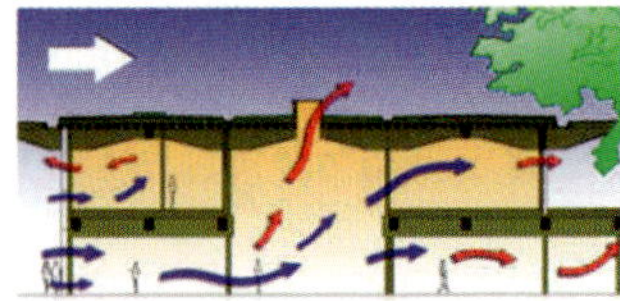

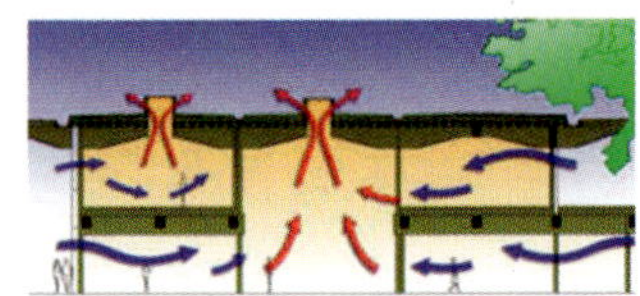

5.30 The building was designed for cross and stack ventilation. EDWARD CULLINAN ARCHITECTS

Strategies

The John Hope Gateway uses passive strategies and low-carbon energy sources to achieve status as a high-performance, low-carbon building. Max Fordham Engineers minimized overall energy consumption by combining enhanced U-factors, passive ventilation, and low-energy lighting with the use of wind power, biomass, solar thermal, and PVs. Moreover, the design team paid great attention to the selection of materials to assure a durable, healthy building with low embedded energy. The architect affirms: "As befits a building in the Botanic Garden, we have endeavored, wherever possible, to make the building out of natural materials with low embodied energy, including a predominantly timber structure." Structural elements throughout the building are exposed as finish materials to demonstrate their natural beauty and reduce the total amount of material required.

Natural ventilation and shading. The building is naturally ventilated using both cross and stack ventilation with windows opening automatically depending on internal and external conditions. Mechanical ventilation is provided to high-heat-gain areas like the kitchen. Summertime night-flush ventilation (via secure high-level windows) acts in conjunction with the exposed, polished concrete ground floor and interior mass walls to smooth internal diurnal temperatures throughout the cooling season. A 4-m overhang shades the south and east building facades from summer sun, reducing overheating, while low winter sun will penetrate the glazed public areas bringing heat and light when it is most needed and appreciated.

5.31 A tent structure (using the same structural grid as the steel and glulam system) protects the outdoor plant sale area from sun and rain while also shading the west facade of the ground floor. MATT LAVER PHOTOGRAPHY

Photovoltaics. A 118-ft^2 [11 m^2] array of roof-mounted, non-crystalline flat-panel photovoltaic modules (facing due south and set at the optimum angle for annual energy production) will provide a peak electrical output of 1.5 kW—enough power to run six office desktop computers. The PV system will reduce the energy required from the national grid by about 1400 kWh/year, which equates to a saving of 1323 lb [600 kg] of CO_2 per year.

Solar thermal collectors. Five 32-ft^2 [3 m^2] evacuated-tube solar thermal panels are mounted on the roof. They will generate an estimated peak output of 41,000 Btuh [12 kW], providing all hot water for the building in the summer and hot water preheating in the winter, reducing the demand on the biomass boiler. If this water was heated by a modern condensing gas boiler, it would result in the emission of around 4400 lb [2000 kg] of CO_2 per year.

Wind turbine. Entry to the Gardens is marked by the Quiet Revolution 5 (QR5) vertical-axis wind turbine mounted high (59 ft [18 m]) atop the stone encased stair tower. Designed to tackle the two major issues that face urban wind turbines—turbulence and noise—the QR5 provides a peak electrical output of 6 kW. The wind turbine will reduce the amount of energy required from the national grid by 8500 kWh/year, which equates to a carbon saving of 7700 lb [3500 kg] of CO_2 per year. Because the trees in the gardens cause considerable turbulence, it was essential to choose a turbine designed to work with turbulent air. The turbine was carefully located on the building's tallest element to reduce turbulence and benefit from higher wind speeds. As the Royal Botanic Gardens Edinburgh allows city dwellers to escape the city without leaving the city center, the quiet operating QR5 turbine is an ideal choice for a place where peace is held in high regard.

5.32 The roof houses solar thermal panels, PV panels, roof monitors with ETFE skylights, a sedum-planted green roof, and a wind turbine. MATT LAVER PHOTOGRAPHY

Building envelope. The building envelope is heavily insulated to a thermal performance 20% better than current building regulations. As good practice, the building was tested for air tightness (though not a statutory requirement in Scotland), and leakage measured 24.8 ft^3/ft^2 @ 50 Pa [7.55 m^3/m^2 @ 50 Pa], exceeding the minimum target of 32.8 ft^3/ft^2 @ 50 Pa [10 m^3/m^2 @ 50 Pa]. Airlock entries are used to mitigate heat loss. The brise-soleil, or sun shading devices, used on the west facade and high-performance glazing reduce heat gain to the first floor offices. The glazing and shading configuration was extensively modeled to achieve balance among views, daylight penetration, and internal temperature control.

5.33 Vertically lapped larch boards provide a rainscreen above and below the office windows. The 8-in. [200 mm] deep fins spaced 20 in. [500 mm] apart were modeled to ensure adequate shading for west-facing windows. EDWARD CULLINAN ARCHITECTS

Daylighting. Clerestory and view glazing allow views for awareness of the surrounding gardens and deep daylight penetration to reduce lighting costs and improve visual comfort. Thermally efficient ETFE pillow roof lights allow daylight into the heart of the building to stimulate plant growth and provide core daylighting. When heavy rains fall on the skylights, they resound like drums, creating an acoustic celebration of nature that the RBGE staff heartily endorsed as being in line with the principles of "bringing the outside in" and "connection with the environment." Daylight harvesting throughout the building, under which lighting fixtures dim or brighten automatically, reduces the energy consumed for electric lighting. External light sensors monitor the ambient light levels to ensure that electric lighting is switched off or dimmed when adequate daylight is available. Automatic movement sensors in the bathrooms and service spaces turn lights off when these rooms are not in use, also saving energy. External ponds act as light shelves that reflect light onto the soffits and ceilings, and also provide some cooling and humidification.

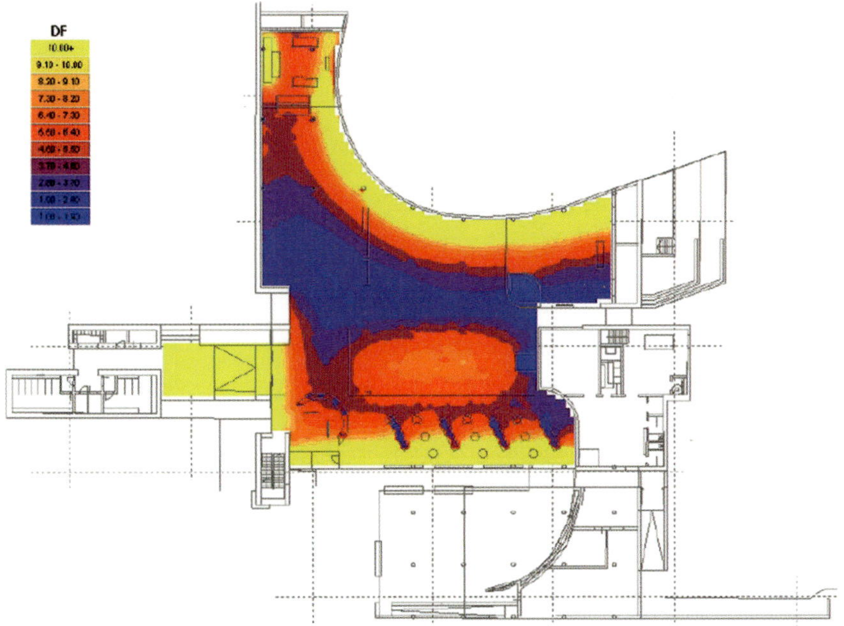

5.34 Ground floor plan daylight factors. EDWARD CULLINAN ARCHITECTS

Water conservation. The building has two rainwater collection systems, each with a 1850-gal [7000 L] tank for a total catchment volume of 3700 gal [14,000 L]. The most visible tank captures water from the north end of the main roof in a tank located on the roof of the restroom at the main entrance. To fully illustrate water collection, two drainpipes stop short of the tank so that discharging water is on full display.

5.35 The green roof (shown left) drains to a cistern (shown right) then demonstrates a gravity-fed journey of water from roof to cistern to toilet. MATT LAVER PHOTOGRAPHY | MAX FORDAM LLP

5.36 Daylighting was designed to illuminate the occupied edges and central atrium, while leaving the exhibition area relatively dark. The offices (clerestory) and restaurant (half wall) on the first floor also harvest daylight from the atrium. MATT LAVER PHOTOGRAPHY

This water is filtered cyclonically and fed by gravity to the toilets below. A second system collects water from the other half of the roof in a tank beneath the south service yard. The filtered water serves water closets in the main building. Based on annual rainfall data and expected occupancy, rainwater harvesting will reduce the amount of potable water that is needlessly flushed down toilets by at least 36% per year.

5.37 The ground floor concrete slab is equipped with hydronic tubing for radiant heating. EDWARD CULLINAN ARCHITECTS

Green roofs. A sedum roof was used for its biodiversity advantages as well as to help attenuate stormwater runoff. Although the green roof may cause browning of runoff (and possible staining of toilets), the RBGE felt this wasn't a problem, but part of the story of rainwater harvesting and the hydrologic cycle.

Mechanical systems. The combination of biomass boiler and solar thermal system will reduce the CO_2 output related to heating and hot water by 85% compared with a typical condensing gas boiler setup. Radiant heating is used in the ground floor slab and at the building perimeters on both floors to allow reduced internal air temperatures, saving energy while still providing comfortable conditions for visitors and staff. The first-floor office and restaurant are served by an underfloor displacement heating and ventilation system. The building management system, (BMS), adjusts the temperature and flow rate of the heating and natural ventilation system depending on outside weather conditions, to achieve maximum heating energy savings.

Biomass boiler. The primary low-carbon energy for heating and hot water for the Gateway comes from a biomass boiler fueled by prepared wood collected locally. A clean burning 200-kW Binder biomass boiler addresses 90% of the heating loads throughout the year. Locally sourced fuel (from within 50 miles [80 km]) is stored in a 2331-ft^3 [66 m^3] silo under the service yard. Backup for the biomass boiler is provided by two high-efficiency condensing gas boilers, which ensures heating system reliability.

Materials. To minimize transport distances and reduce embedded energy, materials sourcing was prioritized—first Scottish, then British, then European materials. The initial goal was to procure 80% of the materials from the UK. Durable European engineered timber (glulam beams, structural veneered lumber, and cross-laminated timber decking) was used extensively in the structure and finishes of the building, demonstrating the uses, beauty, and importance of wood and trees as a renewable, low-carbon material, compared with high-carbon materials such as steel and concrete. Durable, riven-faced, coursed Scottish Caithness slate clads three concrete retaining walls—the long terrace wall, the stair tower, and the restroom drum. Vertically lapped, untreated Scottish larch boards act as rainscreen cladding, protecting the weathertight insulated wall construction. The well-shaded, east-facing glass wall of the biodiversity garden is made of facetted, double-glazed, low-emissivity (low-ε), argon-filled panels that exceed "innovative practice" for thermal performance. Some internal walls are plastered block walls providing good acoustics as well as thermal mass to even out daily temperatures. Likewise, the ground floor is an exposed polished concrete screed that provides thermal mass and durability in the heavily trafficked public

5.38 Scottish Caithness slate clads the long terrace retaining wall. BRUCE HAGLUND

areas. On the first floor, the exposed solid Douglas Fir floor extends out into the landscape as the roof deck and shading device over the exhibition hall. Custom chairs and tables for the restaurant were made of timber previously felled and seasoned from the four Royal Botanic Gardens in Scotland.

Construction. Construction waste was minimized by design—the predominantly timber structure is an assembly of components prefabricated off-site. The impact of construction was also reduced by avoiding the wide-scale use of concrete and by replacing elements that are traditionally cast-in-place with precast elements.

5.39 Bespoke chairs and tables were constructed from trees felled on the grounds of the four Royal Botanic Garden properties in Scotland. MATT LAVER PHOTOGRAPHY

How Is It Working?

> "The Scottish Government has set out ambitious plans to cut greenhouse gas emissions dramatically. We have a part to play in delivering that agenda—not just by placing renewable technology in public places so it becomes familiar, as we have in the John Hope Gateway, but by reducing the environmental impact of everything we do. So we have two roles: as a catalyst for change in society and as direct contributors to achieving a more sustainable relationship with our planet."
>
> *Stephen Blackmore, Regius Keeper*

5.40 Glu-lam beams on slender metal columns support the cross-laminated timber decking. EDWARD CULLINAN ARCHITECTS

Although the clients considered a BREEAM assessment an unnecessary expense, the design team aimed to exceed the requirements for a BREEAM "Excellent" rating. The Gateway is predicted to achieve an Energy Performance Certificate (EPC) rating of "A," with a score of 1.4 $lb/CO_2/ft^2/yr$ [7 $kg/CO_2/m^2/yr$]. This figure does not include display lighting (in the exhibition areas) or small power (computers and plug loads). If excluding the display lighting is disallowed, the expected rating could be as high as "C" (6.3–9.2 $lb/CO_2/ft^2/yr$ [31–45 kg/ CO_2/m^2/year]). All public buildings in the UK must display an EPC, showing actual performance over the most recent three years. Starting October 2010, visitors will be aware of building performance in terms of carbon emissions, energy use, and renewable energy generated. Although it has not yet been implemented, visual displays of real-time and cumulative energy production by each of the renewable sources as well as overall carbon count are planned for a prominent location in the atrium.

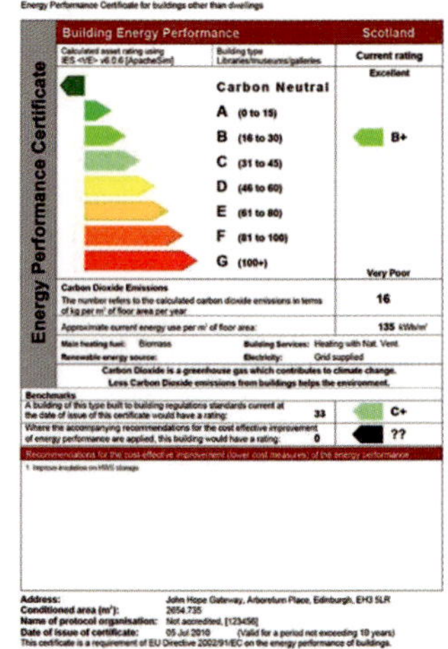

Energy Performance Certificate for buildings other than dwellings

Energy Performance Certificate

Building Energy Performance — Scotland

Calculated asset rating using IES <VE> v6.0.6 [ApacheSim]

Building type Libraries/museums/galleries

Current rating

Excellent

Carbon Neutral

A (0 to 15)

B (16 to 30) — B+

C (31 to 45)

D (46 to 60)

E (61 to 80)

F (81 to 100)

G (100+)

Very Poor

Carbon Dioxide Emissions
The number refers to the calculated carbon dioxide emissions in terms of kg per m² of floor area per year — 16

Approximate current energy use per m² of floor area: 135 kWh/m²

Main heating fuel: Biomass — Building Services: Heating with Nat. Vent

Renewable energy source: — Electricity: Grid supplied

Carbon Dioxide is a greenhouse gas which contributes to climate change.
Less Carbon Dioxide emissions from buildings helps the environment.

Benchmarks

A building of this type built to building regulations standards current at the date of issue of this certificate would have a rating: 33 — C+

Where the accompanying recommendations for the cost effective improvement of energy performance are applied, this building would have a rating: 0 — ??

Recommendations for the cost-effective improvement (lower cost measures) of the energy performance

1. Improve insulation on HWS storage

Address: John Hope Gateway, Arboretum Place, Edinburgh, EH3 5LR
Conditioned area (m²): 2654.735
Name of protocol organisation: Not accredited, [123456]
Date of issue of certificate: 05 Jul 2010 (Valid for a period not exceeding 10 years)
This certificate is a requirement of EU Directive 2002/91/EC on the energy performance of buildings.
NB THIS CERTIFICATE MUST BE AFFIXED TO THE BUILDING AND NOT REMOVED UNLESS REPLACED WITH AN UPDATED VERSION AND FOR PUBLIC BUILDINGS DISPLAYED IN A PROMINENT PLACE

5.41 EPC-like performance indicators—the Gateway will achieve an A, B, or C rating, depending on the status of some display lighting and plug loads. MAX FORDAM LLP

Water meters measure the water consumption of the following: general water use (toilets, showers, sinks); water used specifically for toilet flushing (both rainwater and potable water); the kitchen; and irrigation and biodiversity pond. Meters installed on all main and local electrical distribution boards closely monitor the electricity, biomass, and gas consumption of the building in addition to the electricity production from the wind turbine and the PV array and the hot water heating from the solar thermal system. Besides the BMS sensing of some weather data, the RBGE maintains a weather station on site. The station provides detailed data, and graphic output of the last month's data is on display in the Gardens.

Commissioning was in the contract for the building; however, it was not fully completed. An independent specialist was subsequently hired to complete the seasonal commissioning by the end of summer 2010. Fine-tuning of the equipment is on-going. Importantly, the RBGE facilities manager is committed to monitoring the Gateway's performance over time and to making adjustments of internal conditions and systems to optimize performance.

5.42 The RBGE weather station, with the previous month's data displayed. BRUCE HAGLUND

5.43 Weather station data on display in the Gardens. BRUCE HAGLUND

Further Information

Beatty, R. 2010. "Green Begins at Home," *Botanics*, 41, 4–6 (*Botanics* is the quarterly news magazine distributed to friends and members of the RBGE.)

Edward Cullinan Architects. www.edwardcullinanarchitects.com/projects/rbge.html (The architect's website, which includes photographs and a description of the project.)

RGBE. www.rbge.org.uk/about-us/corporate-information/environmental-responsibility/ (The RGBE environmental responsibility web page, which includes links to documents and reports related to strategies and policies.)

RGBE. www.rbge.org.uk/the-gardens/edinburgh/the-gateway (The main RBGE website, which includes visitor information, photographs, and links to frequently asked questions, the restaurant, and a calendar of events for the John Hope Gateway.)

NOTES

Background and Context

Kenyon House is an affordable housing project located on Kenyon Street in the southeast section of Seattle, Washington. The facility contains 18 dwelling units for extremely low-income individuals, many of whom were previously homeless and have significant mental or physical health issues including HIV/AIDS. The project was conceived of and initiated by Building Changes, an organization focused on ending homelessness in Washington State. It was constructed by Housing Resources Group (HRG), the developer and present owner, and Sound Mental Health, the property manager and part future owner. Kenyon House provides residents with a safe, home-like atmosphere where they have both autonomy and access to services.

The building occupies a 0.5-acre [0.2 ha] site that previously contained four abandoned houses and illegal squatters. The Kenyon House building replaced these derelict properties with a 12,700-ft^2 [1180 m^2] facility containing 18 apartment units, common dining room and lounge spaces, offices for case workers/staff, and laundry facilities. The building provides secure access in addition to outdoor "back yard" spaces for gathering, gardening, and contemplation. The long facade is oriented along an east–west axis with the front of the building facing south along Kenyon Street.

5.44 View of Kenyon House from Kenyon Street. JOSH PARTEE

Design Intent and Validation

Kenyon House was envisioned, designed, and constructed to be a permanent home for people transitioning out of homelessness or experiencing extreme poverty. The client was very clear that the facility was not intended as temporary housing similar to group or halfway houses. Kenyon House was to be a "softer kind of place"

5.45 Front entrance to Kenyon House. HOUSING RESOURCES GROUP

LOCATION
Seattle, WA, USA
Latitude 47.5 °N
Longitude 122.3 °W

HEATING DEGREE DAYS
4729 base 65 °F
[2627 base 18.3 °C]

COOLING DEGREE DAYS
2034 base 50 °F
[1130 base 10 °C]

DESIGN DRY-BULB WINTER (99%)
29.1 °F [−1.6 °C]

DESIGN DRY-BULB & MEAN COINCIDENT WET-BULB SUMMER (1%)
81.3/63.6 °F [27.4/17.6 °C]

SOLAR RADIATION
Jan 262 Btu/ft^2/day
[0.83 kWh/m^2/day]
Jun 2248 Btu/ft^2/day
[7.09 kWh/m^2/day]

ANNUAL PRECIPITATION
37 in. [940 mm]

where residents could have privacy and autonomy in a setting that also offered access to services, social opportunities, and supervision.

The primary design objectives for the project were to provide affordable housing that would be simple to construct, durable over time, comfortable for occupants, and energy efficient. The design team focused on a wide variety of design considerations in pursuit of these goals.

Simple slab-on-grade wood frame construction was used for the project. The design team, however, upgraded certain materials (such as roofing and exterior wall cladding) to ensure long-term durability and performance. The LEED for Homes (Multi-family) v.1.0 certification process necessitated that certain material substitutions be made during construction, which would not have been possible without effective collaboration between the design team and the contractor. The design team relied heavily on input from other design professionals (who had completed similar affordable housing projects) to help validate design decisions amidst the tight constraints imposed by the project budget.

Universal design played a critical role in the design process due to the fragile health of many residents. The design team worked closely with case workers, doctors, and nurses at the Bailey-Boushay Adult Day Health Center and Lifelong AIDS Alliance to ensure that the facility was easily accessible, navigable, and adaptable to account for a wide range of resident needs and abilities. All scales of the building-user interface were investigated, from the overall layout of the building to the operable window-opening mechanisms.

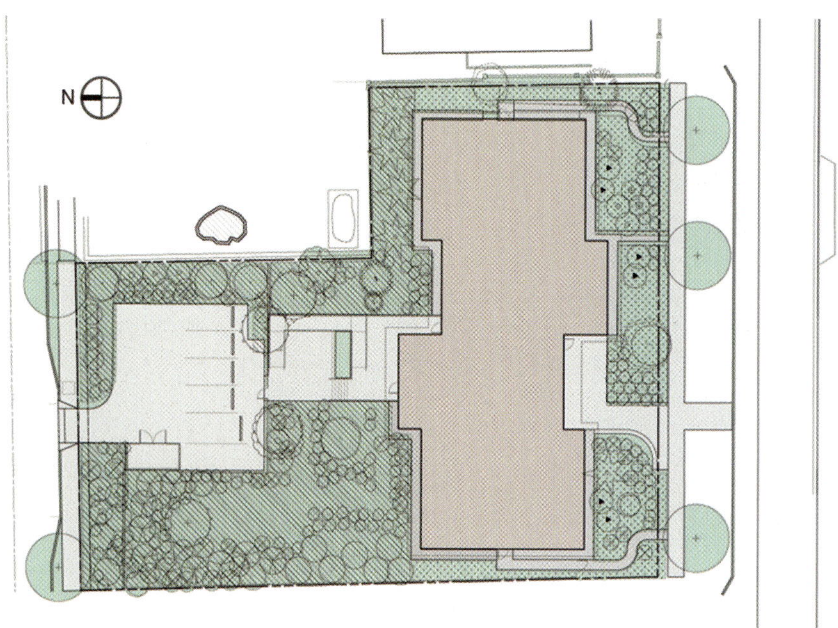

5.46 Site plan showing the building oriented with its long facade along Kenyon Street creating a public front yard and a private back yard. SMR ARCHITECTS

BUILDING TYPE
Multi-family Housing

AREA
12,700 ft^2 [1180 m^2]

CLIENT
Developer/Owner, Housing Resources Group (HRG); Property Manager/Owner, Sound Mental Health

DESIGN TEAM
Architect, SMR Architects

Mechanical Engineer, SIDER + BYERS Associates Inc.

Lighting Designer, Cierra Electrical Group

Green Consulting, O'Brien & Company

Universal Design, ADAPTations, Inc.

Landscape Architect, Graysmith Landscape Architects

General Contractor, Walsh Construction Company

COMPLETION
September 2008

PERFORMANCE METRICS
Energy Utilization Index (EUI):
Actual:
86,000 Btu/ft^2/yr
[271 kWh/m^2/yr] (2008–2009)

Carbon Emissions:
Not Available

Water Use:
Not Available

The design team faced a number of challenges in providing a facility that looked and felt like a home for residents. One problem was that Kenyon House would have to be considerably larger than most homes in the neighborhood to accommodate the 18 living units, common spaces, and offices. In order to have a public front yard and a private back yard, the building would have to have a wide frontage along Kenyon Street. This optimal orientation was not allowed by city ordinances, but the design team went through a lengthy design review process for approval. The team also addressed neighborhood concerns about the project through community involvement in the design process. The result is a large building broken into four volumes or sections, which responds to the scale of the surrounding neighborhood and looks more like a lodge than an apartment building.

5.47 Construction photograph showing the wood framing. SMR ARCHITECTS

5.48 View of Kenyon House from Kenyon Street. JOSH PARTEE

Energy efficiency was a key objective for the client because the residents do not pay their own utility bills. Because owners of affordable housing often have greater access to funding for construction than they do for operations and maintenance, the design team focused on incorporating features up front that would help save energy and resources once the building was occupied. Validation came in the form of documenting these design features through the LEED for Homes certification process.

5.49 The facility was designed to feel like a home and includes common lounge spaces in which residents can socialize. JOSH PARTEE

Strategies

Tight budgets for affordable housing projects often prevent design teams from using sophisticated or innovative green design strategies prevalent in other building types. The design team for Kenyon House, however, employed a variety of simple, low-cost strategies and took advantage of available grants and incentives to provide an exemplary living environment that addresses energy efficiency and occupant health.

Site. The building wanted to be oriented toward the south to take advantage of opportunities for daylighting and passive solar heating. The local building ordinance did not allow this optimal orientation because of limits on building width. The design team felt that a longer building facing the street would provide greater opportunities for residents to watch the street from their windows and allow for more private "back yard" space behind the building. The southern orientation would allow for greater access to daylight and solar radiation. Several mature trees could be saved that would help provide shading for the building and outdoor spaces in warm months—and patio, gathering, and garden spaces could be located on the cooler north side of the building. The team elected to go through a complicated design review process in order to take advantage of the preferred orientation. Such "big moves" were only justified if they were able to address many different design considerations or issues.

Natural ventilation. Occupants have access to operable windows in the apartments and common spaces throughout the building. The ability to open a window when the indoor conditions are uncomfortable gives residents and staff a degree of control over their thermal comfort. Interconnected lounge spaces and windows on three sides of the dining room allow for cross ventilation through common interior spaces. Ceiling fans are provided in common areas. Housing units are designed to accommodate ceiling fans, and several residents have installed these devices.

Passive solar heating. The 120-ft [36.6 m] long front elevation faces south to take advantage of passive solar heating opportunities. Large, tall windows on the south side of the building allow solar radiation to warm the interior spaces during cold months. Roof overhangs and deciduous trees on the site help to shade this orientation during the warm months. Less glazing was provided on the north side of the building to minimize heat loss during cool months.

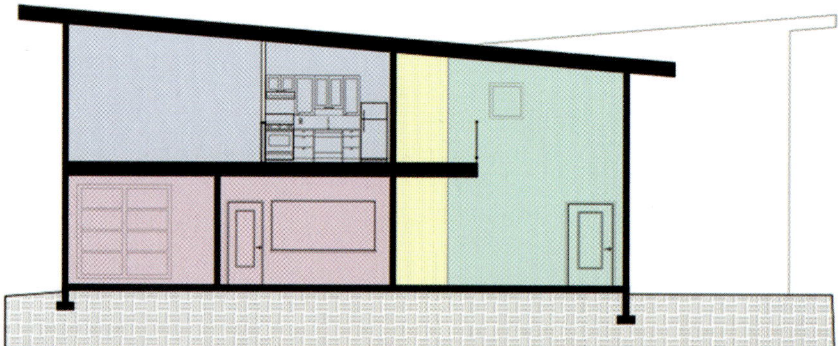

5.50 Building section showing the high point of the shed roof facing south and the double-height common lounge space. SMR ARCHITECTS

5.51 Storefront glazing in the dining room looks out on an outdoor patio and backyard space. JOSH PARTEE

Daylighting. The site orientation offers ample opportunities for daylighting, which helps reduce energy consumption for electric lighting and creates bright, cheerful interior spaces for the residents. The double-loaded corridor layout results in half the units facing north and half the units facing south. The architectural form and fenestration respond to these two orientations and offer residents different daylighting qualities within their living spaces. Shed roofs typically pitch from north to south, which gives the units facing the street higher ceilings and taller windows. Daylight can penetrate deeply into the floor plan in these units. On the north side of the building, ceiling heights are lower and smaller windows admit diffuse daylight into the space. Few windows were placed on the east and west elevations to help control the glare responses that might result from low sun angles on these orientations.

5.52 Ground floor plan illustrating the double-loaded corridor arrangement with common spaces between the residential units. SMR ARCHITECTS

5.53 Tall windows in the residential units and large areas of storefront glazing in common spaces provide ample daylighting within the building. JOSH PARTEE

Resource conservation. A sophisticated building management and lighting control system was not possible given the project budget, but several simple, inexpensive strategies were employed to minimize water and energy usage. Twin gas-fired, high-efficiency (95%) boilers were used to provide domestic and space heating hot water. Each boiler can be operated at or below design capacity. The system was selected because it would require minimal maintenance over time, reducing overhead costs for the owners—and they were able to take advantage of a grant from the gas utility. The building is not air-conditioned. Operable windows and ceiling fans are used for cooling and ventilation. Large windows throughout the building deliver abundant daylight to interior spaces reducing the need for electric lighting. Occupancy sensors throughout the facility further reduce the use of electric lighting. Residents do not pay directly for their heat, water, or electricity. Units were wired, however, to allow individual metering to be installed in the future.

5.54 Site landscaping includes plantings that are easy to maintain and do not require irrigation. JOSH PARTEE

Low-flow plumbing fixtures, including faucets, toilets, and showerheads, were specified to reduce water consumption. Site landscaping is not irrigated. Bathroom ceiling fans run continuously to exhaust stale air from units because many residents smoke. These fans exhaust heat unnecessarily, but are critical to the provision of adequate indoor air quality. Range hood fans are designed to run only when the range is being operated, which helps to save energy by not relying on occupants to turn the devices off. The bathroom and the range hood fans are both Energy Star certified. Extensive air barrier testing was performed using blower doors.

Indoor air quality (IAQ). Indoor air quality was a major concern for the client due to the poor health of many of the residents. Operable windows throughout the facility offer occupants access to fresh air. Materials were carefully chosen to be non-toxic. Low-VOC carpets and paints and zero-VOC adhesives, plywood, countertops, and casework were used in the project. Heating is provided through hydronic fin-tube radiators in units and common spaces. Using a central hot water heating system meant that ductwork could be eliminated and airborne allergens and contaminants could be more easily controlled if air was not being blown into each unit. Corridors are positively pressurized and unit doors are undercut to allow fresh air into the apartments. Stale or moist air is exhausted from the residential units through bathroom ceiling fans that run continuously and intermittent range hood fan operation.

5.55 Residential units are spacious, light-filled, and designed for universal access. JOSH PARTEE

Climate control. Simple thermostat controls in each unit allow occupants to adjust the temperature in their units according to a 1–5 scale. Operable windows allow residents control over their individual thermal comfort conditions, which is particularly important in the summer months because the units are not air-conditioned.

Materials. Durability was a primary concern when selecting materials for Kenyon House. City funding requires that affordable housing projects last for at least 50 years. The design team chose to use a standing-seam metal roof and a cement board rainscreen cladding system on the exterior of the building—materials ideally suited to the wet Seattle climate. To reduce costs, rigid polystyrene insulation was only used on the roof. Glass fiber batt insulation was used in wall cavities throughout the building. More than 65% of the waste generated during construction was diverted from landfills. During construction the contingency budget was used for material substitutions

5.56 Exterior rainscreen system. SMR ARCHITECTS

necessary for the LEED application process. The client, general contractor, and architects worked closely to make these changes within the constraints of the construction schedule. As a result, Kenyon House received the maximum number of LEED materials and resources credits for section MR2.2.

5.57 Standing-seam metal roof installation. SMR ARCHITECTS

Alternative transportation. The site for Kenyon House was carefully selected for its close proximity to public transportation. In addition to nearby bus routes, the building is conveniently located less than 0.5 miles [0.8 km] from the Othello Light Rail Station. Alternative modes of transportation were a critical consideration for the client because many of the residents were homeless prior to moving into the building and do not have their own vehicles. A small parking lot at the rear of the site provides four spots for staff. Currently only one resident parks a vehicle in this lot. Bike racks for staff were installed outside the building. Residents store their bikes inside their units for added theft protection.

How Is It Working?

The budget did not allow for a post-occupancy evaluation (POE) of the building-in-use. SMR Architects performed a walk-through of the building one year after completion. "Lessons learned" were documented and shared with other designers in the office as a form of knowledge transfer. Although the building appears to be performing well and occupant feedback is mostly positive, the design team acknowledges that: sound isolation between the units could be improved; carpet should have been avoided entirely; and the bathroom fans exhaust too much conditioned air in the winter.

The project was the first building in Washington State to receive a LEED for Homes (Multi-family) v.1.0 Platinum Certification from the U.S. Green Building Council. Kenyon House also received the Northwest Housing Best of 2009 Award. The project was given a 2009 10 × 10 × 10 Green Building Slam Selection award from the Northwest EcoBuilding Guild.

Residents have expressed interest in the "green" features of the building and want to know what they can do to help. Sound Mental Health has used bi-monthly house meetings to discuss, among other things, how tenants are using the building. A "Kenyon Healthy Home Guide," developed by SMR Architects, assists residents with operational issues. Sound Mental Health, the property manager, uses the "green" features within the building to engage tenants in discussions of how to use and maintain their living environments. This approach has helped residents develop effective routines.

In addition to a manual for residents, SMR Architects developed a separate manual to show staff how to use and maintain the building. Walsh Construction Company, the contractor, even developed an operations and maintenance training video to assist in future facilities management transitions.

Further Information

Building Changes. http://www.buildingchanges.org/our-work/the-buzz/Kenyon-House-Green-Building-at-its-Best.html (A website with a press release describing the Kenyon House project with links to the project team and partner websites.)

Housing Resources Group (HRG). http://www.hrg.org/htm/about/press.htm (A website with a press release containing a description and a photograph of the Kenyon House project.)

Northwest Construction. http://northwest.construction.com/northwest_construction_projects/2009/1201_KenyonHouse.asp (An online article describing the project entitled "Kenyon House: Best Green Housing.")

SMR Architects. http://www.smrarchitects.com/?p=affordable_housing (A website with photographs and a description of the project.)

OFFICES FOR THE KfW BANKING GROUP, FRANKFURT

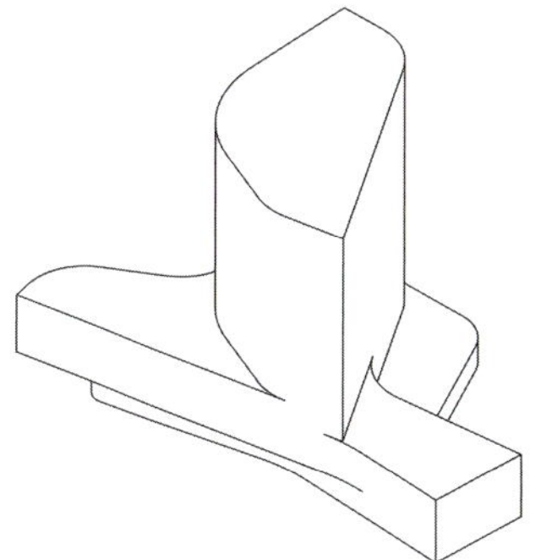

5.59 A conceptual massing diagram showing the tower sitting atop a low podium base. SAUERBRUCH HUTTON

Background and Context

The KfW Banking Group was established in 1948 by the German government with funding from the Marshall Plan and the United Nations to assist with post-World War II redevelopment. For more than 60 years KfW has been a completely state-owned bank. Public ownership clearly distinguishes KfW from its development-banking peers and has allowed the company a high degree of flexibility in its lending practices. Today KfW is the world's largest lender for renewable energy projects deployed in developing countries. Based in Frankfurt, Germany, the KfW Banking Group employs more than 4000 people in 50 locations around the world.

A strong sense of environmental responsibility within the organization extends far deeper than the company's renewable energy lending practices. The bank has implemented an "in-house environmental protection" program to assess and manage the environmental impact of its business operations within its German offices. The program focuses on: transportation and business travel; energy, water, and paper consumption; and carbon emissions. These environmental considerations played a significant role in the renovation and construction of the bank's corporate office buildings over the past 10 years.

5.58 The building viewed from Zeppelinallee, a busy arterial road adjacent to the site. JAN BITTER FOTOGRAFIE

LOCATION
Frankfurt am Main, Germany
Latitude 50.1 °N
Longitude 8.7 °E

HEATING DEGREE DAYS
5657 base 65 °F
[3143 base 18.3 °C]

COOLING DEGREE DAYS
2124 base 50 °F
[1180 base 10 °C]

DESIGN DRY-BULB WINTER (99%)
17.9 °F [−7.8 °C]

DESIGN DRY-BULB & MEAN COINCIDENT WET-BULB SUMMER (1%)
84.0/65.6 °F [28.9/18.7 °C]

SOLAR RADIATION
Jan 279 Btu/ft^2/day
[0.88 kWh/m^2/day]
Jun 1547 Btu/ft^2/day
[4.88 kWh/m^2/day]

ANNUAL PRECIPITATION
26 in. [658 mm]

In 2004, KfW launched a design competition for a new Westarkade office building with room for 700 employees. The facility was to be located on their existing corporate campus in Frankfurt's West End neighborhood adjacent to the Palmengarten botanical gardens. Sauerbruch Hutton won the competition. Their proposal included a slender 15-story office tower atop a low, curving three-story podium that connected to existing adjacent structures built in the 1970s, 1980s, and 1990s. An existing storage building on the site was not suitable for reuse and was subsequently demolished to make way for the new structure.

5.60 The first four floors form a broad podium along Zeppelinallee (left) upon which the 10-story tower (right) is positioned to take advantage of prevailing winds on the site.
SAUERBRUCH HUTTON

Design Intent and Validation

In keeping with KfW Banking Group's interest in environmental impact and stewardship, the primary design objective for the new facility was to set a new standard for energy consumption in high-rise office buildings. The goal was to design a building that would use less than 31,696 Btu/ft^2/yr [100 kWh/m^2/yr] of primary energy, to include operable windows for occupant control and natural ventilation, and to provide for a maximum summer temperature of 79 °F [26 °C].

To achieve their ambitious energy target, the design team relied heavily on modeling and simulations as both design tools and validation for design decisions. Analysis of prevailing wind conditions, computational fluid dynamic (CFD) modeling, and wind tunnel testing allowed designers to optimize the shape, form, and orientation of the building to take full advantage of passive, low-energy environmental control strategies. Because the tower facades primarily face east and west, thermal and daylight modeling were used to evaluate solar control strategies and to ensure the client that occupant thermal and visual comfort would be possible. Testing provided validation for the design team and the client that innovative design solutions would satisfy project goals and objectives.

The design team also looked carefully at the relationship between the new building and its surrounding urban context. The massing, color scheme, setbacks, and heights of the building components respond to specific existing conditions at the site perimeter. The

BUILDING TYPE
High-rise office tower and conference center

AREA
409,000 ft^2 [38,000 m^2]

CLIENT
KfW Banking Group, Frankfurt

DESIGN TEAM
Architect, Sauerbruch Hutton Architekten

Energy/Climate Engineer, Transsolar Energietechnik

HVAC Engineer, Zibell, Willner & Partner

Structural Engineer, Werner Sobek Frankfurt

Facade, Werner Sobek Stuttgart

Electrical Engineer, Reuter/ Mosbacher & Roll Rührgartner GmbH

Fire Protection, hhpberlin Ingenieure für Brandschutz GmbH

Transportation Systems, Jappsen + Stangier Oberwesel GmbH

Landscape Architect, Sommerlad Haase Kuhli

Acoustics & Physics, Müller-BBM

Lighting, Licht Kunst Licht

Traffic Planning, Durth Roos Consulting GmbH

Project Management, Weber Baumanagement, Architekten Theiss

COMPLETION
July 2010

PERFORMANCE METRICS
Energy Utilization Index (EUI):
Target:
31,696 Btu/ft^2/yr [100 kWh/m^2/yr]

Actual:
Not Available

Carbon Emissions:
Not Available

Water Use:
Not Available

architecture of the new building makes a bold statement without turning its back on the surrounding urban fabric.

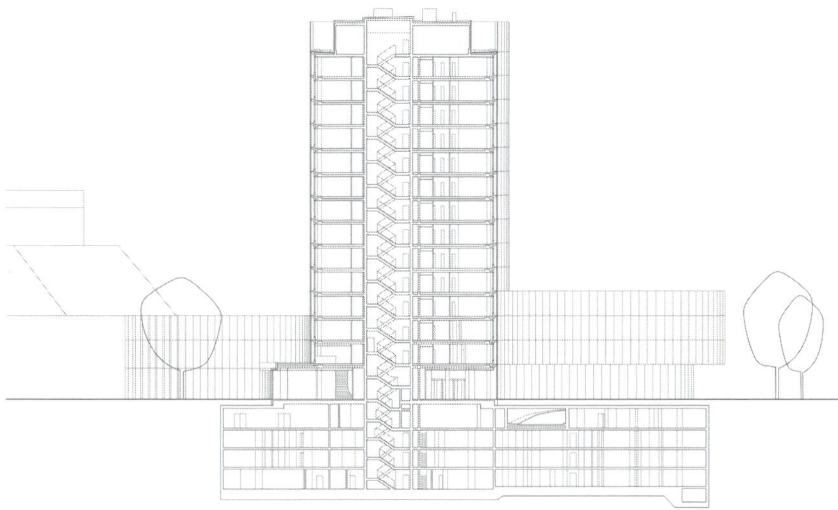

5.61 Building section showing the tower, podium, and basement. SAUERBRUCH HUTTON

5.62 Site plan showing the new building in relation to the existing KfW campus, the Palmengarten, and the intersection of two busy arterial roads. SAUERBRUCH HUTTON

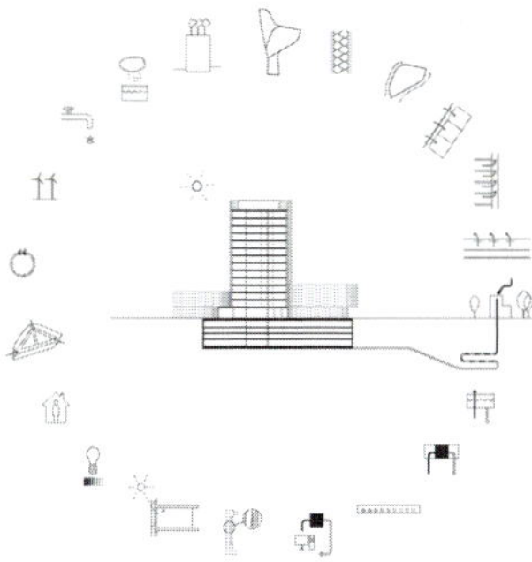

5.63 Diagram illustrating the energy concepts the design team incorporated into the Westarkade building. SAUERBRUCH HUTTON

Strategies

The site context played a critical role in the green strategies pursued in the Westarkade project. The shape and orientation of the building respond directly to local solar and wind conditions, which enabled the design team to employ a host of strategies intended to optimize energy efficiency and occupant satisfaction.

Site. The building responds to three distinct urban conditions at the periphery of the site. Along the busy Zeppelinallee arterial road to the west, a long, three-story podium forms a street wall and acts as a base for the tower. To the south, the three-story podium is connected to an existing KfW building. The new building matches the floor-to-floor heights of the neighboring building. The building faces a botanical garden to the northeast. This green landscape element is pulled into the project site creating an outdoor urban oasis that is separated from the noise and vehicles of the streetscape to the west by the podium element and to the south by the existing KfW campus facilities.

Double envelope. The design team devised a unique double envelope facade system for the building that they call the "pressure ring." The tower is oriented in the direction of the prevailing winds and the shape of the floor plan resembles an airfoil. As air moves around the envelope, an area of positive pressure results on the windward side and a larger area of negative pressure results on the leeward side. The facade consists of an inner layer of insulated glazing separated from an outer layer of single-pane glazing by a cavity space that is 28 in. [710 mm] at its deepest point. Floor slabs extend to the outer layer of glazing, closing off the cavity between floors. The inner layer of glazing uses a conventional aluminum curtainwall system fitted with low-emissivity (low-ε) coated insulated glazing units (IGUs). The outer layer of glazing consists of triangular projections with wide fixed single-pane glazing units and narrow operable flaps. The facade is intended to operate in three different modes—flaps are closed in winter to create a thermal buffer and wind is directed around the envelope; flaps are opened in the "shoulder seasons" to funnel air into the cavity, which is used to naturally ventilate the interior spaces; flaps are open in the summer, air is not admitted into the interior, and pressure differentials pull warm air through and from the cavity space.

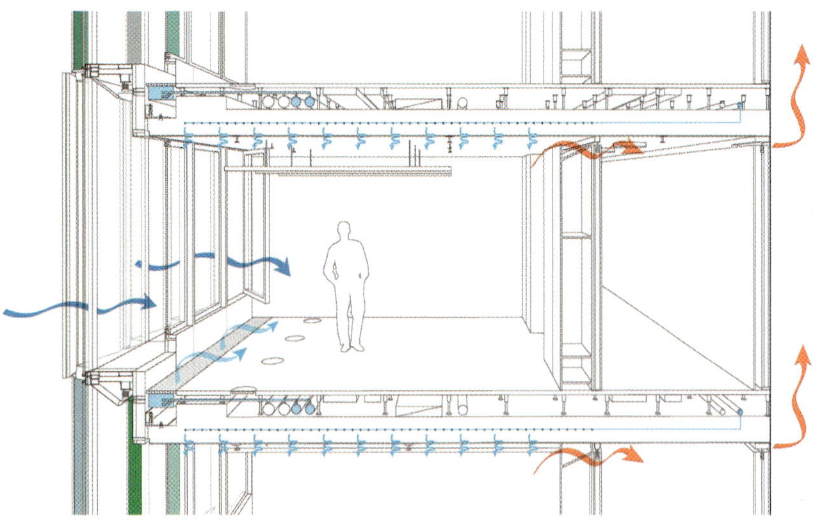

5.64 Natural ventilation diagram shows air moving through the offices and being exhausted into a shaft at the building core. SAUERBRUCH HUTTON

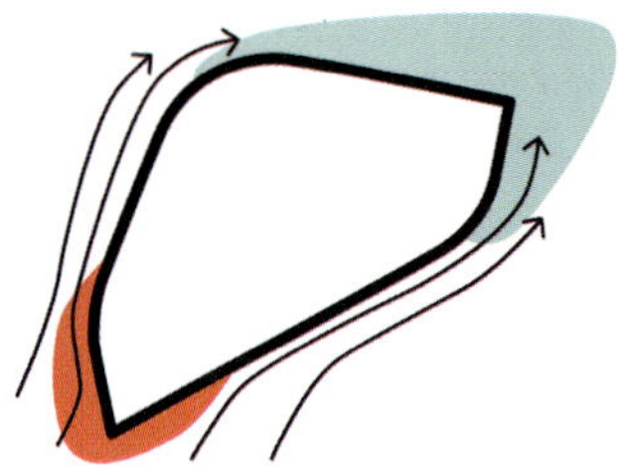

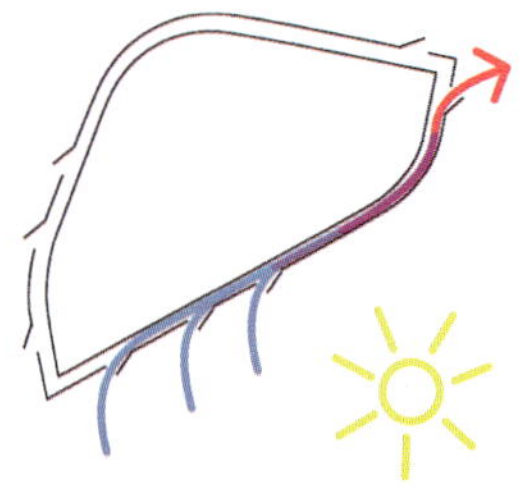

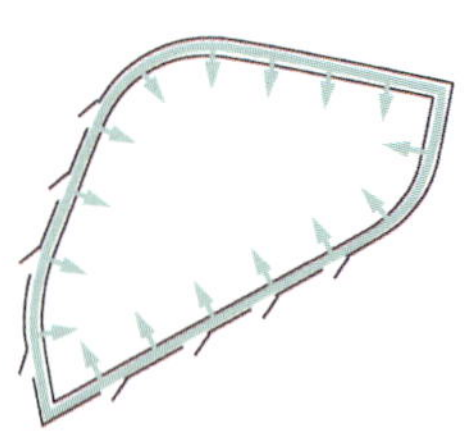

5.65 Diagrams showing the "pressure ring" concept for the double envelope. SAUERBRUCH HUTTON | TRANSSOLAR

Natural ventilation. The building is designed to operate in either a natural ventilation mode or a mechanical ventilation mode depending on the outdoor temperature. In natural ventilation mode, prevailing winds are admitted into the double envelope cavity space through operable flaps on the outer layer of glazing. These automated flaps adjust to create evenly distributed wind pressure on the inner layer of glazing, which helps to minimize excessive cross ventilation through the interior. Ventilation air is admitted into the building either through operable windows controlled by occupants or through air inlets. The design intent was for air to move from the facade, through the offices and into the corridors where it would be exhausted through a shaft via stack effect. Placing the operable windows on the inner layer of glazing allows a degree of individual control of natural ventilation without draft and acoustical disturbances for other employees.

5.66 The double envelope is composed of a large plane of glass with narrow, colored operable panels for ventilation. JAN BITTER FOTOGRAFIE

Passive solar heating. The thermal mass of the concrete floor slabs absorbs solar radiation and stores and reradiates heat in the winter months, which helps to passively heat the interior spaces and reduces the need for mechanical heating. Automated shading devices within the double envelope's cavity space assist in controlling unwanted solar heat gain in the summer months. Slabs within the double envelope cavity space absorb direct solar radiation, helping to preheat ventilation air before it is admitted to the building through operable windows or ventilation inlets in the fall and spring "shoulder seasons."

Daylighting. All offices are located along the building perimeter, which allows workers ample access to daylight in their workspaces and reduces the amount of energy used for electric lighting. Workspaces, where occupants spend the most time, have the greatest access to daylight. Spaces where occupants spend little time (such as elevators, stairs, rest rooms, and corridors) are located at the core of the building away from the facades. Circulation corridors extend to the building facade at three locations on each office floor to admit some daylight into the spaces at the building core.

5.67 Internal circulation corridors extend to the facade at three locations on each floor of the tower to allow daylight to reach the core of the building. JAN BITTER FOTOGRAPHIE

Earth duct. When outside air temperatures rise above 77 °F [25 °C] or fall below 50 °F [10 °C], interior spaces are mechanically ventilated. Outside air is pulled into a 98-ft [30 m] long geothermal earth duct located at the edge of the building site. The location, adjacent to the Palmengarten botanical gardens, was chosen because it offered the least risk of pulling contaminated air into the system. The consistent temperature of the ground is used to precondition air before sending it into the building ventilation system. In the summer, ground temperatures are cooler than the ambient air, which cools air being pulled through the system. In the winter ground temperatures are warmer than the ambient air, which warms air being pulled through the system. The preconditioned air is carried to the floors through a series of vertical shafts that connect to raised-floor plenums. Ventilation air is introduced to the offices near the facade and exhausted through the corridors in the same manner as occurs in the natural ventilation mode.

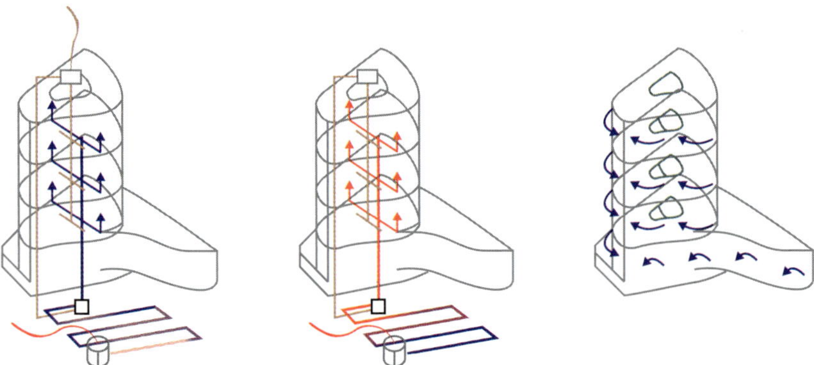

5.68 Concept diagrams showing the earth duct system for preconditioning ventilation air (left and center) and the natural ventilation mode (right). SAUERBRUCH HUTTON | TRANSSOLAR

Heating and cooling. The building is connected to a high-efficiency district hot and chilled water system capable of handling the base heating and cooling loads for the building. Thermo-active slabs provide radiant heating and cooling for the building. This energy-efficient radiant system maintains comfortable indoor temperatures without the need for forced-air ductwork in the ceilings. Electric convector units help to mitigate the cold conditions at the facades during winter months. A rooftop cooling tower provides "free" night-time cooling for the radiant cooling system in the summer by storing coolth in the thermal mass of the slabs at night, which absorbs heat the next day to maintain thermal comfort conditions. Heat recovered from ventilation air is used to heat water for the radiant slabs via a heat exchange system. Decentralized chillers at the Westarkade satisfy any peak cooling loads.

Energy-efficient support equipment. The building employs an innovative smart elevator system to conserve electricity and reduce employee wait time. Rather than simply pushing the elevator call button, occupants enter their floor destination on a keypad or scan their ID badge. The system clusters or groups employees into specific elevators which reduces the number of floor stops and the shuttling of empty cars and thereby conserves energy.

Water conservation. Low-flow plumbing fixtures are used throughout the Westarkade project. A rainwater harvesting system captures rainwater and stores it in a cistern. The water that is captured is not used as a non-potable water source in building fixtures, but for other purposes.

Green roofs. An intensive green roof system was used on the three-story podium in an effort to harmonize with the adjacent Palmengarden landscape, to protect and insulate the roof membrane, and to provide green space for employees to view from several outdoor patios.

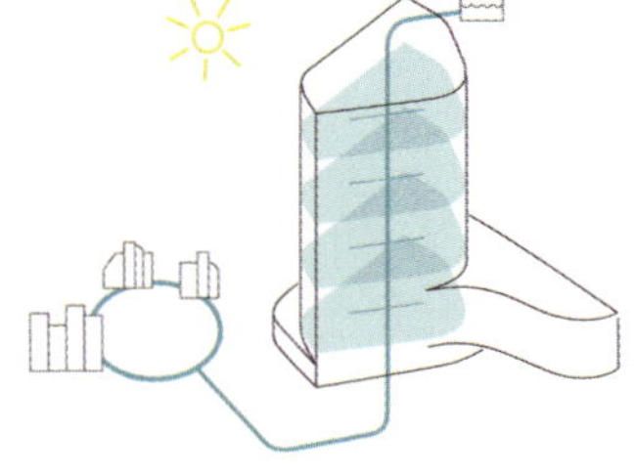

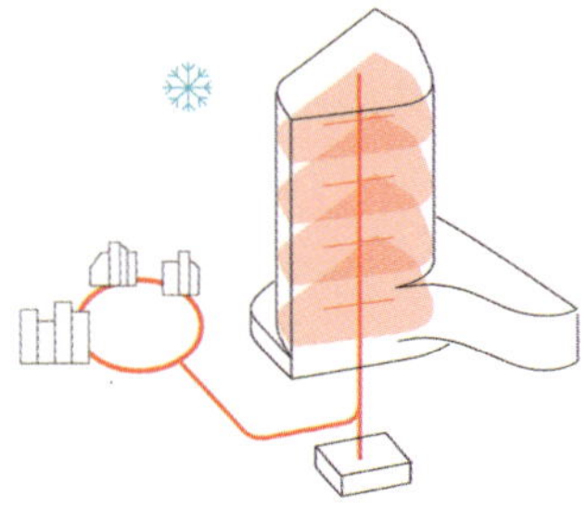

5.69 Heating and cooling loads are handled by a district hot and chilled water system. SAUERBRUCH HUTTON | TRANSSOLAR

Alternative transportation. The building is conveniently located 1/4 mile [0.4 km] from the Brockenheimer Warte subway station and street tramline. A variety of public transportation options reduces the need for employees to drive to work.

Materials. The building structure is concrete. Raised floors are used throughout the building as a ventilation plenum. Office partitions are constructed of laminated wood-composite materials for easy future modification. The design team made extensive use of conventional aluminum curtainwall for the inner layer of the double envelope. The exterior layer of the double envelope uses opaque panels for the ventilation flaps. The colors of these flaps harmonize with the colors present in the urban context—red tones for the facades along Zeppelinalle, blue tones on the facade facing the existing KfW campus buildings, and green tones on the facade facing the Palmengarten botanical gardens.

5.70 Exterior envelope of the Westarkade building with colorful operable wind flaps for ventilation. The color scheme responds specifically to facade orientations. JAN BITTER FOTOGRAFIE

How Is It Working?

A post-occupancy evaluation of the building-in-use has not yet been performed. A third-party organization, however, will be responsible for monitoring ongoing building performance and operations. Actual performance data will be compared with predictions made through modeling, simulations, and calculations during the design phase to determine whether the building is performing as intended.

The design team evaluated a number of country-specific building certification systems such as the Leadership in Energy and Environmental Design (LEED) system used in the U.S., the British

Research Establishment Environmental Assessment Method (BREEAM) used in Great Britain, and Solarbau used in Germany. Although the various certification methodologies, procedures, calculations, and guidelines proved useful during the design of the Westarkade building, none was deemed comprehensive enough on its own to be selected as a suitable system to be used for certifying the building.

Further Information

Gonchar, J. 2010. "More Than Skin Deep." *Architectural Record* July 2010: 102–104. (A print article, which describes the project and the double-skin facade system.)

KfW Bankengruppe. www.kfw.de/EN_Home/KfW_Bankengruppe/Our_Actions/Sustainability/In-house_environmental_protection.jsp (A website outlining KfW Bank's "in-house environmental protection" program, which includes information on the new office tower in Frankfurt.)

Sauerbruch Hutton. www.sauerbruchhutton.de/images/kfwbanking_group_en.pdf (A two-page downloadable document that includes project information, design strategies employed, and color images and diagrams.)

Background and Context

Manitoba Hydro is the fourth largest electricity and natural gas provider in Canada. The company is provincially owned and most of the electricity sold comes from renewable hydroelectric power sources. Manitoba Hydro offers some of the lowest utility rates available anywhere in the world.

Prior to the completion of this new corporate headquarters, employees were scattered among multiple offices located in the Winnipeg suburbs. The new building was intended to consolidate these offices into one complex that would allow consolidation of employees from the suburban offices into downtown Winnipeg—where they would have greater access to transportation options and downtown amenities. The site was specifically chosen because of its close proximity to Winnipeg's public transportation routes and for the potential that it offered to design and construct a building that would strengthen and revitalize the city's urban core.

5.71 North and east elevations of Manitoba Hydro Place showing the tower sitting on the three-story podium and the solar chimney rising above the tower roof. EDUARD HUEBER | ARCHPHOTO INC.

5.72 An early design sketch of the two tower sections and winter gardens atop the arcade podium. BRUCE KUWABARA | KPMB ARCHITECTS

LOCATION
Winnipeg, Manitoba, Canada
Latitude 49.9 °N
Longitude 97.1 °E

HEATING DEGREE DAYS
10,350 base 65 °F
[5750 base 18.3 °C]

COOLING DEGREE DAYS
1819 base 50 °F
[1011 base 10 °C]

DESIGN DRY-BULB WINTER (99%)
−21.8 °F [−29.9 °C]

DESIGN DRY-BULB & MEAN COINCIDENT WET-BULB SUMMER (1%)
84.1/68.6 °F [28.9/20.3 °C]

SOLAR RADIATION
Jan 461 Btu/ft^2/day
[1.45 kWh/m^2/day]
Jun 2025 Btu/ft^2/day
[6.39 kWh/m^2/day]

ANNUAL PRECIPITATION
19 in. [483 mm]

The 695,250 ft^2 [64,591 m^2] Manitoba Hydro Place complex, completed in September 2009, consists of two 18-story office towers for 1800 employees atop a three-story public arcade that includes retail and commercial space. A solar chimney was placed on the north side of the building and rises above the 18-story towers, leaving the top of the chimney and the other building facades with unobstructed access to solar radiation and prevailing winds.

Design Intent and Validation

Being a large producer of renewable power, Manitoba Hydro envisioned a building that would set new standards for energy efficiency, at least 60% lower than conventional office buildings in milder climates. Manitoba Hydro also wanted to create an architectural statement, to improve the surrounding urban context, and to provide for the comfort and productivity of employees using the building.

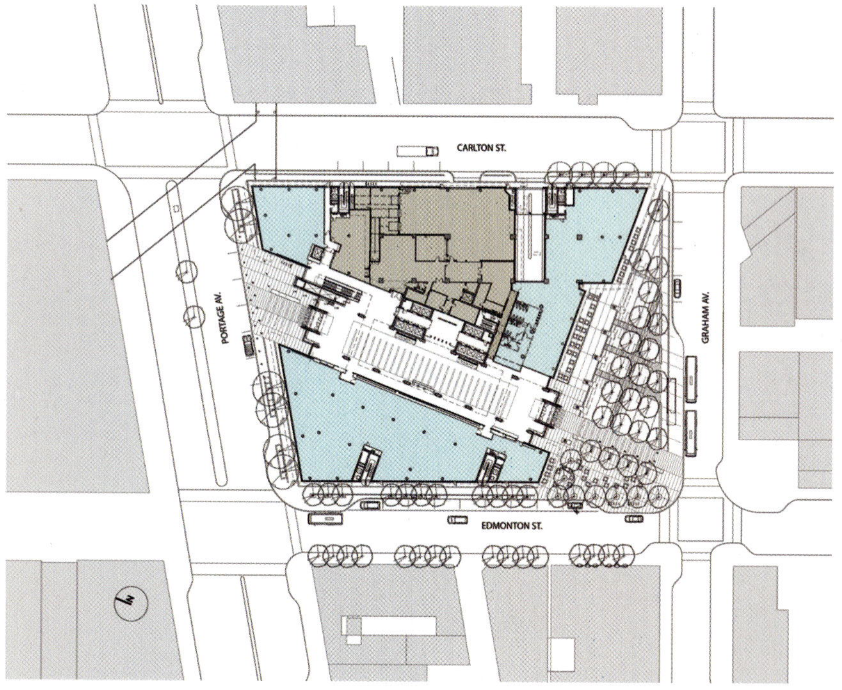

5.73 Site plan of Manitoba Hydro Place showing the public ground floor arcade and outdoor plaza. KPMB ARCHITECTS

Kuwabara Payne McKenna Blumberg Architects (KPMB) was chosen from a large list of renowned architecture firms to design the building. Other consultants (an extensive team of designers, engineers, and specialists) were similarly interviewed and selected by the client. Once assembled, the full design team began a lengthy integrated design process.

One of the most challenging aspects of the project was the location. Winnipeg has a severe climate that can range from −30 °F [−34 °C] with 20-mph [8.9 m/s] winds in the winter to 95 °F [35 °C] in the

BUILDING TYPE
Mixed-use (office/retail)

AREA
695,250 ft^2 [64,591 m^2]

CLIENT
Manitoba Hydro

DESIGN TEAM
Design Architect, Kuwabara Payne McKenna Blumberg Architects (KPMB)

Architect of Record, Smith Carter Architects and Engineers

Advocate Architect, Prairie Architects Inc.

Energy/Climate Engineer, Transsolar Energietechnik

Mechanical/Electrical Engineer, Earth Tech Canada Inc.

Structural Engineer, Crosier Kilgour

Building Envelope, Brook Van Dalen & Associates

Construction Manager, PCL Constructors Canada Inc.

COMPLETION
September 2009

PERFORMANCE METRICS
Energy Utilization Index (EUI):
Target:
31,700 Btu/ft^2/year
[100 kWh/m^2/yr]

Actual:
29,000 Btu/ft^2/year
[92 kWh/m^2/yr]

Carbon Emissions:
1.1 lb CO_2/ft^2
[5.4 kg CO_2/m^2]

Water Use:
Not Available

summer. A thorough analysis of climate conditions revealed that Winnipeg may be extremely cold in the winter, but it's also sunnier than most cities in cold, harsh climates. The design team realized that Winnipeg was an ideal location to employ passive solar heating (and daylighting) strategies. The orientation and the massing of the complex were carefully calibrated to harness the solar potential of the site.

Validation of design moves involved extensive computer modeling and simulation. Thermal modeling of temperatures in the workspaces (both radiant and air temperatures) allowed the design team to justify the use of a dynamic double envelope because of the benefits that it would have for occupant thermal comfort. Computational fluid dynamic (CFD) models were used to study wind conditions around the perimeter of the building and the flow of ventilation air horizontally across the floor plates and vertically in the solar chimney. Daylighting was also modeled to reinforce the idea that workers would have close access to the facades, resulting in less need for energy-consuming electric lighting and greater access to views.

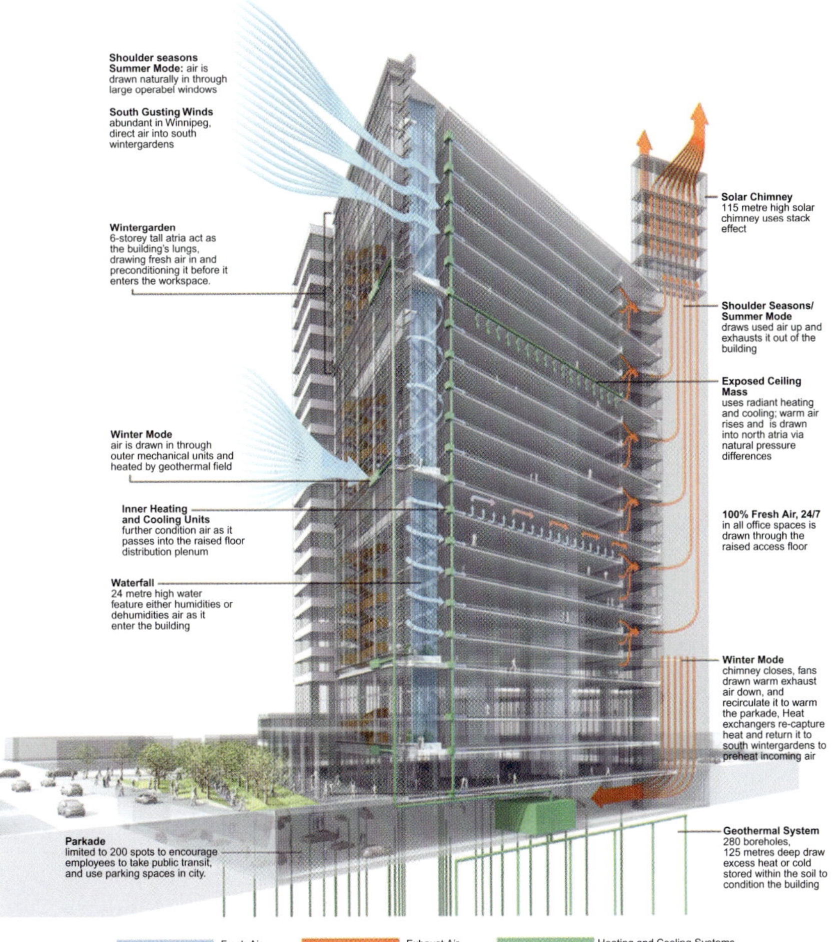
Shoulder seasons Summer Mode: air is drawn naturally in through large operabel windows
South Gusting Winds abundant in Winnipeg, direct air into south wintergardens
Wintergarden 6-storey tall atria act as the building's lungs, drawing fresh air in and preconditioning it before it enters the workspace.
Winter Mode air is drawn in through outer mechanical units and heated by geothermal field
Inner Heating and Cooling Units further condition air as it passes into the raised floor distribution plenum
Waterfall 24 metre high water feature either humidities or dehumidities air as it enter the building
Parkade limited to 200 spots to encourage employees to take public transit, and use parking spaces in city.
Solar Chimney 115 metre high solar chimney uses stack effect
Shoulder Seasons/ Summer Mode draws used air up and exhausts it out of the building
Exposed Ceiling Mass uses radiant heating and cooling; warm air rises and is drawn into north atria via natural pressure differences
100% Fresh Air, 24/7 in all office spaces is drawn through the raised access floor
Winter Mode chimney closes, fans drawn warm exhaust air down, and recirculate it to warm the parkade, Heat exchangers re-capture heat and return it to south wintergardens to preheat incoming air
Geothermal System 280 boreholes, 125 metres deep draw excess heat or cold stored within the soil to condition the building
Fresh Air
Exhaust Air
Heating and Cooling Systems

5.74 Diagram illustrating the integrated "green" design strategies used in the project. BRYAN CHRISTIE DESIGN

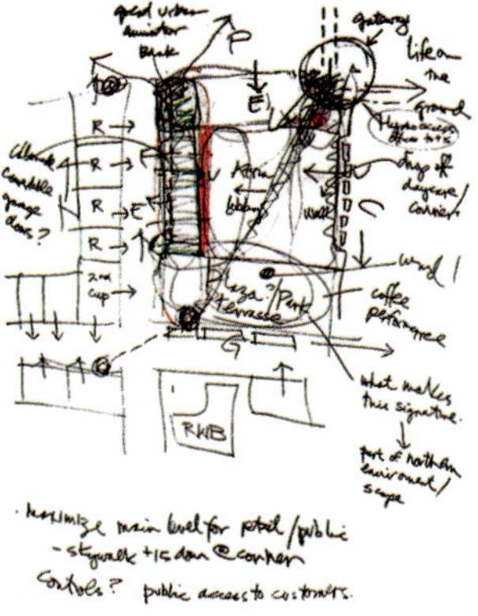

5.75 A conceptual sketch generated during the integrated design process. KPMB ARCHITECTS

5.76 A conceptual sketch of the ground level public arcade. KAEL OPIE | KPMB ARCHITECTS

Strategies

Manitoba Hydro Place employs a host of strategies designed to take advantage of the climatic resources in Winnipeg and the project's specific site orientation, to produce a workplace that is both energy-efficient and comfortable for occupants.

Site. The relationship between Manitoba Hydro Place and its site in downtown Winnipeg was critical to both the design team and the client. Manitoba Hydro chose to consolidate multiple suburban offices into one central complex to allow workers greater access to public transportation. The majority of Manitoba Hydro employees now take public transportation to and from work, which lessens the impact on the environment of vehicle miles traveled. The building also occupies a prominent place in the heart of the city, which was intended to positively impact the revitalization of the urban downtown core. A public arcade with retail and commercial spaces allows the general public to use the building. The design team carefully studied the impact of the building massing on the surrounding context. Canopies help to redirect wind away from the building to shelter sidewalks where pedestrians stroll. The adjacent Air Canada Plaza, where workers often sit outside to eat their lunches, was protected from potential shading by Hydro Place during the summer months.

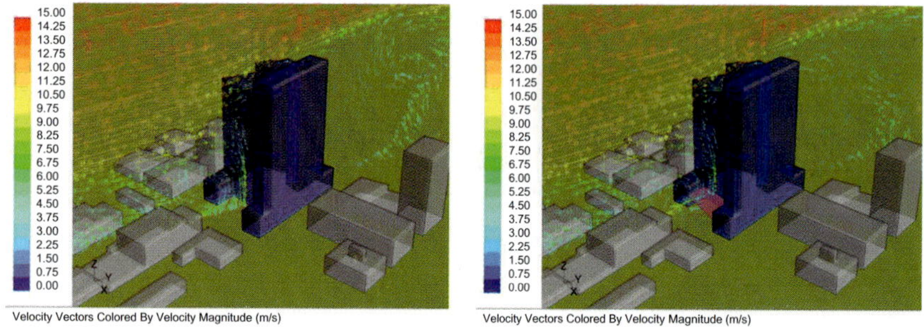

5.77 Computational fluid dynamic (CFD) models showing the impact of the building form on wind effects in the urban context. A canopy (right) was introduced to redirect wind away from the sidewalks surrounding the site. TRANSSOLAR

Natural ventilation. Operable windows within the double facade allow occupants a measure of personal control over thermal conditions in their workspaces during the spring and fall transitional seasons. Three six-story winter gardens capture prevailing winds from the south and precondition outside air before it is used in the raised-floor displacement ventilation system. Humidification and dehumidification of intake air is achieved through the use of Mylar ribbon water features in the atria. Warm water humidifies dry winter intake air and chilled water dehumidifies humid intake air in the summer. At the north end of the building, six three-story atria capture return air from the office spaces and channel it into the 377-ft [115 m] tall solar chimney. In the summer months the sun heats elements in the top of the chimney enclosure, which increases the buoyancy of the air within and pulls the air upward. Sand-filled pipes at the top of the chimney absorb solar radiation during the day and release the resulting heat at night to warm the air in the chimney when temperatures are cooler.

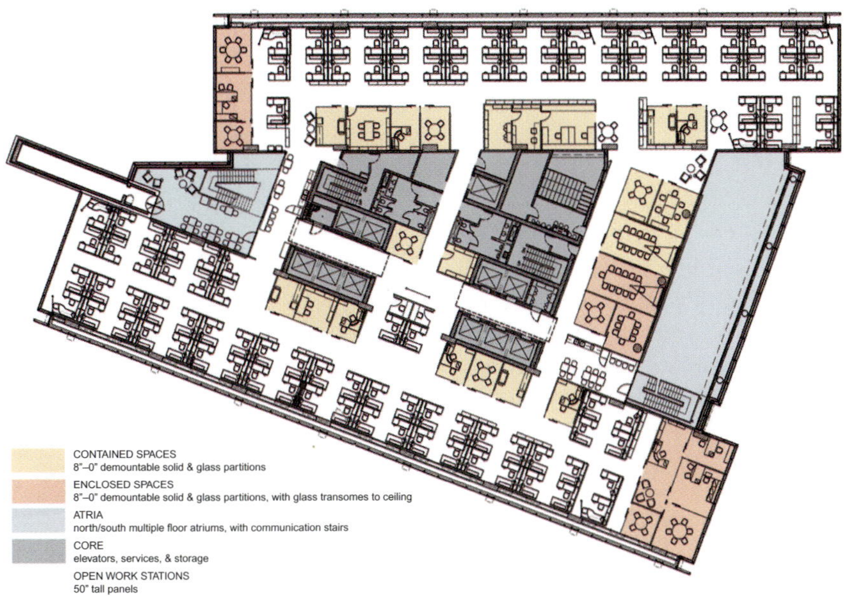

5.78 Typical tower floor plan showing the winter gardens and solar chimney positioned between the two rectilinear office wings. KPMB ARCHITECTS

Passive solar heating. Winnipeg has the beneficial characteristic of being sunny when the temperatures are extremely cold. For this reason, a passive solar heating strategy was appropriate for Manitoba Hydro Place. The three south-facing winter gardens are intended to function as sunspaces, where concrete floor slabs absorb solar radiation and release heat to preheat the intake air. This air moves across the sunspaces into displacement ventilation plenums (located beneath raised floors in the office spaces) for distribution. Additional heating or cooling of intake air is performed as needed through the use of fan-coil units at the intake louvers, but the design team expects that the passive solar preheating will conserve energy. Radiant tubing embedded in concrete slabs within the double envelope cavities and atria spaces is also designed to capture and store heat within the thermal mass elements and transmit it to a geothermal storage field via a heat exchange system.

5.79 Operable windows controlled by the building management system (BMS) on the outer layer of the double envelope. TOM ARBAN | TOM ARBAN PHOTOGRAPHY

Double envelope. The dynamic facades on the east and west sides of the building consist of two layers of glazing separated by a 3-ft [0.9 m] cavity space. The outer layer consists of fixed and operable low-iron, low-emissivity (low-ε) coated insulated glazing units (IGU). The inner layer consists of fixed and operable low-emissivity (low-ε) coated single-pane glazing. Windows on the outer layer of the facade are opened and closed by the building management system (BMS) to vent the cavity, while windows on the inner layer of glazing are manually operated by the occupants. The low-iron, low-emissivity (low-ε) coated glass was intended to maximize daylight transmission into the interior, while maintaining high thermal resistance.

Daylighting. Daylighting was used extensively to reduce the amount of energy used by electric lighting fixtures. The winter gardens at Manitoba Hydro Place (used for passive solar heating and natural ventilation) occupy the southern side of the building. As a result, the two office floor plates are oriented west and northeast. The floor plates were kept long and narrow so that no worker is more than 30 ft [9 m] from a window. In addition, closed offices were located away from the facade, close to the service core, to increase the distribution of daylight into the workspaces. Ceiling heights are high (10.8 ft [3.3 m]) to allow daylight to reach deep into the floor plane. Automated window shades were integrated into the facade system to help control glare that might result from low sun angles on the east and west orientations and to prevent excessive solar heat gain. These devices are perforated to allow some transparency even when fully extended. The electric lighting and shading systems respond to changing daylight conditions throughout the day.

5.81 Automated shading devices within the double envelope cavity space. KPMB ARCHITECTS

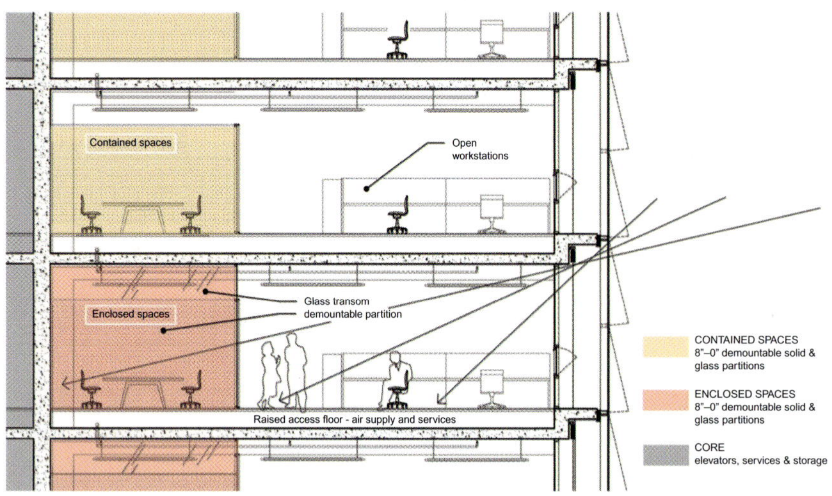

5.80 Section illustrating the winter and summer daylighting conditions within the office spaces. High ceilings and glass partitions allow light to reach deep into the floor plan. KPMB ARCHITECTS

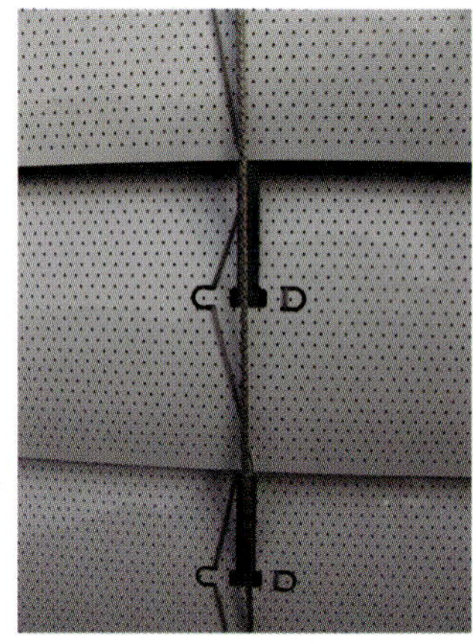

5.82 Detail view of the microperforated shading devices (shown in the closed position). KPMB ARCHITECTS

Ground source heat pumps. A ground source heat exchange system feeds the building chiller and subsequently the radiant ceilings in the office spaces. The closed-loop system consists of 280 ground source wells that were bored vertically 410 ft [125 m] into the ground beneath the building. The system takes advantage of consistent ground temperatures year round and incorporates a long-term-storage field where heat captured during the summer is stored for use in the winter. A radiant ceiling system absorbs heat from the interior spaces, improving summer thermal comfort via mean radiant temperature modification. Approximately 60% of the building heating in the winter is supplied by the underground storage field.

Energy recovery. In the winter months, exhaust air entering the solar chimney is redirected downward by fans rather than being

5.83 Construction photograph showing the boreholes for the ground source wells being drilled. MANITOBA HYDRO

allowed to rise, via stack effect, up the chimney and out of the building. A heat recovery system extracts some heat from the exhaust air, sends the heat to fan-coil units at the winter garden intake fan-coil units (for preheating), and distributes the air to the public ground floor arcade space.

Indoor air quality (IAQ). The building uses 100% fresh air. This means that the supply (and ventilation) air moves through the interior of the building only once before being exhausted through the solar chimney. This strategy was intended to reduce the risk of contaminated or stale air negatively impacting occupant health and productivity and differs from standard HVAC system design where a percentage of air within the building is routinely returned, filtered, and mixed with incoming fresh air. The energy "penalty" associated with a 100% fresh air ventilation system was mitigated through the use of a heat recovery system and a high-performance envelope that reduces heat gains and losses.

Green roof. A green roof was installed atop the three-story podium. The system helps to protect the underlying roof membrane from ultraviolet (UV) degradation and acts as added thermal insulation.

5.84 Construction photograph of a rigger drilling the boreholes for the ground source wells. MANITOBA HYDRO

How Is It Working?

Manitoba Hydro Place opened in September 2009. It generally takes a year or two of calibration before an uncommissioned building performs as designed. However, by all accounts the building is performing better than expected. The limited energy data available show savings of 66% over typical office building energy consumption, which exceeds the goal of 60% that the client and design team established.

The building has received a host of design awards since its completion. These include:

- 2010 AIA COTE Top Ten Green Projects;
- 2009 Council on Tall Buildings and Urban Habitat (CTBUH) Best Tall Building Americas;
- 2008 International Building Skin-tech (IBS) Award, Highly Commended;
- 2006 Mipim Architectural Review Awards, Commended for Innovation; and
- 2006 Canadian Architect Award of Excellence.

The project is currently pursuing a LEED NC 3.0 certification through the U.S. Green Building Council. A Platinum rating is anticipated.

5.85 Green roof atop the three-story podium with the tower and solar chimney in the background. EDUARD HUEBER | ARCHPHOTO INC.

Further Information

Gonchar, J. 2010. "More Than Skin Deep," *Architectural Record*. July 2010: 104–110. (A print article that describes the project and the double-skin facade system.)

5.86 Occupants enjoying a corner of the three-story north atrium space beside the solar chimney. TOM ARBAN | TOM ARBAN PHOTOGRAPHY

Kuwabara Payne McKenna Blumberg. www.kpmbarchitects.com (The architect's website, which includes photographs, project facts, awards received, and a project description.)

Linn, C. 2010. "Cold Comfort: Manitoba Hydro Place—One of North America's Most Complex Energy-efficient Buildings is also Sited in One of its Most Challenging Climates." *Greensource*, 5, No. 2, 52–57. (A print article, which includes building metrics data, material sources, and descriptions of the green design features.)

Manitoba Hydro. www.manitobahydroplace.com/ (The owner's website, which includes information related to building performance, the integrated design process, the design team, and green design strategies.)

Transsolar Energietechnik. www.transsolar.com/download/e/pb_manitoba_hydro_winnipeg_e.pdf (A document that includes photographs and information related to the project team, design process, climate strategies, and predicted performance.)

5.87 One of three six-story south atrium spaces. EDUARD HUEBER | ARCHPHOTO INC.

MARIN COUNTRY DAY SCHOOL, LEARNING RESOURCE CENTER

Background and Context

Marin Country Day School (MCDS) is located in Corte Madera, California—about 10 miles [16 km] north of San Francisco, across the Golden Gate Bridge. The school serves more than 500 students from kindergarten through eighth grade. The 35-acre [14.2 ha] campus is situated on a site bounded by San Francisco Bay to the north and the Marin County Open Space District uphill to the southwest and east. The campus property, which was terraced for agriculture prior to the construction of the school, constitutes a self-contained watershed area that supports habitats for local flora and fauna. The proximity and beauty of the natural setting have become indelibly linked to one of the school's educational missions—to encourage students to connect with and learn from the natural environment around them.

Rather than one large facility, MCDS takes the form of a campus in which the Upper Division (grades 5–8) and the Lower Division (grades K–4) are organized into smaller buildings, each housing various educational functions. Connections between the indoors and outdoors are strengthened through the use of outdoor educational spaces and outdoor circulation between the buildings.

The Learning Resource Center (LRC) was completed in 2009 as part of the second phase (Step 2) of a 25-year master plan that EHDD Architecture began in 1999. The 23,592 ft^2 [2192 m^2] LRC building includes space for a library, classrooms, laboratories, and art studios. The building is "L" shaped in plan and organized around an outdoor courtyard space. The elevation change across the site allows the building to be vertically zoned according to occupant uses—the Upper Division classrooms are on the upper floor with easy access to other Upper Division buildings further uphill on the campus and the Lower Division classrooms are on the lower floor with access to other Lower Division buildings on campus. The library and Step-up Courtyard amphitheater vertically link the Upper and Lower Division areas.

5.88 The entrance to the Learning Resource Center library at dusk. JOSH PARTEE

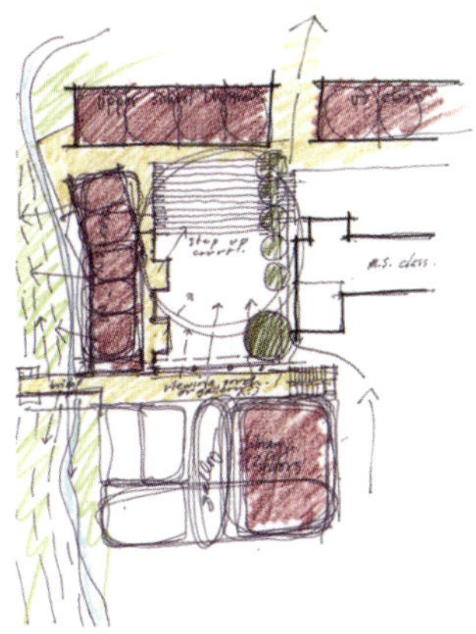

5.89 Conceptual sketch showing the LRC in relation to the creek, Step-up Courtyard, and existing campus buildings. EHDD ARCHITECTURE

LOCATION
Corte Madera, California, USA
Latitude 37.9 °N
Longitude 122.5 °W

HEATING DEGREE DAYS
2708 base 65 °F
[1504 base 18.3 °C]
San Francisco, CA data

COOLING DEGREE DAYS
3026 base 50 °F
[1681 base 10 °C]
San Francisco, CA data

DESIGN DRY-BULB WINTER (99%)
40.8 °F [4.9 °C]
San Francisco, CA data

DESIGN DRY-BULB & MEAN COINCIDENT WET-BULB SUMMER (1%)
78.3/62.1 °F [25.7/16.7 °C]
San Francisco, CA data

SOLAR RADIATION
Jan 708 Btu/ft^2/day
[2.23 kWh/m^2/day]
Jun 2392 Btu/ft^2/day
[7.55 kWh/m^2/day]
San Francisco, CA data

ANNUAL PRECIPITATION
34 in. [864 mm]
San Rafael, CA data

Design Intent and Validation

The design intent for the Learning Resource Center was to integrate the natural surroundings, as an immersion learning experience for the students, within the curriculum and the physical environment. The school, nestled in a natural watershed, did not follow the typical approach of an east–west orientation. The buildings that follow the creek are provided with shade by a neighboring hill on the east side and the west side features deep, shaded walkways that provide ample protection from the sun.

5.90 Kite aerial photograph of the MCDS campus looking south toward the Marin County Open Space district. CHARLES C. BENTON

The architects took a "zero net energy" building approach both for planning the MCDS campus and for embedding such principles in the educational curriculum. Specific design goals included:

- Using site-specific architectural strategies to minimize resource consumption for heating, cooling, ventilation, lighting, and water supply/waste, while providing thermal comfort and control capabilities to occupants throughout the year.
- Utilizing on-site renewable energy resources to produce more energy than the building uses during the year. This goal was motivated by climate change concerns in California and by a desire to use the energy generating capability of the building as a teaching tool to raise students' awareness of their impact on the natural environment. EHDD was able to convince the client that a "zero net energy" building could be accomplished in a cost-effective manner.
- Integrating a new building into an existing campus context through the use of natural materials, sensitive scaling and

BUILDING TYPE
School

AREA
23,592 ft^2 [2192 m^2]

CLIENT
Marin Country Day School

DESIGN TEAM
Architect, EHDD Architecture

MEP Engineer, Stantec Consulting

Civil Engineer, Sherwood Engineers

Structural Engineer, Tipping + Mar Associates

Landscape Architect, CMG Landscape Architecture

Acoustics, Charles M. Salter Associates, Inc.

Contractor, Oliver & Company

COMPLETION
2009

METRICS
Energy Utilization Index (EUI):
Predicted:
21,000 Btu/ft^2/yr
[66.2 kWh/m^2/yr]

Actual:
Not Available

Carbon Emissions:
Not Available

Water Use:
Not Available

massing of building components, relationships to adjacent existing structures, and connections to site landscape features.

There are three primary means by which the design intent and goals for this project were validated by the design team. First, energy modeling showed that the energy produced through on-site renewable energy sources exceeds the total energy usage of the building each year. The result is a "zero net energy" building. Second, thermal comfort conditions were modeled during the design process to demonstrate to the client that occupants would be satisfied with the environmental conditions in a building utilizing passive architectural strategies such as natural ventilation. Finally, the integrated design process used by the design team and the client resulted in a completed building that fits nicely into the existing campus and the intellectual life of the school. Indeed, the LRC is so tightly connected to its setting that it is challenging to know which architectural and landscape elements were existing and which are new.

An integrated design process (sometimes called "whole building" design) was used on the LRC project. The key to integrated design is that team members (architects, engineers, cost consultants, specialists, facilities managers, and others) are actively involved in the design process from the very beginning. Collaboration, exchange of ideas/information, and synthesis of complex design considerations are hallmarks of the integrated design process and allowed the team to evaluate design decisions continuously and to predict performance outcomes. A case in point—Stantec and EHDD coordinated the mechanical systems early in the design process in an effort to place hot equipment on the cooler, north side of the building, which had implications for the floor plan layout of the building.

Third-party validation has come in the form of a LEED for Schools 2.0 Platinum certification. The design intent was to obtain all of the Energy and Atmosphere credits—a goal that design teams routinely have difficulty accomplishing.

5.91 Longitudinal north–south site section. EHDD ARCHITECTURE

Strategies

The design team employed a number of simple architectural and adaptive behavioral strategies to achieve a zero net energy building that responds to institutional goals, provides for occupant comfort, and acts as a tool to teach children about their impact on the environment.

5.92 Exterior gathering and classroom spaces provide students with opportunities to be outside and to connect with the site landscape of the MCDS campus. JOSH PARTEE

5.93 The MCDS campus sits in a natural watershed, which provides rich habitat for local flora and fauna. JOSH PARTEE

5.94 A reconstructed stream hugs the east side of the LRC and channels stormwater runoff from the campus site watershed to San Francisco Bay. EHDD ARCHITECTURE

Site. The Learning Resource Center maintained a close connection with the outdoors through its relationship to existing campus buildings and site features. Spaces between buildings create microclimates suitable for educational and ceremonial activities at various scales, such as for those that will occur in the new Step-up Courtyard amphitheater. Circulation routes run through and next to outdoor gathering spaces, which give them an active and dynamic character. Existing paved surfaces were reduced in extent and the new site landscape design features a combination of dry-laid pavers and permeable gravel to reduce stormwater runoff and to increase infiltration of stormwater back into the ground for water table recharge. A stream on the periphery of the campus and adjacent to the LRC, part of the natural watershed on the site, was restored as a natural riparian habitat and provides a unique educational opportunity for students to learn about the ecology of the area. Stormwater runoff from large areas of playground paving flows into a new series of bioswales that filter the water before sending it into the reconstructed stream, marshland, and then the Bay. Although many existing buildings at MCDS are low, one-story structures, the design team chose a two-story layout for LRC to preserve unspoiled land on the campus.

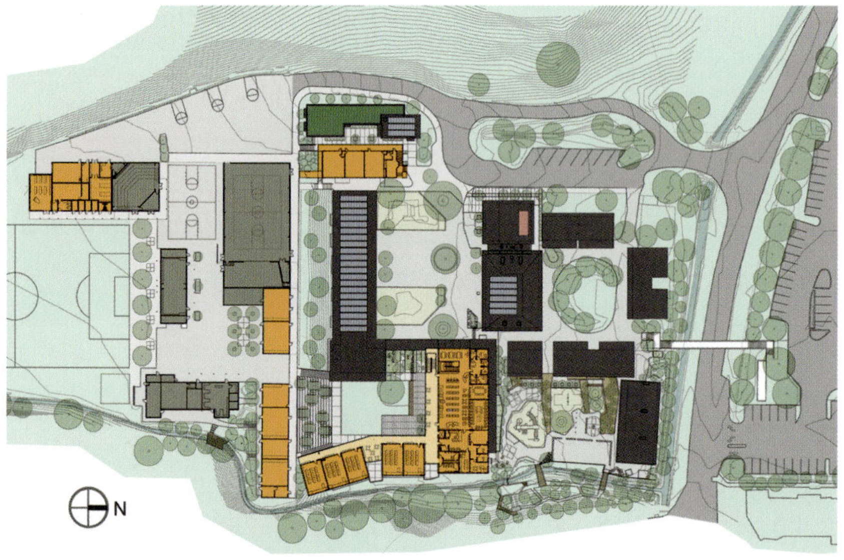

5.95 Site plan showing MCDS campus improvements in yellow, including the new "L" shaped LRC building at the bottom center of the plan. EHDD ARCHITECTURE

Transitional spaces. Because the building maintains a close relationship with adjacent outdoor spaces, landscaped courtyards and outdoor classroom/art studio spaces provide opportunities for occupants to migrate from indoor to outdoor environments. This strategy takes advantage of the mild climate of the Bay Area to extend usable program space and provide for occupant comfort. Trees, covered walkways, courtyard connections to the existing buildings, and shading devices on various sides of the LRC create unique microclimates and transitional spaces that can be enjoyed at various times of the day and throughout the year.

5.96 Stormwater is carried through a reconstructed stream on the MCDS campus to the marshes at the edge of the Bay. JOSH PARTEE

5.97 Courtyard space with stepped seating/stairs allowing vertical circulation between the Lower Division and Upper Division at MCDS. JOSH PARTEE

5.98 Covered walkways provide transitional spaces between the classroom wing and the outdoor Step-up Courtyard space. JOSH PARTEE

5.99 View of the Step-up Courtyard from above. CHRIS PROEHL for EHDD ARCHITECTURE

5.100 Exterior wood shading devices reduce glare potential and block unwanted solar heat gain.

5.101 Radiant tubing embedded in the concrete slabs is ganged and connected to the hydronic heating and cooling system. EHDD ARCHITECTURE

Natural ventilation. The building was designed with "passive solutions for active occupants." Operable windows allow occupants to interact with their ambient environment and provide opportunities for user control. Skylights in some spaces open to allow for stack ventilation. Extensive thermal modeling conducted during the design phase demonstrated to the client that thermal comfort conditions would be maintained in the building when both natural and mechanical ventilation strategies were used.

Daylighting and solar heating. Varying orientations are handled with appropriate shading strategies and take full advantage of daylighting opportunities. Strategically designed shading devices and wood screens minimize direct solar radiation heat gain in the summer months when the sun is higher in the sky, and provide for solar heating potential in the winter months when the sun is lower in the sky. A steep hillside along the creek and adjacent to the building helps to shade the east side of the building from the summer sun. Covered exterior walkways help to shade the west side of the building from low sun angles (reducing glare potential and excessive solar heat gain). The design goal was to provide light on at least two sides of every interior space. Having no overhead ductwork in the classroom spaces allowed the design team to eliminate suspended ceilings, which raised ceiling and window head heights and allows daylight to penetrate the floor plan more deeply. Skylights with operable shading baffles were used to provide daylight closer to where the teachers sit.

5.102 Insulated pipes carry water for the radiant slabs between the campus buildings. EHDD ARCHITECTURE

Night-time cooling. In order to maintain thermal comfort conditions throughout the year, the building employs a night-time cooling regime in which water is circulated between a 15,000-gallon [56,780 L] underground cistern (or tank) and a rooftop evaporative cooling tower unit. The cooling tower operates in a manner similar to a swamp cooler, where water is sprayed across a fan, heat is rejected into the cooler night air, and the chilled water is pumped back to the cistern for use the following day. During the daytime, the chilled water is circulated through radiant tubing embedded in the floor slabs to address the cooling loads in the building. The system does not use a mechanical compressor to chill the water for the hydronic system, which results in lower energy consumption. Night-time cooling is also achieved through the use of high and low operable windows. Heat gains are absorbed by the floor slabs during the day, reradiated to the spaces at night, and vented from the building through the operable windows. The campus also uses two aboveground storage tanks each holding 500 gal [1893 L] of emergency water, but this system is separate from the night-time cooling system used for the LRC.

5.104 Mechanical room showing hydronic piping and electrical panels. EHDD ARCHITECTURE

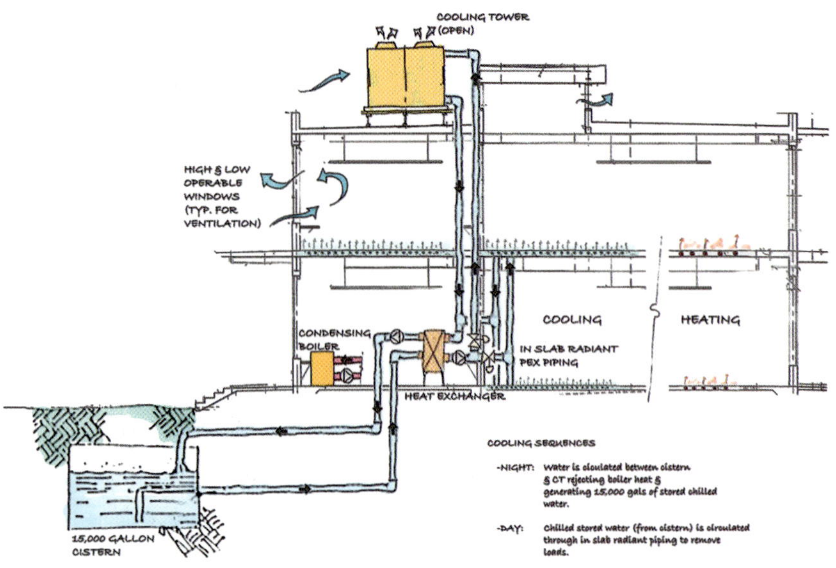

5.103 A sectional diagram showing the heating and cooling systems at the LRC. STANTEC

5.105 PV array atop an existing building at MCDS. JOSH PARTEE

Photovoltaics. A 95.5-kW (peak) photovoltaic (PV) array of 190-W crystalline panels was placed on south-facing roofs of four existing campus buildings and functions as the primary means of on-site energy generation. The array was designed to produce more energy than the campus buildings use over the course of a year. This strategy, known as zero net energy, has become a valuable benchmark for high-performance buildings responding to building energy consumption and climate change concerns. The grid-connected PV system at MCDS was designed to generate 168,536 kWh/year, which would amount to more than 115% of the annual energy used by the Learning Resource Center. The system does not have battery backup capability.

5.106 Site view prominently features the expanse of rooftop PV.

Solar thermal collectors. A flat plate collector solar thermal system, located on the roof of an older campus building, was installed during Step 1 of the masterplan to provide 50% of the hot water needed by a new commercial kitchen. The remaining hot water is heated by a natural gas hot water heater. The commercial kitchen, incidentally, features locally grown foods for student lunches.

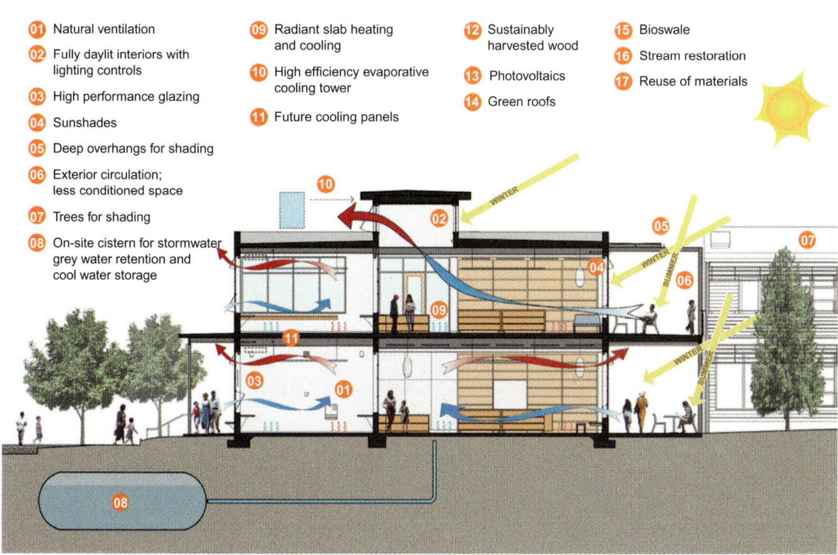

5.107 A section diagram showing the high-performance design strategies adopted at the LRC. EHDD ARCHITECTURE

Water conservation. Rainwater falling on the LRC roof is captured in a 15,000-gal [56,780 L] cistern rather than being discharged onto the site. This approach mitigates the adverse effects of stormwater runoff and provides a valuable source of greywater (non-potable water) to be used for flushing toilets and heat sink purposes, whereby excess heat generated or collected by building systems (including the boiler and the radiant slabs) is shed into the water through a heat exchanger unit. Due to lack of room on the site, the cistern is not sized for the dry summer season.

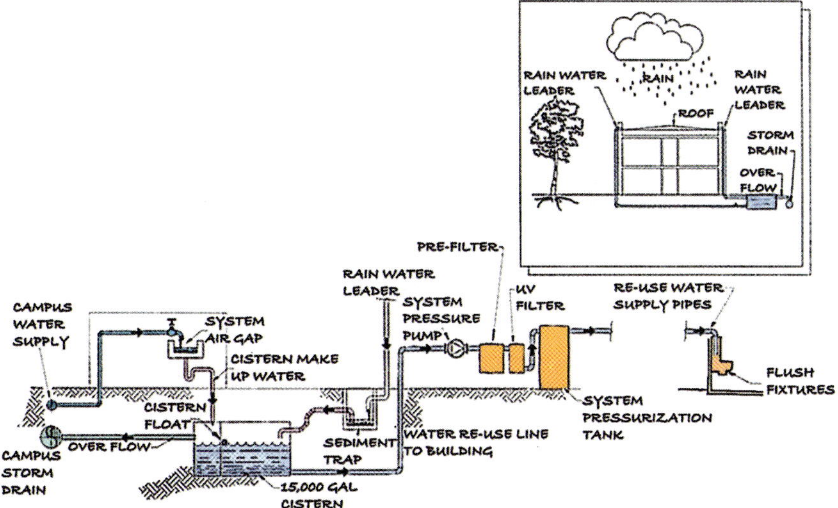

5.108 A conceptual diagram showing rainwater harvesting, storage, and reuse at the LRC. STANTEC

5.109 Boxes of locally grown fruit, freely available to students, are found outside of the cafeteria.

Materials. Cedar and mahogany wood used at the LRC was Forest Stewardship Council (FSC) certified. Modern fire codes prevented the design team from using cedar shingle cladding, a material common on existing campus buildings. The team chose instead to use wood screens, shading devices, and rainscreen systems to unite the building with the MCDS context. Several buildings were demolished to make way for the new facility, but the concrete slabs were reused for landscape pavers and redwood timbers were reused to create a series of unique exterior benches. Low-VOC paints and carpets were used throughout the building. Fly ash, a waste product generated from steel smelting, was used as a cement substitute in the new concrete slabs, although the percentage of this material used had to be limited to produce a workable concrete mix for the contractor.

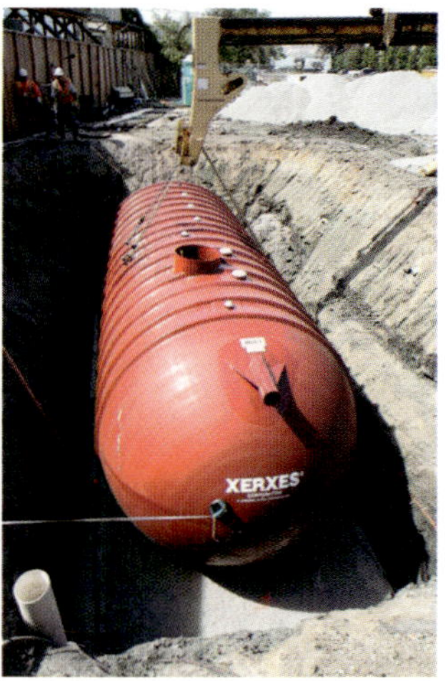

5.110 A construction photograph showing the installation of the underground cistern. EHDD ARCHITECTURE

Real-time monitoring. The LRC was designed for real-time monitoring and display of energy production and consumption. The school has not yet installed the building management system that would make this possible. When this system is put online, it will provide feedback to students, staff, and administrators through campus computers. The long-term objective is to raise awareness and understanding of the environmental impact of the buildings on the MCDS campus.

5.111 MCDS students assisting with campus compost collection. MCDS STAFF

Curriculum integration. Many of the teachers and staff have embraced the new environment and have developed exercises and projects, such as measuring and comparing roof (dark and light colored) surface temperatures and growing native plants, fruits, and vegetables for the kitchen. Boxes of fresh fruits are available to students throughout the school day and the school features "lights out" days several times each month where everyone in the school works by daylight.

How Is It Working?

Energy modeling conducted during the design process predicted that the building would use 6.0 kWh/ft^2/yr and that the on-site PV and solar thermal systems would produce 7.1 kWh/ft^2/yr, which would result in a building that produces more energy than it uses. It is anticipated that the LRC will be the first zero net energy classroom building in North America. The completed building is performing well, however, the building management and real-time monitoring systems have not yet been installed. The hope is that these systems will be in operation in the near future, which will enable the design team and the client to compare the predicted and the actual energy consumption and production.

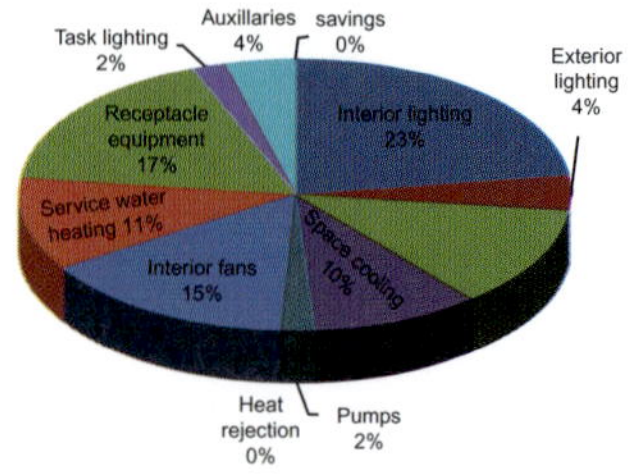

5.112 Pie chart showing a breakdown of the predicted total energy use by building system. STANTEC

MCDS Step 2, which includes the Learning Resource Center, has received a LEED for Schools 2.0 Platinum certification from the U.S. Green Building Council—providing third-party validation of exemplary building design.

According to the Head of School, attendance at MCDS has increased since the completion of the LRC and the new outdoor transitional spaces have been popular with both students and staff. The design team hopes to conduct a post-occupancy evaluation (POE) on the building once it has been occupied for several years.

Further Information

CMG Landscape Architecture. www.cmgsite.com/projects/campuses/marin-country-day-school/ (The landscape architect's website, which includes a brief description of the project in addition to an extensive series of site landscape photographs and design sketches/renderings.)

EHDD Architecture. www.ehdd.com/#/2296 (The architect's website, which includes photographs, information, and a description of the project. There is also a link to a Net Zero Energy Building Case Study document.)

Sherwood Design Engineers. www.sherwoodengineers.com/projects.html (The civil engineer's website, which includes a site plan and a brief description of site, stormwater, and landscape features of the project.)

NOTES

Background and Context

The historic seaside city of Brighton, England is located about 80 miles [130 km] south of London. In the New England Quarter—near the city center on what previously had been a small, derelict site—stands One Brighton, one of the most innovative residential developments in the United Kingdom. The project was developed as a joint venture between BioRegional Quintain and Crest Nicholson. Designed by Feilden Clegg Bradley Studios, One Brighton takes a holistic approach to green living that is economical for both the developer and the buyers and addresses the impact of an innovative residential development on local, national, and global environmental issues.

The project was conceived as the first of a series of worldwide residential developments to adopt the One Planet Living principles created by BioRegional Quintain and WWF (formerly World Wildlife Fund). The 10 principles include: zero carbon; zero waste; sustainable transportation access; sustainable materials use; local and sustainable food; sustainable water usage; providing natural habitats for wildlife; contributing to the cultural heritage of the site; equity and fair trade with the local economy; and providing for health and happiness of residents.

5.113 Ground level terraces at One Brighton. TIM CROCKER

One Brighton consists of two eight-story linear buildings on a tight urban site. The 172 residential units are located above ground-level commercial, community, and garage space. Numerous apartment types and sizes are available: 19 small "eco-studios" intended for first-time homebuyers, 68 one-bedroom units, 81 two-bedroom units, and four three-bedroom units. Approximately one-third of the

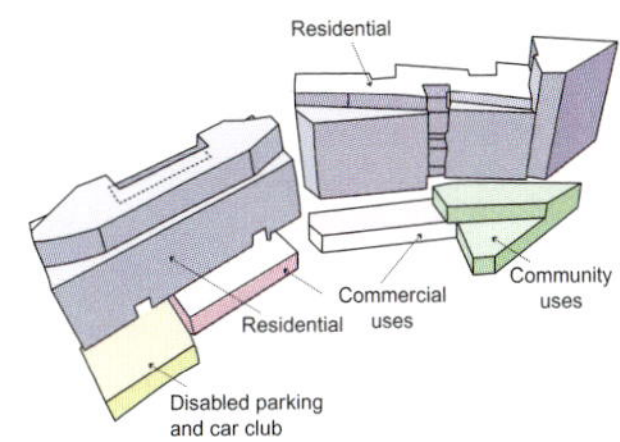

5.114 Sketch illustrating the building massing concept. FEILDEN CLEGG BRADLEY STUDIOS

LOCATION
Brighton, East Sussex, UK
Latitude 50.8 °N
Longitude 0.1 °W

HEATING DEGREE DAYS
5019 base 65 °F
[2788 base 18.3 °C]

COOLING DEGREE DAYS
1648 base 50 °F
[916 base 10 °C]

DESIGN DRY-BULB WINTER (99%)
29.5 °F [−1.4 °C]

DESIGN DRY-BULB & MEAN COINCIDENT WET-BULB SUMMER (1%)
73.0/64.9 °F [22.8/18.3 °C]

SOLAR RADIATION
Jan 285 Btu/ft^2/day
[0.90 kWh/m^2/day]
Jun 1759 Btu/ft^2/day
[5.55 kWh/m^2/day]

ANNUAL PRECIPITATION
31 in. [790 mm]

residential units are designated as affordable housing, creating the potential for establishing a diverse community of residents within the development.

Design Intent and Validation

The overall objective for One Brighton was to demonstrate that it is possible to build a high-performance, well-designed residential complex that is affordable and appealing to potential buyers and also economically viable for the developers. The 10 principles developed by the One Planet Living initiative helped the project team address a wide range of environmental considerations and validate specific design decisions throughout the design process.

5.115 Rendering of building elevations along Fleet and New England Streets. FEILDEN CLEGG BRADLEY STUDIOS

Zero Carbon Hub prepared an LZ Zero Carbon Profile for One Brighton. The organization is a non-profit involved with helping the UK to achieve its goal of all new homes being zero-carbon by 2016. The profile document outlines the environmental strategies employed and predicts expected performance.

Additional design validation came in the form of an EcoHomes "Excellent" designation, achieved by satisfying 19 of the 20 credit opportunities available under the program's Energy category.

Strategies

The One Planet Living principles served as a framework for the project team and ensured that a variety of environmental design strategies were explored and employed at One Brighton. A large number of synergies existed among the comprehensive list of specific strategies described below. It should also be mentioned that an on-site "sustainability coordinator" lives at the complex, assisting residents with the building's many green features and managing ongoing sustainability efforts at the development.

BUILDING TYPE
Mixed-use housing/commercial

AREA
157,584 ft^2 [14,640 m^2]

CLIENT
Crest Nicholson BioRegional Quintain LLP

DESIGN TEAM
Architect, Feilden Clegg Bradley Studios (FCBS)

Mechanical/Electrical Engineer, Fulcrum/MLM

Structural Engineer, Scott Wilson

Project Manager, Crest Nicholson BioRegional Quintain LLP

Landscape Consultant, Nicholas Pearson Associates

Cost Consultant, Jones Lang Lasalle

Contractor, Denne Construction

COMPLETION
September 2009 (Phase 1), July 2010 (Phase 2)

METRICS
Energy Utilization Index (EUI): Not Available

Carbon Emissions: Not Available

Water Use: Not Available

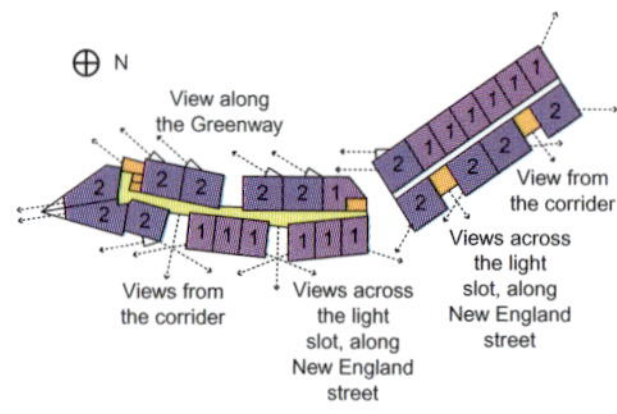

5.116 Plan diagram showing the open space "slots" inserted between residential units. FEILDEN CLEGG BRADLEY STUDIOS

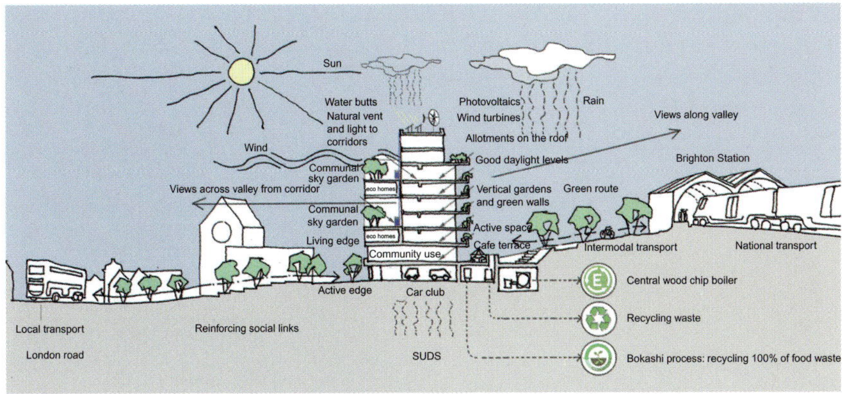

5.117 Diagram illustrating environmental connections to the urban context. FEILDEN CLEGG BRADLEY STUDIOS

Site. One Brighton is closely connected with its site context. The development responds to the dense urban surroundings by occupying a formerly empty and neglected parcel of land. Ground-floor commercial spaces, including an outdoor terrace for a café, allow the public to access and use the building. The project was also deliberately sited to provide close proximity to public and alternative transportation options. A car club allows residents access to a vehicle when needed without having to provide parking for every residential unit. A communal bicycle storage area at ground level allows a resident to easily access his/her bike without having to carry it into the building and store it in the apartment. The small areas of landscaping available within the tight urban site use native plantings that do not have to be irrigated. These areas, combined with vertical green walls and "sky gardens" provide habitats for local wildlife. Ground-level plazas, sky gardens for growing food, and private apartment balconies collectively provide plentiful outdoor access. The balconies are angled to direct views up and down the adjacent streets rather than across the streets to adjacent buildings.

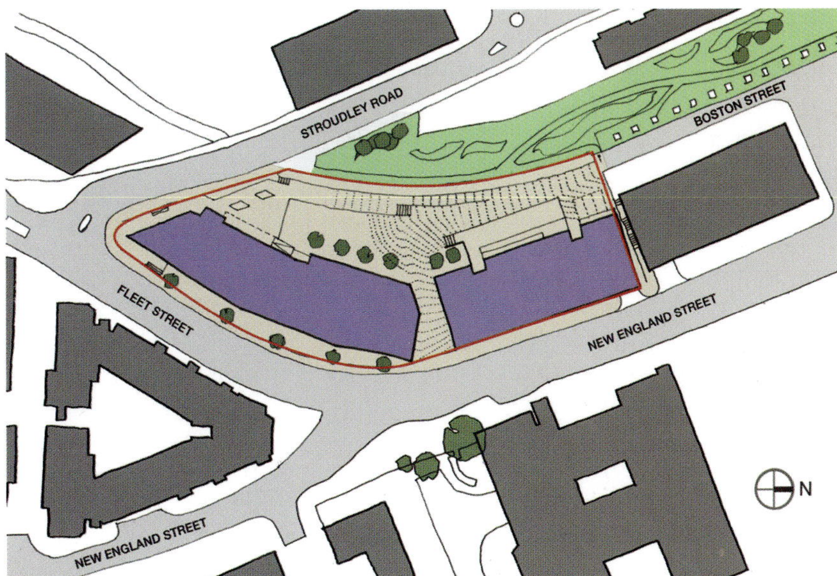

5.118 Site plan showing the two apartment buildings (blue) with the outdoor terrace space to the west. FEILDEN CLEGG BRADLEY STUDIOS

5.119 3D rendering of the eco-studio residential units. FEILDEN CLEGG BRADLEY STUDIOS

Photovoltaics (PV). A portion of the electricity used at One Brighton is provided by an on-site PV system that consists of 52 panels with a peak output of 9.36 kW, which provides 7600 kWh/year of renewable energy. Eventually, this system will be used for electric charging stations for the car club in the parking garage. The remaining electricity used by the complex is from off-site renewable sources such as wind. This combination of on-site and off-site renewable energy results in annual net-zero CO_2 emissions.

Energy conservation. Energy conservation strategies played a vital role in helping the design team produce a zero-carbon building. One Brighton uses a central boiler for space heating and hot water rather than separate systems in each unit. Heat recovery and heat exchanger systems capture waste heat from exhaust air. A tank is used to store hot water for the residential units, but also acts as a heat sink by absorbing excess heat from the building through a heat exchange system. A tight thermal envelope was designed to minimize heat loss. High R-value insulation and high-performance windows (triple-glazed, low-ε, argon filled) were used throughout the complex. Daylighting and energy-efficient lighting fixtures were used in building corridors and common spaces to reduce electricity consumption.

5.120 Roof planes showing brown roof (a form of green roof) and PV array. TIM CROCKER

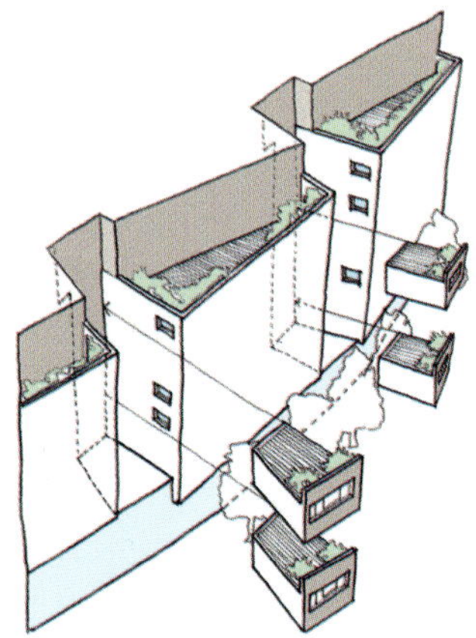

5.121 Conceptual diagram showing how the sky gardens atop residential units were inserted into "slots" in the building massing. FEILDEN CLEGG BRADLEY STUDIOS

Green roofs. Sky gardens and brown roofs are the two types of green roof features used at One Brighton. The "sky gardens" provide allotments where the residents can grow their own food. Rainwater is used for irrigation of these gardens and compost generated from resident food waste is used as a fertilizer. Other roof surfaces are covered with brown roofs, which are a type of green roof in which the planting medium or soil is sourced from the site.

Water conservation. Rainwater collected from the roofs and paved surfaces is stored and used to irrigate the sky gardens. Harvesting rainwater reduces the need to use expensive, potable water for site landscaping purposes. Low-flow plumbing fixtures and water-saving appliances (such as washing machines and dishwashers) were also provided in each residential unit. All of these water conservation strategies provide the added benefit of reducing the amount of wastewater sent into the municipal system.

Materials. Local, recycled, and non-toxic materials were used extensively at One Brighton. The concrete used 100% recycled aggregate, and 50% of the cement was replaced with ground granulated blast furnace slag (GGBS). This resulted in the greenest concrete structural frame in the UK. Wood products for the interiors and exterior cladding were FSC certified and locally sourced from UK forests. Paints and finishes with low-VOC content were specified throughout the buildings. Exterior wall construction consisted of wood fiber insulation board on hollow clay blocks with a clay-based interior plaster finish, which resulted in a breathable wall assembly and a tight thermal envelope. Crushed, recycled glass was used under exterior paving and landscape features. A Bakor bitumen membrane with 25% post-consumer recycled content was used for the roofing.

Alternative fuels. A biomass boiler with a peak output of 500 kW is used for space and water heating. The system uses locally sourced woodchips for fuel. The developer established a community-owned energy company called ESCO to procure the fuel and manage the system. A natural-gas boiler was provided as a backup system.

Waste management. A comprehensive recycling program at One Brighton includes Bokashi composting systems, which enable residents to make compost in small, odorless, containers that break down organic material through an anaerobic process. This method differs from traditional composting, which takes longer and uses organisms and oxygen to break down organic matter. The compost that is generated is used to fertilize the sky gardens. Composting also reduces food waste going into the municipal wastewater system. In addition, the biomass boilers use local woodchips that are diverted from landfills.

Construction. Environmental stewardship was also an integral part of the construction process at One Brighton. Equipment, such as cranes, used biodiesel fuel. The contractor created a "Green Café" that provided local and organic food for the construction crew. Great attention was paid to the segregation and recycling of construction waste on the site. Temporary site trailers used by the construction crews were fully insulated. The contractor also began using electricity generated by the PV panels as soon as the system became operational (prior to the completion of construction).

How Is It Working?

The first phase of One Brighton was completed in September 2009. As the building has only been occupied for a short time, available performance data are limited and a post-occupancy evaluation (POE) has not yet been conducted. The development won the Royal Town

Planning Institute (RTPI) Planning Awards: Sustainable Communities Award 2009 and was shortlisted for the Building Awards 2010: Housing Project of the Year.

5.122 View of balcony projections and skygarden "slots." TIM CROCKER

Further Information

Feilden Clegg Bradley Studios. www.fcbstudios.com (The architect's website, which includes information and professional photographs of the One Brighton project under the Housing/Private tabs.)

Zero Carbon Hub Profile. www.zerocarbonhub.org/downloads/Profile003-OneBrighton.pdf (A 7-page downloadable document that includes project information, descriptions of green strategies, and predicted performance figures.)

Camco. www.camcoglobal.com/en/onebrighton.html (A webpage that includes a brief description of the One Brighton project.)

One Planet Living. www.oneplanetliving.com (A webpage with descriptions of the 10 principles of the One Planet Living [OPL] initiative and links to the WWF and Bioregional websites.)

Background and Context

The Passive House concept embodies a stringent energy standard and design-build method that promises to reduce energy use by 90% compared with conventional buildings. The Passive House method sets target performance criteria that must be met during construction before the walls are closed in, virtually eliminates the need for an active climate control system, and requires verification testing after the walls are sealed. Under such criteria "the devil is in the details," which demands extensive modeling using Passive House Planning Package (PHPP) software, consideration of details to prevent thermal bridging, specification of high-performance building components, and compliance to air tightness and ventilation standards. Although most Passive House buildings in the U.S. are residential, there are more than 20,000 residential and commercial Passive House buildings in Europe. Current wind and solar technologies/practices cannot alone reasonably meet expectations of the 2030 Challenge. The Passive House approach is an aggressive way to address a targeted 100% reduction in carbon emissions by 2030.

The Passive House Institute U.S. (PHIUS), based in Urbana, Illinois, is a non-profit organization assisted and supported by Dr. Wolfgang Feist, who in 1996 founded The Passivhaus Institut (PHI) in Germany. PHIUS leads and conducts research in the U.S. on Passive House science topics; provides education and training for design professionals, builders, engineers, developers, and policymakers; trains, tests, and certifies Passive House consultants; certifies Passive Houses; and supports Passive House design-build demonstrations for research and education.

5.123 Team Germany, the 2009 U.S. Solar Decathlon winner, wrapped a two-story cube with an 11.1-kW PV system—using panels on the roof (single-crystal silicon), sides, and front (thin-film copper indium gallium diselenide). Designed to Passive House standards, the house was a net energy producer.

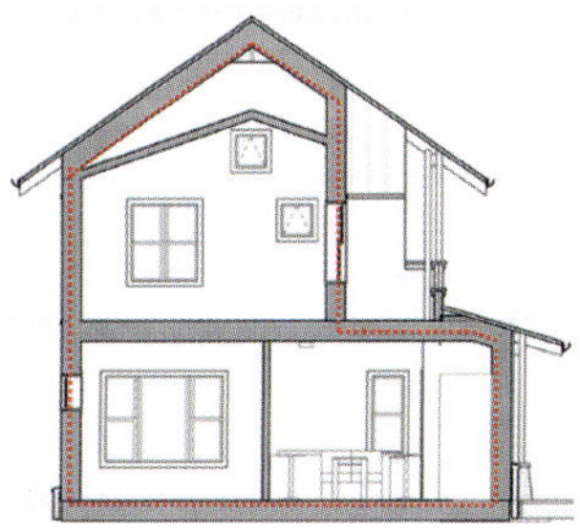

5.124 Continuous insulation concept diagrammed for a single family residence in Eugene, Oregon. STUDIO-E ARCHITECTURE

LOCATION
Varies

HEATING DEGREE DAYS
Varies by location

COOLING DEGREE DAYS
Varies by location

DESIGN DRY-BULB WINTER (99%)
Varies by location

DESIGN DRY-BULB & MEAN COINCIDENT WET-BULB SUMMER (1%)
Varies by location

SOLAR RADIATION
Varies by location

ANNUAL PRECIPITATION
Varies by location

A Passive House is a well-insulated, airtight building that is primarily heated by solar and internal gains (people, equipment, animals, etc.). Energy losses through openings and thermal bridging are minimized. Shading and window orientation help to reduce heat gains in an effort to minimize building cooling load. A heat or energy recovery ventilator provides a constant fresh air supply.

This case study covers the schematic design phase aspects of the Passive House approach, describes several projects underway in the United States, and provides sample construction details and images. A successful schematic design process, coupled with quality construction and detailing, will result in a high-performance building.

BUILDING TYPE
Single- and multi-family residential, schools, commercial

AREA
Compact plans are better suited to achieve Passive House standards

CLIENT
Many

DESIGN TEAM
A dedicated and collaborative design team, willing to develop innovative design-build practices that work well in the locale

COMPLETION
Growing number of U.S. examples

PERFORMANCE METRICS
Energy Utilization Index (EUI): Varies (but pretty good)

Carbon Emissions: Varies (but pretty low)

Water Use: Varies by location

5.125 The 2009 U.S. Solar Decathlon's 2nd place winner from the University of Illinois was designed to meet Passive House standards and responded to a rural farmhouse vernacular by reusing wood from an Illinois barn. JIM TETRO PHOTOGRAPHY FOR U.S. DOE.

Design Intent and Validation

The design intent of the Passive House is to optimize both building envelope and thermal comfort, so that a building can meet its heating and cooling needs solely through conditioning of the incoming fresh air volume required for good indoor air quality. The ability to do so is validated (or invalidated) by demanding performance requirements for the building components evaluated within the PHPP spreadsheet.

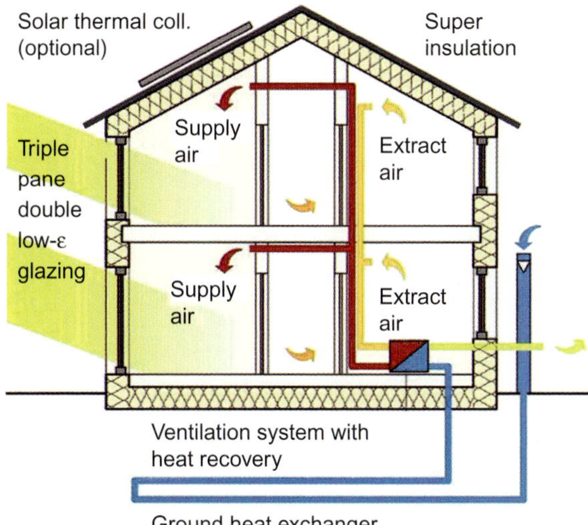

5.126 Passive House conceptual cross-section. WIKIMEDIA COMMONS (licensed under a GFDL agreement)

5.127 Double wall framing, showing the load-bearing (and shear-resisting) interior wall and the exterior frame that will house the insulation.

In summary, a Passive House building must meet these performance-based energy benchmarks before any application of active solar systems:

Heating energy use <4750 Btu/ft^2 yr [15 kWh/m^2 yr]

Peak heat load <3.2 Btu/hr ft^2 [10 W/m^2]

Air tightness <0.6 ACH at 50 Pascal (a typical residence is 5)

Total primary energy use <38,000 Btu/ft^2 yr [120 kWh/m^2 yr]

Additionally, exterior building elements and glazing must meet or exceed specific U-factor requirements; air tightness of the building envelope must be verified by an on-site air leakage test; and ventilation systems must comply with Passive House Institute certification for energy efficiency. The primary energy limit noted above describes the amount of non-renewable primary energy that can be used on a project. Primary energy (source energy) includes extraction, distribution, conversion, and delivery to the end user. Passive House standards have defined requirements for minimum ventilation rates based on German DIN standards. In terms of cooling, the current PHPP does not set upper limits on cooling use as it does for heating, although cooling loads are calculated in the planning software. Designers may examine building envelope performance using WUFI-ORNL/IBP software, which predicts moisture transfer within the building envelope over time.

5.128 Blower door test is used to determine air tightness. BILYEU HOMES, INC.

5.129 All exterior planes are air-sealed. BILYEU HOMES, INC.

Strategies

Eight guiding principles help to reduce energy use and increase thermal comfort in buildings built to the Passive House standard. Even though all the guiding principles must work in concert, the first three principles are critical in the schematic design phase of a project. As the design progresses, thermal bridging and air tightness can be tested and the design optimized through PHPP. The principles are:

1. **Compact Building Shape:** Design for compact building shapes, as opposed to long and narrow forms, for low surface-to-volume ratios (<1).
2. **Optimal Solar Orientation and Shading**: Maximize solar gains for winter through transparent openings and minimize summer solar gains with shading.
3. **Continuous Insulation:** Create steady indoor temperatures that will not go below 50 °F [10 °C] in the absence of a heating system by designing highly insulative envelopes and using window assemblies with thermal breaks.
4. **Thermal-Bridge-Free Construction:** Minimize any transfer of heat and moisture through the envelope to prevent energy loss, condensation, or building deterioration. The effectiveness of construction details may be checked using THERM (a free program provided by the Lawrence Berkeley National Laboratory that analyzes two-dimensional heat transfer through building assemblies).
5. **Air Tightness:** Minimize air infiltration into/through wall assemblies.
6. **Balanced Ventilation with Heat Recovery:** Specify a heat recovery ventilator or energy recovery ventilator to provide exceptional efficiency, indoor air quality, and thermal comfort.
7. **Energy-Efficient Appliances and Lighting:** Specify highly efficient appliances and lighting to minimize overall energy use.
8. **User Manual**: Develop a user-friendly building operations manual to give to the owner.

5.131 Schematic design sketch for the Lonefir residence—a Passive House in Portland, Oregon. BEN GATES, MARGO RETTIG

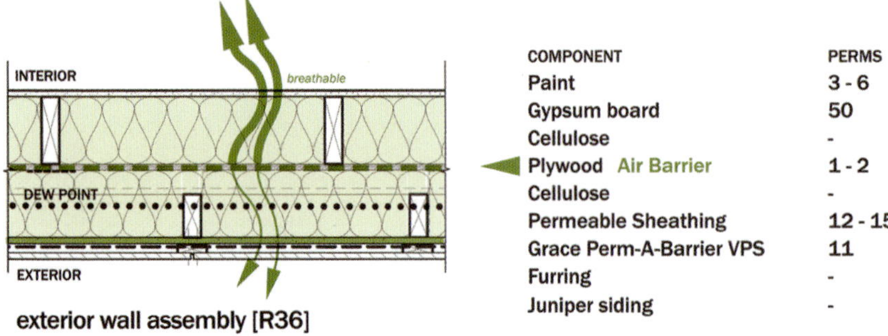

COMPONENT	PERMS
Paint	3 - 6
Gypsum board	50
Cellulose	-
Plywood Air Barrier	1 - 2
Cellulose	-
Permeable Sheathing	12 - 15
Grace Perm-A-Barrier VPS	11
Furring	-
Juniper siding	-

5.130 Wall assembly diagram showing air barrier and permeability rating. BEN GATES, MARGO RETTIG

5.132 Construction of Lonefir foundation with foam underlay. BEN GATES, MARGO RETTIG

5.133 Alternative framing with insulation netting attached just prior to filling with dense-packed cellulose insulation. BILYEU HOMES, INC.

5.134 (Left) Mechanical closet showing the water heater, heat recovery unit (above) and insulated air intake through the exterior wall. (Right) Labeled water lines (hot and tempered water) are "home-runned" and indicate the connected fixture. The copper Power-Pipe® recovers heat from the shower and laundry fixtures in the room above. BILYEU HOMES, INC.

5.135 Single-family residence in Salem, Oregon—upon completion and prior to Passive House certification. BILYEU HOMES, INC.

How Is It Working?

Occupants of Passive House buildings are the best post-occupancy evaluators of how well their investment is paying off. Katrin

Klingenberg, Director of the Passive House Institute (U.S.), recently completed a post-occupancy evaluation of her own residence in Illinois. The PHPP modeling software accurately predicted (within 10%) her actual energy consumption—which was 70% lower than the typical American home. Frequently asked questions always include, "Is this cost-effective?" There are several Passive House projects under construction in the Northwest U.S. and, like other green certified buildings, reported first cost increases range from 0–18%. Life-cycle cost analysis will show this to be offset by energy savings—and as energy costs increase and our resources decrease, the long-term cost justification for a Passive House will only get stronger.

During the recent construction of a registered Passive House in Salem, Oregon, Blake Bilyeu (Bilyeu Homes, Inc.) conducted a blower door test for air tightness on an 1800-ft^2 [167 m^2] house prior to the installation of foam insulation (but with a carefully taped plywood shell) to identify any remaining points of air leakage in the envelope. At 50 Pascal pressure differential, the house performed at 0.26 ACH, well under the 0.6 ACH that the Passive House standard requires. Upon completion of the enclosure, the test was performed again and resulted in 0.20 ACH50. This type of pre-occupancy/post-occupancy test assures performance during occupancy. The owners were equally engaged in the process and have maintained a planning, construction, and occupancy blog.

Further Information

Gordon, J. 2009. "The Aggressive Standard of a Passive House," *Dwell*, November 2009. www.passivehouse.us/passiveHouse/Articles_files/Dwell.PassiveAcceptance.pdf

Jenkins, J. 2010. Certified PH Consultant responds: "Passive House: Isn't it a bit of overkill?" June 16, 2010, *Building Capacity Blog*, buildingcapacity.typepad.com/blog/

Klingenberg, K., M. Kernagis, and M. James. 2009. *Homes for a Changing Climate, Passive Houses in the U.S.*, Passive House Institute US, Urbana, IL.

Kolle, J. 2010. "The Passive House: Green Without Gizmos," *Fine Homebuilding*, April/May 2010, no. 210. www.passivehouse.us/passiveHouse/Articles_files/passivehouse.pdf

Passive House Institute US (PHIUS): www.passivehouse.us/passiveHouse/PHIUSHome.html

Passivhaus Institut (PHI): www.passiv.de/

THERM: software for modeling two-dimensional heat-transfer effects in building components. windows.lbl.gov/software/therm/therm.html

WUFI-ORNL/IBP: software for modeling heat and moisture transport in building envelopes.
www.ornl.gov/sci/btc/apps/moisture/index.html

YODAKANDIYA COMMUNITY COMPLEX

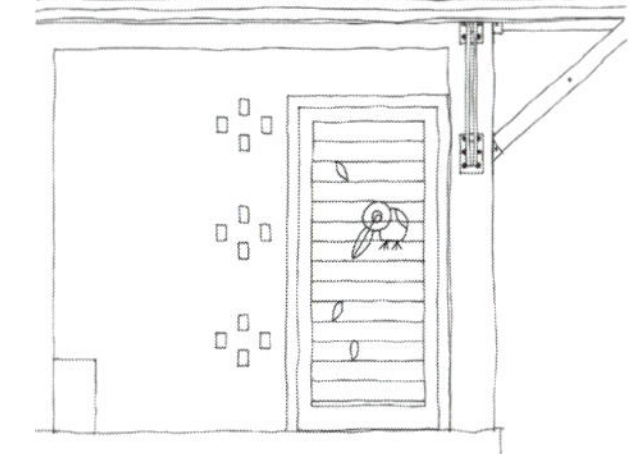

5.137 Design sketch of the main entry to the preschool. SUSI PLATT | ARCHITECTURE FOR HUMANITY

Background and Context

Tissamaharama is located in the Hambantota district of southeastern Sri Lanka overlooking the ancient Yoda Wewa reservoir and the Yala National Park wildlife sanctuary. The coastal fishing village of Kirinda, where many locals work, is approximately 7 miles [11 km] to the southeast. The climate in Hambantota is characterized by a long dry season that lasts from February through September and a short wet season that lasts from October to January. The region, which is subject to the Northeast Monsoon rains, was one of the most severely devastated by the 2004 tsunami. Reports estimate more than 1300 deaths, 6600 injuries, and 12,000 people displaced by the disaster. Nearly half of the housing stock in the area was lost or beyond repair.

Part of the massive rebuilding effort involved the creation of the new Yodakandiya settlement outside of Tissamaharama to house 218 families impacted by the tsunami. Much of the planning and construction was community-focused with help from UN-Habitat, a program run by the United Nations to promote environmentally sustainable human settlement, and funded by the Italian government.

5.136 The community center building is one of three structures at the Yodakandiya Community Complex. SUSI PLATT | ARCHITECTURE FOR HUMANITY

The Yodakandiya Community Complex was designed by Architecture for Humanity, a non-profit organization that provides design and construction services to communities, in close collaboration with UN-Habitat, with the local citizens standing to benefit most from the new facilities. The project directly involved the community at all stages of the process—from the creation of the design brief (or building program), through the construction of the buildings and landscaping, to the ongoing maintenance and operations of the complex.

The community complex consists of three buildings situated on a 3.3-acre [1.3 ha] site. Outdoor space was provided for a cricket field, volleyball courts, and shaded gathering areas. Indoor space was divided between three separate structures: a 3165-ft^2 [295 m^2]

LOCATION
Tissamaharama, Hambantota, Sri Lanka
Latitude 6.3 °N
Longitude 81.3 °E

HEATING DEGREE DAYS
0 base 65 °F
[0 base 18.3 °C]
Katunayake, Sri Lanka data

COOLING DEGREE DAYS
11,617 base 50 °F
[6454 base 10 °C]
Katunayake, Sri Lanka data

DESIGN DRY-BULB WINTER (99%)
71.5 °F [22.0 °C]
Katunayake, Sri Lanka data

DESIGN DRY-BULB & MEAN COINCIDENT WET-BULB SUMMER (1%)
90.6/77.8 °F [32.6/25.5 °C]
Katunayake, Sri Lanka data

SOLAR RADIATION
Jan 1427 Btu/ft^2/day
[4.50 kWh/m^2/day]
Jun 1610 Btu/ft^2/day
[5.08 kWh/m^2/day]

ANNUAL PRECIPITATION
43 in. [1092 mm]

community center with space for a main hall, a stage, a kitchen, offices, a store, and bathrooms; a 1735-ft^2 [161 m^2] library and health clinic; and a 1815-ft^2 [169 m^2] preschool with space for worship, offices, a sick room, bathrooms, and an outdoor play area. Funding for the library, health center, and preschool was initiated by Do Something, an organization focused on getting teens involved in community service—with funds raised primarily by student efforts at Pace Academy in Atlanta, Georgia.

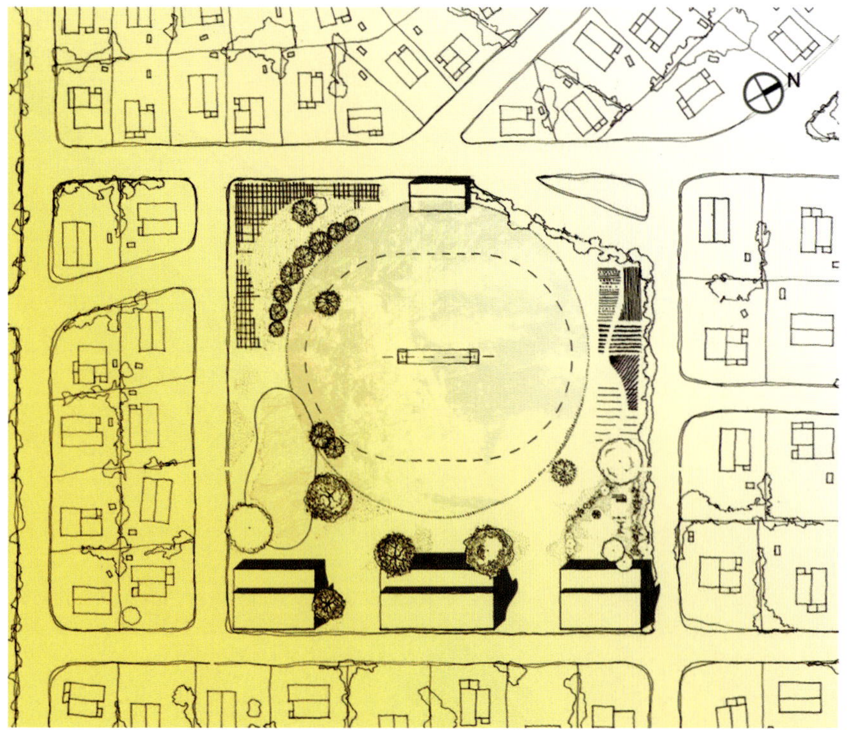

5.138 Site plan of complex showing how the three buildings are located at the southeast perimeter of the parcel and overlook the outdoor athletic space to the north. SUSI PLATT | ARCHITECTURE FOR HUMANITY

Design Intent and Validation

Three primary goals guided the design for the Yodakandiya Community Complex:

- Engaging the local community in the design process.
- Taking advantage of low-cost, passive climate control strategies.
- Respecting the rich history of Sri Lankan architecture.

It was critical to the design team that the community be actively involved in the planning and construction of the new complex. In the aftermath of such a devastating natural disaster, the intent was to bring local citizens together to help repair social relationships that had been damaged or disrupted as a result of death, injury, or displacement. The community members developed the design brief,

BUILDING TYPE
Mixed-use: community center, preschool, library/medical clinic, athletic fields

AREA
Community Center:
3165 ft^2 [295 m^2]
Library/Clinic:
1735 ft^2 [161 m^2]
Preschool: 1815 ft^2 [169 m^2]

Total: 6715 ft^2 [624 m^2]

CLIENT
Pinsara Federation of Community Development Councils

DESIGN TEAM
Architect, Architecture for Humanity | Susi Jane Platt

COMPLETION
2007

PERFORMANCE METRICS
Energy Utilization Index (EUI): Not Available

Carbon Emissions: Not Available

Water Use: Not Available

which ensured that the complex would satisfy their specific programmatic desires and needs. Citizens also invested considerable "sweat equity" in the construction of the complex. Training seminars allowed individuals to develop construction skills that could be used on the project and after its completion. As a result of learning new construction skills, several community members started new businesses after construction of the complex was complete. A strong sense of empowerment and ownership resulted from this community involvement in the design and construction processes.

The hot and humid tropical climate of Sri Lanka presented unique challenges for the design team because the project budget and the environmental agenda for the complex did not allow for air-conditioning of the buildings. The intent was to maximize opportunities for passive cooling via natural ventilation—using strategies common to traditional Sri Lankan vernacular architecture, which include careful attention to site conditions, solar orientation, prevailing winds, building massing, and the use of masonry materials for insulation and thermal mass. Low-cost, low-tech, local materials were used extensively in the construction of the complex. The results were buildings and site features intimately connected to the climate, geography, history, and local economy of southeastern Sri Lanka.

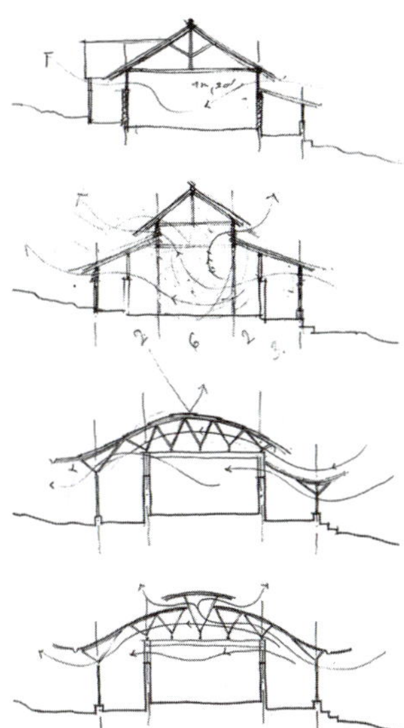

5.140 Conceptual sketches showing natural ventilation through various building section configurations. SUSI PLATT | ARCHITECTURE FOR HUMANITY

5.139 Perspective sketch of the three buildings in the Yodakandiya complex. SUSI PLATT | ARCHITECTURE FOR HUMANITY

5.141 A local citizen constructing a brick retaining wall. SUSI PLATT | ARCHITECTURE FOR HUMANITY

Strategies

Environmental control strategies stressed energy efficiency and natural ventilation in lieu of sophisticated mechanical systems. The approach was deliberately low tech, which responded to budgetary constraints and local building traditions.

Site. Careful attention was devoted to site analysis on the Yodakandiya Community Complex project. The site has stunning views of the Yala National Park forests to the southeast. The proximity to the park, however, meant that the placement of buildings and site features had to take into account elephant migration paths. Human–elephant conflicts were thus minimized. Buildings were also sited for beneficial solar orientation and access to prevailing winds. The large site allowed for a cricket field, volleyball courts, organic

5.142 Local citizens pouring concrete into formwork for the landscape stairs leading from the buildings to the athletic fields. SUSI PLATT | ARCHITECTURE FOR HUMANITY

gardens, and community gathering places. Masonry retaining walls and steps double as spectator seating for the athletic activities occurring on the site.

5.143 Construction of the site landscape features. SUSI PLATT | ARCHITECTURE FOR HUMANITY

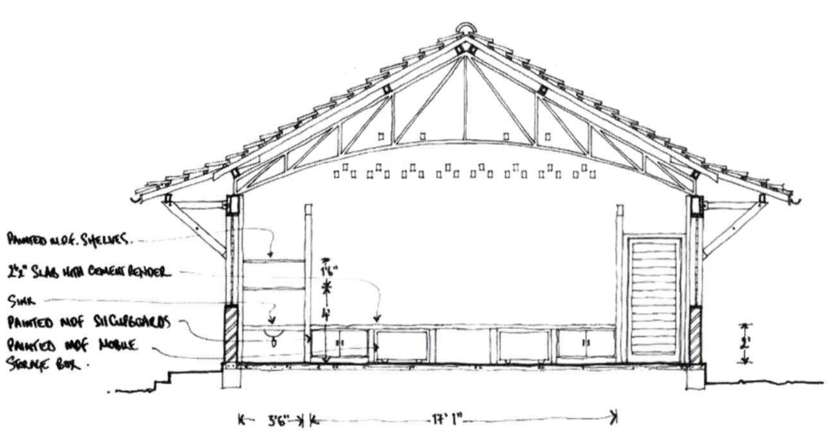

5.144 Section drawing of the preschool building showing roof overhangs, load-bearing masonry walls, and the tube-steel trusses supporting the roof. SUSI PLATT | ARCHITECTURE FOR HUMANITY

5.145 Community members using the shade provided by the broad roof overhangs surrounding the complex buildings. SUSI PLATT | ARCHITECTURE FOR HUMANITY

Passive cooling. Several green design strategies work in concert to passively cool the Yodakandiya Community Complex buildings. Deep roof overhangs shade the exterior masonry walls and window openings, helping to control interior heat gains during the day. Load-bearing masonry walls (composed of outer and inner wythes of brick filled with rubble and mortar) provide thermal insulation. Masonry walls, concrete floor slabs, and clay roof tiles act as thermal mass, which slowly absorbs solar radiation during the day and reradiates it at night, with the heat being picked up by the cooler night air. Skillful building orientation takes full advantage of prevailing winds on the site for cross ventilation. Vaulted ceilings with ridge vents and open eaves allow for stack ventilation of the interior spaces.

Natural ventilation. Provisions for maximizing natural ventilation in the three buildings were made early in the design process. The program requirements were allocated among three separate buildings in an effort to place all spaces along an exterior wall with access to

5.146 Clay tile roofs and outlet for stack ventilation. SUSI PLATT | ARCHITECTURE FOR HUMANITY

windows or openings. The rectangular buildings are oriented with their long facades perpendicular to the prevailing winds, which reverse seasonally. Large openings in the masonry exterior walls, many without window frames or glazing, and narrow floor plans allow for cross ventilation through the interior spaces. High, open ceilings and large ridge vents within the buildings allow for stack ventilation. The space between the top of the load-bearing masonry walls and the roof rafters was left open to further aid ventilation and to help prevent moisture problems that can result from the high humidity in this tropical climate. Clay roof tiles are hung from thin furring strips attached to the roof rafters, and no continuous decking is used. The open eaves and ridge vents aid in exhausting the hot air from the open attic space.

5.148 Brick screens filter daylight on the east and west facades. SUSI PLATT | ARCHITECTURE FOR HUMANITY

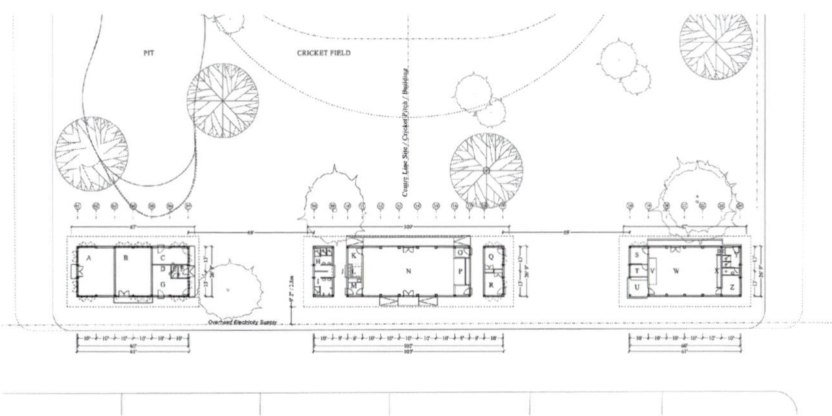

5.147 Floor plans of the Library/Health Clinic (left), Community Center (middle), and Preschool (right), which are arranged in a straight line along the periphery of the site. SUSI PLATT | ARCHITECTURE FOR HUMANITY

5.149 Load-bearing masonry walls support wooden roof brackets and stop short of the roof rafters to allow air movement between the interior and exterior. SUSI PLATT | ARCHITECTURE FOR HUMANITY

Solar control. Hipped roofs with broad overhangs shade the exterior walls of the three buildings. The overhangs are deeper on the east and west orientations to address the difficult solar heat gain and glare potentials associated with these facades. Apertures on the east and west facades are minimized through the use of unglazed brick screens, which filter daylight entering the buildings. Shaded areas beneath the roof overhangs create cooler microclimates around the building perimeter throughout the day. Benches provide shady outdoor gathering spaces for occupants. Roof overhangs also direct rainwater away from the buildings, which helps to keep the interiors dry during the wet season.

Energy conservation. The reliance on natural ventilation cooling strategies resulted in buildings that use very little energy. Energy conservation measures were incorporated into the design at the very beginning. This resulted in lower construction costs (because expensive equipment was not necessary), and lower operating costs (a critical consideration for a poor community with few resources that was recovering from a catastrophic natural disaster).

5.150 A local child stands at a rainwater receptacle; rain chains connect receptacles to roof gutters. SUSI PLATT | ARCHITECTURE FOR HUMANITY

Water conservation. The complex responded directly to the acute lack of drinking water in this area by employing a rainwater harvesting system. Gutters collect rainwater from the roofs via rain chains, rather than traditional enclosed downspouts, and transport the water from the gutters to ground-level receptacles around the perimeter of the buildings. The collected water is stored in two underground cisterns and is used during the dry season for drinking water and landscape irrigation. The rain chains visually display the process by which rainwater is harvested.

Materials. Budgetary constraints and a preference for traditional building methods led the design team to use predominantly local materials in the construction of the complex. Bricks were handmade using local clay that was fired in open pit furnaces fueled by rice husk waste sourced from nearby farms. Brick walls and clay tile roofs provide thermal mass, which keeps the interior of the buildings cool in the tropical climate. Bricks also have the added benefit of being a simple, modular material, which enabled local citizens to assist in the construction of the buildings even with little prior masonry construction experience. Rubble from buildings demolished on the site was used as aggregate for the foundations of the three new structures.

Construction. The complex was constructed by the Yodakandiya citizens, which made possible the incorporation of bespoke (custom) artwork, motifs, and details into the masonry, woodwork, and paving. A series of training sessions, focused on contract administration, masonry construction techniques, and carpentry skills, gave community members the skills necessary to complete the project. The buildings were designed to use simple, yet durable, construction materials: brick walls and partitions, concrete slabs, wood rafters and overhang brackets, light tubular steel trusses, and clay tile roofing.

5.151 Local materials were used in the construction: clay brick (above) and recycled tile (below). SUSI PLATT | ARCHITECTURE FOR HUMANITY

5.152 Artistic motifs incorporated into stone masonry retaining walls on the site by community craftsmen. SUSI PLATT | ARCHITECTURE FOR HUMANITY

How Is It Working?

Additional funding, secured after the complex was completed, allowed the design team to conduct a post-occupancy evaluation (POE) of the building-in-use and to pay for necessary adjustments or modifications to the complex. Detailed building performance measurements and data are, unfortunately, not available at this time.

The complex was the first Architecture for Humanity project to secure a Creative Commons "Developing Nations" license, which enables the protection of intellectual property rights in developed countries while allowing distribution of information to the developing world. In addition, information about the project has been "open sourced" on the Open Architecture Network, a website that allows for the free exchange of ideas, designs, and plans as a no-cost form of knowledge transfer.

The Yodakandiya Community Complex project was one of 19 projects shortlisted for the 2010 Aga Khan Award for Architecture.

5.153 A local child standing beside a load-bearing brick wall under construction. SUSI PLATT | ARCHITECTURE FOR HUMANITY

Further Information

Aga Khan Development Network. www.akdn.org/architecture/project.asp?id=3955 (Includes downloadable images, information, and a description of the project.)

Architecture for Humanity. architectureforhumanity.org/node/781 (Includes photographs, a detailed description of the design process, and project information.)

Architecture for Humanity. architectureforhumanity.org/updates/2010-05-25-susi-platt-and-architecture-for-humanity-shortlisted-for-the (An online article on the Architecture for Humanity website which includes a project description, video, and news update.)

Architecture for Humanity. architectureforhumanity.org/files/four_seasons_article.pdf (An online article from Four Seasons Magazine [Issue Four 2009] about the Yodakandiya Community Complex.)

Open Architecture Network. openarchitecturenetwork.org/node/385 (Includes downloadable photographs, a detailed description of the design process, project information, and a link to project updates.)

5.154 Citizens gathered in the Main Community Hall. SUSI PLATT | ARCHITECTURE FOR HUMANITY

5.155 Colorful children's work tables in the Preschool building. SUSI PLATT | ARCHITECTURE FOR HUMANITY

NOTES

APPENDIX 1

ESTIMATING DESIGN HEAT LOSS AND DESIGN COOLING LOAD

The preliminary sizing of heating and cooling systems during schematic design depends upon having a reasonable estimate of design heat loss and design cooling load. Well-developed manual and computer-based methodologies for calculating these loads are readily available—but require more information than is (or should be) available during schematic design. To avoid this problem, the following estimates are presented. These are to be used with caution and judgment—and only for preliminary design purposes.

Estimated Design Heat Loss:

The following values assume code-compliant energy performance and are "conservative" (not a bad thing for schematic design); where higher performance is anticipated (for green buildings with a focus on energy efficiency, for example) it is suggested that these values be *divided* by a factor of 1.3. The area (ft^2, m^2) refers to conditioned floor area.

Warm Climates: 20 Btuh/ft^2 [63 W/m^2]

Temperate Climates: 30 Btuh/ft^2 [95 W/m^2]

Cold Climates: 40–50 Btuh/ft^2 [125–160 W/m^2]

Estimated Design Cooling Load

The following values assume code-compliant energy performance and are "conservative" (again, not a bad thing for schematic design); where higher performance is anticipated (for green buildings with a focus on energy efficiency, for example) it is suggested that these values be *multiplied* by a factor of 1.3. The area refers to conditioned floor area.

Light-Occupancy Buildings (residential and the like):
560 ft^2/ton [14.8 m^2/kW]

Moderate-Occupancy Buildings (office/institutional):
360 ft^2/ton [9.5 m^2/kW]

Dense-Occupancy Buildings (theaters and the like):
220 ft^2/ton [5.8 m^2/kW]

Additional values for estimating design cooling load can be found in Table 4.15 (in the Absorption Chillers strategy).

NOTES

APPENDIX 2 PSYCHROMETRIC CHARTS

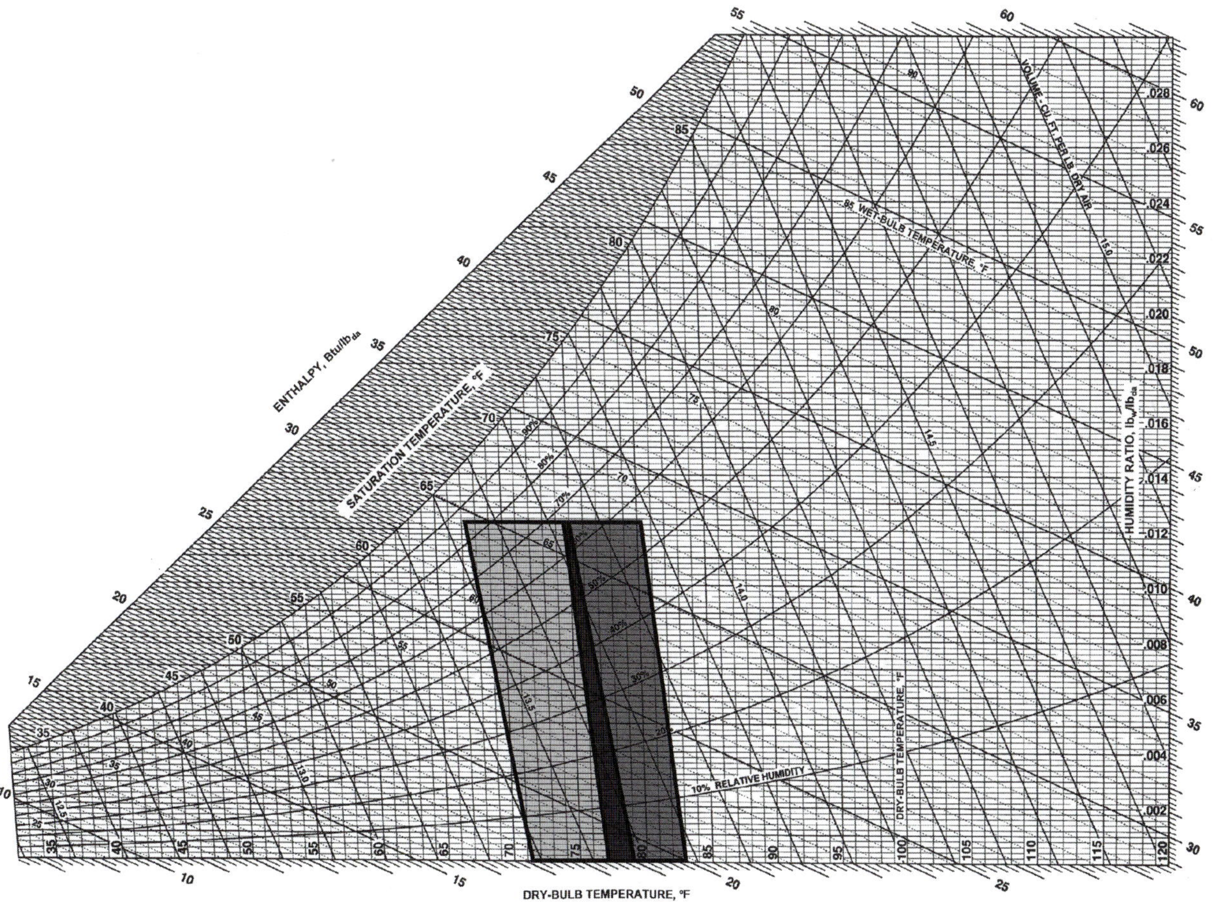

A.1 Psychrometric chart (I-P units) showing *ASHRAE Standard 55* thermal comfort zone.

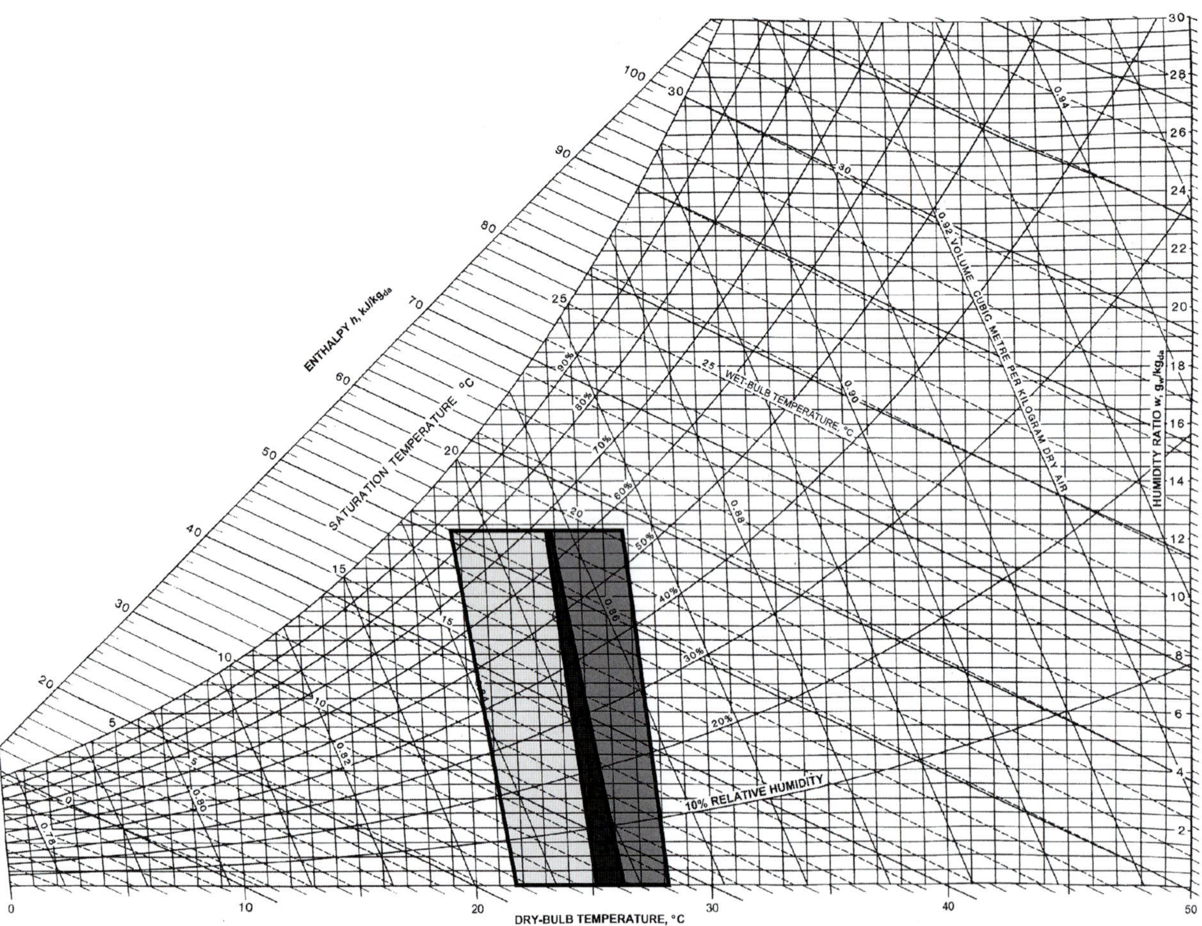

A.2 Psychrometric chart (SI units) showing *ASHRAE Standard 55* thermal comfort zone. © Reprinted with permission of the American Society of Heating, Refrigerating and Air-Conditioning Engineers, Inc., Atlanta, GA

GLOSSARY OF BUILDINGS

The buildings described in the strategies and case studies are listed here with their geographic location and the primary design architect.

BUILDING	LOCATION	ARCHITECT
1 Finsbury Square	London, UK	Arup Associates
4 Times Square (Condé Nast)	New York, NY, USA	FXFOWLE Architects
Adam J. Lewis Center for Environmental Studies	Oberlin, OH, USA	William McDonough & Partners
Aldo Leopold Legacy Center	Baraboo, WI, USA	The Kubala, Washatko Architects, Inc
Armour Academic Center, Westminster School	Simsbury, CT, USA	GUND Partnership
Arup Campus Solihull	Blythe Valley Park, Solihull, England, UK	Arup Associates
Arup Headquarters Building	London, England, UK	Arup Associates
Ash Creek Intermediate School	Independence, OR, USA	BOORA Architects
Bad Aibling Spa	Bavaria, Germany	Behnisch Architekten
Bayerische Vereinsbank	Stuttgart, Germany	Behnisch, Behnisch & Partner
Becton Engineering and Applied Science Center, Yale University	New Haven, CT, USA	Marcel Breuer
Beddington Zero Energy Development	Beddington, Sutton, England, UK	Bill Dunster Architects
Biodesign Institute, Arizona State University	Tempe, AZ, USA	Gould Evans
Blue Ridge Parkway Destination Center	Asheville, NC, USA	Lord, Aeck & Sargent
Building Research Establishment (BRE) Offices	Garston, Hertfordshire, England, UK	Feilden Clegg Architects
British Museum of London—Glass Shell	London, UK	Foster and Partners with Buro Happold
Burton Barr Central Library	Phoenix, AZ, USA	Will Bruder Architects, Ltd
California Polytechnic University-San Luis Obispo Solar Decathlon House 2005	San Luis Obispo, CA, USA	California Polytechnic University-San Luis Obispo
Cambridge Public Library Main Branch	Cambridge, MA, USA	William Rawn Associates
Casa Nueva, Santa Barbara County Office Building	Santa Barbara, CA, USA	Blackbird Architects, Inc.
Center for Global Ecology, Stanford University	Stanford, CA, USA	EHDD
Chesapeake Bay Foundation	Annapolis, MD, USA	SmithGroup

BUILDING	LOCATION	ARCHITECT
Christopher Center, Valparaiso University	Valparaiso, IN, USA	EHDD
Clackamas High School	Clackamas, OR, USA	BOORA Architects
Cornell Solar Decathlon House 2005	Ithaca, NY, USA	Cornell University
Cornell Solar Decathlon House 2009	Ithaca, NY, USA	Cornell University
Dockside Green	Victoria, British Columbia, Canada	Busby Perkins + Will
Domaine Carneros Winery (Pinot Noir Facility)	Napa, CA, USA	Valley Architects of St. Helena
Druk White Lotus School	Shey, Ladakh, India	ARUP + ARUP Associates
EcoHouse	Oxford, England, UK	Susan Roaf
Eden Project	Outside St. Austell, Cornwall, England, UK	Sir Nicholas Grimshaw
Emerald People's Utility District Headquarters	Eugene, OR, USA	Equinox Design, Inc.
Fisher Pavilion	Seattle, WA, USA	Miller/Hull Partnership
Ford Premier Automotive Group Headquarters	Irvine, CA, USA	LPA with William McDonough + Partners
GAAG Architecture Gallery	Gelsenkirchen, Germany	Pfeiffer, Ellermann und Partner
Genzyme Center	Cambridge, MA, USA	Behnisch Architekten
Germany Solar Decathlon House 2007	Darmstadt, Germany	Darmstadt University of Technology
Global Ecology Research Center, Stanford University	Palo Alto, CA, USA	EHDD
Goodlife Fitness Club	Toronto, Canada	unknown
Guangdong Pei Zheng Commercial College	Huadi, China	Mui Ho Architect
Habitat Research and Development Centre	Windhoek, Namibia	Nina Maritz Architect
Hearst Memorial Gym, University of California Berkeley	Berkeley, CA, USA	Julia Morgan and Bernard Maybeck
The Helena Apartment Tower	New York, NY, USA	FXFOWLE Architects, PC
Hong Kong and Shanghai Bank	Hong Kong, China	Foster and Partners
Honolulu Academy of Arts	Honolulu, HI, USA	John Hara & Associates
Hood River Public Library	Hood River, OR, USA	Fletcher, Farr, Ayotte
Hyatt Olive 8 Hotel	Seattle, WA, USA	Gluckman Mayner Architects
IBN-DLO Institute for Forestry and Nature Research	Wageningen, The Netherlands	Behnisch, Behnisch & Partner Architects

BUILDING	LOCATION	ARCHITECT
Ironmacannie Mill Holiday Cottage	Castle Douglas, Scotland	unknown
Islandwood Campus	Bainbridge Island, WA, USA	Mithūn Architects
Jean Vollum Natural Capital Center (The Ecotrust Building)	Portland, OR, USA	Holst Architecture PC
John E Jaqua Academic Center for Student Athletes, University of Oregon	Eugene, OR, USA	Zimmer Gunsul Frasca Architects
John Hope Gateway at RBGE	Edinburgh, Scotland, UK	Edward Cullinan Architects
Kenyon House	Seattle, WA, USA	SMR Architects
KfW Banking Group Offices	Frankfurt am Main, Germany	Sauerbruch Hutton Architekten
Kindergarten, 2008 Olympic Village	Beijing, China	Beijing Tianhong Yuanfang Architecture Design Co., Ltd
Kroon Hall, Yale School of Forestry and Environmental Studies	New Haven, CT, USA	Hopkins Architects
Kuntshaus Bregenz	Bregenz, Austria	Peter Zumthor
Laban Centre	London, UK	Herzog and de Meuron
Lady Bird Johnson Wildflower Center	Austin, TX, USA	Overland Partners Architects
Lanchester Library, Coventry University	Coventry, UK	Short & Associates
Lillis Business Complex	Eugene, OR, USA	SRG Partnership
Logan House	Tampa, FL, USA	Rowe Holmes Associates
Manitoba Hydro Place	Winnipeg, Manitoba, CA	Kuwabara Payne McKenna Blumburg Architects
Marin Country Day School, Learning Resources Center	Corte Madera, CA, USA	EHDD Architecture
Martin Luther King Jr. Student Union	Berkeley, CA, USA	Vernon DeMars
Menara Mesiniaga	Subang Jaya, Malaysia	T.R. Hamzah & Yeang International
Mod 05 Living Hotel	Verona, Italy	Studio Fusina 6
Mt. Angel Abbey Annunciation Academic Center	St. Benedict, OR, USA	SRG Partnership
Mt. Angel Abbey Library	St. Benedict, OR, USA	Alvar Aalto
Multnomah County Central Library	Portland, OR, USA	Carleton Hart Architecture
The Not So Big House	Orlando, FL, USA	Sarah Susanka
New York Institute of Technology Solar Decathlon House 2005	New York, NY, USA	New York Institute of Technology
Nine Canyon Wind Project	Kennewick, WA, USA	Energy Northwest
Oak Lodge, Our Lady of the Oaks Retreat Center	Applegate, CA, USA	Siegel & Strain Architects

BUILDING	LOCATION	ARCHITECT
ODS School of Dental Hygiene	Bend, OR, USA	GBD Architects
One Brighton	Brighton, England, UK	Feilden Clegg Bradley Studios
One Peking Road	Hong Kong, China	Rocco Design Ltd
Oregon Health Sciences University Center for Health & Healing	Portland, OR, USA	GBD Architects various
Passive House US	various	
Patagonia Headquarters, Ventura	Ventura, CA, USA	Miller/Hull Partnership
Penn State Solar Decathlon House 2009	University Park, PA, USA	Pennsylvania State University
Queen's Building at De Montfort University	Coventry, England, UK	Short and Associates
Raffles Hotel	Singapore	Renovation: Fredrick Gibberd and Partners
Ridge Vineyard—Lytton Springs Winery	Healdsburg, CA, USA	Freebairn-Smith & Crane
RiverEast Center	Portland, OR, USA	Group MacKenzie
Roddy/Bale Garage/Studio	Seattle, WA, USA	Miller/Hull Partnership
Ronald Reagan Library	Simi Valley, CA, USA	Pei Cobb Freed & Partners
Royal Danish Embassy	Berlin, Germany	Nielsen, Nielsen & Nielsen A/S
Sabre Holdings Headquarters	Southlake, TX, USA	HKS, Inc.
San Francisco Public Library	San Francisco, CA, USA	Pei Cobb Freed & Partners
Shaw Residence	Taos, NM, USA	John Shaw
Sokol Blosser Winery	Dundee, OR, USA	SERA Architects
Springs Preserve	Las Vegas, NV	Lucchesi Galati Architects
St. Ignatius Chapel at Seattle University	Seattle, WA, USA	Steven Holl Architects
Tanfield Mill	West Tanfield, UK	unknown
Texas A&M Solar Decathlon House 2007	College Station, TX, USA	Texas A&M University
Water Pollution Control Laboratory	Portland, OR, USA	Miller/Hull Partnership
Westhaven Tower	Frankfurt, Germany	Schneider + Schumacher
Woods Hole Research Center	Falmouth, MA, USA	William McDonough + Partners
University of Texas-Austin Solar Decathlon House 2005	Austin, TX, USA	University of Texas-Austin
Virginia Polytechnic Institute Solar Decathlon House 2009	Blacksburg, VA, USA	Virginia Polytechnic Institute
Yodakandiya Community Complex	Tissamaharama, Sri Lanka	Susi Jane Platt (Architecture for Humanity)
Yokohama National University	Yokohama, Japan	unknown
Zion National Park Visitor's Center	Springdale, UT, USA	James Crockett, AIA

APPENDIX 4

CASE STUDY BUILDINGS (FROM 1ST EDITION)

The following buildings were featured as case studies in the first edition of *The Green Studio Handbook*. They are not available in the second edition—but may be accessed via the website for this book: www.greenstudiohandbook.org/

BUILDING	LOCATION	ARCHITECT
Arup Campus Solihull	Blythe Valley Park, Solihull, England, UK	Arup Associates
Beddington Zero Energy Development	Beddington, Sutton, England, UK	Bill Dunster Architects
Cornell Solar Decathlon House 2005	Ithaca, NY, USA	Cornell University
Druk White Lotus School	Shey, Ladakh, India	ARUP + ARUP Associates
Habitat Research and Development Centre	Windhoek, Namibia	Nina Maritz Architect
The Helena Apartment Tower	New York, NY, USA	FXFOWLE Architects, PC
Lillis Business Complex	Eugene, OR, USA	SRG Partnership
National Association of Realtors Headquarters	Washington, DC, USA	Gund Partnership
One Peking Road	Hong Kong, China	Rocco Design Ltd

NOTES

How many green strategies can you identify in the following proposal (for a small house designed around a shipping container)—and what strategies would you add?

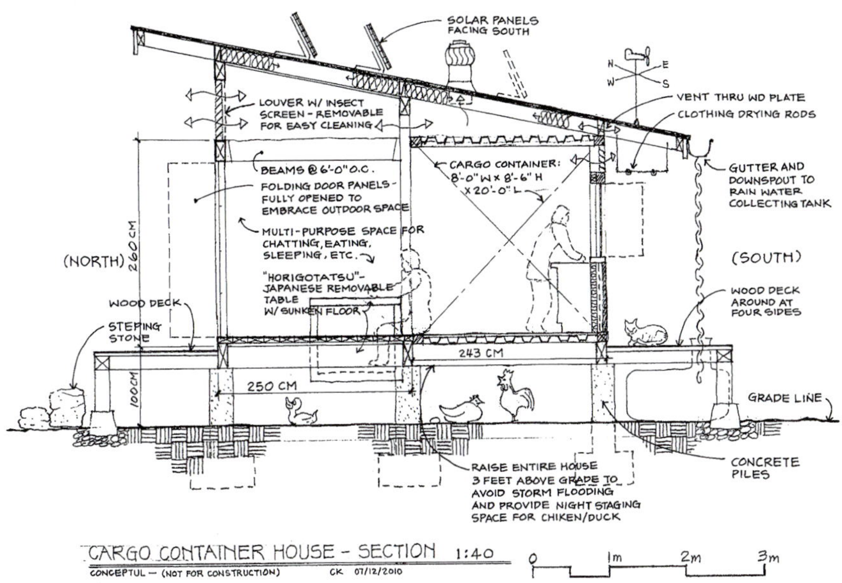

A.3 Schematic design for a cargo house in a tropical climate. CLEMENT KING

NOTES

GLOSSARY OF TERMS

absorption refrigeration system—a cooling device that transfers heat from an evaporator to a condenser by means of the cyclical condensation and vaporization of a water-salt solution; driven by heat input to a chemical process (versus electrical input).

active facade—a facade that responds to changing weather conditions by modifying its performance (by varying apertures, shading, etc.).

airflow rate—a measure of the quantity of air that passes through a defined area (window, duct) in a unit of time; expressed in cfm (cubic feet per minute) [L/s (liters per second)].

alternating current (AC)—the flow of electricity from high potential to low potential in a stream that varies sinusoidally in amplitude and direction over time; grid or mains electricity is AC.

altitude angle—a solar angle that indicates the height of the sun in the sky.

ambient—referring to conditions in the immediate surroundings; sometimes used to describe naturally occurring (or unaltered) conditions; in lighting, usually referring to general or area-wide conditions.

amorphous PV—a photovoltaic module manufactured using a thin film of silicon; amorphous modules do not have the circular cell structure characteristic of mono-crystalline PV modules.

anidolic zenithal collector—a toplighting device that collects daylight from a view of the north sky and delivers the daylight into a space via a diffusing element; the daylight is reflected and redirected as it passes through the device.

anode side—the negatively charged side of a fuel cell.

array—an assemblage of photovoltaic modules; PV manufacturers sell modules that are assembled on site into larger capacity units called arrays.

ASHRAE—American Society of Heating, Refrigerating and Air-Conditioning Engineers.

azimuth angle—a solar angle that indicates the position of the sun relative to a reference orientation (typically solar south).

balance of system—describes the components of a photovoltaic system beyond the PV modules themselves (this usually includes batteries, inverters, controllers).

base load—a "typical" average electrical load for a building or generating system.

berm—an earthen construction rising above the surrounding ground plane; typically built to block views, channel wind, water, or circulation, or partially earth shelter a building.

bilateral (daylighting)—a daylighting system that introduces light into a space from two (generally opposite) directions.

biodegradable—a material (organic) that will degrade under the action of microorganisms; generally describes a material that will decompose in nature in a reasonable time period.

biodiversity—the existence of a large number and variety of species in a given geographic area; often used as an indicator of ecological health.

biofuel—a fuel derived from unfossilized plant material (such as wood, garbage, rapeseed, manure, soybeans).

biomass—unfossilized biological matter (wood, straw, dung) that can be processed (burned, decomposed) to produce energy (typically heat).

bioregional development—development consistent with the constraints of a bioregion (a geographical area with common ecological processes and systems).

bioremediation—a process that uses microorganisms to break down environmental pollution.

boiler—active mechanical equipment that heats water (or produces steam) for space heating or domestic hot water.

brownfield—an unused/underused former industrial or commercial site that is environmentally contaminated, with the contamination limiting its potential reuse.

building integrated photovoltaics (BIPV)—photovoltaics modules that are integrated into a building enclosure element (such as a roof shingle, glazing unit, spandrel panel); see also "glazing integrated photovoltaics."

Building Use Survey—a formal means of obtaining information from occupants regarding building performance (see www.usablebuildings.co.uk/).

carbon neutral—a carbon neutral building balances the amount of carbon dioxide released on an annual basis with an equal amount (or more) of carbon-emissions-free renewable energy production and/or purchased offsets.

cathode side—the positively charged side of a fuel cell.

cell—a unit of a photovoltaic collector panel; PV cells are assembled into modules by the manufacturer, modules are then assembled into arrays by the design team.

CFD—computational fluid dynamics; refers to numerical simulation of the motion of a fluid (typically air) in a space; commonly used to predict the performance of natural ventilation and active air distribution systems.

charge controller—a device that regulates the flow of electric voltage and current.

chiller—active mechanical equipment that cools water for space cooling.

cistern—a storage container for rainwater.

clarifier—a settling tank that separates residual solids from treated wastewater.

CO_2 emissions—the release of carbon dioxide into the atmosphere; identified as a principal cause of global warming and a focus of many green design efforts.

coefficient of performance (COP)—a dimensionless number used to express the efficiency of chillers (and heat pumps); COP is the ratio of the cooling output to the energy input (in consistent units).

coefficient of utilization (CU)—a measure of the ability of a lighting fixture and space to deliver light from a lamp to a task plane; the delivery efficiency of a fixture/space combination; expressed as a decimal value.

cogeneration—an electrical generation process that produces useful (versus waste) heat as a by-product; the process of co-producing electricity and heat on site.

coincident loads—loads that occur at the same time; used to describe thermal loads that contribute to system capacity requirements; also used to describe thermal and electrical load patterns (for cogeneration systems).

color rendering index (CRI)—a measure of the ability of a given light source to accurately present object color; expressed as a whole number value.

commissioning—a process that ensures that the owner's project requirements have been met; this involves design validation, testing of equipment and systems, and training and documentation for owner's personnel.

compact fluorescent—a small fluorescent lamp, marketed primarily as a replacement for less efficient incandescent lamps.

conduction—the transfer of heat through direct molecular contact within or between solid objects.

contrast—a measure of the difference in luminance (brightness) between two objects within the field of view; contrast enables vision, but too much contrast can cause glare.

convection—the transfer of heat through the action of a fluid (typically air in building design situations); natural convection occurs without mechanical assist while forced convection involves mechanical assist.

cooling capacity—a measure of the cooling load that can be met by a given system; expressed in Btu/h [Watts].

cooling degree day (CDD)—a measure of the summer severity of a climate (or current weather); the CDDs for a 24-hour period equal the average daily temperature minus a reference temperature (often 65°F [18°C]) that represents the balance point temperature of a building.

coolth—a term used to describe a beneficial flow of heat during the cooling season, as in "the roof pond provides a source of coolth during the morning hours."

daily heat gain—the amount of heat from various sources gained during the course of a 24-hour period.

daylight factor (DF)—the ratio of daylight illuminance at a given point within a building to the horizontal illuminance at an exterior reference point; daylight factor represents the efficiency of a daylighting system in delivering daylight to a specified location; expressed as a decimal or percentage.

Decibel—a dimensionless unit used to express sound pressure level or sound power level.

deconstruction—the philosophy and practice of designing a building to facilitate ease of disassembly to encourage reuse of components.

deforestation—the large-scale and long-term removal of trees from a region, typically due to over-cutting for fuel or building materials.

desiccant—a material with a high affinity for water vapor; used as a dehumidifying compound; also used as a coating on an energy (enthalpy) wheel.

design cooling load—a statistically significant cooling load (heat gain) that serves as the basis for system design and equipment sizing; expressed in Btu/h [Watts].

design development—a phase in the design process where design decisions are finalized, equipment and materials are selected, detailed and specified, and construction documents are begun or prepared; design development follows schematic design.

diffuse reflection—a reflection from a matte (non-specular) surface, in which light (or solar radiation) leaves a surface in generally random directions not directly related to the angle of incidence; no clear image can be seen via diffuse reflection.

direct current (DC)—the flow of electricity from high potential to low potential in a continuous, unidirectional stream; electricity from a battery or directly from a PV module is DC.

diurnal—referring to a 24-hour (daily) cycle.

diurnal temperature range—the daily range of temperature; the daily maximum temperature minus the daily minimum temperature; expressed in degrees F [C].

dry-bulb temperature—a temperature measurement taken using a dry-bulb thermometer; an indicator of sensible heat density; expressed in degrees F [C].

dynamic glazing—glazing that can change one or more properties (such as visible transmittance) in response to environmental conditions or a human control signal.

earthship—a building design approach that relies upon passive heating/cooling and renewable energy, rainwater harvesting, on-site sewage treatment, food production, and the use of societal by-products as building materials.

ecological footprint—a measure of the land area required to sustain an individual, community, or country; typically expressed in acres [ha] per capita.

electrochemical—a chemical process that results in an electrical charge.

embodied energy—the energy required to produce a product (from extraction of raw materials, through manufacturing, and including transportation to the point of use); expressed as Btu/lb [kJ/kg].

energy recovery ventilator (ERV)—a device (usually self-contained) that transfers heat and moisture between incoming and outgoing air streams as part of a building ventilation system.

Energy Star—a (U.S.) certification system for energy-efficient appliances.

enthalpy—a measure of the total (sensible and latent) energy content of air; expressed as Btu/lb [kJ/kg].

enthalpy wheel—a type of rotary heat exchanger that transfers both heat and moisture.

equinox—when day and night are of equal length (approximately March 21 and September 21).

evaporation—the process of changing from the liquid to the vapor phase (or state); evaporation can be an effective cooling process because of the amount of heat required to break molecular bonds to effect this change.

expanded polystyrene (EPS)—a form of thermal insulation manufactured by molding expanded polystyrene; commonly called beadboard.

extensive green roof—a vegetated roof with fairly short plantings and a limited depth of soil.

external daylight illuminance—the daylight illuminance at a reference point outside of a building.

extruded polystyrene (XEPS)—a form of thermal insulation manufactured by extruding polystyrene; XEPS has a higher R-value and higher compressive strength than expanded polystyrene (EPS).

first cost—the cost to acquire a facility, not including operating, maintenance, and repair costs.

flow—the volume of fluid that passes a given point per unit of time; a factor in determining the potential power generation of a wind or hydro system; airflow is a key factor in the design of natural ventilation and most HVAC systems.

fluorescent—a low-pressure gaseous discharge electric lamp that operates on the basis of electron flow through an arc tube.

footcandles—I-P unit of illuminance; lumens per square foot.

Forest Stewardship Council (FSC)—an international non-profit organization that promotes sustainable forestry and timber use practices.

glare—a negative visual sensation caused by excessive brightness or contrast; glare may be classified as direct or reflected and as discomforting, disabling, or blinding.

glazing integrated photovoltaics—a type of building integrated photovoltaics where PV elements are an integral part of a glazing element (a window or skylight, for example).

green—a building, project, or philosophy based upon reducing environmental impacts related to energy, water, and materials use; green buildings respect building occupants as well as those who are indirectly affected by building construction/operation.

green travel plan—a management policy to encourage environmentally-friendly travel for employees.

grid-connected—an on-site power generation system that is linked to the local utility system.

ground source heat pump—a heat pump that transfers heat to/from the below-ground environment rather than to/from the ambient air; more energy-efficient than a conventional heat pump; sometimes inaccurately called a geothermal heat pump (which implies tapping into deep earth heat reservoirs).

halogen—a relatively small, long-life incandescent lamp; the terms "quartz-halogen" or "tungsten-halogen" are also used.

head—the vertical height (depth) of water that exerts pressure on a turbine; a factor in determining the potential power generation of a hydro system.

heat exchanger—a device that transfers heat from one medium (air, water, steam) to another without mixing of the media.

heat gain—a flow of heat that will increase the temperature of a building or space; heat gains include radiant, convective, and conductive heat flows through the building envelope and the flow of heat from lights, people, and equipment within a building; cooling load is heat gain that directly affects air temperature (excluding stored radiation gains).

heat loss—a flow of heat that will decrease the temperature of a building or space; heat losses include radiant, convective, and conductive heat flows through the building envelope, infiltration, and/or heat flows due to evaporation.

heat pipe heat exchanger—a heat exchanger that employs refrigerant-filled tubes to exchange heat between two media through the cyclic vaporization and condensation of the refrigerant in the tubes.

heat pump—a mechanical-electrical heating/cooling device that transfers heat from a condenser to an evaporator by means of the cyclical vaporization and condensation of a refrigerant circulated by a compressor.

heat recovery system—a system that captures "waste" heat (which would otherwise be rejected) as a means of increasing building energy efficiency.

heat recovery ventilator (HRV)—a device (usually self-contained) that transfers heat between incoming and outgoing air streams as part of a building ventilation system.

heat sink—a location with a lower temperature that will accept heat flow from a location with a higher temperature; a place to dump heat from a building that is being cooled.

heating degree day (HDD)—a measure of the winter severity of a climate (or current weather); the HDDs for a 24-hour period equal a reference temperature minus the average daily temperature (the reference temperature is often 65°F [18°C] and represents the balance point temperature of a building).

high pressure sodium—a high-intensity gaseous discharge electric lamp that operates on the basis of electron flow through an arc tube.

horizontal axis wind turbine (HAWT)—a wind machine with the axis of rotation parallel to the ground (as opposed to a vertical axis machine with the axis of rotation perpendicular to the ground).

humus—an organic substance consisting of decayed vegetable or animal matter; the output of a composting toilet; humus can provide nutrients for plants.

HVAC system—heating, ventilating, and air-conditioning; an active climate control system.

hybrid system—an on-site power generation system that includes alternative devices (such as PV, wind, or fuel cells) as well as conventional devices (such as a diesel generator).

hydrocarbon fuel—any fuel that is principally composed of molecules containing hydrogen and carbon; fossil fuels are hydrocarbons.

hydrogen fuel cell—a device that generates electricity via the chemical reaction of hydrogen with oxygen.

hydroponic reactor—an element in a wastewater treatment system in which aquatic plants floating atop liquid in a tank provide aquatic-root-zone treatment of the wastewater.

hypothesis—a formal statement that predicts the behavior of a system; a testable statement; building design proposals are hypotheses.

IESNA—Illuminating Engineering Society of North America.

Illuminance—the density of light falling on a given surface; expressed as fc [lux], which is lumens per unit area.

impervious (surface)—a material that prevents the passage or diffusion of a fluid (such as water).

impulse turbine—a type of microhydro turbine that relies on the kinetic energy of water jets to rotate the turbine; the turbine can be open and not fully immersed in water.

indoor air quality—the collective condition of air within a building relative to occupant health and olfactory comfort; acceptable indoor air quality is typically a fundamental design intent.

infrared radiation—radiation bordering the visible spectrum (light) but with longer wavelengths; radiation emitted by objects near room temperature.

inlet area—the collective size of opening(s) through which air is admitted for natural ventilation; typically net area (less the effects of mullions, screens, etc.) is of interest; expressed in square feet or square meters.

insolation—the intensity of solar radiation that reaches a given surface (wall, ground, solar collector) at a specific time; typically expressed as W/ft^2 $[W/m^2]$.

intensive green roof—a vegetated roof with some tall plantings and a fairly deep soil cover.

internal daylight illuminance—the illuminance caused solely by daylight at a defined location within a building.

interreflections—light (or solar radiation) reflected from surface to surface.

inverter—a device that converts direct current (DC) to alternating current (AC); used with on-site power generation systems such as wind or photovoltaics.

isolux—a line connecting points of equal illuminance (or equal daylight factors).

kinetic energy—energy embodied in an object or fluid due to its motion.

lamp—any manufactured source of light.

latent heat—heat that is an increase or decrease in the moisture content of air in a building; heat is absorbed by the evaporation of moisture and released by the condensation of moisture; the heat required to change the phase (state) of a material; the latent heat of vaporization is related to a change from the liquid to the vapor state—the latent heat of condensation is related to the opposite phase change; in buildings, latent heat is typically experienced as an increase or decrease in the moisture content of air.

life-cycle analysis—in building design, an analysis of the energy and environmental implications of a material from “cradle to grave.”

life-cycle cost—the cost to obtain, operate, repair, and decommission (or salvage) a building over a defined period of time.

light—radiation that is visible (can be seen by the human eye).

light scoop—an architectural device used to collect and bring light into a building.

light shelf—a device that is installed at the building facade to more evenly introduce daylight into a space to improve daylight distribution; light shelves may be external to the daylight aperture, internal, or both.

low-ε—low emissivity; a coating applied to glass to improve its thermal performance by reducing longwave radiation heat transfer through the glass.

lowest mass temperature—the minimum temperature reached by thermal mass in a passive cooling system; an indicator of the feasibility and capacity of the night ventilation of mass strategy.

lumen maintenance—a measure of the consistency of luminous flux over time; used to describe lamp performance or lighting system output.

luminaire—a lighting fixture.

luminance—the density of light leaving a surface or source; expressed in lumens per square foot [candelas per square meter]; the qualitative evaluation of luminance is termed "brightness."

luminous efficacy—a measure of the efficiency of a light source; the ratio of light output by the source to energy (electric) input; expressed in lumens per Watt.

luminous flux—a flow of light; expressed in lumens.

lux—SI unit of illuminance; lumens per square meter.

maintenance factor—an adjustment factor that accounts for the loss of illuminance (in electric lighting or daylighting systems) due to the deterioration of reflective surfaces and lamps, and the collection of dirt on glazing; expressed as a decimal value.

mercury vapor—a high-intensity gaseous discharge electric lamp that operates on the basis of electron flow through an arc tube; this lamp has generally been displaced by metal halide lamps.

metal halide—a high-intensity gaseous discharge electric lamp that operates on the basis of electron flow through an arc tube.

microclimate—a localized area of differential climate relative to the larger surrounding macroclimate; examples include the climate under a shade tree (versus in the open), the climate on a south-facing slope (versus a north-facing one), the climate at an airport (versus a downtown location in the same city).

mixed-mode cooling system—a cooling solution that employs both active and passive strategies to achieve comfort (e.g., natural ventilation and an active HVAC system).

module (PV)—a photovoltaic panel; modules are assembled on site into PV arrays.

natural ventilation—the flow of outdoor air through a building via a passive system, using naturally occurring forces (wind, stratification, pressure differences); natural ventilation can provide cooling and/or improve indoor air quality.

net metering—an arrangement whereby a utility customer with an on-site power generation system is billed based upon a "net" electrical meter reading that represents the difference between site draws from the grid ("purchases") and site input to the grid ("sales").

net-zero energy—a net-zero energy building balances the off-site energy used over an annual period with on-site energy production from renewable resources; sometimes referred to as zero net energy.

non-potable water—water that is not fit for human consumption.

optimization—a design process that attempts to determine the most beneficial size of a system or component based upon a balancing of costs and savings; optimization seeks the highest life-cycle return on investment.

overcast sky—a design sky (with complete cloud cover, no direct solar radiation, and fully diffuse light distribution) that is used as the basis for much daylighting design; an overcast sky is brighter at the zenith than at the horizon (making a unit of horizontal aperture more effective than a unit of vertical aperture).

parasitic energy—energy "losses" from a system due to components necessary for the system operation (such as pumping energy in a solar thermal system); parasitic energy demands decrease system efficiency.

passive downdraft evaporative cooling (PDEC)—an alternative name for a cool tower.

payback—the time that it takes for a system (investment) to pay for itself through accrued savings (often energy cost savings); both economic and energy payback may be of interest in green design; energy payback is the time it takes for a device or system to save or generate the amount of energy required to produce and install the device or system.

peak load—the maximum electrical load for a building or generating system in a given time period.

peak oil—a term used to describe the occurrence of maximum oil production as a function of resource availability; once peak oil has been reached, production (and oil availability) will necessarily decrease.

penstock—valve or gate that controls the flow of water in a microhydro system; sometimes this term is also used to describe the channel connected with this control device.

permeable medium heat exchanger—a heat exchanger that permits the transfer of moisture as well as heat.

pervious (surface)—a material that readily permits the passage or diffusion of a fluid (such as water).

phantom load—an electrical load that appears to occur without explanation, typically due to background power draw by appliances and equipment that are seemingly not in use (such as power consumed by instant start lamps and dormant televisions).

phosphoric acid fuel cell (PAFC)—a fuel cell that uses phosphoric acid as the electrolyte (which acts as a differential barrier allowing positive charge to pass through, while inhibiting negative charge, thereby creating current).

photosensor—a light-sensitive sensor used to control the operation of an electric lighting system; often used in daylight-integrated electric lighting systems and to control exterior lighting elements.

plate heat exchanger—a heat exchanger that uses flat plates to separate two media while transfering heat between them.

post-occupancy evaluation (POE)—a formal investigation into some aspect of building performance conducted after a building has been placed into normal use.

potable water—water fit for human consumption.

prevailing wind—the predominant direction from which wind blows; this is often seasonal and sometimes changes diurnally.

profile angle—an angle that relates the position of the sun to the plane of glazing; defined as the angle between a plane perpendicular to the plane of the glass and the rays of the sun traced in a plane parallel to the window plane; profile angle is used in the design of shading devices.

proton exchange fuel cell (PEM)—a fuel cell that uses a plastic polymer as the electrolyte (which acts as a differential barrier allowing positive charge to pass through, while inhibiting negative charge, thereby creating current).

psychrometric process—one of several processes that change the condition of moist air; the psychrometric processes include sensible heating, sensible and latent cooling, evaporative cooling, and dehumidification (among others).

Radiance—software program used to model lighting conditions; provides high-end simulation capabilities.

radiation—the transfer of heat between two objects not in contact (but within view of each other) through the action of electromagnetic radiation.

rammed earth—a building construction technique that produces walls by compressing soil (and additives) in forms on site.

reaction turbine—a type of microhydro turbine that relies on the pressure difference between inlet and outlet to rotate the turbine; the turbine must be encased and immersed in water.

reclaimed materials—materials that are being reused, but have not been significantly altered from their physical form in a previous application.

recycled content materials—new materials that contain a substantial percentage of feedstock provided by recycling.

reflectance—the characteristic property of a material (or surface coating) that allows it to redirect incident radiation without changing the nature of the radiation; expressed as a percentage of incident radiation.

relative humidity—a measure of the moisture content of the air; the amount of moisture actually held by the air compared with the maximum amount that could be held at the same temperature; expressed as a percentage.

renewable energy—energy produced by a resource that is rapidly replaceable by a natural process (examples include wood, biofuels, wind, and solar radiation).

room surface dirt depreciation factor—an adjustment factor that accounts for the negative impact of dirt, dust, and aging on room surfaces (which result in lowered reflectance over time); expressed as a decimal value.

rotary heat exchanger—a heat exchanger that employs a rotating wheel to transfer heat between two adjacent air streams; heat wheel (sensible only) and enthalpy wheel (sensible and latent exchange) options are available.

runaround coil—connected coils that are used to exchange heat between two air streams located some distance apart through the action of a water loop that connects the coils.

R-value—a measure of thermal resistance; the inverse of the thermal conductance of a material; expressed as ft^2 h °F/Btu [m^2 K/W].

sanitary drainage—building wastewater that contains biological pollutants and must be treated before discharge into the environment.

selective surface—a surface coating applied to solar collectors to increase absorptivity and decrease emissivity, thereby increasing the effectiveness of the absorber surface.

sensible heat—heat that is connected to an increase or decrease in the temperature of air or objects in a building.

shading coefficient (SC)—the ratio of solar radiation (heat) transferred by the transparent portion of a window or skylight to the radiation incident on the window/skylight; expressed as a decimal value; solar heat gain coefficient (SHGC) is replacing SC for most building design applications.

skin-load-dominated building—a building in which the climate control needs are determined principally by exterior climate conditions acting through the building envelope; also termed "envelope-load dominated."

soil moisture content—a measure of the water content of soil; affects the conductivity of the soil and impacts the performance of earth tubes, earth sheltering, ground source heat pumps, and green roof plantings.

solar chimney—an architectural device that collects solar radiation to enhance the stack effect (typically as part of a natural ventilation system).

solar heat gain coefficient (SHGC)—the percentage of solar heat gain that passes through a glazing assembly (including both glazing and frame components); SHGC is replacing shading coefficient in building regulations.

solar loads—cooling loads resulting from the impact of solar radiation on a building.

solar transit—a device used to sight and make angular measurements of obstructions to direct solar radiation on a site.

sound transmission class (STC)—a single-number index that represents sound transmission loss across a range of frequencies; indicates the viability of an assembly as a sound barrier.

specific heat—a fundamental thermo-physical property of a material; the amount of heat required to raise the temperature of a unit mass of a material by one degree relative to the amount of heat required to raise the temperature of a similar mass of water by one degree; specific heat (along with material density) is a factor in determining thermal capacity.

specular reflection—a reflection from a specular (mirror-like) surface, in which light (or solar radiation) leaves a surface at an angle equal to the angle of incidence; specular reflection can produce a viable image of a source or object.

stack effect—a naturally occurring phenomenon wherein hot air rises and establishes a vertical circulation of air; employed in some natural ventilation systems.

stand-alone—an on-site power generation system that is not linked to the local utility system; also known as off-the-grid.

standard incandescent—an electric lamp that operates on the basis of a heated filament that glows; "standard" distinguishes this type lamp from a quartz-halogen incandescent.

stick-framing—a construction method that predominates in the North American single-family housing market, using small-dimension wood members assembled on site into a structural frame.

stormwater—rainwater that is not immediately absorbed on site and must be dealt with through on-site or off-site means.

stratification—the naturally occurring separation of a vertical volume of fluid (for example, air in an atrium or water in a storage tank) into temperature zones (hot high, cool low).

Sun Angle Calculator—a proprietary product that presents horizontal projection sun angle charts for a range of latitudes.

sun angle chart—a two-dimensional plot that represents the position of the sun in the sky vault over the course of a year; horizontal and vertical projection charts are readily available; the Sun Angle Calculator is a form of sun angle chart.

sunpeg chart—a type of sun angle chart used with physical model shading studies; a gnomon on the chart projects a shadow corresponding to a selected date and time of day.

sun-tracking photovoltaics—a photovoltaic module mounted on a movable frame that rotates to follow the sun's path, maximizing total insolation exposure and thereby electrical energy production.

superinsulation—the use of extensive insulation in the building envelope (substantially beyond code minimums) such that the building becomes an internal-load-dominated building.

sustainable—a building, project, or philosophy that is based upon allowing this generation to meet its needs without impeding the ability of future generations to meet their needs; in essence a project with no net negative environmental impacts.

swept area—area delineated by the rotation of the propeller of a wind turbine; equal to $(\pi)(r^2)$, where r is the radius of the propeller.

task lighting—lighting for a specific use or area (as opposed to ambient lighting).

temperature—a measure of the density of heat in a substance (not the absolute quantity of heat); heat flow is proportional to temperature difference; expressed in degrees F [C].

temperature stratification—the layering of a fluid, due to differential density, that results in a measurable vertical temperature gradient (e.g. hot air high, cool air low).

thermal capacity—the heat storing capability of a material; the amount of heat stored by a thermal mass.

thermal mass—a material that is selected and/or used based upon its ability to store heat; usable thermal mass will have high thermal capacity (density times specific heat).

throat area—the smallest unobstructed cross-sectional area through which air passes on its way from inlet to outlet in a natural ventilation system.

time lag—a delay in the flow of heat through a material caused by the thermal capacity of the material; time lag can be used to shift loads across time.

tower exiting airflow rate—the volume of air leaving a cool tower per unit of time; a partial measure of tower capacity.

transmission loss (TL)—the reduction of sound pressure (at one particular frequency) caused by an assembly; TL is an indicator of the effectiveness of a sound barrier.

transmittance—the amount of light (or solar radiation) that passes untransformed through a substance; expressed as a percentage of incident light (or solar radiation).

trickle vent—an opening in a building envelope that allows a steady and controlled flow of outdoor air to enter the building.

U-factor—the overall coefficient of heat transfer; a measure of the thermal conductance of a building assembly; the inverse of the sum of the thermal resistances of an assembly; expressed as Btu/h ft^2 °F [W/m^2 K].

ultraviolet radiation—radiation bordering the visible spectrum (light) but with shorter wavelengths; ultraviolet radiation is part of the solar radiation spectrum.

unilateral (daylighting)—a daylighting system that introduces light into a space from only one direction.

urban heat island effect—the tendency for urban areas to maintain a higher ambient temperature than surrounding suburbs or rural areas; caused by the absorption of solar radiation by built surfaces and heat emissions from buildings.

vapor compression refrigeration system—a mechanical-electrical cooling device that transfers heat from an evaporator to a condenser by means of the cyclical vaporization and condensation of a refrigerant circulated by a compressor; driven by electrical input to the compressor.

vertical axis wind turbine (VAWT)—a wind machine with the axis of rotation perpendicular to the ground (as opposed to a horizontal axis machine with the axis of rotation parallel to the ground).

visible transmittance (VT)—the transmittance of a glazing material relative to radiation in the visible portion of the spectrum (excluding infrared and ultraviolet radiation); visible transmittance may differ substantially from solar transmittance for selective glazings.

volatile organic compounds (VOCs)—compounds that vaporize (evaporate) at room temperature; VOCs are produced by many building materials and furnishings; an indoor air pollutant; low- or no-VOC options are available for many products.

waste heat—heat produced as a generally unusable by-product of some process.

wastewater—water that must be treated for proper disposal; sanitary drainage.

wet-bulb depression—the difference between coincident wet-bulb and dry-bulb temperatures.

wet-bulb temperature—a temperature measurement taken using a wet-bulb thermometer; an indicator of sensible heat density and air moisture content; wet-bulb and dry-bulb temperatures are identical at saturation (100% relative humidity); expressed in degrees F [C].

wind farm—a grouping of wind turbines used to generate electricity; usually for commercial purposes.

windward—in the direction (or on the side) from which the wind is blowing.

zone—an area of a building with characteristics or needs that substantively differ from those of other areas; for example a daylighting, thermal, or fire zone.

INDEX